FOREIGN POLICY AND PARTY POLITICS

Pearl Harbor to Korea

FOREIGN POLICY

and PARTY POLITICS

Pearl Harbor to Korea

H. BRADFORD WESTERFIELD

1972
OCTAGON BOOKS
New York

Reprinted 1972

by special arrangement with Yale University Press

OCTAGON BOOKS

A Division of Farrar, Straus & Giroux, Inc.

19 Union Square West

New York, N. Y. 10003

Reprinted from the original edition in the Wesleyan University Library.

Library of Congress Catalog Card Number: 70-159236

ISBN 0-374-98363-1

Manufactured by Braun-Brumfield, Inc.
Ann Arbor, Michigan

Printed in the United States of America

For Putney and my mother and father

ACKNOWLEDGMENTS

IT WAS William Yandell Elliott of Harvard University who stirred my interest in the problems of administering America's foreign relations, and his encouragement and advice have been instrumental in the preparation of this volume. Many others at Harvard have also shared with me their insight and counsel, notably McGeorge Bundy, Arthur N. Holcombe, and V. O. Key. The final responsibility is of course mine alone.

Several dozen men in government gave me freely of their limited time in personal interviews. They include numerous senators, representatives, congressional staff assistants, and executive officials. I am grateful also to the American Political Science Association and the Edgar B. Stern Family Fund for having made it possible for me to spend a recent year working in influential congressional offices concerned with foreign affairs.

In the preparation of my manuscript for publication I have relied heavily on the able assistance of David Horne and others at the Yale University Press. For permission to quote from published works I am indebted to Congressional Quarterly News Features, Harper and Brothers, Houghton Mifflin Company, the Macmillan Company, and the Viking Press, Inc.

Finally, I want to express a small part of the affectionate gratitude I feel to my own family for manifold assistance I often needed during my work on this book.

H. B. W.

Cambridge, Mass.
February, 1955

CONTENTS

ix

INTRODUCTION

THE BROAD PROBLEM of this study is how to foster a truly democratic control of the foreign relations of the United States in this period of its history.

There are good reasons to value such control. In all democratic institutions the aim is to increase popular understanding of the policies pursued by men of authority in political, social, and economic life and to secure free popular consent to their decisions. This view, that the citizen as far as possible should give his assent willingly and comprehendingly, rests on concern for the individual human personality as such and for its unobstructed development, as well as on the premise that the efficiency and stability of a society are enhanced when there is a minimum of need to resort to coercion to accomplish social purposes. Today, particularly, when it seems likely that for many years to come the public will be called upon to sacrifice in order to preserve the nation in competitive international society, the lives of millions may actually depend on the results of these sacrifices. But if they are not made willingly, it is much less likely that they will be made effectively.

Democratic control does not require the public to announce its will in "majoritarian" referenda. Rather it calls for a society pluralistic in structure and animated by democratic purposes, with continuous competition in many fields of activity among men seeking leadership by means which are respected in that society. Most of the pluralist competition in a democracy is not immediately directed at the electorate as such; the drive is to get members for clubs and churches, employees and contracts for businesses, audiences for meetings and broadcasts, readers for books and periodicals, etc. The response of individual citizens, one way or another, indicates varying degrees of affiliation with different groups, and correspondingly there are gradual shifts in the power of group leaders to make decisions affecting society at large. Only a few of these decisions (not always the most important ones) are made through *government,* and only a few of those which are made through government can be determined in any detail by the results of national elections. But elections at least furnish the ultimate popular sanction, and in the sphere of foreign affairs this is especially important, for there the groups of private citizens are less able than in the domestic sphere to make major decisions of public policy independent of government approval. The great unions and corporations, for example, can influence the domestic price level more directly and decisively than they can the balance of trade.

The "people's choice" for elective office in a democracy may be regarded as a *local delegate,* the chosen spokesman of local views and interests; or as an *independent representative,* of the sort Edmund Burke idealized, chosen to exercise his own judgment; or as a *partisan,* personally seeking to influence the decisions of his party from within but prepared to support it fully against outsiders. In the United States the local delegate conception has long been predominant; it has served to ensure strong representation for the diversity of interests in a continental republic. But in the Congress inevitably there has been an admixture of the attitudes of independent "Burkean" representatives, who retain their right to attack problems of general policy according to their personal views of how best to serve the people as a whole. The reason is that constituents are often very little interested in public policy; those who do show an interest commonly reveal to their delegate conflicting mental pictures of reality, conflicting values engaged by the same problems, conflicting goals, and conflicting notions of the proper means to reach any agreed goal. All these elements of indifference, ignorance, and disagreement over fact and the application of value are particularly prevalent in the "distant" sphere of foreign affairs.[1] This gives elected officials exceptionally wide discretion in that area. Often they are further encouraged to disregard their constituents by the survivals in politics of traditional Protestant respect for the individual conscience: men are honored

1. Martin Kriesberg argued in 1949 from opinion-polling research that approximately 30 per cent of the voters are "unaware of almost any given event" in American foreign policy. He found that 45 per cent are "aware but uninformed," retaining little information and unable to "frame intelligent arguments" about the foreign affairs they hear and see discussed. The remaining quarter of the electorate does show "knowledge of foreign problems." These figures must be regarded as giving the voter the maximum benefit of doubt. Lester Markel, ed., *Public Opinion and Foreign Policy* (New York, Harper, 1949), p. 51.

in American politics for independence, even for insurgence against their party.

Thus the American congressman is almost always what may be called an "independent delegate," who combines the exercise of personal judgment with his subservience to constituents. On matters of policy he may, of course, choose the role of *partisan,* but almost no discipline exists compelling him to do so. American political parties are remarkably stable coalitions, but they exist primarily to elect the President; they do not formulate legislative policy, which is actually made by independent delegates in fluctuating coalitions which are not submitted to the voting public for approval.

PARTISANSHIP

Would a stronger party system be generally preferable for the democratic control of government policy in the United States? Should the parties each be more unified, with more clear-cut lines drawn between them on national issues? Is it reasonable to suppose that such partisanship would promote *public understanding* and provide *expressed consent* to a *feasible program* of *coordinated government action?* Each of the italicized words involves important considerations.

First of all, if the parties each had greater unity of outlook and stronger organizational discipline, the debate between them would probably educate the electorate more fully, because there would be greater concentration on issues which confront the whole nation and because of the increased sense of responsibility in utterance which comes from an awareness that as a member of a group one will be held accountable for its failure to carry out what has been promised or to eliminate what has been criticized.

In the second place, although stronger parties would not eliminate the essential need for political compromise of interests and ideals—a situation which some purists consider destructive to integrity—they would force the major compromises to be made during the process of organizing party coalitions *before* elections, so that alternative combinations could then be passed on by the voters. (In most vital aspects of policy America has been governed for many years by a congressional coalition of Republicans and Southern Democrats which the national electorate cannot directly approve or disapprove.)

Thirdly, if the leaders of each major party were expected to agree in advance on the shape of a program which they would be strong enough to have some real hope of implementing after the majority of the voters expressed their consent, the winning party would be under obligation to do what it promised, and hence would be less likely in the first place to promise the impossible. Furthermore, it could implement its program far more effectively by being better able to coordinate the numerous government agencies.

However, changes in party *institutions* would not in themselves be sufficient to produce party responsibility unless they were activated by a basic realignment of the country's major interests. What are needed are two new party coalitions, each concerned with interests which are mutually compatible. The interests in each party could then formulate a program and seek majority support of the electorate to carry it out.

In the long run, to be durable and efficient in domestic policy making, such coalitions in America would almost certainly have to rest fundamentally on an urban class basis. But great areas of the United States are still not urbanized. Until they are, the power of rural interests, which have defied effective and enduring organization along class lines, will impede and very probably prevent the achievement of a new factional alignment adequate to permit responsible party programing and implementation. There are other obstacles to be overcome, too: the tremendous importance of nationality and sectarian differences in American voting today. Consider the solidarity produced in the South by fear of Negro equality—to say nothing of constitutional barriers in federalism, separation of powers, and the pattern of uncoordinated elections for different important offices. It appears that the prospects for party responsibility are very remote in the United States, however desirable it may be.

Moreover, the arguments for a higher degree of party discipline may not be equally applicable to all areas of public policy. In some spheres special considerations may override the general values of partisanship as a means of democratic control. One such sphere is that of foreign affairs. On balance it appears that to present the national electorate in the foreseeable future with a choice between sharply contrasting partisan policies on all-important foreign relations would seriously endanger the international position of the United States, and hence the future of American democracy. The several reasons for this may be briefly stated:

(1) American policy needs to appear dependable to the outside world. This would be true even if she were "going it alone" while the Soviet Union sparred and watched for an opening, but in a multilateral strategy of alliances the appearance of dependability is even more important. Apart from concern for preserving the heritage of the West, it seems doubtful that the effective range of American bombers can suffice to insure victory in an intercontinental war for many years to come, if Europe and Asia are lost. For its very survival the United States very probably will continue to need allies overseas. But it is hard to exaggerate the risks which must be taken by allied leaders who side with America virtually under the guns of the Communists. Such risks are hardly likely to be accepted if there appears to be much danger that a national election in the United States may abruptly cause an about-face in American foreign policy. The point which is particularly important is the *abruptness* of an electoral decision between presidential candidates contesting foreign policy. Changes in such policy are to be expected in the United States, as in any democracy, but as long as they can proceed gradually, with due negotiation and preparation of allied opinion, they are less likely to impair confidence than is the possible election of a new President who proclaims a sharply contrasting foreign policy—even if with greater information and under bureaucratic influence, he should later decide not to alter the policy of his predecessor very drastically.

(2) The effective conduct of foreign relations requires flexibility to meet changing developments. This is at least as important as dependable continuity and in practice much more likely to be achieved, unless partisanship intervenes. The need for flexibility

can hardly be overestimated in an essentially defensive foreign policy based on the principle that Communist aggression must be contained and deterred; there must be a wide enough measure of mutual confidence in both American parties to permit local psychological warfare sorties and swift retaliation against particular foreign attacks. For an *aggressive* American foreign policy which would seek to move toward ultimatums and preventive war, considerable flexibility would also be desirable, but it may be conceded that in this case the desired purposefulness, taken by itself, would be enhanced by disciplined majority partisanship.

(3) In the cold war America needs to appear united—to her own people as well as to the outside world, both allied and enemy. This necessity may not be continuous. Insofar as it involves an element of self-deception, one hopes it is not. But at least in periods of emergency the sacrifices certain to be demanded are such that no simple majority party can risk carrying them through on its own responsibility over heavy opposition by the minority party. The majority will be strongly tempted to use shock techniques virtually to coerce wider support. Alternatively, in an emergency the "responsible" majority would feel it necessary to make sudden drastic concessions to the opposition party to win immediate support and break any existing or developing partisan deadlock. That would damage both the continuity and the inner consistency of the general foreign policy being pursued. This eventuality should be pondered by any who seek to commit their own party to a much more hazardous program in foreign affairs than is acceptable to the other major party.

A similar obstacle confronts those who might be content to espouse the side of "extreme" caution as basic foreign policy for their party, in defiance of an "aggressive" opposition. A partisan program of international noninvolvement could be undercut at any moment by an *external* act of aggression, and the party would then find itself suddenly and onerously constrained for the sake of national "unity" to come to terms with the apparently more farsighted domestic opposition. A price would have to be paid in the prestige of the party and in the sacrifice of essentially unrefuted elements of its earlier policy. How great the cost, to the party and the country, might well depend on how deep a division had been allowed to develop in more peaceful times between conflicting partisan foreign policies.

Also, not only would the appearance of dependability and unity and the reality of flexibility—all internationally valuable—be seriously impaired by partisanship in foreign affairs, but there is grave doubt that a sociological basis exists which would permit cleavage between disciplined, responsible parties along the same lines on foreign as on domestic problems. If it does not, by an election victory in which foreign and domestic issues were mixed, no clear mandate could be drawn regarding majority preference in foreign policy.

Certainly as long as some degree of resistance to Communist aggression remains the core of American foreign relations, there seems little reason to suppose that differences of opinion on *means* will run continuously along the *class* lines appropriate to domestic partisanship. Although upper class groups, by and large, have a continuing special interest in "cheap" government, which can be expected to affect foreign as well as domestic programs, the other groups which have no such general aversion to government spending are nevertheless likely to have a private interest of their own in directing it toward domestic rather than foreign purposes. Both sets of interests, which may loosely be called economy-mindedness and welfare-mindedness, are, to be sure, class oriented; and both affect foreign policy—but not in clearly conflicting directions. Both can be offset by views of foreign requirements which do not themselves run along class lines—most obviously and simply, by nationality background.

Of course it may properly be argued that the real foreign policy cleavage is a complex *regionalism*—not simply area against area, but an elaborate pattern which reflects the contrasting attitudes of the groups which dominate each party in each separate region of the country; that the regional factions which act together in either national party may not agree with one another, but that within each party some area appears predominant on foreign affairs and colors the whole. In the Republican party that dominant region would seem normally to be the Midwest and Mountain states, and in the Democratic the Atlantic seaboard. This line of argument can be extended: a strong partisan disagreement on foreign affairs might well have run along lines which are roughly those of the *present* party alignment, if in recent years the special conditions of hot and cold war and the idealization of "bipartisanship" had not distorted the pattern. On such a theory the tightening of party discipline along the existing lines, with no attempt at realignment, would provide an appropriate basis for offering the public genuinely alternative foreign policies.

One trouble with this theory is that it pays too little attention to the crucial importance of the huge Northeastern urban industrial states in the election of the President under a system which gives the entire electoral vote of each state to the winner of a mere plurality. It has often been noted that this situation is likely to make presidential candidates devote particular attention to attempts to win the support of metropolitan masses, and hence that the tone of their campaigns, and their behavior if elected, are likely to be somewhat to the left of the average sentiment of the active members of their respective parties. It should also be observed that the electoral system may tend in both parties to make the drafters of national platforms and presidential campaign speeches—and even those who determine the nominations for highest office—pay particular attention to the *foreign policy* views of influential elements in the Northeastern states.[2] In the Republican party especially this has the effect of offsetting to an important degree the distinctive record made for the GOP in Congress by its predominant Interior faction. Strategy in a presidential election is likely to dictate soft-pedaling that record rather than attempting to capitalize on it by offering it openly for the choice of the national electorate. Partly for the same reason the contrasting views and behavior of the Eastern wing of the party in the Senate have significance out of proportion to the numerical size and seniority status of that faction. It is easy to recognize this when an eastward-oriented Republican is in the White House. But it is also worth

2. In the Democratic party the special weight of New York voters has in recent years been a determining influence on Middle East policy and was a considerable reason for the delay in "getting tough with Russia" after World War II.

remembering at *all* times that East and Midwest, Coast and Interior are nearly equally represented in any GOP National Convention. Interior Republicans with their distinctive foreign policy viewpoint are not likely to show the special strength in nominating a President that they show in the United States Senate.

A further important objection to tightening current party lines very much more firmly for the sake of achieving party responsibility on the most important issues in foreign affairs is that it would put additional obstacles in the way of the realignment which seems to be necessary for party responsibility on domestic problems, whereas the public is usually more interested and always better informed in domestic matters. After extensive study of public opinion polls Gabriel Almond has offered a shrewd conclusion as to the lack of basic concern with world affairs which lies beneath the surface regard often accorded them by the American people:

> What [the] studies suggest is that there is no mass market for detailed information on foreign affairs. The general public looks for *cues* for *mood responses* in public discussion of foreign policy. It does not listen to the content of discussion but to its tone. A presidential statement that a crisis exists will ordinarily be registered in the form of apprehension. A reassuring statement will be received with complacency reactions. In both cases the reaction has no depth and no structure.[3]

To be sure, these studies were made before the Korean War. Almost certainly a series of such shocks as this will broaden public horizons, at least to the extent of generating interest. Ignorance is much more difficult to overcome. It is arguable that intense partisan debate on foreign policy would speed the educational process. In all aspects of government policy this is an important reason for favoring partisanship. But on foreign affairs the educational effects at best could be only very distant, given the complexity of the problems which stump experts. And there remain the

3. Gabriel A. Almond, *The American People and Foreign Policy* (New York, Harcourt, Brace, 1950), p. 232. The italics are Almond's.

immediate serious dangers which have been suggested in the last few pages. Caution, however, must indeed be taken to avoid unnecessary muffling of educational debate when considering preferable alternatives to partisanship as a device for the democratic control of current American foreign relations.

ALTERNATIVES TO PARTISANSHIP

What are the alternatives?

The term which naturally leaps to mind in America at the mid-century is "bipartisanship," but its meaning is cloudy. As commonly used it has involved *some measure of consultation among leaders of both major parties on foreign affairs with the object and/or the result of dampening opposition on foreign policy in Congress and in national elections.* That, be it emphasized, is a description of common usage rather than a definition adequate for precise thinking. But in a study of foreign policy in American politics in recent years it is hardly possible to avoid entirely the loose usage of the term "bipartisanship" which has been so generally prevalent. Therefore in this study when the word appears in quotation marks the *popular* meaning is intended, as described above. The neutral phrase *two-party collaboration* is also used to convey this same imprecise meaning.

But what would a really complete bipartisanship require? Study reveals that the key questions are: Who should consult? On what? At what stage? The following would appear to be the necessary answers for an all-embracing bipartisanship in American foreign relations:

(1) Collaborators with an administration of the opposition party would have to be delegated by their own party, not merely selected by executive authorities. This requirement could be modified to the extent that the opposition collaborators might be men chosen by their party simply to be its leaders on foreign affairs rather than explicitly selected to cooperate with the administration; but the administration would have no discretion to refuse to consult sincerely with the recognized leaders of the opposition in the foreign field.

(2) They would have to be consulted on all major foreign policy problems, to be defined by joint agreement. What is or is not a major problem, or even primarily a foreign policy problem at all, is by no means self-evident in every case. But on this principle both the administration and opposition leaders would have to be satisfied with the compromise on scope worked out between them. Except by mutual agreement neither side could deliberately exclude a major area of foreign relations from consultation.

(3) Consultation would have to take place before any final decision was reached by a politically responsible official of the administration. This principle is designed to recognize the constitutional prerogatives of the executive to act, and also the fact of bureaucratic planning. It would not insist that the opposition leaders be brought in the moment a problem arises, before the experts have had time to consider it. But it would insist that those collaborators be given real opportunity to express themselves before the ranking official actually makes up his mind, not just before he signs the final order.

(4) On those subjects where agreement was reached by consultation, the leaders of both parties would also collaborate in the use of all currently available devices of party discipline to rally their respective party cohorts behind the policy decisions. To be sure, the techniques of party control now available are not substantial. But in the theory of full bipartisanship, disciplinary devices within each party should be strengthened at the same time that two-party collaboration is improved.

When the term *bipartisanship* is used in this study without quotation marks it has general reference to the above four principles, especially to points 1 and 3, the *delegate character of the party consultants* and the *prior nature of the consultation* (because number 2 has been so rarely observed and number 4 is so little available).

No such full merger of American parties on foreign affairs is actually feasible on any continuous basis. There are a number of reasons for this:

(1) Leading members of Congress simply do not have the time to devote to such extensive consultation. They probably have

even less than do top executive officials, for the latter are better staffed and need not add to their respective regular duties as administrators or legislators the continuous chore of appeasing constituents in order to stay in office. Long drawn-out meetings and endless briefings on foreign affairs would be beyond the physical capacity of most congressional leaders whose seats are not absolutely safe.

(2) There is grave doubt of the ability of many congressional leaders to make a useful contribution in consultation on foreign policy, even if they had the time to devote to it. Participation by individuals relatively ignorant of the field might cause the sessions to degenerate into mere briefing by executive officials, which would drive away the able members and might embarrass even the ill informed.

(3) Especially serious is the problem of secrecy in foreign affairs if the administration were to lose power to select the members of the opposition—and even of its own party—with whom it would consult. The preservation of secrecy with a minimum loss of democratic responsibility and confidence is an important potential advantage to be derived from two-party collaboration. But to risk it with every opposition leader selected by his own party is too dangerous, given the existing pressures upon politicians to secure personal publicity and make partisan capital out of leaks to the press. Neither in the parties nor in Congress as a whole are disciplinary devices strong enough to protect even the most important secrets if they are revealed to basically unsympathetic individuals.

(4) At present the two parties—especially the opposition—are not organized to produce leaders who can commit their fellow partisans in the various branches of government. (That will be illustrated at length in the discussion of Congress in Part II.) But of course, if increased party discipline could be transcended by full bipartisanship, this particular and most serious practical difficulty would disappear.

However, even if such disciplined bipartisanship should become feasible and leaders of both parties find time to devote to it, the system would be a less democratic device for the control of foreign

relations than the existing practices. It would deliberately minimize the measure of popular control over foreign relations which
now results from the competition of would-be "independent delegates" before the electorate, without substituting even the limited
benefits of a system in which alternative partisan foreign affairs
programs would be submitted for the voters' mandate. The intensity of public debate would be further limited. And strongly
held alternative policies would be foreclosed from the choice of
regional voting blocs even in congressional elections.

The very real dangers of general partisanship in the control of
American foreign relations do not require any such drastic cure.
The essential requirement is to keep the most important foreign
policy issues out of presidential election campaigns. Given the
localistic American party system—especially as it is reflected in
the choice of congressmen—only in a *presidential* election can it
be easily argued that a national mandate has been given, producing
the special evils of partisanship which have already been mentioned: (a) threatening to bring about abrupt shifts in policy, (b)
severely limiting flexibility by partisan commitments, (c) running
the risk of stalemate, (d) tempting the President to use shock
techniques to coerce support, or else (e) in an emergency forcing
him to upset the consistency of his general foreign policy by sudden
drastic concessions to the opposition—all with no assurance, given
the make-up of the parties and the mixture of foreign and domestic
issues, that a truly popular mandate is possible. These dangers
can be kept within manageable limits if the presidential candidates do not contend sharply over major foreign policies in the
quadrennial campaigns.

But the party lines almost certainly will be drawn on foreign
policy in the presidential elections if they are drawn regularly and
tightly *between* elections at the times when Congress considers
foreign affairs. Yet an opposition party cannot be indefinitely expected (except perhaps in time of all-out war) to give mere passive
acquiescence to the major foreign policies of the administration.
Indeed, if it did, the educational and corrective values of moderate
debate would be lost (a real danger in wartime). Normally some

active participation by some leaders of both parties in the formulation of foreign policy is necessary if party lines are to be kept from hardening.

A President is constitutionally charged with leadership in foreign affairs. It seems appropriate for him to *seek to associate in active collaboration with his administration's conduct of foreign relations enough influential members of the opposition party to prevent its lines from solidifying against basic administration foreign policies—while at the same time the President's position as leader of his own party is used to mobilize support for those policies, to the limited extent that it can safely be done without causing the opposition party to consolidate in counteraction.* This practice may be labeled "extrapartisanship"—the administration working outside party lines while maintaining a base of support in its own party.

This extrapartisanship is an additional alternative to partisanship and bipartisanship as a democratic device for the control of American foreign relations. Some may feel it smacks so much of trying to have one's cake and eat it too that it may be regarded as unfeasible. To others the idea may appear trite and the label perhaps pretentious.[4]

This study, then, seeks to examine evidence for and against these three solutions to the problems of achieving democratic control of foreign policy: partisanship, bipartisanship, and extrapartisanship. Three general approaches are utilized:

(1) A statistical analysis of congressional voting to see what it reveals concerning the relative feasibility of the three systems for

4. This extreme observation was made in a recent imposing study of Congress: "Despite abstract talk about the two-party system and the importance of party responsibility, when it comes down to specific issues and campaigns, nobody really wants rigid party lines. A President, for example, who is trying to unify his own party must necessarily try to divide the opposing party. Hence party conflict in the legislative arena becomes a matter of coalition strategy. Both Franklin Roosevelt and Truman suffered from the fact that the opponents to their legislative programs succeeded in maintaining a deep split within the Democratic party ranks. Yet they themselves, while trying to heal this split, were always eagerly looking for sources of support within the Republican party." Bertram M. Gross, *The Legislative Struggle* (New York, McGraw-Hill, 1953), p. 237.

foreign affairs in general and for particular areas of foreign relations.

(2) A descriptive analysis of party organization in Congress for the control of foreign relations. Congressional party organizations are not, of course, the only party organizations. But for all their weakness they are certainly more continuously operative on most foreign affairs than state or local organizations or the national committees. The state of the parties in Congress needs special attention for a practical understanding of their actual and potential role in American foreign relations. The partisan activity of the presidency and of national nominating conventions is also of course of great importance. It will be illustrated by historical examples in Parts I and III. But if Congress cannot somehow be carried along, the President cannot go very far or very fast.

(3) A historical analysis of the role of the parties in American foreign relations from the beginning of World War II to the outbreak of the Korean War, with emphasis on the interwar period. This has proved to be an adequate period for finding examples of passive acquiescence, of partisanship, bipartisanship, and extra-partisanship—with their causes and consequences through a trend of historical evolution. The time is recent enough to suggest some patterns which are still definitely relevant to current developments, while the use of the Korean War as a cutoff date for the detailed analysis makes it possible to examine the course of events with some perspective.

PART ONE

A Statistical Survey of Voting
in Congress on Foreign Affairs

CHAPTER 1

A Method for Analyzing Congressional Voting

DURING the eight-year period from 1943 through 1950 members of the United States Congress put themselves on record 316 times in roll calls relating significantly to foreign affairs. This total includes practically every record vote on a treaty, bill, or resolution (and amendments thereto) dealing with foreign aid, foreign trade, international organizations, international claims, peacetime defense appropriations, the draft, large-scale immigration, and the administration of American foreign relations.[1] Table 1 shows the distribution of these roll calls between House and Senate and in different sessions of Congress.

TABLE 1. Number of Roll Calls Relating to
Foreign Affairs

	House	Senate	Total
78th Congress	10	23	33
79th Congress	21	33	54
80th Congress	23	41	64
81st Congress	41	124	165
ALL	95	221	316

1. Every substantial doubt regarding a particular roll call has been resolved in favor of inclusiveness, but there remain a very few votes which were disregarded because on careful consideration they seemed wholly without significance. Usually these involved questions of legislative procedure exclusively, with no sign of

This constitutes a very substantial body of concrete data which can be used to determine how tightly party lines have actually been drawn, on what issues, and in what parts of the country. Such a record of actual voting behavior in foreign affairs should give some indication of the feasibility of sharpening partisan differences for the choice of the voter, or of encouraging extrapartisan cooperation between the administration and sympathetic individuals of both parties, or even of achieving fully bipartisan collaboration between the recognized leaders of two disciplined parties.

If a highly consistent pattern should emerge within Congress, it could provide a key which would fit far beyond the Capitol buildings and open a door to the structure of opinion within and between the parties in the nation at large. There the "payoff" for the active partisans is the nomination and election of a President once every four years. Especially in foreign affairs the position of the President is pre-eminent among the branches of government. Hence in the long run the levels of partisanship on foreign affairs in either house of Congress are of *special* importance if they reflect a structure of political forces which may vitally affect the outcome of a national convention, shaping the behavior of a nominee in his presidential campaign and perhaps in the White House. Thus for an understanding of the role of American parties in foreign affairs it is important to observe relationships between Congress and the national conventions and to examine roll call data in such a way as to facilitate such comparisons wherever they are pertinent.

One must concede, of course, that record votes do not always approximate the division of opinion even among congressmen, to say nothing of divisions among other individuals across the country who are effective in national politics. At the Capitol members often switch their votes on the same subject, both in committee and on the floor. Votes are affected by momentary surges of passion among the interested public or simply among the legislators. Motivation behind a congressman's vote is usually mixed and unclear, even to the legislator himself. The resulting risks in interpretation are

substantive policy implications. Also ignored were some roll calls involving only Mexican-American relations; for practical purposes these seemed to be domestic issues.

somewhat reduced for the student dealing with statistical aggregates, but they are never eliminated. Another difficulty derives from the fact that parliamentary tactics and the shortage of time cause surprisingly many important issues to be handled on the floor by various types of votes in which individuals are not recorded at all.[2] Finally, the problem of classification is always of fundamental importance in studying roll calls. At what should one look? For what should one look? Data become meaningful only when fitted into categories of analysis; but if those categories should in fact be irrelevant, or wrongly delimited, the significance which seems to reveal itself is purely superficial. Care can minimize but not entirely obviate arbitrariness in drawing the necessary lines.

CLASSIFICATION

Roll Calls. With such reservations, but also with persistent confidence, a study was undertaken of recent congressional roll calls on foreign affairs. The first problem was to select the record votes. The Seventy-eighth Congress (1943–44) was chosen as the starting point, since it was the first post-Pearl Harbor Congress and witnessed the first determined efforts at collaboration across party lines in concrete planning for postwar international relations. A few years later the Eighty-first Congress was, until its final months in 1950, the last "peacetime" Congress before the pattern of American political life was once again twisted by the special tensions of a fighting war, this time in Korea. For that reason, and to permit some degree of time perspective, December 1950 became the cutoff point for this study. In the selection of issues which arose during the intervening years inclusiveness was a prime objective, but such questions as Communist control in the United States, the organization of the military establishment, and arms appropriations *in time of war* were arbitrarily omitted as not bearing a sufficiently

---

2. If unsatisfactory to the managers of the bill, such votes can be reversed more easily than can record votes. The reversal may be sought in a later roll call, more opportunely timed, or else in the ultimate meetings of a Conference Committee between the two houses.

close relationship to foreign affairs. The types of issues ultimately chosen have been indicated at the beginning of this chapter.

Voting Behavior. Once the subjects were identified and the roll calls in House and Senate in each of the four congresses classified accordingly, the data stood arranged for inspection, ready to be analyzed for levels of party loyalty. But party loyalty is an exceedingly vague concept. It was clear that the readiness of a member to go along with most of his fellow partisans might differ markedly according to whether the two parties were arrayed against each other or were in general agreement. Therefore at least two categories of party-support analysis would be needed: "party line" and "two party." And it was also evident that not every two-party majority or every Democratic party-line vote actually supported the *administration's* position. Hence a third, omnibus, classification of "administration support" was required, which would embrace all roll calls.

But what constitutes a "party-line" vote? What percentage of each of the parties must be lined up in opposition to each other? It could be easily argued that the figure ought to be set at 70 or 80 per cent at least, otherwise the party line would be so loose as to be almost accidental, but if this high percentage is used there is danger of biasing the results toward the conclusion that party lines were hardly ever drawn in foreign affairs. Therefore a straight 50 per cent line of division has been chosen. If over half of one party stood against more than half of the other, it was called a party-line vote. If they stood together, it was a two-party vote.[3]

A congressman, then, was credited with "administration support" when his recorded, announced, or paired vote on a particular roll call seemed to conform to what was being sought at the time by the executive authorities primarily concerned. "Two-party support" was credited to an individual when he voted, announced, or paired in company with majorities of the voting members of

3. A lesser problem was posed by the recording of pairs and announcements in addition to votes actually cast. Since votes were being analyzed mainly as a key to the attitudes which congressmen from different parties and regions were willing to have formally recorded, it seemed a mistake to exclude such concrete evidence of a disposition to vote in a definite way. So announced votes and specific yes-and-no pairs were counted as fully recorded votes.

both parties. "Party-line support" occurred when a member registered his vote, announcement, or pair in favor of a position supported by a majority of the voting members of his own party while a majority of the voting members of the other party were opposed.[4]

NUMERATION

It then became possible to make these computations:[5] (1) the times a member went on record in each subject category and what percentage he was recorded in support of the administration; (2) the times the member went on record on two-party majority roll calls on each subject and what percentage he was recorded in support of that majority; (3) the times the member went on record on party-line roll calls on each subject and what percentage he was recorded in support of his own party. The calculations were made separately for each Congress.

Table 2 is a sample page indicating the results of this stage of the calculations. Column A shows the percentage of support which some congressmen in the Eighty-first House gave to the administration, B the support to two-party majorities, and P the support to their own party on party-line votes dealing with foreign aid and tariffs.[6]

4. When the voting members of either party were evenly split on a particular roll call, it was usually possible to decide how to count it by taking into consideration the pairs and announced votes of other members of that party. In a very few cases, however, the party-line or two-party character of the vote remained indeterminate, and the roll call could be counted only for administration-support analysis.

5. For convenience the sessions of the Senate, like those of the House, were labeled with the number of the Congress, although it was recognized that the Senate is a continuing body. Mimeographed lists were prepared for the House and for the Senate in each of the four Congresses with the names of all members arranged by states, including those congressmen who sat for only part of a session. All roll calls were then transcribed to these sheets. Keys were devised which pointed out the different subject categories of roll calls (foreign aid, tariffs, etc.) and showed whether each of a member's votes on a particular subject supported the administration, a two-party majority, or his own party in a party-line situation.

6. This particular example was derived from 23 foreign aid roll calls—16 of which were party line and 7 two party (to one of which the administration was op-

TABLE 2. Sample Compilation of Individuals' Support-Percentages

	FOREIGN AID			TARIFFS		
	A	B	P	A	B	P
MICHIGAN						
12 Bennett (R)	4	29	100	25	50	100
6 Blackney (R)	38	80	75	67	[100]	50
8 Crawford (R)	10	43	100	25	50	100
15 Dingell (D)	100	67	100	[100]		[100]
17 Dondero (R)	17	71	100	0	[0]	[100]
9 Engel (R)	47	80	60	50	[100]	[100]
5 Ford (R)	52	100	63	50	100	100
4 Hoffman (R)	4	29	100	25	50	100
16 Lesinski (D)	100	100	100	100	[100]	[100]
2 Michener (R)	56	100	56	75	100	50
13 O'Brien (D)	79	100	80	100	100	100
11 Potter (R)	14	80	100	25	50	100
14 Rabaut (D)	100	86	100	100	100	100
1 Sadowski (D)	13	25	8	100	[100]	[100]
3 Shafer (R)	14	67	100	25	0	50
7 Wolcott (R)	29	100	92	25	0	50
10 Woodruff (R)	10	40	94	0	0	100
MINNESOTA						
7 Andersen (R)	17	71	100	33	50	[100]
1 Andresen (R)	19	83	100	25	50	100
8 Blatnik (D)	70	86	69	100	100	[100]
9 Hagen (R)	30	71	81	25	50	100
5 Judd (R)	82	86	27	100	100	[0]
6 Marshall (D)	90	83	87	100	100	100
4 McCarthy (D)	89	100	92	100	[100]	[100]
2 O'Hara (R)	9	43	100	0	0	100
3 Wier (D)	77	71	73	100	100	100
MISSISSIPPI						
4 Abernethy (D)	26	43	13	100	100	100
6 Colmer (D)	48	100	29	100	100	100
1 Rankin (D)	4	29	0	100	100	100
2 Whitten (D)	37	80	27	100	100	100
3 Whittington (D)	95	100	100	100	100	100
7 Williams (D)	9	43	0	100	[100]	[100]
5 Winstead (D)	26	43	25	100	100	100

Highlighting Regionalism. With such figures it would of course have been possible to compute the average national depth of these three types of loyalty to party and administration in congressional roll calls dealing with different subjects. Deviations from such averages could then have been measured for members representing different types of constituencies. *Regional* divergencies within the parties could no doubt have been disclosed by this method. But then each "national party average" from which the divergencies were measured would reflect the way in which the sectional composition itself differs within each party between House and Senate and between different sessions of Congress. The overweighting of Mountain states in the Senate is the best example of this. And since the broader purpose of our roll call investigation was not to emphasize the peculiarities of Senate politics but rather to generalize about foreign policy in national politics at large, it seemed preferable to use a method which would highlight any existing similarity in the sectional conflicts which appear in *both* Houses; if very similar they might be found to have significance also for the line-up of forces in presidential nominating conventions where numerically the sections are weighted differently.[7]

---

posed)—and 4 tariff roll calls (2 party line and 2 two party). All were recorded in the Eighty-first House.

There is a serious methodological weakness in the fact that no effort was made to weight the different roll calls within a particular category according to some standard of relative importance, but since any simple standard seemed excessively subjective and a complex standard unworkable, all were allowed to count equally. This means that for validation of the final results it was especially important to find a high degree of consistency; fortunately that proved to be possible.

Another possible objection is that a member's failure to record himself at all on a roll call did not necessarily harm his support record, its only effect being to cause a relative overweighting of the votes he did cast in the same category. However, this potential distortion seems less serious than that which would come from counting every absence as evidence of nonsupport. And when a man was found to have recorded himself only once in a category in which most other members had voted at least twice, his "record" was bracketed as negligible and ignored in later regional averaging in order to minimize accidental distortions.

7. For example, if the Republican party should grow much stronger in the Mountain states, a situation might easily arise in which Eastern Republicans would appear to deviate widely from the average GOP position in the Senate; and yet the Easterners' foreign policies could continue to be dominant in the action of Republican National Conventions. These House-Senate-Convention relationships are discussed at greater length in the next chapter.

Therefore the method adopted was to compare *regional* voting records within each party *directly,* without attempting to compute any *national* party records which would be affected by the relative strength of the regions in a particular party, House, and session.

Of course this approach involved an initial assumption that *regional* conflicts within the parties are of special importance for foreign affairs. The following chapters show that that assumption is valid. The regional divergencies often reflected the varying strength of other divisive factors, such as nationality, religion, and urbanism, but usually the social composition of a particular party in a particular area is sufficiently well recognized to allow pertinent inferences to be drawn from regional data alone, without further detailed statistical measurement of the impact of other factors.[8] In general, such nonstatistical inferences seemed adequate for the purpose of this study, but *metropolitanism* is given special attention in the next chapter.

The next problem was to identify the regions. In order to simplify the statistical task the smallest reasonable number of sections—five—was utilized: Northeast, Midwest, South, Mountain, and Pacific. And state boundaries were used so that Senate and House would be consistent, although the boundaries of political regions in the United States may be drawn more accurately if they cut across various states. The lines that were drawn were of course largely arbitrary. This was because the convenient device of a "border states" category seemed inappropriate for foreign affairs unless further divided into east border and midwest border —sections too small to handle profitably. The assignment of border states was finally made on two grounds: a desire to keep the South as "solid" as possible (since scattered Republican votes there would indicate very little) and a comparison of the foreign aid record of each of the border states in the Eightieth House with that of each of the adjacent regions to see if it was markedly more similar to one than the other. Maryland and Delaware were thus assigned to the Northeast; West Virginia, Kentucky, and Missouri

8. Ensuing analysis will point out, for example, the nationality influences at work on German plant dismantling, religious factors in aid to Franco Spain, economic interests in foreign agricultural policy, and many forces of similar character.

to the Midwest; and Tennessee and Oklahoma to the South. Presumably a different mapping would be more precise for other issues and other sessions of Congress, but consistent use of the same geographical divisions facilitates statistical comparisons.

Regional Computations. Regional averaging constituted the next stage of operations. A calculating machine was used to average the individual percentages of support achieved by all members of each party in each region, with the exception noted above. This was done for each of the categories exemplified by the vertical columns of figures in Table 2. And of course it was done separately for House and Senate in each of the four Congresses.

For the sake of clarity the resulting regional averages were placed in position on blank maps, as shown by those included in the Appendix. A key to their use may be found on page 413. The preparation of about seventy such maps completed the basic calculations required for this study. The records thus tallied and arranged could then be compared by inspection and simple computations.

CHAPTER 2

The Foreign Aid Model

APART from the Korean War itself, the fundamental tool of American postwar foreign policy has been foreign aid. A wide variety of programs has been utilized in an attempt to win for the United States the friendship and if possible the effective support of different foreign peoples and governments. There have been many moods, ranging all the way from the amiable humanitarianism of UNRRA to the calculated power politics of aid to Yugoslavia. There have been varied instruments, national and international, and varied conditions have been placed on the transfers. But the underlying motive has been recurrent—helping others to help themselves, more or less in the American national interest.

Any kind of assistance costs money. It is hardly surprising, therefore, that the most common subject which has confronted Congress in foreign affairs in the past decade has been aid to other nations. Foreign assistance bills of one kind or another—authorizations and appropriations—tend to become the focal points for debate on all aspects of our foreign policy, at least in the area immediately concerned and often in the whole world. Attempts are made to define the objectives of a program more precisely by adding "climate language." Congressmen also seek to turn grants into loans (although insisting at the same time that the loans will never be repaid). Administrative organization is a recurrent issue. There are efforts to alter the emphasis of the aid program (as from economic to military) or to extend it to other parts of the world. The support of domestic interests must be bought by special concessions. Most of these questions, of course, are settled in the committees of Congress or handled in nonrecord votes on the floor, but many require roll calls. The result is that a composite of all significant roll calls on bills and amendments dealing with authorizations or appropriations for assistance to foreign countries constitutes a very broad sampling of congressional opinion on a wide variety of foreign policy questions, though all are related to the basic device of recent American foreign policy—foreign aid.

The foreign aid category in this study remained an omnibus, although separate ratings were also made for most of the lesser subjects which arose more than once during voting on foreign assistance bills. Despite their diversity, such issues did at least reach some focus in the concept of "foreign aid," but no attempt was made to go further and compile statistics collectively on all the 316 roll calls relating to different subjects in foreign *affairs* between 1943 and 1950. There seemed to be too much danger of distorting the results by combining too many variables.

Moreover, even by themselves, the foreign aid roll calls seemed numerous enough to be statistically significant. Table 3 indicates the distribution of the roll calls on which were based foreign aid maps 1–8 in the Appendix.

TABLE 3. Number of Roll Calls Relating to Foreign Aid

	House				Senate			
Congress	All	Two-party	Party line	Per cent party line	All	Two-party	Party line	Per cent party line
78th	8	6	2	25%	7	6	1	14%
79th	12	7	5	42%	15	8	7	47%
80th	10	8	2	20%	17	15	2	12%
81st	23	7	16	70%	66	23	42	64%
TOTAL	53	28	25	47%	105	52	52	50%

(1 roll call indeterminate)

A comparison of Table 3 with Table 1 (p. 21) shows that usually about half of all the foreign affairs roll calls studied were concerned with foreign aid.[1] It was reasonable to suppose that careful examination of the foreign aid maps could suggest a model of interparty and intra-party division on foreign affairs which might then be applied to the more limited and specific subjects.

It was evident at once and confirmed by various checks that within each party there were significant regional variations. This was true in the Democratic party between North and South, with the Mountains going along with the South. It was even more true in the Republican party, between the two Coasts and the Interior.

REPUBLICAN CLEAVAGE

Regional Averages. Inside the Republican party the same regional cleavage appeared on the party-line ballots, the two-party votes, and over-all administration support: almost always Coasts vs. Interior. In the House of Representatives the record was especially clear cut. In every Congress Pacific Republicans had about the same point margin over the Midwest GOP in average two-party support as the Midwesterners had over them in average party-line support. The parallel was strikingly precise, and what was more it also held between Northeast Republicans and their Midwest colleagues, with the former maintaining the same margin in two-party support that the latter secured in party-line support.

1. Table 3 shows further that there was a great variation from one Congress to another in the percentage of all foreign aid roll calls which ran along party lines. But significantly the shifting trends affected both houses similarly. There was no really marked difference between the House and Senate in any one session as to the percentage of all roll calls which were party line—despite the greater facilities in the House for party discipline. This suggests that the rising and falling congressional partisanship was linked in a process of interaction to changes in the national mood which extended far beyond Capitol Hill. Further investigation shows that during World War II party differences were in fact minimized as the Republicans sought by all-out support of the war effort to compensate for their politically embarrassing pre-Pearl Harbor "obstructionism." Then during the Republican Eightieth Congress GOP leaders sought to prevent party-line roll calls at times when there was danger of so many of their members defecting that the Democratic minority would carry the day anyway, and thus earn partisan credit from a public apparently sympathetic to administration foreign policies. But in the Seventy-ninth and Eighty-first Congresses, the Republicans who were hostile were less inhibited; even then only about two-thirds of the foreign aid roll calls were partisan.

In the Senate the respective margins were more varied (except during the Eightieth Congress), but between the East and Midwest similar differences certainly existed.[2] Only the size of the margins was involved. Midwestern Republicans always shrank from two-party majorities; Eastern Republicans recoiled from the party line. The party was consistently divided.

Session by session over the eight-year span the Republican regional pattern showed little change in the relative willingness of different sections to support the party line. In the Eightieth Congress, to be sure, Republicans from the Coasts were even less willing than usual to join their colleagues in a partisan front—and for once the Midwest Senators seemed to feel the same way; Vandenberg's leadership was certainly important in holding the latter's party-line average down to 59 per cent in 1947 and 1948. But with that single exception, in not one Congress, House or Senate, was the average of Midwest party-line support ever *less* than 75 per cent. And in no Congress, House or Senate, was the average of East or Pacific "party-lining" ever *higher* than 75 per cent. Only once did it reach as high as 75; usually it stood in the sixties.

Plainly it would be very difficult to tighten up the foreign policy discipline of a party as deeply divided as this—one major section practically always more partisan than other vital sections *ever* were, and those other sections so recalcitrant that they were unwilling to go along much more than half the time when their own party was arrayed against the opposition party.

This cleavage has been variously identified with Willkie, Dewey, Vandenberg, and Eisenhower, who have been champions of one set of forces, Hoover, MacArthur, and Taft of another. No doubt new leaders will emerge. But the likelihood of uniting East and West on a "Republican" foreign policy seems exceedingly remote. *Distribution of Individual Averages in the Regions.* The question may well be raised, however, to what extent these regional averages may have concealed a wide and perhaps important diversity of Republican voting records within each section. How large a proportion of Eastern Republicans were Midwestern on foreign af-

2. The Pacific Republican Senate delegation was too small to justify comparisons in this connection.

fairs, and vice versa? Was the concentration of strongly contrary Republican attitudes in the different regional camps really as great as the averages would suggest, or was there actually a predominant middle-of-the-road GOP bloc sharing the same views in all sections?

A partial test was made to answer these questions. In the Eightieth and Eighty-first Congresses the administration-support records of individual Republican Representatives on foreign aid were subjected to a frequency distribution analysis.[3] The results are indicated in Chart 1, which shows the number of individual GOP Congressmen from each of the northern sections who supported the administration on foreign aid 0–19 per cent of the time, or 20–39 per cent, 40–59 per cent, etc. On this evidence a number of observations can be made:

(1) The pattern of *distribution* of Eastern GOP records was indeed the same as that of Pacific GOP records, just as their respective regional *averages* were found to be similar.

(2) In the Eightieth Congress the concentration of this Coastal Republican opinion was overwhelmingly in favor of foreign aid policies.

(3) Antiadministration GOP sentiment increased in all sections in the Eighty-first Congress, and there did appear a conspicuous bloc of "Midwestern" Easterners. But nearly three-fifths of the Eastern Republicans were still willing to support the administration at least 40 per cent of the time, while only about one-seventh of the Midwesterners would do so. The regional difference in the distribution of opinion was still very clear.

(4) At least a third of the Midwestern Republicans in the Eightieth Congress constituted an irreconcilably isolationist bloc. The rest of them, in varying degrees along a normal distribution curve, were willing to heed appeals to go along with "bipartisan" policies.

(5) A bell-shaped distribution curve also appeared among Coastal Republicans in the Eighty-first Congress—but this time there was no evidence of an irreconcilable internationalist bloc

3. The figures on *administration support*, on the issue of *foreign aid*, 1947–50, were chosen because these included the greatest number of relevant roll calls which was conveniently available under the general method employed in this study; and the *House* records were used because the larger number of members permitted a deeper frequency distribution count.

CHART *1*. The Distribution of Republican Representatives as to Frequency of Their Support of the Truman Administration on Foreign Aid

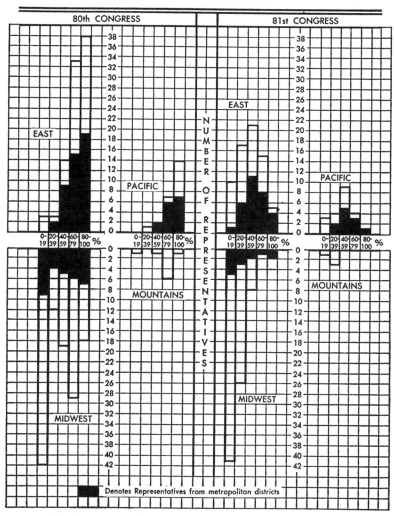

comparable in size to the Midwest opposition faction in the previous years. This might suggest that the Easterners were less doggedly determined about their foreign policies than the Midwesterners, but the evidence would be very sketchy.[4]

(6) In each section there did appear to exist an important

4. Cf. p. 38.

"swing group" whose regional predilections were not intense; this group tended one way in the "Vandenberg era," the other way in the "age of Acheson." It did seem numerous enough in each section to shade together the contrasting regional complexion of the party, but not to blur very much the intensity of either extreme, especially the Midwestern. The middle-of-the-road partisans could scarcely be called predominant over the regionalists.

Foreign Aid Partisanship vs. Over-all Partisanship. Thus the frequency distribution analysis generally confirms, with clarifying details, the pattern of GOP cleavage on foreign policy which appeared through the simpler process of averaging the records of regional party delegations. It may not be thought enough, however, merely to show that there is a concentration of Republicans in the Interior whose views on foreign affairs differ strongly from those of other GOP members who are most numerous on the Coasts. Obviously there are also many *domestic* questions on which Eastern Republicans differ considerably from their Midwestern colleagues. Are the foreign policy conflicts significantly greater than conflicts over GOP policy in general?

With available figures it can be shown that they were measurably greater in the Eighty-first Congress at least. The Congressional Quarterly News Features service has compiled over-all "party unity" percentage figures for the members of Senate and House in that biennium.[5] These were derived in the same manner as the party-line support figures in this study, except that the *Congressional Quarterly* used *all* party-line roll calls, whatever their subject.[6] It has therefore been possible to compare the partisanship level of named congressmen on foreign aid questions with their general record of partisanship.

Accordingly, Table 4 shows the number of Republican congressmen from different parts of the country whose percentage of party-line support on foreign aid roll calls differed more or less from their percentage of party-line support on all roll calls combined.

5. *Congressional Quarterly Almanac* (Washington, Congressional Quarterly News Features, 1950), *6*, 59–61.

6. The *Congressional Quarterly* found 138 party-line roll calls in the Eighty-first House; this study found 16 on foreign aid or 12 per cent. Party-line roll calls in the Senate totaled 292, of which 42 were on foreign aid or 14 per cent.

These figures demonstrate that in the Eighty-first House virtually half of all Eastern Republicans were substantially less willing to vote the party line on foreign aid than to vote it on all issues combined, and in the Senate well *over* half shared the same reluctance. Only a negligible number of Eastern Republicans in the House and none at all in the Senate felt more than usually partisan when it came to foreign aid.

TABLE 4. Republican Foreign Aid Partisanship vs. Over-all Partisanship in the Eighty-first Congress

	Total	F.A.P. 30-plus points Less than O.P.	F.A.P. 20-29 points Less than O.P.	F.A.P. 10-19 points Less than O.P.	F.A.P. like O.P.	F.A.P. 10-19 points More than O.P.	F.A.P. 20-29 points More than O.P.	F.A.P. 30-plus points More than O.P.
East Sens.	13	3	4	1	5	—	—	—
East Reps.	67	18	7	7	26	6	2	1
M'west Sens.	20	2	—	3	8	4	2	1
M'west Reps.	74	3	2	3	33	24	3	6
South Sens.	—	—	—	—	—	—	—	—
South Reps.	3	—	—	—	2	1	—	—
Mount. Sens.	5	—	—	—	1	4	—	—
Mount. Reps.	4	—	—	—	2	2	—	—
Pacif. Sens.	4	—	—	1	3	—	—	—
Pacif. Reps.	20	1	5	—	10	4	—	—

On the other hand, Midwest and Mountain Republicans in the House were about evenly divided between those who were *as* partisan and those who were *more* partisan than usual where foreign aid was involved; only a negligible number in these states acted *less* partisan in regard to foreign aid. Even in the Senate the number of Midwest Republicans who were more partisan exceeded those who were less, while among the Mountain men the difference was overwhelming.

Moving westward to the Pacific Coast, we find the familiar pattern repeating itself with the re-emergence of a large minority much less partisan on foreign aid than on other issues. It is plain that throughout the country foreign affairs widened the divisions between Coastal Republicans and their colleagues from the great Interior. A large segment of the Old Guard became even more orthodox than usual when it looked at the outside world, while the heterodox "me-tooers" became positively heretic.

This does not reveal the whole story, however. Fully a quarter of Eastern Republicans had foreign aid records more than 30 points lower than their general average of partisanship—some ranging down 50 and 60 points. Many of these men were highly orthodox Republicans, except in foreign affairs. They included leaders like James Wadsworth (down from 90 per cent to 55 per cent), Richard B. Wigglesworth (down from 81 to 44), and to a slightly less degree Joseph W. Martin himself (down from 89 to 63). Remember that 12 per cent of all the party-line roll calls were *on* foreign aid. It follows plainly that there were a substantial number of Easterners who practically never voted against their party except on foreign affairs—and then did so quite frequently. They were witnesses to the fact that the foreign policy conflict in the Republican party is not just warfare between the generations. It is a disagreement within the Old Guard itself.

Metropolitanism. The regional cleavage on foreign affairs cuts across rural-urban lines of division in the GOP. That was another lesson of this study. Reference to Chart 1 above will make the point clear. There the heavy shading indicates the division of opinion among Republican Representatives from within the commuters' environs (broadly construed) of the two dozen largest metropolitan areas in America (those of at least a half million population each).[7] It will be readily observed that there was no striking difference in the distribution of administration support on foreign aid between the metropolitan and nonmetropolitan GOP congressmen from any particular region. The *regional* records differed markedly, but within any one of them the weight of recorded opinion was spread about the same, whether a member's district lay inside or outside the environs of one of the biggest cities. On the part of Republicans from the greatest population centers, supposedly more cosmopolitan, only a very slight tendency could be observed toward a support of foreign aid greater than their colleagues' from smaller cities and rural areas within their same region. The similarities in their records are much more impressive than these slight differences.

Much more detailed breakdowns would be required if the object were to measure the relative pull of regionalism against various *degrees* of urbanism in population centers of several different sizes. For the purpose of this study, however, a simple demonstration like that above should suffice to show that urbanism is not a simple explanation of the GOP regional cleavage on foreign affairs. No doubt it is one factor involved, as are foreign commerce, nationalities, and religion. The result is a set of biases dividing Republicans very largely along geographical lines. For present purposes it is enough simply to re-emphasize how that fact—the existence of a Coast-Interior cleavage—is confirmed by varied analysis of the congressional voting record on foreign aid, 1943–50. *Nominating a President.* Can it also be confirmed in the voting at a Republican National Convention? In the period covered in detail in the historical chapters below there were two nominating conventions, 1944 and 1948. The reality of sectional cleavage on foreign policy was evident on both occasions, but for special reasons it did not erupt explicitly in balloting on the floor. The Taft-Eisenhower battle of 1952 was a much more clear-cut case. Hence

7. Selection was based generally upon the 1950 United States Census Bureau determinations. But where one of these super-cities was found to have very large satellite cities nearby, they were included within the core of the metropolitan area, on the assumption that such constituencies would share many of the cultural traits of a great metropolis.

that episode will be considered briefly here, although as a whole it is outside the chronological limits of this study.

Of course foreign policy was not the only important issue between Taft and Eisenhower in 1952, but it was an outstanding issue in the minds of most delegates and interested citizens, and continued to be even after John Foster Dulles had achieved a formal agreement between the candidates on the foreign policy plank in the platform. Without minimizing the potency of Eisenhower's personality, the argument that "Taft can't win," or the apparent revulsion from Taft's "grab" for Texas delegates, it seems certain that the line-up of forces in the 1952 Republican Convention was very largely a reflection of differences on foreign policy between powerful camps of GOP politicians, together with their respective backers among the mass media, the big campaign contributors, and the vocal public. And consequently the record of votes at the convention might well be expected to be indicative—though by no means conclusive—of the structure of politically effective Republican opinion on foreign policy. That did indeed prove to be the case—and the Coast-Interior cleavage so familiar in Congress was once again decisively demonstrated.

The convention is the payoff for the factions of a national party. See Chart 2 for the Taft strength in different regions of the country as the 1952 Convention progressed. The graphs move chronologically from one issue to another and from one forum to another. They show on each point the pro-Taft percentage of all the delegate votes which were officially counted from the indicated region. Conspicuous is the die-hard Taftite determination of more than half the Midwesterners; also the very similar division of opinion in the Mountains, though there the weaker GOP organizations did crack in the end and join Eisenhower; obvious too is Taft's mastery of the Southern "pocket-boroughs," until Eisenhower wrested a third of them from him and then the others (patronage hungry) rapidly hailed their new master. On the other side, it is clear that GOP leaders on both Coasts became nearly unanimous in their determination to block Taft at the convention, although the substantial pro-Taft vote of Eastern National committeemen on the Texas-delegate "compromise" suggests that their later show of

CHART 2. Taft Strength at the 1952 GOP Convention

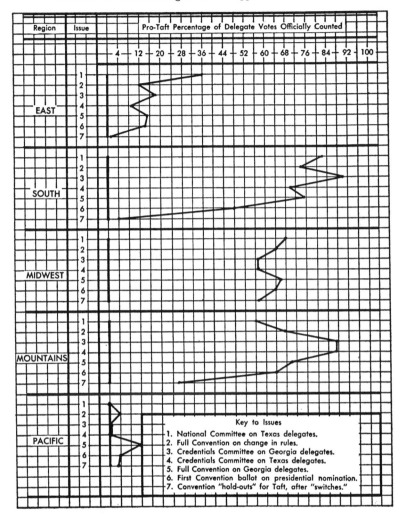

Region	Issue	Pro-Taft Percentage of Delegate Votes Officially Counted

Key to Issues
1. National Committee on Texas delegates.
2. Full Convention on change in rules.
3. Credentials Committee on Georgia delegates.
4. Credentials Committee on Texas delegates.
5. Full Convention on Georgia delegates.
6. First Convention ballot on presidential nomination.
7. Convention "hold-outs" for Taft, after "switches."

unanimity was somewhat forced, and on the Pacific seaboard Earl
Warren was able to deprive Taft of delegates only by holding them
to the very end himself; he could not, if he would, deliver them all
to Eisenhower.

In short, at the 1952 Convention there was actually considerable
Taft support (concealed) from the Coasts, and much Eisenhower

support (open) from the Interior; there was no impassable gulf between them. But the *preponderance* of preference in the one region differed strongly from that in the other. The voting pattern is very nearly the same as that which had appeared on foreign aid in Congress, which is not surprising, since the two phenomena are related. They both largely reflect the structure of effective Republican opinion on foreign affairs.

It seems clear that if foreign policy issues are allowed to come to a head in a Republican National Convention they reveal the party divided region by region, very much as it is on such issues in Congress. But the regions are weighted differently in a convention from their balance in the House or in the Senate. That is highly important. It is one reason why there can be no presumption that a general record on foreign affairs which is made by any small majority of the GOP congressmen will be confirmed at their presidential nominating convention. An Eisenhower could be nominated after an Eighty-second Congress in which most of the vocal Republicans had *seemed* to be preoccupied with anti-Achesonism, under the leadership of Taft, MacArthur, and McCarthy. Actually, of course, the GOP was divided on foreign affairs before Eisenhower's nomination and continued to be thereafter. In large measure what had happened was simply that the convention registered a different balance between the same conflicting forces (not being able to avoid the issue as it had in 1944 and 1948). And the different balance was heavily affected by the regional apportionment of convention delegates as contrasted with that of Senators and Representatives.[8]

What then are the differences? Chart 3 should help to clarify them. It shows for each Congress from 1943 through 1954 what percentage of all the GOP members of the House and Senate respectively came from each region, and what the regional division of delegates was at Republican National Conventions during the same period. A number of observations may be made:

8. Of course it is recognized that other major factors were at work. Aspects of the 1952 Convention are being utilized here only to illustrate some general characteristics of the Republican party which are of recurring importance when it deals with foreign affairs.

CHART 3. Regional Distribution of Republican Congressmen and Convention Delegates

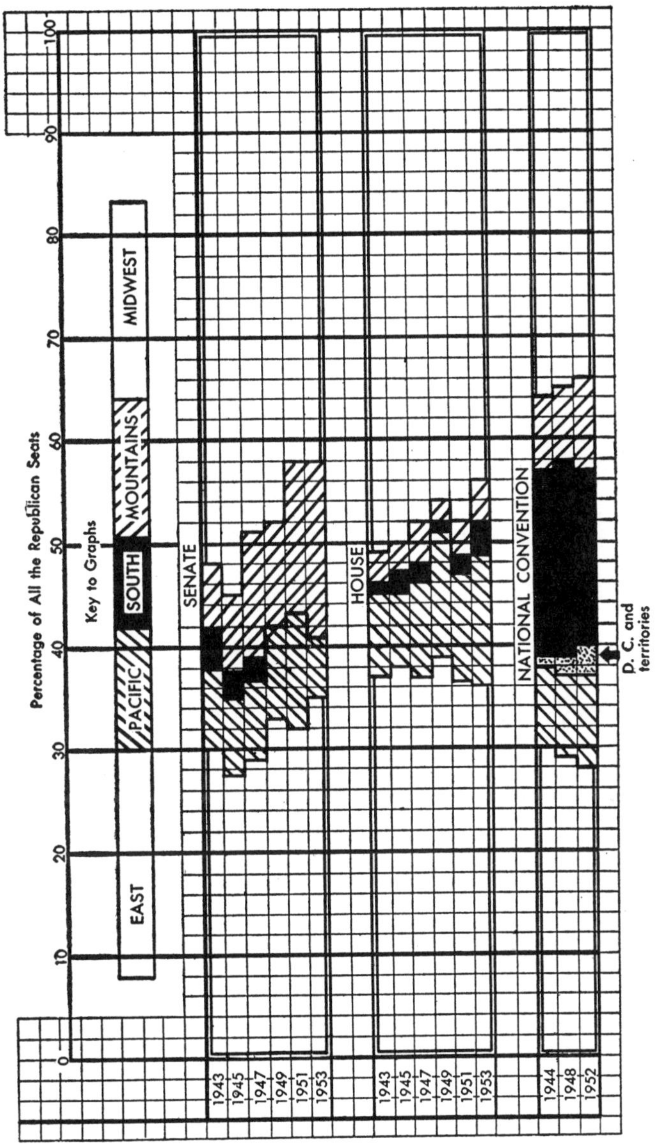

(1) Through a dozen years of electoral victories and defeats, the relative regional balance of the party did not change very much in the House or in the Senate or in the conventions. The only shifts that seem noteworthy were the growing strength of Pacific Representatives and Mountain Senators in the GOP. As the result of related population movements and electoral successes, the strength of both these western regions increased a little in the 1952 Convention, and is likely to continue to do so. But these increases will cancel each other out in their impact on the foreign policy determinations of GOP National Conventions if the Mountain and Pacific Republicans continue to differ as much on world affairs as have the Easterners and Midwesterners.

(2) In the House of Representatives the proportion of Republicans from the Coasts (Northeast plus Pacific) was just about equal to that from the Interior (Midwest plus Mountains). Likewise in the National Convention the Coastal GOP almost equaled the Interior.

(3) In the Senate, however, the Interior outweighed the coasts about three to two. Moreover, the impact of that overbalance may have been amplified by another development of the last ten years —the steady internal shift of numerical strength from the Midwest toward the Mountains, where GOP opinion was, if anything, even more hostile to the foreign policies prevalent on the seaboard.

(4) In short, when evaluating the foreign affairs record of the Republican party as a whole, it is well always to keep in mind that its members from the Interior are not likely to show the strength at a presidential nominating convention that they show in the United States Senate.

(5) In a Coast-Interior showdown at a National Convention, the balance of power is likely to be in the hands of Southern delegates. The weakness of the Southern organizations has in the past made these men very manipulatable by Northern politicians. But if a vitalized GOP in the South becomes self-reliant, one may anticipate a tendency of its leaders to find common ground with Coastal Republicans, when foreign policy is the issue. Correspondingly, the *Senate* Republicans might become increasingly atypical of the party as a whole on foreign affairs.

But this last observation rests on evidence which has not yet been presented. The foreign policies of a future vital Southern GOP can hardly be predicted without a prior examination of the record of the Democrats who would have to be won over to build it.

DEMOCRATIC CLEAVAGE

Up to this point analysis has concentrated on cleavages in the Republican party. But the Democrats also had their differences on foreign affairs, which, like the GOP conflicts, can be observed in the record of congressional voting on foreign aid legislation during the period 1943–50.[9]

Regional Differences. The Democratic differences shown then were mainly North against South, as was to be expected. A little more surprising was the solidarity of Midwestern Democrats and their Eastern colleagues. On roll calls relating to foreign aid the administration always received virtually the same average level of support from Democrats from the Northeast, the Midwest, and the Pacific Coast. And it was never less than 90 per cent, except in the Eighty-first Senate. On that occasion the average was 87, thanks to the lower support record of Guy Gillette of Iowa. This is a matter of consequence, because in the years under consideration there were very few other "Prairie Democrats" in Congress; the Great Plains states sent almost solid Republican delegations to Washington. Back in the thirties the then more numerous Democratic congressmen from this region had shown marked isolationist tendencies, like their GOP neighbors.[10] Probably in the forties also the Midwestern Democrats would not have averaged such very high support of administration foreign aid policies if the membership component from the Prairies had still been substantial. In the adjacent Mountain region, which did continue to have large Democratic representation, the congressmen showed strong doubts about the administration's proposals in foreign affairs—very much as did their fellow partisans from the South.

9. Cf. foreign aid maps 1–8 in the Appendix.

10. George L. Grassmuck, *Sectional Biases in Congress on Foreign Policy* (Baltimore, Johns Hopkins, 1951), p. 101. This whole work is a valuable statistical study of the period 1921–41.

In general during the period 1943–50 it appeared that in foreign as in domestic affairs, in the places where the Democratic party was predominantly urban, its congressmen were quite willing to take their cue from the executive; but where agriculture and mining were the major forces, recalcitrance emerged. The presence of a Democratic administration was plainly of great importance in holding the party together on foreign affairs. If thrown into opposition for a substantial period of time, Democrats might well become as conspicuously divided on foreign policy as Republicans. Actually in the twenties, on legislation resembling foreign aid, the range of regional attitudes in the Democratic party was much greater than that in the GOP.[11] And even with a Democrat in the White House the South-Northeast difference among Democrats on foreign aid, 1947–50, was almost as great as the Midwest-Northeast difference among Republicans. By the statistics compiled for this study the percentage-point disparities on average administration support were much the same. Republicans all stood at a somewhat lower level, but within the respective parties those regional margins were quite similar.

Further examination of the Southerners' foreign aid record showed that they were relatively cooperative when a two-party consensus existed. To go along with a two-party majority usually also meant going along with a New Deal Administration, but still the Southerners would do it to the same degree as Eastern Republicans and far more than Midwestern Republicans. When it came to a party-line vote, however, Democrats from the South and Mountains shied away. Their support percentages on such roll calls hovered in and around the seventies, while their Northern colleagues rarely sank below 90. In the Eightieth and Eighty-first Congresses Southern defections from party-line support were about as great as those of Eastern Republicans from Midwestern GOP standards. The North-South disagreement was real and persistent throughout the 1943–50 period. Moreover, these conflicts seemed likely to become more noticeable when there was no longer a Democratic President in the White House to give a lead to his party on foreign affairs, taking advantage of the special executive prerogatives in this field.

11. *Ibid.*, p. 103.

Distortion in Representation. A further consideration now presents itself. On issues where North and South are divided, the Democrats in Congress, if deprived of presidential leadership, are especially likely to drift in a direction contrary to that which would probably be espoused by a Democratic President. This tendency results in large part from the peculiar balance of power in the party. Since the 1936 abolition of the two-thirds rule in Democratic conventions, there has been an extreme disparity between the strength of various regions of the party in Congress and their power at conventions. Chart 4 shows how very great the difference is. Between 1943 and 1954 the Southerners consistently held around 45 per cent of the Democratic seats in the Senate and around 50 per cent of those in the House—but only about 25 per cent of the votes at national conventions. The problem may be stated another way: East, Midwest, and Pacific Democrats together generally constituted one-third of their party in the Senate, one-half in the House, and two-thirds at the conventions. As long as policy differences in the Democratic party are largely regional, even on foreign affairs, such extreme disparities vastly complicate all the other difficulties which would be involved in trying to formulate an agreed party program which could really be implemented. Indeed, in a sense, the demise of the two-thirds rule constitutes an admission that agreement on program is less important to the party than the nomination of a potential winner for the presidency. Democratic experience would indicate that the party can scarcely ever win the White House if Southerners have as strong a voice in picking the candidates as they are bound to have in Congress. So a platform and a presidential nomination can now be made by a simple majority of the convention, and if the election is won, the North-South disagreements among Democrats can simply be superimposed upon the other traditional rivalries between President and Congress. This pattern has now become fairly familiar in domestic affairs; it could also produce serious confusion and tension on international relations. It is an important obstacle to any durably disciplined Democratic foreign policy—at least under the existing party alignment.

CHART 4. Regional Distribution of Democratic Congressmen and Convention Delegates

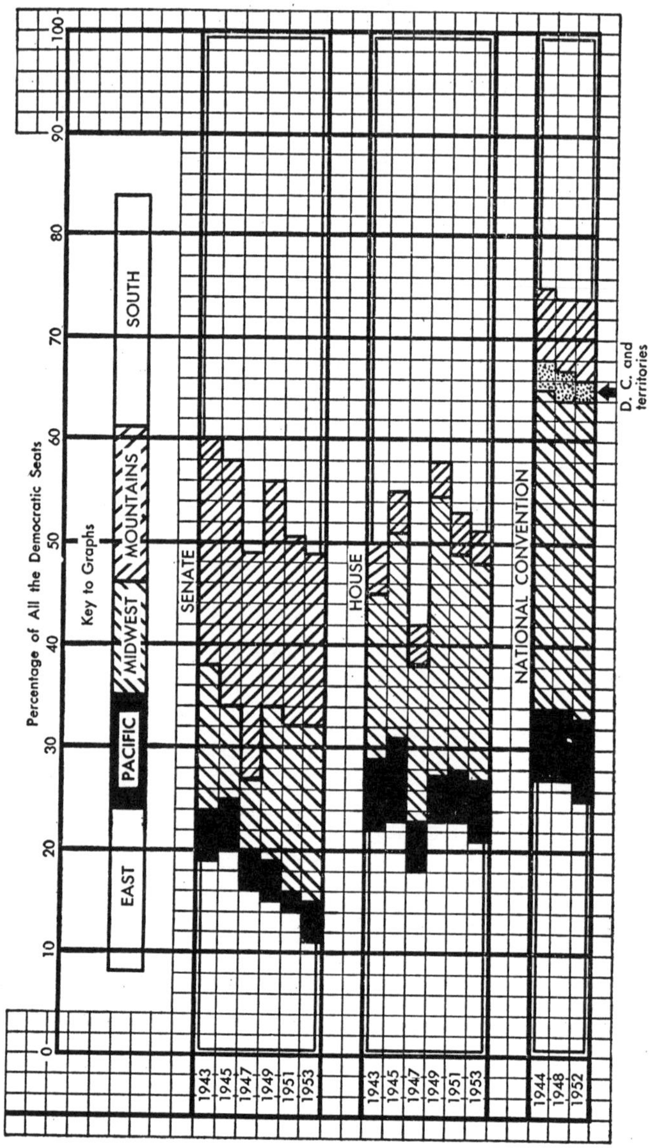

But what of the prospects for realignment? What bearing would foreign affairs have on the breakup of the Solid South? To what extent has foreign policy been a net unifying force in the Democratic party, granted that the party has been significantly divided on this as on other subjects?

To test this question, the *Congressional Quarterly's* figures were again used as they had been for the Republicans. From the *CQ* this time came the Democrats' individual percentages of over-all party-line support in the Eighty-first Congress, and they were compared, man for man, with the individual foreign aid percentages which were computed for this study. Table 5 summarizes the evidence. It was much less clear cut than that of the Republicans. Major differences existed between House and Senate. Only in the House could it be asserted that foreign affairs were a unifying factor for Democrats. In the Senate the evidence pointed the other way.

Such largely contradictory evidence from a single Congress must be handled very cautiously. But this much can be said. The proportion of Southerners who differentiated sharply between most of their party's policies and its foreign aid policies—supporting the latter much more than the former—was much smaller than the proportion of Eastern Republicans who made a similar distinction. It could be hazarded that foreign policy considerations would not seriously impede a breakup of the Solid South on other grounds, unless Midwestern Republicans were to try to impose their foreign policies on the resulting conservative coalition.

That exception seems important, for the evidence has indicated that on foreign affairs most Southern conservatives found a common meeting ground with Eastern Republicans only. For example, on foreign aid in the Eighty-first Congress only a fifth of the Southern Democrats in the House and a quarter in the Senate had percentages of administration support smaller than the Eastern Republican average, which of course was the administration's peak among Republicans. And throughout the postwar period the Midwest GOP not only upheld its party line but definitely shied away

TABLE 5. Democratic Foreign Aid Partisanship vs. Over-all Partisanship in the Eighty-first Congress

	Total	F.A.P. 30–plus points Less than O.P.	F.A.P. 20–29 points Less than O.P.	F.A.P. 10–19 points Less than O.P.	F.A.P. like O.P.	F.A.P. 10–19 points More than O.P.	F.A.P. 20–29 points More than O.P.	F.A.P. 30–plus points More than O.P.
East Sens.	9	—	—	—	4	4	1	—
East Reps.	59	4	—	1	43	10	1	—
M'west Sens.	8	—	1	—	6	1	—	—
M'west Reps.	67	3	2	4	37	21	—	—
South Sens.	24	2	4	4	11	3	—	—
South Reps.	108	12	3	6	22	37	18	10
Mount. Sens.	11	2	—	3	5	1	—	—
Mount. Reps.	11	—	—	—	7	3	1	—
Pacif. Sens.	2	—	—	—	2	—	—	—
Pacif. Reps.	13	1	—	—	10	2	—	—

from two-party majorities in which Southerners and Eastern Republicans were glad to participate. In no biennium of House or Senate did either of those groups have two-party support averages of less than 80 per cent on foreign aid; Midwest Republicans never once stood so high. Thus, to generalize, Midwestern conservatives seem to be in a position where, if they were to succeed in committing the Republican party to their foreign policy position, they would thereby jeopardize their chance to make deep inroads on the conservative South, just as they would risk serious friction with conservatives in the East. On the other hand, one might anticipate that Eastern and Southern conservatives in a left-right realignment would not find it safe to try to impose the discipline of *their* foreign policy on Midwesterners.

What of the hypothetical "liberal" opposition? From the postwar record it would appear that the Northern Democrats and their allies among progressive Southerners would be in general agreement on foreign policy. But there seems good reason to doubt that this solidarity would be reliable, especially when the party was in opposition. Potentially grave divisive factors would remain, such as nationality, religion, special economic interests in foreign relations, and a deep-seated belligerency and isolationism among many lower class voters which might well be set against the conciliatory cosmopolitanism of liberal intellectuals. Powerful forces like these could often be expected to resist party consolidation on foreign policy, inasmuch as the alignment was one where the basis of genuine intra-party agreement lay in *domestic* interests and programs. Policy makers among the liberals would be unwise to rely on party solidarity to enable them to get along safely on foreign affairs without collaboration with sympathetic members of the conservative party—almost as unwise as either foreign policy faction of the conservatives would be if it should look only to the right for support. Thus the distant possibility of achieving a new party alignment on domestic issues would probably be improved if some kind of fluidity across the lines were deliberately maintained on foreign affairs.

In reaching the conclusions in this chapter heavy reliance has been placed on the record of congressional voting on foreign aid legislation, including amendments and appropriations, during the years 1943–50. The implications of that record for the action of presidential nominating conventions have been suggested, and in one case partially checked (GOP, 1952). But the foreign aid roll calls remain the core of the evidence thus far; so the resulting description of interparty and regional intra-party differences on international relations may appropriately be called a "foreign aid model." It is a picture of Democrats divided North and South, Republicans divided Coast and Interior, with whole regions colored accordingly, and with no assurance that even a realignment would bring clear-cut party programs on foreign policy.

But is this model an adequate description of congressional voting on other issues in world affairs, some of which have cut across foreign aid questions, some of which were handled quite independently? Foreign aid roll calls, despite their omnibus subject matter, totaled only about half of all the record votes on international policy from 1943 to 1950. Did the voting on narrower topics resemble that on foreign aid? Could the same model structure, with minor deviations, be found to recur again and again in the roll calls on most of the other separate subjects? If so, the risk would be minimized that "foreign aid" embraced either too many or too few record votes. Any consistency which could be found in the voting on different questions would tend to confirm a presumptive pattern of voting behavior and lend weight to its implications. The foreign aid model must therefore be compared with the record on other subjects, to see how far it may be validated.

CHAPTER 3

The Foreign Aid Model Confirmed

ROLL CALLS on a large majority of subjects in the Seventy-eighth through the Eighty-first Congresses did in fact fit the foreign aid model more or less closely in that levels of party solidarity rose and fell on different issues, but the familiar regional cleavages were only rarely bridged in the Democratic party and almost never in the Republican. To be sure, there were a few issues on which unusual lines of cleavage or extraordinary depths appeared, making the foreign aid model largely inapplicable. Those will be dealt with in the next chapter. Here we are concerned with the subjects to which it was generally applicable.

These can be subdivided into four classes: (1) issues on which records of both parties fitted the model closely, (2) issues on which the Democrats closed ranks but the Republicans remained divided as usual, (3) issues on which both parties solidified in opposition to each other, and (4) issues on which both parties joined in near consensus. Common to all of these, however, was the absence of any striking divergence from the intra-party lineup of forces which was evident on foreign assistance.

CONGRESS DIVIDED AS ON FOREIGN AID

Of the subjects which fitted the model most closely in the years 1943–50, those of enduring importance were Point Four and benefits to American agriculture under tariff and foreign assistance laws.

Point Four. In the Eighty-first Congress the Senate held five roll calls on the program for underdeveloped countries which President Truman announced in his inaugural address of January 17, 1949. This was explicitly a special kind of foreign aid project; so it is not surprising that the Senate record showed cleavages within and between the parties which were not very different from those which appeared on average foreign aid roll calls. Partisanship was somewhat greater than usual—considerably more so in the House, where fewer record votes were taken. But it is difficult to escape the conclusion that this discrepancy would not have been conspicuous if President Truman had not persisted in identifying the program as his personal creation, even after two Republican congressmen, Herter and Saltonstall, had rescued part of it from probable defeat by revising it.

Agricultural Benefits. It may be said that attitudes toward Point Four are obviously akin to attitudes toward foreign aid in general. But there is no such transparent relationship between support of foreign aid and resistance to farm-bloc "grabs." Yet in fact a connection appears. There were repeated efforts in the forties to secure special advantages for American agriculture under the foreign aid and tariff laws. Most of them could be handled without record votes. But when roll calls were required they followed the foreign aid model, except that the Republican party showed itself even more deeply divided East and West than was usual on foreign policy questions. Compared with their fellow partisans, Northeasterners in both parties were the least interested in benefits for farmers, but Southern Democrats did maintain as high an average of administration support as did Northeastern Republicans—both much higher than Interior Republicans. That may be seen on maps 9-12 in the Appendix. In part, it reflected the greater sympathy Southerners and Eastern Republicans felt for foreign aid and low tariffs; they had inhibitions against impairing broad international programs. But the recorded willingness of Southern agriculturalists to go along also reflected the fact that they were satisfied with what they could obtain *without roll calls.* (The classic example was tobacco shipments under the Economic Cooperation Administration.) Record votes were usually needed only on Interior "Republican" crops.

It seems worth while to go into some historical detail to illustrate this pattern of farm-bloc impact upon the parties in Congress when they handled foreign affairs legislation in the forties. This should serve incidentally as a brief case study in resistance to pressures from a powerful domestic economic interest upon the conduct of American foreign relations. What were the issues on which the struggle actually came to a head in formal roll calls?

Tracing the record votes, we find first that in the Seventy-eighth Senate Langer forced a roll call on April 10, 1945, in a vain effort to prevent the lend-leasing of farm machinery; this restriction would have helped the growers of a variety of crops in different parts of the country but would have upset the aid program for restoring European agriculture. Then on June 20 three Senators who were mainly interested in cheese, wool, and cattle sought to amend the reciprocal trade extension to prohibit tariff cuts on more commodities than even they could identify.[1] That failing, the secondary objective was import quotas on wool, also rejected. The crops known to be involved in these June amendments were of concern to a larger proportion of Republican than of Democratic Senators. So it was not surprising that Democrats stood at least four to one against the amendments as they had in April, while Republicans were very much divided.

Among record votes in the Eightieth Congress the foreign policy agricultural issue was the Wool bill. In the House a Senate price-support measure for American wool producers had been amended to provide import fees if wool imports threatened the program. Despite the State Department's protests that the Geneva trade conference then in progress was being endangered, the inter-House Conference Committee authorized import quotas as well as fees. Democratic opposition was made easy by the narrow geographic base of the particular farm interest involved. In the only House roll call on the subject (June 16, 1947) Minority Leader Rayburn sought in vain to have the bill recommitted to conference. Both

1. *Congressional Record,* June 19, 1945, p. 6266.

parties were internally divided about four to one. The cleavage
was heavily sectional. Practically all Republican opposition to the
bill came from the East, where it included more than half of the
delegation; Democratic support for the measure was concentrated
in the grazing areas of the country. In the Senate the same pattern
reappeared on June 19, when the conference report was approved
on a roll call. A presidential veto, however, ultimately killed the
bill.

In the Eighty-first House there was no record vote on benefits
for American agriculture under our tariff or foreign aid policy,
but in the Senate there were no less than seven roll calls in this
category. The main struggle came in 1949 during the consideration of the authorization and appropriation for the second year of
the European recovery program. Agricultural surpluses were then
a major issue in domestic politics, and the temptation was strong
to use ECA to dump farm commodities abroad. The wheat growers
proved to be the agricultural interest least content to trust ECA to
dispose of their surpluses under the partly discretionary authority
provided in the basic enactment. Canadian wheat was being
bought even though the American product was selling below
parity. The wheat belt is predominantly Republican, so that naturally the plea on behalf of wheat attracted Republican support—
three out of every four recorded GOP members. And, as was
equally understandable, given the emphasis on wheat Democrats
were able to mobilize six-to-one opposition when those Republicans tried to prohibit ECA from purchasing commodities abroad
which were selling below parity in the United States. But both
parties were much more evenly divided when Senator Gillette
undertook to take care of the corn processors (just as the wheat
processors were being benefited) by requiring that a fixed percentage of ECA corn shipments be milled before export.

The major struggle over farm exports under the European Recovery Program came, however, during the summer, on the McClellan amendment to the ECA appropriation bill. Agency officials had
sought to protect their full budget request by pointing out to farm
Senators how much of it was scheduled to go for surplus agricultural commodities. But Senator McClellan nearly outfoxed them;

the Appropriations Committee reported a bill with the total reduced, but including a proviso that the amount originally requested for farm products could not be spent for anything else. Even the major farm organizations then joined the administration in protesting this particular technique for disposing of farm surpluses. On the floor it ran into a parliamentary tangle in which the Senate first voted that the proviso was germane, but then that it was unacceptable as legislation in an appropriations bill. To unsnarl the situation, the measure was recommitted, but it came back to the Senate with the agricultural amendment only slightly reworded. Its effect now was to require ECA to spend *proportionately* as much for farm commodities as had originally been requested, making allowance for the over-all appropriations cut. The Senate, however, was still in a mood to rebuke the committee for its frequent highhandedness in rewriting legislation through money bills. Once again the farm amendment was ruled out, and McClellan was driven to seek suspension of the rules in order to include it. He failed by one vote to get even a simple majority; that was of course far short of the two-thirds vote required.

All four record votes (germaneness, money-bill legislation, money-bill legislation again, and suspension) found both parties deeply divided. Unquestionably, the power of the Senate Appropriations Committee was an independent issue throughout the battle. But the geographic division of votes in both parties showed that, whatever the expressed sentiments of the farm organizations, some supposed advantage for agriculture was a prime consideration among many of McClellan's supporters. To be sure, the government would pay for farm surpluses one way or another. It was mainly a question whether the crops would pile up in United States warehouses for CCC money or go to Europe for ECA money, but the latter was a shrewder way of preserving public consent to an expensive price-support program. ECA might at least be prevented from changing its own mind about the size of its payments to American farmers. Southern Democrats, however, showed themselves more willing than the Interior (also rural) Republicans to take a chance on ECA for the sake of the European Recovery Program.

On May 5, 1950, Senator Young repeated the attempt that had been made the year before on behalf of the wheat growers, to eliminate all ECA discretion regarding purchase *abroad* of commodities selling below parity in the United States. Again the amendment failed, this time on the third year's authorization for the European recovery program. The margins in both parties were the same as in 1949. Wheat still interested Republicans far more than Democrats.

When regional party records were computed for all seven roll calls in the Eighty-first Senate, it was evident that Eastern Republicans and Southern Democrats had exactly the same average percentage of administration support—much lower than the urban Northeast Democrats, but more than 40 points higher than that of Interior Republicans. The pattern was the same as in previous years when the subject of congressional roll calls was benefits for American farmers under the country's tariff or foreign aid laws. Most Eastern Republicans and Southern Democrats had far more affinity for each other than either group had for the other wing of its own party, and in the Republican party sectional cleavage was extraordinarily great. The evidence, to be sure, was limited, and its significance was diminished by the fact that so many of the roll calls concerned crops from Interior Republican regions of the country. Conceivably on cotton or tobacco there could have been more Republican solidarity. But roll calls were not required to protect the special interests of Southern farmers, largely because Interior Republicans did not care about safeguarding foreign aid programs against Southern "grabs," but instead wanted to secure further advantages from them for their own farmers. Southern Democrats and Eastern Republicans, on the other hand, once they had satisfied themselves, were willing to defend the program against demands made on behalf of other farm interests. The Southerners and the Eastern GOP were of course not nearly so deaf to farmers' demands as were Northeastern (urban) Democratic Senators. But they were all often willing to uphold foreign policy principles at the expense of some farmers—especially Midwesterners. The latter, in contrast, had foreign policy principles which gave them no special incentive to retaliate in kind against the Southerners: "Any American farmer would be more deserving than Europeans."

This appeared to be the situation: The normal operation of farm-bloc logrolling and "liberum veto" was complicated by basic disagreement on the broad policy of the programs from which domestic interest benefits could incidentally be extracted. At home, for instance, most congressional representatives of agriculture were agreed on a policy of price supports, regardless of party or section. In that context, trading on details between particular farm interests could proceed more easily than on a foreign affairs measure, where its friends recognized that no practicable concessions to the economic interests of its enemies would win their final support, and where correspondingly the enemies were not strong enough (nor perhaps justified by their own principles) to hold up the bill's supporters and prevent them from taking a cut for themselves unless they lavishly paid off the uncooperative opposition. Thus agricultural logrolling failed substantially to moderate sectional cleavages on foreign policy. Indeed, on the limited evidence of congressional roll calls from 1943 to 1950, the depth of cleavage was only rendered greater by the dissatisfaction of Midwest farmers (even export farmers like wheat growers) with their private gains under a public policy which they did not approve anyway.

DEMOCRATS UNITED—REPUBLICANS DIVIDED

In the Seventy-eighth through the Eighty-first Congresses there were three important subjects on which the foreign aid model of cleavage on American foreign policy was modified by an exceptional heightening of Democratic party solidarity—accompanied by no comparable harmony among Republicans. The topics were: (1) appointments in the area of foreign affairs, (2) tariffs, and (3) international organizations.

Appointments. Taking first the matter of appointments, there was need for caution in the study of a category which embraced such a wide variety of cases. Each man posed separate problems. Since mere averaging of confirmation votes might conceal individual circumstances, they ought to be elaborated in some detail. But at least the Democratic party's solidarity was always impressive. The old cement of American politics—jobs—was clearly at work in foreign affairs.

In the Seventy-eighth Senate the issue was one of confirming Mr. Stettinius' "reactionary" crew in the State Department. Joseph Grew, James Dunn, Julius Holmes, and Nelson Rockefeller were ultimately approved by votes of approximately 60 to 10, with Northern New Dealers the main holdouts. William Clayton, as a very wealthy middleman, endured in addition the opposition of several farm Senators, led by Russell of Georgia. The one "radical," Archibald MacLeish, encountered conservative hostility, 43-25. Only in his case was the vote along party lines, but it was interesting that Southern Democrats stood solidly with the administration (95 per cent), while Eastern Republicans mustered only 64 per cent against him.

Acheson's appointment as Under Secretary of State was the only one in the foreign sphere to be brought to a roll call vote in the Seventy-ninth Congress. Recorded opposition was exclusively Republican and was led by Senator Wherry, who based his objections on Acheson's recent dispute with General MacArthur over the size of the occupation forces necessary for Japan.[2] On September 24, 1945, Wherry attracted nearly solid support of *recorded* Republicans from the Midwest and Mountains for his motion to recommit (defeated 66-12; abstentions were widespread). But no Republican from either coast, and no Democrat at all, went on record against Acheson.[3]

The Senate did not have to take another roll call on a foreign relations appointment for more than three years; when it did, Acheson was again the man. On January 18, 1949, he was confirmed, 83-6, as Secretary of State. The opposition was all Republican: four isolationists—Capehart, Jenner, Wherry, and Langer—and two world-wide interventionists—Bridges and Knowland—who were disturbed by the administration's "do-nothing" policy in China. Asia was more emphatically an issue in the other State Department roll call taken that year to confirm Walton Butterworth

2. At that time Acheson's estimate was the larger.
3. On final confirmation Wherry stood alone in opposition.

as Assistant Secretary of State for Far Eastern Affairs, September 27, 1949. Butterworth had no recorded Democratic opposition, but only five Republicans voted for him; three of those were from New England and one from the Pacific Coast.

In mid-July 1950 maverick Senator Morse had negligible support from both parties when he tried to get four Export-Import Bank nominations recommitted pending investigation of its Latin American lending policies. The move was defeated 50-8. But partisanship was intense when the O'Dwyer appointment to Mexico came before the Senate on September 18. Two Democrats were willing to postpone action for two days; none was willing to recommit or to vote directly against confirmation. One Republican opposed the delaying motion; two opposed recommittal; and four ultimately voted to confirm the appointment. Two of those were from New England, one from the Pacific Coast.

The final fight was over Truman's nomination of General Marshall to be Secretary of Defense in September 1950. That required a special act of Congress to permit a military career officer to hold the position; so the House of Representatives got a chance to express itself. Again the Democratic party held solid—100 per cent in the North, 93 per cent in the South. And again the Republican opposition was divided, with more than a third of the GOP from the Northeast and nearly half from the Coast supporting the permissive legislation, while Midwestern Republicans were almost solidly against it. In the Senate the story was similar. Among the Democrats only McCarran of Nevada opposed the authorization when it passed, 47-21; no Democrat voted against the 57-11 final confirmation. Half of the Pacific Republican Senators and 57 per cent of their Eastern colleagues supported the enabling legislation, and the Eastern percentage went up to 89 for confirmation.

The eight-year record on appointments, taken together, showed that Republicans were discriminating in their opposition. Very few appointments in foreign relations were ever even pushed to a roll call vote. That of course was largely a reaction to the normal solidarity of the controlling party when jobs were at stake. If Democrats could not be persuaded to divide on appointments, Republicans stood to gain little by forcing roll calls. But even when record votes *were* held, familiar lines of cleavage in the Republican party evidenced a *discriminating* opposition which could not easily be mobilized against administration appointments.

Tariffs. The most enduring major issue between the two parties in American politics has been the tariff question. Very interesting, therefore, was the breakup of Republican solidarity on that issue in the 1940's. Not yet was there any such split in the Democratic party, though the men from the Mountains were usually recalcitrant. See maps 13–20 in the Appendix.

In the Seventy-eighth Congress the only tariff question was the 1943 extension of the reciprocal trade agreements program. Since it was wartime, American business was not being affected, and the House was willing, after a teller vote of 122-188 on recommittal, to vote an extension by the two-party majority of 343-65. Average Eastern Republican support was 22 percentage points higher than Midwestern, and Pacific support was 11 points higher. *Senate* Republicans and their Mountain Democratic allies were not disposed to let the measure through so easily. Five times by votes of about 50 to 30 administration forces beat down crippling amendments in party-line roll calls. Only then was the bill passed by a two-party majority of 59-23. Midwestern Republicans were somewhat less partisan than usual on tariff questions; they averaged only 74 per cent party-line support. But Eastern Republicans were still lower, and on the final two-party vote for passage the intra-party regional difference was 26 percentage points. Among the Democrats the Mountain men gave the administration only 50 per cent support, even less on the party-line test votes. Elsewhere party solidarity was high.

The tariff roll calls in the Seventy-ninth Congress were again on an extension of reciprocal trade. The administration was now seeking authority to lower duties 50 per cent further. Party lines were tightly drawn in the House. Only seven Republicans crossed those lines on recommittal, but 33 did on passage, with the result that Eastern Republicans averaged 18 per cent support of the administration, 12 points higher than the Midwest GOP. Democrats held firm in all parts of the country, suffering only a dozen desertions on either roll call. In the Senate there were six record votes, all of them party line. On the crucial vote to permit additional tariff cuts, 47-33, only nine Republicans deserted their party; six of them were from the Northeast. Other amendments and final passage were by votes of about 50 to 20 or 30. On the average, Eastern Republicans supported the administration considerably more often than they did their own party; they differed from the Midwestern-ers by nearly 40 points. Once again the Mountain Senators in both parties showed the least support for the administration's program. In other sections the Democrats were still united.

Tariff controversy in the Eightieth Congress centered on the Wool bill and on another extension of reciprocal trade in 1948.[4] The program had been watered down this time in the Republican Ways and Means Committee, principally by the addition of a congressional veto, and this time Democratic strategy in an elec-tion year was to kill the whole program—"better nothing than this." A gag rule in the House prevented any positive amendment. In four roll call votes (two on the rule, one on recommittal, and one on passage) party lines held very tight, the largest Republican defection being 17, the largest Democratic 16. In the Senate deter-mined intervention by Vandenberg, supported by Finance Com-mittee Chairman Millikin, caused the Representatives' proposed congressional veto over trade agreements to be modified to a mere requirement for publicity whenever tariffs were cut below what the Tariff Commission regarded as "peril points" for home pro-ducers. But still the Democrats fought the bill. For the record, Senator Barkley forced three party-line roll calls on straight ex-tension of the existing program for different periods of time. Then the bill was passed by a two-party vote despite the Democratic leaders. "Defections" were heaviest among Eastern Democrats. What was really most noteworthy about the whole performance was the moderation of the final Senate Republican policy, and the wide-

4. The Wool bill was a party-line measure with predictable regional cleavages. It was discussed (p. 55) in the category of "agricultural benefits." There was also a relatively unimportant party-line vote on a provision of the Sugar Act of 1948 which was intended to allow the Secretary of State, if he chose, to put pressure on Cuba for payment of private debts by denying sugar quota increases. The Chavez motion to strike this out was just barely defeated, 40–42. Both parties were internally divided about four to one.

spread support which members from all parts of the country were now willing to give to the trade agreements principle.

"Peril points," however, were still anathema to the victorious Democratic administration in 1949. The demand was for repeal of the 1948 Act and unrestricted extension of earlier acts, and Democrats once more rallied to their party's call. So did House Republicans on a recommittal motion (only a half dozen crossed the lines from either party), but so many went along with the administration on final passage that the vote actually constituted a two-party majority. The other two roll calls relating to imports in the Eighty-first House came in mid-1950 on suspension of copper duties and on a Republican attempt to extend import controls to butter. These were plainly regional issues. On copper only about 30 men from each party defected from the two-party majority. On butter the Democrats were practically solid and the Republicans almost evenly divided. Averages for the biennium in the House showed the usual high level of Democratic party regularity outside the Mountains, and the usual Coast-Interior cleavage among Republicans.

In the Eighty-first Senate there were ten significant tariff roll calls, all but one of them on trade agreements extension.[5] The critical Millikin amendment to restore "peril points" found only four Democrats recorded with the Republicans; three of those were from the Mountains. The GOP was 100 per cent united on this proposal, but when Senator Malone sought to scrap the whole program, a majority of Republicans (17-16) voted with the Democrats to preserve it, and on final passage of the administration's bill, unamended, the Republicans were almost evenly divided. Only two Democrats, both from the Mountains, were opposed. Averages for the Eighty-first Senate showed Eastern Republicans 26 percentage points higher than their Midwestern colleagues in administration support, 26 points lower in party-line support; indeed they supported their own party only a little more than half the time in opposition to the Democrats. The latter, everywhere

5. The only exception was a 100 per cent party-line roll call by which the Senate agreed to accept a Conference Committee report which failed to require the President to protect the domestic fur industry against Russian competition. It had to be decided by the vote of the Vice-President, June 5, 1950.

except in the Mountains, averaged more than 90 per cent support of party and administration.

Generalizing eight years of tariff controversy in Congress, the conclusion was clear that the Republican party was far from united any longer on a policy of higher tariffs, or even in opposition to the reciprocal lowering of tariffs to levels one-quarter of those set in the Smoot-Hawley Act. GOP party unity after 1945 could be achieved only on a mild "peril points" amendment to the Democratic program, a modification which the Eighty-second Congress finally accepted by a voice vote.[6] Moreover, it was clear that the regional lines of cleavage on tariffs in the Republican party ran East-West even more than on foreign aid, since Pacific Coast Republicans were relatively orthodox. Mountain Republicans stood for high tariffs more rigidly than any regional party in the country. Their Democratic neighbors tended to share that attitude, though much less intensely on the average. Democrats in all other regions, however, were united on a low-tariff policy. How long that Southern tradition would continue to survive the increasing industrialization and crop diversification in the region it would be impossible to predict, but as yet there was little evidence of disillusionment with the old credo.

International Organization. In addition to tariffs and appointments, international organization was another subject on which Democrats in all parts of the country tended to maintain their solidarity while Republicans characteristically divided. But only in the Seventy-ninth Congress was there a substantial number of roll calls on this topic; so the evidence is severely limited. Yet it seems worth mentioning because there is a significant, continuing Wilsonian tradition in the Democratic party, of which this voting record was in part a consequent example.[7] The Republican party has lacked a comparable unifying tradition in this field, either for or against the idea of international organization.

6. Republican unity on something more restrictive (but still not completely destructive) was attained in the Eightieth House only by the imposition of a gag rule which barred alternatives.

7. Chapter VIII will show the important part which this tradition also played during World War II in focusing upon the formalism of international organization the public attention which should have gone to the realities of power politics.

RIGID PARTISAN DIVISION

In the foreign policy roll calls from 1943 to the beginning of the Korean War three subjects appeared on which truly rigid partisanship was the rule in *both* parties. They included these topics: (1) export controls, (2) expropriation claims settlements, and (3) the Tydings investigation of McCarthy's first charges against the State Department. The first two subjects involved government regulation and private property rights; the other produced contested "votes of confidence" in the Senate leadership and the administration during an election year. In each case the intensity of partisanship reflected exceptional considerations, but even so it rarely reached 100 per cent in either party.

Export Controls. The subject of export controls was a strongly partisan issue in the House of Representatives the only two times it was pressed to a roll call vote. It would be a mistake, however, to take very seriously this overwhelming partisanship shown in just one chamber on two of several occasions on which it dealt with the subject. In the first case (June 19, 1945) the desire to make a record for decontrol at the end of the war, coupled with the unpopularity of the "radical" Foreign Economic Administration (FEA), were major factors involved. And in February 1949 there was a desire to demonstrate against President Truman's anti-inflation program; even the Republicans were asking only that the old law be extended without amendment. The solidarity of the Democrats also indicates that they regarded the Republican opposition primarily as a gesture made for momentary partisan motives on a subject on which there was actually general agreement. To be sure, export controls constituted both "regimentation" and restrictions on American sales abroad; hence they were a fitting vehicle for opportune Republican assaults upon Democrats. But the heat on this issue could be turned on and off too freely to be convincing.

Expropriation Claims. The International Claims Settlement Act of 1950 was another issue on which partisanship in the House of Representatives was virtually unqualified. Again the Senate did not even take a roll call. The administration's object was to set up a special commission to dispose of government and private claims, mainly against Communist countries, using lump-sum settlements negotiated by the State Department with the foreign government involved. Only Yugoslavia had made the necessary agreement, under duress, since the United States held enough of her assets to have covered American claims fully. Actually the settlement was for only 40 per cent. Negotiations with Poland and Czechoslovakia were also in progress, and many members of Congress were concerned about the larger sums involved in those discussions. Only in the House was a voting issue made of it, however; Senate Republicans widely regarded the move as a prima donna act of John Vorys. He was the only member of the House Foreign Affairs Committee to vote against sending the bill to the floor. He attacked the terms of the settlement, insisted it was an invitation to foreign nationalization, and condemned the extrajudicial character of the commission which would allocate the funds. Other opposition came from John Davis Lodge, who, presumably mindful as always of his Polish constituents in Connecticut, wanted to restrict the administration's bill to Yugoslavia. Every single voting Republican backed Vorys' motion to recommit. Democrats were almost as solid in favor of the measure.

In the Senate, action on the bill was delayed for several months, but all objections were then met by amendments to require Senate confirmation of the commissioners and to include as American claimants in any future international settlement persons who had not become American citizens till after their property was seized. This last provision went a long way toward meeting the kind of objection John Lodge was raising, but House Democrats balked in conference, and the amendment was eliminated.[8] Once again Senators accepted the report without objection; yet Vorys and Lodge resumed their fight in the House. Vorys wanted to kill the whole bill; Lodge asked that the report be sent back to conference in order to force reinstatement of the Senate amendment regarding newly naturalized citizens. Party lines held tightly once more; the measure was approved.

8. Some Southern Democrats, led by Beckworth of Texas, had strongly expressed fear that too many foreigners were already being taken care of as stockholders in American corporations.

But as in the case of export controls, the relative indifference of Senate Republicans to the issue indicated that it really aroused no very deep-seated partisanship on either side. Unquestionably John Vorys felt strongly about it, John Davis Lodge only a little less strongly; other Republicans were glad to have a chance to make a gesture against administrative tribunals, influence peddlers, nationalization, and administration "sellouts" to foreigners, and on behalf of native and naturalized constituents—without the usual inhibitions imposed by really critical foreign policy issues. But the subject was not important enough to furnish evidence of a durable focus of partisan controversy in an area of foreign affairs.

The Tydings Investigation. A really important foreign policy issue on which party lines were rigidly drawn during the period 1943–50 was Senator McCarthy's assault on the State Department and the Tydings investigation of his charges. All the accumulated frustrations of the lost peace found an outlet and a justification in McCarthy's accusations. The Democratic strategy was standpat resistance and counterattack, and in Senator Tydings the party thought it had a "safe" conservative Southerner to conduct operations. The administration was successful in preventing solidification of the Republican opposition until the outbreak of the Korean War. But the Democrats' decision to capitalize on the initial war enthusiasm to call off the hearings and "annihilate" McCarthy united the Republican opposition in the Senate. To the Democrats, the alternative—to continue the hearings in an election year with an uncertain war situation—seemed unendurable, but unfortunately they were now in a position where in effect they were gambling on the imponderables of war morale. And Tydings failed to hedge his bets when he led the all-out counteroffensive against McCarthy.

On five roll calls relating to the McCarthy charges and the Tydings investigation in 1950, party lines were crossed only once, and that once saw just two Republican Senators (Morse and Donnell) merely support Tydings' right to have counsel to assist him on the Senate floor.

The preponderance of evidence on foreign policy in Congress in recent years showed that in such a situation Democratic solidarity by itself could be only temporarily expected to sustain the administration. Before very long there would have to be some accommodation made to the public criticism of State Department personnel. Removals and transfers did come gradually in the Eighty-second Congress.

CONSENSUS

At the opposite extreme from intense partisanship, there were three foreign policy subjects during the years 1943–50 on which roll calls were used to demonstrate that a true consensus prevailed in both parties. Those cases developed in the Republican Eightieth Congress: the Italian and satellite peace treaties, the Rio Treaty, and the Vandenberg Resolution foreshadowing the North Atlantic Pact. To be sure, there was some opposition to each of these measures, but it was not expressed in any important number of dissenting votes.[9]

Of course there were many, many more foreign policy questions in the years 1943–50 on which consensus actually prevailed in Congress. But such problems very rarely required a roll call at all. They could be handled without fanfare, as, for example, were export controls on the occasions when Republicans were not looking for an issue. Where consensus existed, a lot of time would be wasted if votes were taken by the laborious method of congressional roll call. Only if there were special reasons for members or their leaders wanting to "make a record" was there likely to be a roll call on a consensus proposition. Important treaties and—as will be seen later—defense appropriations were the most common types of issues on which it seemed desirable to members to register their *agreement* formally in the Seventy-eighth to the Eighty-first Congresses.

SUMMARY

In summary, the evidence is clear that on a large majority of subjects in foreign affairs on which Congress was recorded in the

9. On all occasions but one that was also true of defense appropriations. But that one occasion (Senate, 1949) was so interesting that the subject will receive comment later (pp. 74–5) as an example of unusual Democratic cleavage.

years 1943 to 1950 the patterns of cleavage within and between the two parties remained the same—and resembled those described by the foreign aid model. On some of those subjects it was possible to achieve greater party unity than on others, but traces of the usual disagreement almost always remained, even when party solidarity was highest. Northern Democrats were not to be found giving the administration less support than did Southern Democrats; Eastern Republicans almost never recoiled from an administration proposal as far as did Interior Republicans. Only under exceptional circumstances were the splits within the parties—especially in the Republican party—very much narrowed. Very rarely did an enduring gulf seem to open between Southern Democrats and Eastern Republicans.

Although the next chapter will show that there *were* subjects on which those rules were sometimes broken, such cases were distinctly the exceptions. The foreign aid model was so consistently applicable that it could fairly be called a "foreign policy model" of congressional voting behavior.

CHAPTER 4

Exceptions to the Foreign Aid Model

THE TRUE EXCEPTIONS to the foreign aid model did not come in those instances in which forces of party loyalty found it possible to minimize intra-party cleavage. Traces of basic disagreement on foreign policy almost always remained. The core of the dissident forces in each party continued the same. On particular subjects they attracted varying amounts of support, but it was almost always weighted with the same sectional bias. More important than the fact that intra-party differences could occasionally be overcome was the fact that when they did appear—as they did in the vast majority of roll calls—they always appeared in the same places. Were there no subjects on which one of the familiar components of the model crumbled so far as to leave the administration supported, if at all, by a really unusual combination of forces?

In the Republican party there *were* occasions on which Eastern GOP support for the Democratic administration utterly collapsed, but never when Interior Republicans were willing to defend the administration. In the Democratic party, however, there were a few occasions on which the normally solid support of Northern Democrats actually crumbled, making the administration particularly reliant on Coastal Republicans and Southern Democrats. And there was a smaller number of occasions on which the hesitant but ordinarily very substantial support of Southern Democrats collapsed at times when the administration was still able to count on Coastal Republicans. Those instances of exceptional breakdown in the Democratic party on foreign affairs will be treated in this

71

chapter. Though the resulting alignments were hardly revolution-
ary, they did appear to be significant exceptions to the foreign aid
model.

DISSENSION AMONG ADMINISTRATION DEMOCRATS

Swiss War Claims. There was a Northern Democratic revolt against
the administration in the Eighty-first Congress on the question of
Swiss war claims. This time the Southerners did not join the revolt
in full force. The result was an extraordinary roll call in which
Southern and Mountain Democrats averaged stronger support for
the administration than did Northeast and Midwest Democrats.

Stephen Young of Ohio, Democratic Representative-at-Large,
sparked an anti-Swiss movement almost uniquely his own—much
like John Vorys' campaign against the Yugoslav claims bill. Young
explained that he had negotiated with Swiss officials for the army
during the war, and "I found them callous and hard, conniving and
cold-blooded, and always looking out for their own interests, and
seeking an unfair advantage . . . They have profited while we
have sacrificed and suffered." Therefore, although he never liked
to oppose a bill recommended by the Foreign Affairs Committee,
he would try to prevent the payment of a high rate of interest on
the Swiss damage claims arising from American bombing during
the war.[1] Republican leader Arends had previously announced
that he knew of no GOP opposition to the bill. But with only
fifty members on the floor, Young's campaign proved so successful
that Majority Leader McCormack had to put off the record voting
till the following day, May 10, 1949. Even then barely half of the
recorded Northeastern Democrats were willing to support the interest payments, and less than three-fourths of Midwest Democrats.
Republicans were characteristically divided, Coasts vs. Interior, but
even among the Eastern GOP only a third supported the administration. Southern Democrats were not particularly aroused; 74 per
cent of them voted with their party. And Mountain and Pacific
Democrats remained loyal.

The whole episode, of course, was of little significance; no roll

1. *Congressional Record,* May 9, 1949, pp. 5913–14.

call was required in the Senate. But the incident did demonstrate that the solidarity of Northern Democratic support for the administration in foreign affairs could—at least once—be shaken even on a matter which concerned no important domestic voting blocs.

Spanish Aid. A far more important defection of Northern Democrats which did fit the election-year demands of an important bloc of their constituents came in 1950 on the question of aid for Franco Spain. The strength of catholicism among normally Democratic voters in the North was a force which congressmen of that party found it difficult to ignore as the election of 1950 drew near. The administration, however, did not alter its public position against any special form of aid for Spain until after Congress had finally voted it by a two-party majority. Democratic Senate leaders had decided to desert the administration on this issue. Among the determining factors were the accelerated mobilization following the outbreak of war in Korea and the McCarthy-Tydings investigation, with its presumption of special impact on Catholic voters in the North. Strategic considerations were probably uppermost, but in a climate of opinion dominated by anticommunism it would plainly be very difficult for any major American party to remain long opposed to Franco Spain. The domestic political situation resembled that which surrounded American Zionism. Even parties far more disciplined and responsible than what we now have could be expected to respond to the wishes of a marginal Catholic minority just as soon as the interested public ceased to feel much menaced by fascism.

The Peacetime Draft. There was one important issue in postwar American foreign policy on which the defection of Northern Democrats in the House was so great that the administration actually found stronger support among Southern Democrats and Coastal Republicans. That was the peacetime draft, both in 1946 and 1948. *It was the one subject on which an opposition coalition combining the "far" right and the "far" left generated important voting strength.* To be sure, a few individuals from the left wing of the Democratic party joined Midwest isolationists in opposing other aspects of the administration's foreign policy in the postwar years. But only on the draft—and then only in the House—did they pick up strong support among the normally faithful Northern Democrats at a time when *other* friends of the administration's foreign policy stood relatively firm. And on both occasions the administration finally decided not to utilize for more than a very few months the draft powers thus narrowly obtained.

Both in 1946 and 1948 the record indicated that Northern Democratic Representatives—men who were loyal to the administration in domestic affairs and practically never balked at any other policy or expenditure it advocated in foreign affairs—were unwilling to confront their constituents in a hotly contested peacetime election with a record of support for a military draft. Senators ventured to take a longer view. So did Southern Democrats and Coastal Republicans. But the administration's failure in those years to expand the armed forces must be understood in the context of the demonstrated attitude of its strongest partisans in the House. Dollars they were willing to spend—more than Truman asked for— dollars that probably could have "bought" still more volunteers and equipped them. But really large-scale expansion required use of the draft, and there the administration was on exceptionally shaky political ground, obliged to piece together a nonpartisan coalition without the normal hard core of Northern Democrats. A determined administration might have gone ahead anyway. Its congressional support did not utterly collapse, as it did later, for example, on opposition to Franco Spain. But the task was obviously very difficult.

Defense Appropriations, 1949. Senate voting on defense appropriations in 1949 also revealed unusual complexity in party alignments in a related area of policy. There was virtual unanimity on every other peacetime roll call on defense appropriations. In the Eightieth House only American Laborites were recorded in opposition. In the Eightieth Senate only Glen Taylor and Harry Cain. In the Eighty-first House only one man (Marshall, Democrat from Minnesota) voted (as the administration wished) in opposition to insisting on appropriations for 58 instead of 48 air groups in the Senate-House Conference, and *no* Representative favored accepting the Senate's cuts in stockpile funds. But in the Senate in 1949 there was sharp disagreement. It paralleled the contemporary controversy within the administration over the defense economy program with which Louis Johnson's name was associated. Advocates of military economy attracted support not only from conservatives who wanted to spend less but also from liberals who wanted to use the money for other things.

Taken as a whole the 1949 Senate record was not clear cut like House Democratic defections on draft bills. If some liberals (notably Paul Douglas), like many conservatives in the Democratic party, seriously wanted to spend less for defense than the administration requested, other liberals wanted to spend more. A cue from the administration might have rallied support in the Senate for larger appropriations. But in the absence of such appeals most Northern Democrats were not disposed to press additional defense funds on the administration, and many were glad to make at least a show of willingness to economize still further. That wavering among Northern Democrats, which had some real substance to it, complicated the administration's position at a time when it was confronted with unusually severe defections on the part of Southerners and Eastern Republicans who wanted *deeper* budget cuts.

All in all, these departures from the foreign aid model were not very great in Senate voting on defense appropriations in 1949. But they reflected real political forces which were at work within the administration also—forces contesting a basic allocation of national resources, with the alignments cutting not only across existing party lines but also across liberal-conservative lines. The war in Korea would postpone this budgetary conflict, but it was certain to recur.
The Voice of America. Another question which divided Democratic Senators in all parts of the country was that of the appropriations for the Voice of America in the Eighty-first Congress. Earlier congressional roll calls on the Voice had shown substantial solidarity among Democrats in support of the program, with a familiar pattern of sectional cleavage among Republicans. But in 1949 and 1950 roll call moves to restore the full amounts requested by the President for the Information Service received very lukewarm support even from Northern Democrats. Both moves were defeated by two-party majorities.

Summary. There were, then, five issues in congressional voting on American foreign relations in the years 1943 through 1950 on which the foreign aid model of party cleavage failed to apply because of important cracks in the administration's own base of support among Northern Democrats. Those cracks appeared on the minor question of Swiss war claims, the more meaningful problem of the Voice of America, the important special interest question of Franco Spain, and the very important issues of the draft and defense mobilization. On none of these questions was the administration *always* bucking its normal supporters. But the fact that such dissension arose at all bore witness to the usefulness of preserving some extrapartisan support from cooperative members of the opposition party—as an insurance policy against defeat, not only through the defection of the administration's enemies within its own party but also occasionally by the defection of its friends. The disputes summarized above would presumably have shaken even a realigned and generally "liberal" party. If the administration of such a party should fail to cultivate friends in the opposition, it would probably find its foreign policies even more paralyzed than were those of the Democratic administration in the comparable postwar situations.

LEFT-RIGHT CLEAVAGE ON IMMIGRATION

Granted, then, that there would be limits to foreign policy solidarity and discipline even in a realigned party system. But were there not some foreign policy controversies in the years 1943–50 on which the solidarity of the two parties would have been much greater if they had been realigned "liberal" and "conservative"? In point of fact there were only two subjects in foreign affairs in those years on which Southern Democrats so consistently deserted the administration and allied themselves with *Interior* Republicans as to produce an alignment resembling a clear-cut liberal-conservative division on domestic affairs.

The first and major foreign policy question on which Southerners went far beyond Coastal Republicans to oppose the liberal

Democratic administration was, appropriately, a highly "domestic" issue—immigration of displaced persons (DP's). And the second was similar—*alien* enlistments in the army. On both these questions Eastern Republicans would have been consistently much more heavily outvoted within a realigned "conservative" party than they were in the existing Republican party. In this pattern of voting the alien problem differed from every other problem in foreign affairs which arose in the postwar years. Only on this problem would the same left-right realignment, with the same degree of tight discipline, have been *equally* appropriate for foreign and domestic policy.

Of course alien immigration was in fact as much an issue of domestic as of foreign policy, even when it appeared in such limited forms as the resettlement of a number of displaced Europeans and the enlistment of aliens in our armed forces. Nativism, agrarianism, anti-Marxism, and anti-Semitism formed a mixed brew which roused opposition to *any* immigration beyond the normal small and discriminatory quotas. Those who tended to favor the administration's policy on DP's were in both parties predominantly the representatives of urban, cosmopolitan communities. It would be hard to contend that real *economic* interest was a major factor on either side. Surely DP competition for all sorts of opportunities would hit urban workers far more than farmers; yet Northern Democrats welcomed the DP's. But of course this was only a limited immigration program. On both sides what was involved was essentially a matter of principle (or, if you will, prejudice): whether, for humanitarian or other reasons, it was wise for America at this stage of her history to attempt to absorb large numbers of persons of unfamiliar nationality and probably socialistic views. And the answers given to such a question would reflect the nationality of a congressman and his constituents, and perhaps their view of welfare-state policies. The result on roll calls was a remarkably clear-cut "liberal"-"conservative" division, with only a few Coastal Republicans from urban constituencies conspicuously violating the pattern.

Most revealing in the Eightieth Congress were the Senate

administration-support averages on DP's. These records showed a difference of 26 percentage points between Eastern and Midwestern Republicans, compared with a difference of 68 points between Eastern and Southern Democrats. And in the Eighty-first Senate the respective intra-party divisions were 40 points for the GOP, 52 points for the Democrats. The discrepancy was smaller, but it was still plain to see which party was more deeply split on this, contrasted with almost any other foreign policy question. Indeed the Southern Democrats consistently averaged even *less* support for the administration on displaced persons than did the Midwest Republicans themselves. Here was clearly an issue on which rural conservatives could very readily and durably unite.

Another subject which revealed the same political configuration was the question of encouraging aliens to enlist in the American armed forces abroad. Senator Lodge repeatedly sponsored such a program in the Eightieth and Eighty-first Congresses. On Capitol Hill the voting pattern was plainly similar to that on displaced persons—and what the two issues had in common was immigration.

There was no direct assault on the immigration laws in the years 1943–50. But the evidence on DP's and alien enlistments indicates that immigration could be one clear-cut, unambiguous "foreign policy" issue between a liberal and a conservative party— an issue on which the imposition of party discipline would be minimally repressive of important intra-party differences on foreign policy, and incidentally one on which highly partisan controversy would probably wreak relatively little havoc in international relations. But as an enduring partisan issue even immigration may be a mirage. Would the urban worker as unionist really support the level of immigration which he might sentimentally advocate as "Pole" or "Italian" or "Greek"? Perhaps this conflict of interest would cause some defections in a pro-immigration liberal party, and surely a new conservative party would find it difficult to hold urban congressmen in line with an anti-immigration policy; hence extrapartisan collaboration might seem desirable on this question too.

CONCLUSION

But such collaboration would not necessarily be so desirable as it has seemed to be on nearly all other subjects which arose in Congress in American foreign affairs during the years 1943–50—subjects to which the response was always some variant of the basic foreign aid model of political cleavage, with the result that disciplined solidarity on a foreign problem was rarely feasible under the existing party alignment and gave little promise of being more feasible in a liberal-conservative realignment. That a conservative party would suffer division on foreign policy between its members who lived near the three Coasts and those who lived in the Interior has been repeatedly demonstrated. That a liberal party would also divide, especially if thrown into opposition, must be more conjectural; but the first part of this chapter showed that this has sometimes happened even while there was leadership from a liberal administration. That there would be few foreign policy issues on which the members of realigned parties could stand consistently and unreservedly against each other, as they can so rarely now, must also be conjectural. The impressive fact is that only one such issue was found—immigration.

On this evidence, the alternative to extrapartisan collaboration in foreign affairs, under the existing two-party system or a realignment, would be a party discipline which would be largely *oppressive*. If it were also intended to present the full national electorate with a simultaneous choice between basically different foreign policies, such partisanship would gravely endanger America's international relations. Even the voters' mandate would remain highly dubious, for the reason that solidarity was not spontaneous in all major sections of the party.

PART TWO

*The Organization of the Parties
in Congress for Foreign Affairs*

CHAPTER 5

Political Organization for Foreign Affairs in the House of Representatives

CONGRESSIONAL POLITICAL MACHINERY for the control of American foreign relations is loose and disjointed. Power and responsibility are dispersed through a maze of committee and subcommittee principalities, linked by a web of "royal-cousin" relationships which no Almanach de Gotha would suffice to clarify. Few insiders are confident they can keep abreast of the family quarrels; no outsider can. The legislature is a congeries of personalities that is always in flux.

The rejoinder: *plus ça change, plus c'est la même chose?* Fortunately yes—at least in broad outline and within the span of a score of years or thereabouts. It *is* possible to make a general survey of the structure of political leadership in Congress as it has pertained to foreign affairs in the past decade. A precise analysis would have to be focused on a narrower time span, but it seems worth while at least to attempt to sketch a broad picture first.

This is intended to set the stage for historical analysis of the main developments in the politics of American foreign relations in the 1940's, and especially to indicate both the weakness and the flexibility of the mechanisms through which party leadership has been exercised. These mechanisms seem to be fairly well adapted to the control of foreign relations on an *extrapartisan* basis which encourages the administration to work freely with cooperative individuals in the opposite party, but not to the formulation and

disciplined implementation of alternative *partisan* foreign policies
or of agreed *bipartisan* policies, by the official leaders of either
party.

The approach in Part Two is institutional, but institutions in
Congress have a way of breaking down into personalities, a few of
whom deserve profiles. Elements of personal leadership, recognized
expertness, and outlook generally similar to some congressional
bloc (in various proportions) combine to give some individual
members special authority in special fields. These are the bell-
wethers. Moreover, the outstanding member of a state party delegation, especially one which frequently caucuses, may exercise a
sort of leadership which shades between the bellwether and the
partisan. But here our emphasis is somewhat narrowly on the
central party leadership in the House and Senate, and on the two
committees on foreign affairs, regarded as the most important of
the myriad legislative committees which have jurisdiction over
some aspect of American foreign relations. Most of the instruments
of central control are available to whichever party holds a majority
in the chamber. But to avoid repetition they will in general be
illustrated as used by the Democrats (who have usually had control in recent years), except for those techniques on which the
Republicans have put special reliance. The intention is to show
what party leadership devices are available in Congress for foreign
affairs, how effective they are, and what differences in *emphasis*
there may be between the two parties regarding the choice of instruments. No attempt will be made to evaluate the use of every
technique by each party, nor does any particular omission, without
some definite statement, imply that a particular device has been
unimportant to either of the parties.

CENTRAL LEADERSHIP AMONG THE DEMOCRATS

Individual (Not Corporate). What central, coordinating leadership
there has been in the Democratic party in the House of Representatives in the past decade has been personally in the hands of Sam
Rayburn and John McCormack, and to a lesser extent their assistant chief whip. They of course have to try to work with other

powerful members of the party, most of whom have attained authority by years of seniority in key committees. But the Democratic leaders definitely prefer to operate informally as individuals—not through any organized mechanism resembling a policy committee. This resistance of the Democratic leadership to any effective apparatus of joint decision, or even of regular joint consultation, is a fundamental characteristic of partisan operations in the House. It was publicly evidenced in 1946 when the Representatives struck provisions for policy committees out of the Legislative Reorganization Act.

Certainly one reason for the Democratic leaders' attitude is simply an unwillingness to share power. One of the Democratic leaders, for example, likes to speak of the importance of "self-confident leadership, willing to take the risk of making quick decisions." On one of the very rare occasions in many years when a chairman of the Democratic Steering Committee ever asked to share even a small amount of authority, this leader declined unless ordered by the full Democratic caucus "to abdicate any of the power which I have inherited."

Some loyal Democrats dispute the capacity of that man and the other leaders to exercise effectively the power to which they cling so "self-confidently." The criticism is made that the party members have not even been kept well informed. "The bell rings, and someone at the door says, 'Most of them are voting yea (or no).'" But if the suggestion be made that formal consultative mechanisms would at least have informational value, some of the Democratic leaders use a rejoinder that is probably valid. Given the state of the Democratic party since 1938, any kind of meeting representative of the membership is much more likely to advertise internal controversies than to produce agreement. If the consultation could be kept private, off the record, that problem would be minimized. But privacy can only be achieved, if at all, by adhering to purely informal and individualistic methods of consultation.

Therefore the Democratic Steering Committee usually meets less than half a dozen times a year in the House. It cannot be regarded as a politically significant body. It is not even allowed to consult regularly with the floor leader about the *scheduling* of business, much less about matters of party policy. Actually it was first set up in 1933 mainly as part of a deal for votes in the election of a Speaker. Fifteen of its members are elected as representatives of fifteen geographical zones by the party members from those zones. The others belong ex officio: the Speaker (if a Democrat), the floor leader, chief whip, caucus chairman, and the ranking party members on Rules, Appropriations, and Ways and Means (the Democratic Committee on Committees). It is easy to see that so representative a body could rarely be in agreement in the Democratic party—and why the leaders prefer to ignore it.

Even less useful is the Democratic caucus. Such a meeting of the full party membership is very rarely held—again for fear of advertising party differences. Even when one *is* held no binding vote is attempted, and under the caucus rules even a "binding" vote does not bind a man "upon questions involving a construction of the Constitution of the United States or upon which he made contrary pledges to his constituents prior to his election or received contrary instructions by resolutions or platform from his nominating authority." The leaders know that the use of such binding authority would fail except in cases where it was not really needed anyway, and would alienate cooperative members of the opposition party. Short of a binding caucus, they tend to feel that a mere conference—like that of the Republicans—will be embarrassing rather than helpful, that things will be said which will further embitter relations between members, and, presumably, that in an open forum kinds of action will be demanded which the leaders oppose. Since the power of a congressional leader lies primarily in his capacity to prevent action rather than to accomplish change, such publicity is not welcome.

The Speaker. Some leadership nevertheless exists, even in a party which seeks to operate without formal organs of consultation among the men who wield power. When the Democratic party is in power—as it was during most of the years covered in this study —the traditional powers of the Speaker are available to its leader in the House, and they are very considerable. His foremost power, of course, is that of recognition of Representatives seeking the floor. This power is expected to be utilized for partisan advantage.

In practice the Speaker's discretion is very much limited while a bill is actually under debate in the House. But if unanimous consent is required to bring it up in the first place, he can of course block it, and, more important, he has full discretionary authority to decline to recognize a member who wants suspension of the rules. That means that a bill favored by more than two-thirds of the members but blocked elsewhere in the House can also be blocked—or alternatively can be promoted—by the whim of the Speaker. He can always protect himself by asking, "For what purpose does the gentleman rise?" before deciding whether to grant recognition.

The Speaker's power to recognize members seeking the floor can of course be used directly to support a foreign policy. Thus on February 9, 1950, Rayburn delayed action in the House on a resolution of inquiry offered by Republican Representative John Davis Lodge and intended as a rebuke to the administration on Far Eastern policy. Rayburn arranged that the House vote first on a revised version of the Korean Aid bill, which had been barely defeated by the House three weeks earlier. When that was safely out of the way, Lodge's resolution was brought up and promptly tabled. Criticized for his tactics, Rayburn told the House: "May the Chair say that the gentleman from West Virginia [Chairman Kee of the House Foreign Affairs Committee] is not responsible at all for the bill carrying Korean and other aid coming up before the resolution. The Chair will take responsibility for that himself." [1]

Sometimes the Speaker's power to rule on moot points of order also allows him a small area of discretion for political decision. With the cooperation of a friendly congressman he may even find a technicality by which to block action on a special rule from the Rules Committee itself. Appeal is very rarely successful. Ordinarily even the opposition leaders do not support such "subversion" of powers which they someday hope to exercise themselves. And most Representatives recognize the need for some decisive procedural authority if anything is to be accomplished in a chamber of 435 members.

1. *Congressional Record,* February 9, 1950, p. 1755.

Another function of the Speaker's office which has some room for political discretion is reference of bills to different committees. Many subjects fall in a cloudy area of mixed jurisdiction, especially since the consolidation of committees under the Legislative Reorganization Act of 1946. The choice of one committee or another can be used to burden or support a legislative proposal, and to build up or hold down a committee and its chairman. For example, the decision of the Republican leadership in 1947 and the Democrats thereafter to let the Banking and Currency Committee retain jurisdiction over international banking—apparently contrary to the intent of the Legislative Reorganization Act—was a decision with important political consequences. It probably helped to protect the financial soundness of the Export-Import Bank and the International Bank and Monetary Fund, and correspondingly to complicate the immediate problem of facilitating dollar transfusions abroad. The overworking of the Foreign Affairs Committee in the Eighty-first Congress showed that the devolution of its potential authority was largely justified. But House Foreign Affairs, unlike Senate Foreign Relations, was not forced to share its jurisdiction over military assistance programs with the Armed Services Committee; this was a matter of some importance in areas of disagreement between the State and Defense departments.

Indirectly also, the power to recognize members, to decide points of order, and to refer bills to a committee may be used to secure support for policies favored by the Speaker. Without arousing widespread protests, many minor bills which are important to individual members in their districts—perhaps even to committee chairmen—can be blocked by the Speaker unless he receives reciprocity from the members concerned. In this respect, however, the Speaker is only one of several powerful individuals or small groups of congressmen who can independently exercise a similar veto, e.g., chairmen of legislative authorizing committees or subcommittees and members of the Rules Committee and Appropriations Committee. Not all of them can simultaneously discipline a member on behalf of their contradictory policies; nor can the Speaker always prevail.

When the Speaker is not himself presiding over the House, another member selected by him is. Presumably the reins of political authority remain with the Speaker. He can himself, of course, participate in debate and in voting at any time he chooses, but in practice these are limited to rather important occasions. Sam Rayburn's infrequent floor speeches have constituted the most authoritative stamp of judgment which the Democratic House leadership could put upon a controversial measure, short of calling a caucus, which it is generally unwilling to do.

Another power of the Speaker is the power to appoint the House members of Conference Committees with the Senate. Here his discretion is severely circumscribed by the seniority tradition, which usually dictates the appointments of "managers" from the majority party as well as from the opposition. But some margin of discretion may remain after the prerogatives of the ranking committeemen have been conceded. Personalities and circumstances determine whether the Speaker himself exercises that discretion in order to influence the action of the Conference Committee, or else, as is usually the case, simply accepts the recommendations of the committee chairman and the ranking member of the opposition. In any event the conferees selected must be able to produce a report which will satisfy a majority of the whole House.

The Speaker also makes appointments to the select and special committees which are sometimes formed despite an effort in the Legislative Reorganization Act of 1946 to establish a presumption against them. Here the prerogatives of seniority are considerably weaker—indeed a prime reason for establishing such committees in the past was to circumvent seniority—and the Speaker may have a somewhat freer hand than on appointments to Conference Committees. But again he will find it easier to persuade weak rather than strong chairmen in related areas of policy to endorse his appointees.[2]

Loose Reins. The powers of the Speaker, in short, like those of most men in authority in the House of Representatives, are more

2. In the Republican Eightieth Congress, elderly Chairman Eaton of Foreign Affairs endured with considerable pain the appointments made by Speaker Martin to the Select Committee on Foreign Aid, of which Eaton was officially chairman. Eaton's authority was so obviously nominal that the committee became generally known as the "Herter Committee," after its leading member, Christian Herter.

effective instruments for blocking than for hastening action, but by logrolling he may be able to produce positive developments. When Democrats previously had control in recent years, their leaders—Rayburn, McCormack, and the chief whip—generally avoided intervening in the vital preliminary activity of House committees except at the invitation of the chairman, at least when the chairman was not actively hostile to "must" legislation. A strong, quasi-dictatorial chairman who could grind out Democratic administration legislation and prevent embarrassing questions and investigations was likely to be appreciated by the leadership, whatever the members of his committee might think of him. In Sol Bloom the Foreign Affairs Committee had such a chairman during the Seventy-eighth and Seventy-ninth Congresses; the difference between the high regard in which he is held by at least one of the House Democratic leaders and the low regard felt for him by his fellow committeemen is striking. A more widely respected example of a strong chairman who neither needed nor brooked interference or support from the leadership was Democrat Carl Vinson of Armed Services; fortunately he was also able to secure support from his fellow committeemen of both parties despite his highhanded methods. But a weak chairman, like John Kee of Foreign Affairs in the Eighty-first Congress, was likely to need help from the leaders. If he was being cooperative, they regarded it as their duty to help him out. Thus Kee is said to have appealed to Rayburn to get Democratic members of the committee to attend meetings.

What is particularly significant about the Democratic leaders' relations with the committees—at least until a bill actually reaches the floor—has been the casual informality with which they have learned what was going on and whether anything they might do or say would improve matters. The leaders have not been equipped with investigatory or follow-up staffs adequate to keep them independently abreast of developments. They have had to rely on information and suggestions from executive agencies, ranking committeemen, and individual members. And in acting upon such advice, they have usually had to be careful not to alienate a ranking committeeman by appearing to intrude on his domain. The result is a situation in which McCormack as Majority Leader might first learn the contents of a controversial Foreign Affairs Committee report from the questions of newspapermen.

The degree of informality seems excessive, even when due regard is paid to the reasons why the leaders of a party as divided as the Democrats have preferred to operate casually. To be sure, it would be a mistake to underestimate how useful and well informed an able and hard-working House leader can keep himself simply through informal channels. When, for example, Rayburn heard that a Democratic committee chairman was in fact not in control of the situation in his bailiwick, a few words in the House lobby to a recalcitrant or lazy member whom Rayburn happened to meet could really be very helpful. There is not much reason to doubt the earnestness of a leader who told the author repeatedly, "It's my job to back up the Democratic Chairman"—at least when the chairman was not opposing the Truman administration; but what if he were? Was the leadership organized to act as effectively as it might, even within the limits imposed by the traditional prerogatives of chairmen? Just as party Conferences and Policy Committees have been ruled out because they "fragment leadership" and advertise dissension, so large-scale staffing of the Democratic leaders' offices has been resisted apparently for fear it would offend ranking committeemen who would be unwilling to endure supervision by "underlings." Yet without such staffing a leader, no matter how able, is excessively dependent on accidental leaks of information from within the various committee empires. Fortuitous circumstances can easily be of excessive importance. Who has the leader's ear? Whom does he trust, given his weak investigatory staff? Suppose he doesn't "run into" the man he does trust? It is hard enough to lead informally without also having to learn informally.

The actual rounding up of Democratic votes has been handled by the House party leaders with similarly extreme circumspection. Any one of the three top leaders can direct that a "general whip" be sent out, but this is just a request for *attendance* at a particular time for a particular vote, and goes to every Democratic congressman through a hierarchical organization of whips, who are elected regionally by the members they serve. In effect it is simply a matter of one congressman's secretary calling another congressman's secretary and asking her to ask him to be on the floor. A general whip offers no certainty to the leaders as to how many Democrats will actually show up, or how they will divide, but selectivity in the circulation of the whip is regarded as offensive.

Selectivity is of course not absent in the *personal* solicitation of votes by the leaders and by individual members friendly to a particular bill. But the Democratic whips themselves feel no obligation to cooperate in such solicitation, since they do not owe their appointments to the party leadership. The most they can definitely be expected to do is to poll the members from their particular regions for the information of the leaders, about half a dozen times a session. The result is that on a measure like most of those in foreign affairs, in which domestic lobbyists do not generally besiege the average congressman in an effort to "educate" him, the Democratic Representative has been surprisingly dependent on grapevine reports and snatches of debate even to discover how his party's floor managers for a particular bill would *like* him to vote on an individual amendment before it actually comes up —whether or not he finally decides to heed their wishes.

Of course it is true that the Democratic congressmen for many years have been deeply divided on many issues. The exercise of any kind of authoritative party leadership is bound to be widely offensive to the members. And much can be accomplished in informal relationships. Still it is hard to believe that the House Democratic leaders since World War II have utilized sufficiently all the possible instruments which would have been available to them even in the divided condition of their party.

CORPORATE LEADERSHIP AMONG THE REPUBLICANS

Among the House Republicans in recent years informal leadership activity has gone on continually, as it has among the Democrats. But the frequent supplementary use of formal consultative mechanisms has distinguished GOP House leadership from that of the Democrats.

The foremost corporate organ is the Republican Policy Committee. Its members are seventeen Representatives elected biennially from regional districts by their GOP colleagues, plus the Speaker (when a Republican), floor leader, chief whip, chairman of the Congressional Campaign Committee, and the chairman and secretary of the party Conference. Other Republicans may be invited to participate when the business under discussion especially concerns them. Such invitations are extended by Joseph Martin, who as the House Republican leader is ex officio chairman of the Policy Committee. The committee meets at Martin's call whenever he feels there are important matters to discuss, usually at least once a week. A bill may be considered in that forum at any stage in its progress through Congress, but rarely before the standing committee with original jurisdiction is at least ready to act on the measure.

The Republican leadership has available to it also an organization of whips to be employed at Martin's discretion not only to secure attendance but if necessary to suggest to the members how the leaders want them to vote. This structure of authority is considerably stronger than the Democratic whipping system. And when the GOP commands a majority in the House, its entire membership is called into Conference about once in three weeks. (But such conferences have usually been less frequent when the GOP has been in the minority position.)

The Rules Committee. One other organizational mechanism is particularly important to the central Republican leadership in the House. That is the Rules Committee. With its membership fixed at eight from the majority party and four from the minority, it is an exceedingly reliable mechanism of party control when Republicans are in power. At least three of the four Democrats left on the committee are likely to be conservatives from the South, not strongly opposed to Republican proposals. It is true that on foreign policy the eight senior members (four from each party) can be expected to be more nearly in balance than on domestic affairs, given the foreign policy divisions among conservatives in both parties; but the appointment of four additional Republican members can be used within limits to throw the balance one way or the other.[3] With its predominantly negative powers, usually exercised without great publicity, the Rules Committee is naturally valuable to a party which is deeply concerned with inhibiting rather than advancing numerous widely advocated programs of government action. An actual "gag rule," severely limiting debate and amendments on a particular bill, is only very rarely produced on *foreign* affairs.[4] But the Rules Committee often waives points of order against legislative provisions in appropriations bills affecting foreign policy, and of course on any bill the decision must always be made by Rules whether to grant any special rule at all. As important a measure as universal military training was blocked in the Rules Committee during the Eightieth Congress. Without a special rule, no bill which has substantial opposition can be put through the House, except by very great effort requiring techniques on which leaders of both parties frown because their control of the legislative timetable may be endangered. As long as the Rules Committee fails to act, other action is almost impossible.[5] This is the veto power which the Republican Policy Committee, when in control of the House, can exercise through the Rules Committee. And it is a veto power which may be thrown against the central Democratic leadership even when Democrats are "in control," though the danger does not seem great in foreign affairs.

Despite the utility of the Rules Committee for the Republicans and their regular use of systematic corporate organs of partisan

3. Correspondingly the Democrats, when they control the House, have less trouble with the Rules Committee in foreign than in domestic affairs, for international programs have consistently attracted the support of a few of those senior members from both parties who constitute the conservative core of the committee. Thus a Democratic administration is not doomed in foreign as in domestic policy to finding Rules a roadblock no matter how carefully the four extra Democratic seats are distributed to its reliable supporters. But even so, the committee as constituted under the seniority system remains much more of a nuisance to Democratic leaders than to Republican.

4. An exception was one on extension of reciprocal trade in 1948. See p. 63.

5. During the Eighty-first Congress the Rules Committee veto was only suspensive (for a minimum of twenty-one days) on bills which were favored both by the chairman of the reporting committee and by the Speaker. But this by-passing device was not of consequence in foreign affairs during that biennium, and it was abandoned at the beginning of the Eighty-second Congress.

consultation it would be a mistake to overestimate the superior effectiveness of GOP party leadership to Democratic in the House. No doubt it has generally been more effective in recent years. But in foreign affairs, where the intra-party tensions have been greatest, Joseph Martin's "solution" in the years between Pearl Harbor and Korea was usually not to attempt to exercise any of his leadership authority at all. Generally he took the position that a "bipartisan" foreign policy meant that he should not act as a partisan leader on foreign policy issues. It should be left to the House Committee on Foreign Affairs to bring out and defend anything it wished, with no formal assistance or opposition from the Republican House leadership.[6] Later, with the growing unpopularity of the Korean War, GOP partisan activity became more pronounced. And of course with a Republican in the White House, administration foreign policy has become "must" legislation for GOP House leaders. All the organs of corporate leadership are called into play. But as yet the Democrats, for all their informality, have shown greater solidarity for Eisenhower's foreign policy than have the House Republicans.

To be sure, this situation may be only transitory. And at least, over the past decade, the more systematic organization of the Republican party leadership has probably kept a wider circle of influential individuals better informed of developments in different parts of the House than is likely under casual Democratic methods. That is something. Still the fact remains that disciplinary devices which will ensure the reaching of agreement by consultation are very weak in both parties. In the Democratic party this is most evident in domestic affairs; among the Republicans, in foreign affairs.

6. In the Eightieth Congress there was an important break in this pattern of behavior. During the Interim Aid debate at the end of 1947, John Vorys, the outstanding Republican member of Foreign Affairs, was managing the bill on the floor and privately took Martin to task for not helping him fully. Martin agreed to do so if that was what Vorys wanted. And during 1948—notably on the European recovery legislation—Martin and floor leader Halleck met often with Vorys and sometimes with the full Republican membership of Foreign Affairs to map a position. But during the Eighty-first Congress, back in the minority role, the central Republican leadership once more ceased to give formal support to the policies advocated by Republican leaders of the committee. In general Martin avoided formally mobilizing the party on foreign policy until the end of 1950.

THE HOUSE APPROPRIATIONS COMMITTEE

The House Committee on Appropriations is in a position to exercise a coordinating authority, with coercive power over Representatives, and this should fit it to serve as a major instrument of the central House leadership. But actually it functions, like most other standing committees, very independently. Through the power of the purse Appropriations Committee members can exercise great influence over the content of policy and the forms and personnel of administration—often sharply revising previous legislative decisions of Congress. Available techniques run from explicit language in appropriations bills (the law of the land if enacted), to language in committee reports, statements in the printed hearings, statements deleted from those prints, and private consultations continually in progress with administrators anxious to preserve the members' good will. The very fact that the Appropriations Committee exercises control at the strategic final stage of the legislative process and can discipline congressmen by denying funds for their pet projects gives it strength to take effective *independent* action as easily as to tie together legislative loose ends in support of a consistent *party* program, and the fact that it is selected on the seniority system ensures that many of its members will not hesitate to use their power independently. Here is another group of congressional coordinators who themselves need coordinating. In effect, the coordination function is largely relegated to the Senate Appropriations Committee, where in turn it is indifferently performed. The Senate Committee acts as an appeals board for those who are dissatisfied with the appropriations granted by the House. Secure in the knowledge that there will later be this partial reexamination of their decisions, the House committeemen devote themselves largely to altering *details* of the administration's budget estimates. This practice assures that there will be an extra check on the bureaucracy and on other committees of Congress, but it is not of much assistance in coordinating national policy as a whole in the House of Representatives.

The problem is further complicated by the subcommittee system by which Appropriations operates. For example, in the area of foreign affairs, funds for the Defense Department, State Department, and foreign assistance have in recent years all been handled by separate subcommittees of about a half dozen men each. Such units of the full committee are each a separate satrapy usually dominated by a subcommittee chairman, who often regards secrecy as the keystone of his power. Only toward the chairman of the full Appropriations Committee is he likely to show deference, since the committee chairman has some limited discretion in assigning bills and members to different subcommittees.

The result is that within the committee the main coordinating function—such as it is—is in the hands of the chairman, who works directly with different subcommittee chairmen; in the minority party a similar task is performed by the ranking member of the full committee working with ranking men on the subcommittees. The full committee itself is not organized to coordinate its subcommittees. Usually it considers a subcommittee bill for only a couple of hours before approving or crudely slashing it.[7] Democratic Chairman Cannon's move in 1950 to consolidate all subcommittee bills in one omnibus bill provided the means for making a meaningful review by the full committee a real possibility, but the effort was exceedingly unpopular and was abandoned after one year.

Fortunately in recent years the senior ranking members of both parties on the committee have been men who were not seriously out of line with the majority sentiment of their fellow partisans *in the House.* The familiar problem of recalcitrance on the part of a full committee chairman has not been great on Appropriations; Democrat Cannon's and Republican Taber's exercise of supervisory authority on their committee has usually not conflicted sharply with a major party program. Exceptions can of course be

7. A good example of this was the handling of ECA appropriations in the House in 1949. A friendly subcommittee under J. Vaughn Gary produced a bill satisfactory to the administration, but it was rudely slashed 15 per cent by the full committee. Paul Hoffman deplored this "spur of the moment decision" and observed, "They brought in a new jury this morning that did not hear the evidence." *New York Times,* May 24, 1949. The House leadership on this occasion was strong enough to "coordinate the coordinators" by getting the Rules Committee to facilitate an amendment that the money be spent in about 15 per cent less time. *Ibid.,* May 26, 1949.

cited. The outstanding one was the "Tabering off" of the authorized sum for the European Recovery Program appropriation in 1948.[8] Another was Cannon's battle for 58 air groups in 1949.[9] But even in these cases the main opposition to the committee's action came from outside the House. And in the Eighty-first and Eighty-second congresses Chairman Cannon was very helpful to the administration in setting up subcommittees dealing directly with foreign affairs, well packed to protect its programs.

Nevertheless, the degree of secrecy which permeates the committee's activities renders it largely not responsible to the House of Representatives. No one chairman—though personally "strong" and loyal to his party leadership in the House—can maintain responsible control over the *detailed* action of such diverse subcommittees, even if he were disposed to do so. And the extensive alteration of detail may disrupt an original legislative policy. All the sessions of the committee are "executive"—behind closed doors. It is unduly difficult for other leaders of the House, even in other segments of the Appropriations Committee, to find out what is being plotted by a particular subcommittee in time to try to stop it with the weak techniques available to leaders in the House of Representatives. Often there is no effective recourse except in the Senate. Of course the existence of a senatorial "appeals board" is one reason why the House handles appropriations as it does. But the Senate Committee is not well coordinated either, nor can an appeal be made to it from every damaging pressure which has been exerted in the secrecy of a House Appropriations subcommittee. Some "opening up" of the House Committee would appear to be a prerequisite for impressing upon its members all the important considerations bearing upon their decisions, otherwise an unsure reliance must be placed upon the Senate to correct abuses.

COMMITTEES ON COMMITTEES

To complete this brief survey of the central House leadership of the Republican and Democratic parties it is necessary to men-

8. See pp. 287–90.
9. See pp. 337–8.

tion the Committees on Committees. These bodies are not of direct, day-to-day importance in foreign affairs, except as the members of the Democratic Committee on Committees deal with questions of international trade and tariffs in their dual capacity as members of the Ways and Means Committee. But indirectly the character of appointments to standing committees which are made in each party by its Committee on Committees can affect the work of the standing committees themselves.[10]

However, the possible effect of the party mechanisms is sharply limited. The discretion of a Committee on Committees is restricted by the seniority rule, which ordinarily assures a member of reappointment to the committee he is on if he wants it and if there is room for him after party members with longer continuous service on that committee have been taken care of. The Committee on Committees devotes itself to placing new members and transferring old ones at their request. In most recent House elections too few seats have changed hands to leave much leeway for deliberately "packing" the standing committees. And in practice, within the limits of seniority, a party's Committee on Committees ordinarily defers to preferences for available applicants which may be expressed by that fellow partisan who ranks foremost on the standing committee concerned.

Here again is exhibited the same discreet caution which inhibits most of the central party leaders in the exercise of even the small disciplinary devices available to them. Ordinarily they find it easier to leave initiative and management in the legislative process to

10. The Democratic Committee on Committees is composed of the Democratic members of the Ways and Means Committee. Seniority protects their positions after they have been elected by the Democratic caucus, which acts on the formal nomination of the caucus chairman. Geographical allocation of party strength is an important consideration in their original selection. (In the Eightieth Congress the Democratic Steering Committee was allowed to work with the men from Ways and Means in making other committee assignments because the geographical distribution of Ways and Means Democrats was too narrowly Southern and Eastern.)

The Republican Committee on Committees is more representative of the party membership. The Republican delegation from each state, meeting separately, elects one of its members to serve on the Committee on Committees and to cast a vote proportionate to the size of the delegation. The Republican floor leader is ex-officio chairman and usually fills later vacancies on standing committees.

a standing committee, and to let those of its members on each side who are sufficiently interested set the tone of debate and round up their own support, with perhaps a few public words of endorsement from recognized party leaders, on the floor and in the cloakroom.

Some of the committees dealing with aspects of foreign affairs can usually carry their own load without difficulty: Armed Services, for example, and Agriculture; Appropriations, of course, and Ways and Means; Judiciary, to a lesser extent, and Banking and Currency. Sometimes, indeed, majorities on these committees find it too easy to have their own way with one-sided approaches to foreign policy. That is because the specialized committee in the field—Foreign Affairs—is often not influential enough to prescribe policy, and central party leaders are slow to intervene. The Foreign Affairs Committee's own standing before the House is therefore a matter of consequence.

THE HOUSE FOREIGN AFFAIRS COMMITTEE

Politically the most important fact about the Foreign Affairs Committee is its *weakness*. Until very recent years ambitious members of the House of Representatives rarely sought a seat on Foreign Affairs. There were few votes to be made out of it back home, and very little chance of personal publicity. Compared with the great standing committees handling economic and social legislation and appropriations, the Foreign Affairs Committee had a work load neither interesting nor important. Senators, with their treaty power, asserted their authority in State Department decisions, but not the Representatives, who had few important bills to consider. Men who sought leadership in the House naturally gravitated to other committees where a reputation could be made. Left on Foreign Affairs were many timeservers who were glad to avoid the rough-and-tumble of bitterly contested domestic legislation. Some of them were thoughtful men; others were mainly interested in the embassy receptions to which committee membership was an open sesame. But what they nearly all had in common was a lack of qualities of personal leadership.

Of course that is changing. As the vital importance of foreign affairs bills came to be recognized during and after World War II, the committee became very attractive. The change might have come sooner if Chairman Bloom, during the war years, had not been so dictatorial and had allowed other members of Foreign Affairs a chance to make a reputation for themselves. He went so far to assert his authority as to require nearly all significant legislation reported out of the committee to bear his name (the "Bloom bill"). But Eaton's milder leadership and Kee's weakness freed other members to distinguish themselves if they had the capacity. By 1949 there were more requests for seats on Foreign Affairs than on any other committee in the House. As important a Republican leader as Christian Herter (now Governor of Massachusetts) sought transfer from the Rules Committee itself, and had trouble arranging it until the Eighty-second Congress. The infusion of new blood is raising the political potency of the Foreign Affairs Committee in the House. But under the operations of seniority, this will take a long time unless weak members of long standing are willing to forego their prerogatives.[11]

The past weakness of the Foreign Affairs Committee was reinforced in the mind of House members (including the committeemen themselves) by invidious comparisons with the mighty Foreign Relations Committee in the Senate. In conference the House managers were regarded as spineless tools of the State Department while the Senators gave an appearance of independence. Therefore in 1947 it seemed vitally important to some Foreign Affairs conferees to get reference to China aid included in the Interim Aid bill—not just for the sake of Chiang Kai-shek but for the sake of the House Foreign Affairs Committee. The managers felt they had to prove to the House that they could put over something which the State Department did not want and which the Senators (most important, Vandenberg) regarded with relative indifference.

The prewar tendency of the House membership to sift down in quality to self-conscious mediocrity on the Foreign Affairs Commit-

11. That this is not impossible has been demonstrated by the way Eaton and now Chiperfield have deferred to Vorys as *de facto* Republican leader of the committee.

tee is not the only reason for the political weakness of the committee. It shares with the State Department the vulnerability of a body
which has nothing but hardship to offer the public—hardship all
the more resented as it appears mainly to benefit a lot of foreigners.
The Foreign Affairs Committee has been regarded as a buffer for
the State Department against the rest of the House; the State Department correspondingly is seen as a buffer for foreign governments against American self-interest. Not only "buffers for outsiders," but "milking machines of American lives and treasure." To
say the least, hardly any measure the Foreign Affairs Committee
ever has to present to the House really *pleases* any large number of
Americans; the committee is almost always dealing with the lesser
of two evils, both of them usually very great. No wonder it is relatively unpopular with other members of the House.

When this situation was combined in the Eighty-first Congress
with excessive demands upon the *time* of the House, its patience
with the Foreign Affairs Committee became exhausted. The committee brought nine controversial bills to the floor in 1949 alone;
it was receiving nearly 20 per cent of all special rules granted by
the Rules Committee. Foreign Affairs members were tired of
defending bills on the floor. Finally on March 1, 1950, the House
"revolted" and heavily defeated a trivial proposal to buy books for
European libraries with about $1,400,000 earned by American con-
scientious objectors during the war. The episode dramatized the
weakness of the Foreign Affairs Committee before the House even
in 1950. One needed palliative was "package legislation," for example combining many separate foreign aid programs in one
omnibus bill, in order to reduce the time consumed. But the basic
problem of alleged "foreign-mindedness" remains.

The traditional weakness of the Foreign Affairs Committee and
the painful struggles through which its members have had to go
in defending unpopular measures on the floor brought problems
of committee morale in recent years which were significant in the
politics of American foreign relations. The feeling of corporate
unity and fellowship in the committee was insufficient to hold most
of its members in attendance at its day-to-day work against all the
other manifold responsibilities of a congressman's life. Absentee-

ism was a perennial problem. Of course that is true of many committees in House and Senate, but on Foreign Affairs particular difficulty arose from the fact that absenteeism ran along party lines. Republicans were much more regular in their attendance than were Democrats. Often when they were a minority of the full committee they constituted a majority of the quorum actually present for its deliberations. In a committee where the membership recognized that this situation was likely to occur frequently, there was, of course, special reason for the Democrats to cooperate regularly with the Republicans across party lines.

Vorys and Eaton. The character of the GOP leader, John Vorys of Columbus, Ohio, has also been an important element in the weighting of Foreign Affairs Committee activity on the side of the Republicans. Vorys possesses qualities of personal leadership which most senior members of the committee lack. Vorys is a fighter. He does not like to be beaten in debate. He is willing to work hard to amass the facts and arguments on any issue which attracts his attention. It has been his practice to acquaint himself with upcoming bills sooner than most other members of the committee; the result has been that often he has been able to make himself master of the situation by the sheer weight of his information and the vividness of his presentation. He constantly probes for weak points in an official briefing—searching critically for discrepancies in detail. In any debate he is a tough opponent, with a flair for facts and figures. It is difficult for any congressman to stand against him. He speaks fluently and effectively, and his appearance and manner are vigorous and impressive.

Nevertheless, he has weaknesses. As noted above, some members regard his liking for detail as infatuation. There is an old saying around the Foreign Affairs Committee (repeated in good humor by all concerned) to the effect that if Mr. Vorys had been present when Moses came down from Mount Sinai with the tablets of the Ten Commandments, he would have found something to amend. Perhaps he has carried emphasis on terminology too far. But when Truman was President it was difficult for a generally cooperative Republican to put a "GOP stamp" on foreign affairs legislation any other way. A more serious criticism relates to the erratic and

impulsive character of some of Vorys' past moves. Examples may
be easily cited: defeat of the Korean Aid bill right in the midst of
the Senate Republican assault on Acheson's decision against military aid to Formosa, back in January 1950; an attempt in March
1950 to shift most of the burden of expense for ECA agricultural
purchases to the Commodity Credit Corporation, thereby embarrassing friends of price supports in both parties; a campaign in the
Eighty-first Congress against the Truman administration's plan
for settling American citizens' claims against Communist countries in East Europe. These and other moves have indicated a certain impetuosity in Vorys which has made many members of his
own party regard him as undependable for wise and consistent
leadership of GOP Representatives in foreign affairs. Some believe
that with a Republican in the White House Vorys shows greater
discretion.

In any case the Ohio Republican has been *de facto* GOP leader
of the House Foreign Affairs Committee since the spring of 1947,
although he was then only third-ranking member and still is not
chairman. Leadership devolved upon him largely by default. The
then Chairman Eaton was too old, and the second-ranking Republican, Chiperfield, did not want the job of floor manager, partly
because as a moderate isolationist he was very often opposed to
the committee's bills anyway. During the Eighty-first Congress
Eaton, without abdicating, increasingly transferred responsibility
to Vorys formally; thus, for example, the Democratic leaders Rayburn and McCormack began to come directly to Vorys for nominations to Republican seats on Conference Committees. The result
has been an interesting modification of the seniority system which
has enhanced and formalized Vorys' authority and made the personal characteristics of his leadership, good and bad, very important in foreign affairs.

Charles Eaton, the ranking Republican, was the other GOP
member of the committee whose qualities were probably most important in determining his party's reception of administration
foreign policy proposals in the war and postwar years. His age and
his loyalty to the State Department sharply limited his influence
among Republicans; but his tremendously impressive "old Viking"

appearance, voice, and manner, and his reputation for massive integrity, which was bolstered by his background as a Baptist minister, made him a strong figure, especially in the early years of "bipartisan" collaboration on postwar international organization.[12]

Bloom and Richards. In the Democratic party on the Foreign Affairs Committee during the war and postwar years two men were, like Vorys and Eaton in the GOP, of such special importance as to merit comment even in a brief discussion of the committee. They were Sol Bloom and James Richards.

Bloom's qualities as chairman have been noted elsewhere in this chapter. His hand lay heavy on the committee for several years. For the administration and the Democratic leadership of the House he was for a time a very useful person to have in his position—a strong and loyal congressman in control of a weak committee. He could be relied on to grind out what the State Department wanted and to block what it opposed, except with regard to Palestine. But a large number of the members of his committee regarded him as dictatorial and heartily disliked him.

Some allege that the cumulative effect of Bloom's rule was to depress the caliber of the membership by depriving able congressmen of the opportunity to distinguish themselves. The long-run effects of this would probably have been pernicious even for the State Department, because Bloom could not carry nearly so much weight on the floor as he could in committee simply by determined use of the chairman's prerogatives. Without strong and willing support from other members of the committee he would have had serious trouble putting over the administration's bills in the postwar years, but his treatment of his colleagues might well have deprived him of that support. It seems probable that the advent of Republican leadership in 1947, by freeing the Foreign Affairs Committee of the domination of Sol Bloom and through him of the

12. Eaton's upbringing in Canada, of old Nova Scotian loyalist stock, must have inculcated a sympathetic regard for Great Britain; his heritage also linked him to old and influential families of New England. For a time he served as Canadian correspondent for the Boston *Transcript* and the New York *Tribune* and special correspondent for the London *Times*. From 1925 to 1952 he was a member of Congress.

State Department, helped to transform the committee into a body with prestige which would actually become a more powerful vehicle for major State Department policies.

Bloom's resumption of the chair at the beginning of 1949 threatened to undo the promising developments of the Eightieth Congress in committee organization and morale, but death came very shortly, and the weakness of his successor, Judge Kee, left wide range for the talents of others. The outstanding Democrat was James Richards of South Carolina, who became chairman when Kee died early in 1951.

Richards is an independent Southern Democrat—a Dixiecrat in 1948—who usually went along with the Roosevelt and Truman administrations on foreign policy—but failed to do so often enough and forcefully enough to earn a reputation for moral courage in fighting for his convictions. Democrats, especially from the South, have had confidence that he does not support a measure simply because an administration supports it; therefore when he does go along, many others go with him.

One man who has worked closely with Richards believes that the essential fact about him is that he lives by the code of a Southern gentleman in the best sense of that much-abused term. His active support or opposition are aroused when the values of that code are engaged—more than by considerations of *political* belief. This interpretation may be challenged, but it appears to be applicable in major cases of foreign policy insurgency by Richards against the Roosevelt and Truman administrations. The obverse has been his loyalty to the Foreign Affairs Committee, which has kept him working harder than most Democrats at least, though not so hard as Vorys.[13] When the seniority system finally elevated Richards to the chairmanship of the committee in the Eighty-second Congress, he was equipped to show greater all-round effectiveness—on the floor and in the committeeroom—than any chairman Foreign Affairs has had since before World War II. But the nature of his position in the Democratic party has obviously made

13. Unlike Vorys, Richards likes to concentrate on the broad principles of a piece of legislation rather than search for details to amend; as a learning device he prefers a few hours of cramming with documents to many hours of discussion in committee.

him a man whose support neither the Truman nor Eisenhower administrations could take for granted, even in foreign affairs.

SPECIALISTS AND/OR LEADERS

It is a matter of great significance that Richards and the other members of the Foreign Affairs Committee in recent years—Bloom, Eaton, and Vorys—whose combination of ability and seniority entitled them to make a claim to leadership in the House of Representatives did so only in the limited role of specialist on foreign affairs. A particular member of Foreign Affairs might be influential with one or another faction in the House by reason of his customary alignment with that faction on domestic issues, but rarely as one of its leaders. Notable exceptions in the Eightieth and Eighty-first Congresses were Jacob Javits and Helen Douglas, but their strong factional connections often got in their way on foreign policy by arousing suspicions in other factions regarding *anything* they might advocate. Most of the influential members of Foreign Affairs have relied mainly on their status as foreign policy specialists to win support for their proposals in the House. Indeed one able and conscientious freshman Democrat on the committee in 1949 was advised never to lift his voice in the House on any subject except foreign affairs if he wanted speedily to make a reputation and acquire influence.

The growing measure of authority which Foreign Affairs committeemen have thus independently acquired provides a basis for more ready access to the resources of central leadership in their respective parties. However, it should be clear by now that those resources are very limited and that the will to use them is often even more limited. The rise of Foreign Affairs men to high posts would hardly alter the situation very much. Only some fundamental changes in the structure of party organization in the House would make the individual leaders much less dependent on purely personal esteem. As long as the personal factor remains so important, and so accented by basic intra-party cleavages on foreign policy, the habit of semi-independent activity across party lines by foreign affairs specialists seems likely to survive an elevation of some of them to positions in the central House leadership.

CHAPTER 6

Political Organization for Foreign Affairs in the Senate and between the Chambers

ALTHOUGH systematic party organization is weak in the House, it is weaker still in the Senate. Nor are the hands of the party leaders in either chamber much strengthened by the practice of submitting legislation to small Conference Committees to settle the differences between the houses.

In the upper chamber even the legislative timetable is at the mercy of individual members because of the lack of any effective method of closure or requirement that debate be germane to the matter under consideration. This means that the procedure by which most measures can be handled in the Senate has to be worked out with the unanimous consent of the members. The prime function of the party leaders, then, is to arrange such agreements. Beyond that the work of "leadership" is essentially lobbying. The power of any individual Senator to disrupt the work of the chamber is so great under the rules that he can hardly be coerced.

CENTRAL PARTY LEADERSHIP IN THE SENATE

Primary Organs. The Democratic leadership in the Senate differs from the Republican in much the same manner as it does in the House—in greater reliance on personal, informal methods of consultation rather than on formal corporate devices—and for much the same reason—fear of advertising party dissension. The titular chief is the floor leader, though in recent years there has been no presumption that the Democratic Senator holding that office was in fact particularly influential with his colleagues. Real leadership has often been exercised by others, some of whom have served on the Democratic Policy Committee which was established pursuant to the Legislative Reorganization Act of 1946. Even the Policy Committee has been very slow in developing prestige as an institution. Its members, except for the floor leader himself and the whip and Conference secretary, are selected by the floor leader, who also serves as its chairman. The successive floor leaders have generally been free to make as much or as little use of the Policy Committee as they have respectively seen fit to do.[1]

Full Democratic party conferences in the Senate have been even less useful, though they are held somewhat more often than in the House. One example, notable as much for its abortiveness as for its uniqueness, was the caucus decision on January 17, 1950, to back President Truman's decision not to intervene in Formosa. William S. White of the *New York Times* observed that "it was the first time in years that [Democratic Senators] had so formally proclaimed a party position on an international issue." Lucas announced that "to the best of his knowledge every Democratic Senator was ready to go on to the end with the President on the general decision against intervention itself."[2] Very passively most of them did, until the administration reversed itself step by step under the pressure of the Republican party and the exigencies of the Korean War. But most of the promised active defense of the

1. The most important occasion prior to the Korean War on which the Democratic Policy Committee as such intervened decisively in a foreign affairs issue was to designate the Foreign Relations Committee as the body to investigate Senator McCarthy's first charges. The three Democrats who were members of both these committees were reluctantly persuaded to serve also as the majority of the investigating subcommittee. The appearance of thus politicizing the probe proved in the end to be very unfortunate for the Democratic party.

2. *New York Times*, January 18, 1950. No actual vote was taken but a "consensus" was reached, in Lucas' words, "that the President and State Department are handling this matter in the right fashion and that intervention in Formosa might lead ultimately to war." Not every Democratic Senator, Lucas observed, approved all details of the administration's policy against military assistance. The *Washington Post* (January 18, 1950) quoted him as naming only Ellender of Louisiana an exception.

State Department policy evaporated much sooner than that. A week after the caucus Acheson announced, "I do not intend to turn my back on Alger Hiss"; thereafter it seemed especially dangerous for Democratic Senators to go out of their way to defend administration foreign policy. The effect of the Conference decision at best can have been to silence only temporarily a few anti-administration Democrats. Rarely has even that been attempted by such a formal device as a full conference.

The Republican Senators have for years made much more systematic use of the corporate devices of Policy Committee and Conference. Since 1947 the Senate GOP Policy Committee has met regularly at least once a week when Congress was in session; and conferences of the full party membership are frequent when Republicans control the upper chamber. Even when the Senate majority is Democratic, the GOP caucuses more often than does its opposition. Significantly, the GOP floor leader, Policy Committee chairman, and Conference chairman are three separate individuals, independently elected, not all the same man as in the Democratic party. Nor does the floor leader normally prescribe the membership of the Policy Committee. Senate GOP leadership is *formally* in *commission,* in contrast to the *formal centralization* of Democratic authority in a floor leader. Of course in practice personality factors may make the working relationships in both parties quite opposite from the formal arrangements. But at least the Republican pattern of organization seems fitted to produce under most circumstances a more active and effective leadership in a chamber where the authority of any one member, even the floor leader, is in fact virtually limited to his personal powers of persuasion.

The Presiding Officer. The role of the presiding officer in the Senate as a party leader in that body depends largely on his personal qualities, but in any case it is far less important than that of the Speaker of the House. There is no assurance that the presiding officer, if as usual he is the Vice-President, will even be a member of the majority party in the Senate, much less that he will be a Senate leader of either party by right of long seniority.[3] Be-

3. In the absence of the Vice-President the President pro tempore presides. He is customarily a committee chairman of very long seniority elected by the majority

cause he is not chosen by the Senate, and because of the individualistic tradition in the upper chamber, it has not entrusted nearly
so much authority to its presiding officer as has the House. He is
restricted in his right of recognition to the first Senator who has
addressed him, and cannot demand to know in advance "for what
purpose does the gentleman rise?" Some discretion of course remains as to whom the presiding officer will notice, but when such
failure to recognize is flagrantly prejudiced, Senators are likely to
rise to protect their colleagues.[4] As in the House, the presiding
officer has the formal power to appoint conferees, but in the Senate
that power is even more ineffective than in the lower chamber. The
real decision is made by each committee chairman. Even the chair's
decisions on points of order are much less binding in practice in
the Senate than in the House, as was witnessed in the complex parliamentary tangle over ECA appropriations in the summer of
1949.[5] The same is true of his reference of bills to committees.

But it remains true that the presiding officer has some power,
and if he combines it with a long career of political leadership in
the Senate he can make considerable use of his power in order to
influence legislation. In the Eightieth Congress Arthur Vandenberg, as President pro tempore, and in the Eighty-first Congress
Alben Barkley, as Vice-President, were men of that caliber. (In
earlier years Henry Wallace, an outsider, and Kenneth McKellar,
by reason of infirmity, were not.) Vandenberg and Barkley were
both extraordinarily free about discussing legislative matters from
the chair. And with the cooperation of the floor leaders of both
parties (or the watchdogs designated by them to remain on the
floor) a man in Vandenberg's position was often able to entertain

---

party. In the absence of both of them, the President pro tempore designates a
Senator to fill the chair.

4. An outstanding example of this came on June 19, 1948. Glen Taylor had been
filibustering against selective service in the closing hours of the session and had
finally been silenced because of his language. He sought to regain the floor a
few moments later, before the bill had finally been approved. The presiding officer
ignored him. Colleagues of all political beliefs rallied and demanded that he be
given the floor. He was, but promptly resigned it, grateful for the demonstration of
"devotion to the principles of democracy" in the United States Senate. *Congressional
Record*, June 19, 1948, pp. 8995–9, especially p. 8998.

5. See pp. 56–7, and *Congressional Record*, July 27, 1949, pp. 10262–80, *passim*.

requests for unanimous consent agreements at hours when factional opposition was absent from the chamber. Thus a close associate recalls Vandenberg's smiling satisfaction as he said: "I just got those things through all right. There were only four men on the floor."

Such petty subterfuge would, hardly be necessary if Senate leaders had much real power over their colleagues. Even small minorities find it so easy to demand attention that most leadership and "whipping" can be no more than cloakroom buttonholing. Whether it has the sanction of some policy committee or party conference may mean much or little to the various individual Senators. *Committees on Committees.* The other main organs of central party leadership in the upper chamber are the Committees on Committees. The Democratic one is appointed by the floor leader; the Republican by the chairman of the party Conference. The work of these Committees on Committees is of course important, especially since the Legislative Reorganization Act of 1946 sharply restricted the size of standing committees. In recent years there have been sharp foreign policy disputes involved in the selection of Republican Senators to fill successive vacancies on the Foreign Relations Committee. On the Democratic side in earlier years Claude Pepper was deliberately kept off Foreign Relations during much of the period when he was most uninhibitedly wooing the far left. And still earlier the reorganization and strengthening of that committee late in 1940 was of great importance for lend-lease and postwar planning. But for proper perspective it should be recalled that the operation of seniority in the United States Senate makes it virtually impossible for any Committee on Committees —much less the leader who appoints it—to pack the standing committees on behalf of a general program. The most that can be attempted is to modify the action of a few committees by new appointments from the limited ranks of applicants who have roughly equivalent seniority in the Senate as a whole.

THE SENATE APPROPRIATIONS COMMITTEE

The Committee on Appropriations fails in the Senate as in the House to perform its potential function of program and budget coordinator for the majority party. Again the major obstacle is the seniority system which puts such enormous power in the hands of uncontrollable individuals on subcommittees.

For years before he left the Senate in 1952 Kenneth McKellar's infirmity rendered him incapable as chairman of coordinating his various subcommittees. Fortunately the ranking Democrat on Appropriations, Carl Hayden of Arizona, has been one of the most respected men in the Senate, a real "Senator's Senator" despite his studied avoidance of publicity. But Hayden was clearly in no position to hold down subcommittee chairmen of such independence as McCarran of Nevada, who headed the group handling State Department appropriations.

On the Republican side of the full committee partisan leadership has been stronger. The ranking GOP member, Styles Bridges of New Hampshire, is a major party leader in his own right, combining vigor and hard-bitten determination with long seniority. But as is the case with the House Appropriations Committee, even a strong chairman is unable really to cope with the formidable task of coordinating the work of subcommittees handling such diverse and detailed subject matter as government spending. Especially in the absence of a single, consolidated appropriations bill, it is simply too difficult to evaluate the total effect of the many small changes in the administration's budget requests, which are made independently by various subcommittees. Fortunately the Senators at least do not compound the evil, as do the Representatives, by relying partly on secrecy to shield their operations from congressional leaders outside the Appropriations Committee. The Senate Committee functions openly as a board of appeal from the House of Representatives. The only factor which to some extent inhibits other Senators from making their views known to members of the Appropriations Committee during their deliberations is an awareness of the normal jealousy which any powerful congressional committee feels for its prerogatives. At least, any Senator can find out roughly what is going on, whether or not he chooses to intervene to alter it.

Indeed the collaborative relationship between Appropriations and other Senate committees is partly formalized. Thus, in the area of foreign affairs the Armed Services Committee may designate three of its members to serve with the Appropriations Committee during consideration of the budget for the Defense Department and one member to serve on the important Senate-House Conference Committee handling those appropriations. The Foreign Relations Committee has the same privileges when State Department appropriations are being considered—but significantly *not* on foreign aid funds. Even on foreign aid Vandenberg's spectacular appearance before the Senate Appropriations Committee in 1948 to plead for rejection of the House cut in European recovery funds was only a public dramatization of a common interchange of private views between members of Foreign Relations and Appropriations over the size of foreign aid budgets even while they are still before the Appropriations Committee.

That is a far cry from the cellular exclusiveness of the House Committee on Appropriations. It can be argued that the freer Senate practice leaves the way open for all sorts of pressures—not just those of the leadership—to influence committee action. The Senators' habit of raising House appropriations indicates that that is so. But on balance their procedure seems more likely to ensure full consideration of the elements involved in budget requests than is the practice in the House, where in secret some slight coordination of government expenditures is attempted by a committee chairman who owes his position to seniority, and a few subcommittee chairmen who are only partly subject to his discipline. In the Senate, at least, ordinary members get more of an inkling of what is being projected, and influential men outside the Appropriations Committee can attempt persuasion before it is too late.

The difficulty, of course, is that the Senate leaders commonly feel too weak in the face of the jealousies engendered by committee prerogatives, chairmen's prerogatives, and even individual Senators' prerogatives to take a strong stand on the work of committees until measures have actually been reported out. And then they know that on the floor orderly procedure is dependent on unanimous consent. Lacking, for the most part, even the elementary techniques of discipline which are available in the House, the Senate leaders must restrain themselves from presuming too far on their personal persuasiveness and public prestige when they are dealing with fellow members of the greatest club on earth.

THE SENATE FOREIGN RELATIONS COMMITTEE

Fortunately for recent American foreign policy, the Committee on Foreign Relations stands high before the Senate, well able to look out for itself, in contrast to its counterpart in the House of Representatives. If the most important characteristic of the House Foreign Affairs Committee is its political weakness, it could almost be said that *strength* and effective power have been the most important characteristics of the Senate Foreign Relations Committee. Indeed, Foreign Relations has been surfeited with riches in its membership. For example, in the Eighty-first Congress, of its thirteen members five were committee chairmen, another was the ranking minority member of another committee, and three more were members of a party policy committee. Even the other four members were men of some distinction in the Senate: Fulbright, Lodge, Pepper, and Alexander Smith. With such a galaxy the problem has been not so much how to preserve the authority of the committee vis-à-vis the full Senate and the administration, but rather how to secure the attention of committee members to their responsibilities on Foreign Relations.

Senators as outstanding as these can afford to collaborate closely with an administration without being widely caricatured as its puppets. They do not find it necessary first to establish a reputation for independence as do members of the weak House Foreign Affairs Committee. Successive administrations in recent years have benefited greatly from the buffer of the Foreign Relations Committee. The political power of the members has been an enormous asset to many controversial State Department policies. Probably only some disastrous failures in the "internationalist" programs

with which the committee members have preponderantly associated themselves would suffice to destroy, even temporarily, the
political effectiveness of the Foreign Relations Committee as a
link between Congress and the outside world.

One aspect of the committee's work which is of particular interest in the politics of American foreign relations is the determined
effort which was made in the early postwar years to achieve unanimity among the members. This was carrying collaboration to an
absolute limit, but the committeemen did not in consequence behave obstreperously, as though each could exercise a liberum veto
on the committee's action. In the Eightieth Congress, of about fifty
votes taken in committee, only the strongly sectional issues of the
St. Lawrence Seaway and the Anglo-American Oil Agreement
produced any final division. In the Eighty-first Congress the record
was not much worse; the important exceptions came on the Mutual
Defense Assistance Program, when Foreign Relations functioned
jointly with Armed Services. A unanimous Senate committee can
almost always carry the day on the floor of the chamber; so the
ability to achieve consensus gave Foreign Relations added strength
in pushing its legislation. But of course the unanimity was not
the result merely of good will on the part of its members. More
important was the absence in that period of any "irreconcilable"
Senator from the Republican Midwest. That situation no longer
reliably holds. The seniority system was bound to alter it. But
even if exclusiveness were possible, it would probably be a mistake to select applicants in such a way as to preserve the fetish of
unanimity on Foreign Relations. It is more important to secure
a balanced committee composed of men who command the respect
of their colleagues because they can be counted on to review with
considerable care the recommendations put before them. The inclusion of some reasonable foreign policy critics should help to
preserve the strength of Foreign Relations in the long run. They
are thereby enabled to share in the educational experience of the
committee's work; other Senators can be reassured that diverse
viewpoints receive serious consideration; and there should be less
chance of the continued growth of a foreign policy opposition led
by Senators who lack entirely the experience of Foreign Relations

work. Because of the undisciplined nature of the United States Senate there would be much to fear from the vagaries of a large opposition bloc which felt itself wholly divorced from the Foreign Relations Committee. In the latter years of the Truman administration there was growing evidence of such a tendency.

Vandenberg. For a limited time this outside opposition was combated most effectively by the same person whose efforts were most important in producing unanimity on the Foreign Relations Committee itself—Senator Arthur Vandenberg. The historical section below will discuss his work in detail, but the importance of his political role and also the position of Senator Connally deserve special attention in even a brief discussion of the Foreign Relations Committee in recent years.

George Smith watched Vandenberg at work from a berth as staff director for the Senate Republican Policy Committee. Smith is no friend of a "bipartisan" foreign policy, but his observations on Vandenberg seem exceptionally well balanced:

> By far the greatest architect of bipartisan policy, and responsible for much of its success, is Senator Vandenberg. His sincerity and earnestness cannot be doubted however much the wisdom of his course might be challenged. His ideas on the current role America should play in the world are strictly the product of his own study and reflection on the posture of world affairs. His taste for elder statesmanship (bringing him dangerously close to the pitfalls of vanity) made it easy for the Administration to accept him and to build him up. This does not mean that the State Department or the Administration is solely responsible for his prominence and party leadership. He reached those places by the qualities of his own mind, heart and character. He came by convictions leading to bipartisan policy through profound study of history and by more than a quarter of a century of experience and prominence in national politics. The Administration merely recognized the quality of the man, the unfolding texture of his thought and his place of leadership in Republican circles. Accepting him as a key figure the Administration catered to

him as part of its own strategy, and thereby rendered him a disservice by feeding the suspicions of critics of bipartisan policy.[6]

Another shrewd observer, Richard Rovere, has made these observations about the sources of Vandenberg's strength:

> He owes a lot to virtue, but he owes a lot more to sin. It is the fact that he was once on the wrong side that is the source of his strength today. . . . For what Vandenberg did by switching from isolationism to internationalism was to make it possible, by a process resembling vicarious atonement, for lots of other isolationists who knew, if not that they were wrong, at least that they were licked, to make an honorable peace with the Administration and thereby to give the country something like a workable foreign policy.
>
> Vandenberg was the ideal man to start the bipartisan foreign policy not only because of his isolationist past but because of his genius for compromise and face-saving. His political talent has always been for mediation, melioration, coalition, and decent compromise. He is not a synthesizer, as Roosevelt was, but a kind of creative temporizer. Every politician has to face both ways occasionally, but few can do it as adroitly as Vandenberg can, or with such classy rhetoric. One of the last of the old-time orators, he can make a retreat sound like a call to arms, an evasion like a declaration of lofty principle.[7]

All these were factors in Vandenberg's rise to commanding authority in foreign affairs in the Eightieth Congress: his ambition,

6. George H. E. Smith, "Bipartisan Foreign Policy in Partisan Politics," *American Perspective*, Spring 1950, p. 158.

7. Richard H. Rovere, "The Unassailable Vandenberg," *Harpers*, May 1948, pp. 395–6. Vandenberg's gifts were not in originating policy but in selling to Congress and the public what was proposed by the administration. "He thinks in terms not of ideas but of action. He does not want to philosophize about a thing or pare it down to principles and lay it out, A, B, C, in the Dulles manner; he wants to know whether the damned thing will work." James B. Reston, "John Foster Dulles and His Foreign Policy," *Life*, October 4, 1948, p. 137. Vandenberg "showed great skill, much greater skill than the Administration, at *anticipating* and removing the Capitol Hill arguments that threatened to block Congressional acceptance. And it is in this field that he has made his major contributions."

his seniority, his personal qualities of leadership and skills at compromise, his symbolic conversion, the administration's build-up
of him by propaganda of the deed as well as of the word. Very
rapidly after his "conversion" speech of January 10, 1945, there developed a process of interaction whereby Vandenberg's public role
of "unpartisan" leadership (his own term) in foreign affairs magnified his political importance in his own party, and then in turn
his partisan authority strengthened his hand for "unpartisan" national leadership. Republicans anticipated that the payoff would
come in the 1948 National Convention, and, as the months went
by in Truman's first term, GOP congressmen became increasingly
wary of treading on the toes of a colleague who might become
President and who would in any case probably have a sizable
block of convention votes at his disposal. Most important was Senator Taft's uncertainty where Vandenberg would jump. But after
1948 Vandenberg was out of the running for President. Taft and
others could afford to move in on his foreign affairs domain.

Connally. Tom Connally of Texas, the other chairman of the Foreign Relations Committee in the war and early postwar years, is in
many respects a more complex figure than Vandenberg, but one
thing at least is certain: whatever leadership he was able to exercise
in the Senate on foreign affairs derived from his personality and his
long association with the work of that committee—not, as did
Vandenberg's, from his standing as a fullfledged leader of his
party. Connally was not even a recognized leader of the *Southern*
Democrats like Russell, George, or Byrd. But his work on behalf
of administration foreign policies was by no means as unimportant
as it was usually made to appear because of the superior ability of
Senator Vandenberg and the need for the Truman administration
to build him up.

In foreign affairs, and to a considerable degree even in domestic
affairs, Connally was a loyal administration Senator. He had a
strong sense of the authority of the President in foreign relations.
Although he liked to bluster and flail at State Department officials
with his scathing sarcasm, in the end he almost always went along

Reston, "Events Spotlight Vandenberg's Dual Role," *New York Times Magazine,*
March 28, 1948, p. 51.

and helped them. To some extent Connally's very irascibility and combativeness led to that result, for on the floor he found himself being treated as the most conveniently available foreign policy "spokesman" and being critically questioned about whatever the State Department might be doing. He would rise to defend *himself* along with State, and then become emotionally involved in an argument which intellectually might perhaps have just as easily been cued the other way at the beginning.

Connally's reactions were thus essentially partisan, at least in a situation where he detected partisan motives on the part of critics. His observations on bipartisanship after the 1950 election were most revealing:

> All this talk about "bipartisanship" and "You've got to consult the Republicans"—to hell with all that! If a man is an American he ought to stand for an American foreign policy in the interests of the people of the United States!
>
> All this talk about a bipartisan foreign policy makes me kind of weary. It's not a bipartisan policy that it should be; it should be an American policy.
>
> We will consult the Republicans, yes. But that doesn't mean that we have got to do just what they tell us to do. We are not going to do any such of an infernal thing. We are going to operate not on a Democratic basis and not on a Republican basis but on an American basis that looks after the American people. All the questions to date have been settled on a so-called bipartisan basis.
>
> But the Republicans talk about "re-examination." Well, if they do they will find their tracks all around them. . . . Do they want to go back and undo everything they have joined in doing? I don't think they do. I believe the Republicans are patriotic—most of them—and want to do the right thing.[8]

Connally's reaction to partisan demands for more "bipartisan" collaboration was probably compounded with the jealousy most observers thought he felt for Arthur Vandenberg, that "Johnny-come-lately" to internationalism who was getting all the credit

8. William S. White, *New York Times,* November 28, 1950.

for American foreign policy. Connally's own capacity for contribution to American foreign policy lay partly along the same lines as Vandenberg's—sensitivity to public opinion and to effective presentation techniques for policies originated by the administration. But Connally lacked the concentration to apply himself steadily even to that sort of "sales" work, much less to the critical study of American foreign relations.

If Connally's weakness in sustained effort and thoughtful analysis could have been fully compensated for by his fighting spirit and showmanship, he would have been a more influential Senate leader. But too often his irrepressible wit betrayed him. The lash of his repartee wounded most Senators, and he remains a very controversial character. In an able profile of Connally (generally sympathetic), Washington correspondent Beverly Smith sums up the arguments:

> The extreme opinions run something like this:
>
> Favorable: Connally is a shrewd and wily elder statesman, a chief architect of the bipartisan foreign policy who, along with Republican Senator Vandenberg, has served as an indispensable link between the President and the Senate, thus enabling America to preserve a united front in a dangerous world. His sharp wit deflates diplomatic pomposities; his homely common sense holds policy within bounds which the public will support.
>
> Unfavorable: Connally is an old-time politician who, by the accidents of seniority and the committee system, has been carried to a position of international importance beyond his depth. He is not sufficiently dignified, or studious, or intellectual. His knowledge of the world is shallow. He pays lip service to bipartisanship, but his own ingrained partisanship frequently endangers it. Admittedly he is quick and clever, and when he wants to he can charm the birds off the trees; but he is also irascible, indiscreet, and unpredictable. His sarcasm, his irrepressible witticisms, might sometime upset the international applecart.[9]

9. Beverly Smith, "The Senator Loves a Fight," *Saturday Evening Post,* July 1, 1950, p. 18.

It seems reasonable to conclude that Connally's special talents would probably have made him a more impressive leader of a fully partisan foreign policy than of the partly bipartisan or extrapartisan policy which sought to win collaboration from members of the opposition. But in foreign affairs his own loyalty to the administration, if nothing else, prevented him from putting very serious barriers in the way of the two-party cooperation which the executive usually sought. There is testimony to that in the very record of postwar unanimity on the Foreign Relations Committee, whose members had to work most closely with Connally. He could not bring to the committee the political leadership of a Vandenberg, but neither did he impair the collective prestige, power, and solidarity of its influential membership.

On that membership must continue to rest the major reliance for leadership on foreign affairs in the Senate. Even less than in the House are the *elected* party leaders able to perform such a function. They have at their disposal little more than the arts of persuasion, which may also be exercised by any other Senator who is personally respected and is influential with his colleagues. Fortunately the Committee on Foreign Relations has enough prestige to attract outstanding Senators to its membership even after they have proved themselves on other committees. Reassuring examples may be found in the present chairman and a half dozen ranking members, to say nothing of most of their junior colleagues. The prospect seems good that the Foreign Relations Committee's nonpartisan influence will long continue to exercise a powerful moderating effect in many quarters—with the official and unofficial Senate leaders of both parties as well as with the individual Senators on and off the committee itself, as they shape their tangled, loose, and shifting blocs.

POLITICAL ORGANIZATION BETWEEN THE HOUSES

Relationships between the political leaders of the two houses of Congress are characterized by the phenomenon which is so prominent in each house separately—the independent authority of senior members of the standing committees.

Within Congress the Conference Committee is virtually the only mechanism of detailed bicameral coordination. Of the few House-Senate joint committees existing, only the one on Atomic Energy can be said to be continuously effective as something more than just an umbrella for a joint staff which produces reports that are interesting cross checks on the administration but rarely provide coordination of Congress. Outside Congress, of course, the President and executive officials provide a focus of coordination for action in both houses on bills in which they are interested. But except in a Conference Committee or under executive auspices the leaders of the two houses of Congress do not ordinarily meet together very often to discuss business.

That is true both of the central party leaders in House and Senate and of the leaders of the committees with parallel jurisdiction in the two chambers. In the parallel committees on foreign affairs there has been no frequent consultation between members from different houses. A leading Republican on Foreign Affairs remarked to the author: "There's a Chinese Wall between the two houses. There is more bipartisanship in Congress than there is bicameralism." His primary reference was to relations between the Foreign Affairs and Foreign Relations Committees.

Conference Committees. The Conference Committee, then, at the final stage of congressional activity, remains the basic device for Senate-House collaboration. And it is almost always under the control of senior members of the committees which originally reported the legislation in each house, who may or may not be amenable to suggestions from their party leaders in Congress and the administration. If they are, their agreed "conference report"—which must be voted on as a whole by each house, with no amendment permitted—can be a very useful instrument for "tidying up" legislation which may have passed one or both houses in a form which displeases the party leaders. But if the conferees are recalcitrant, they are in a position to impose their independent will or at least to insist on preserving some objectionable amendment which had previously been added on the floor.

Actually, as has been indicated, the appointing officers—the Speaker of the House and the presiding officer of the Senate—by custom have little real authority over the choice of managers for a conference. Though the Speaker's discretion is less restricted than the Vice-President's, the actual choice is usually made by the chairman and ranking minority member of the committee in each house which is handling the bill, or by other leading committee members designated by them. And during the meetings of the Senate-House conferees the party leaders in the two chambers do not normally keep very close track of the proceedings. The relationship resembles the one between party leaders and the regular standing committees; the party leaders are either not sufficiently staffed to keep themselves fully informed or else are hesitant to intrude on senior committeemen—often both. Only if a cooperative chairman is so patently weak as to need help in dealing with his fellow managers is a party leader likely to intervene very seriously.

A minimum compromise needed to produce agreement between the houses on a particular bill can usually be worked out by the conferees (senior committeemen) and their staffs, but if any very serious effort is to be made to integrate the terms of that compromise into a broad program of policy transcending the jurisdiction of the two committees, that effort generally must come from the executive branch, using appeals which may or may not be partisan.

The officials of the executive agencies immediately concerned are the ones most likely to take an active interest in conference proceedings, but even *their* liaison has often been haphazard and unsystematic. The conference report is their great opportunity to get a "workable" bill which cannot later be amended on the floor. Omnibus "packaging" of foreign aid legislation in recent years has made the conference report an especially potent instrument for straightening out the details of a large number of programs in a single document which Congress as a whole cannot immediately change and, for political reasons, can hardly reject in toto. Shrewd administrators furnish the best possible liaison officers for on-the-spot consultation with full Conference Committees and individual managers. But much depends on the personal influence of the individuals designated and on the degree of foresight and preparation which has gone into establishing good working relations between them and the relevant congressmen and staff personnel on the Hill. In general it may be said that at the last stage of the legislative process as in the early stages executive officials are left to make the best bargain they can with senior committeemen whose partisan loyalty to the administration varies greatly, as does also their regard for the particular agency involved and for its personnel.

CONCLUDING OBSERVATIONS

At the intermediate stages also it is clear that "generalist" *party* leaders have little authority to coordinate the activity of influential "specialists" on various committees of the United States Congress. The looseness of the whole system certainly lends itself to initiative on the part of any administration which may seek to enlist the cooperation of influential individuals from the opposition party who are willing to associate themselves with the administration's conduct of foreign affairs. Indeed the discipline is so loose, even in a party which formally controls all the branches of government, that the President does not secure from his own position as party leader even the full potential advantage which he might obtain without losing his opposition collaborators as a reaction. Some tightening of the structure of the President's party in Congress on world affairs could make extrapartisanship more efficient while no less feasible politically; this was true when Truman was in the White House as it is now under Eisenhower.

If in addition the much more ambitious goal be sought of increasing *all* party discipline for the sake of party responsibility and bipartisanship, these must be clearly recognized as very remote objectives in Congress. And if it be decided that such far-reaching changes are not wise in the particular field of foreign affairs, it is likely that congressmen would welcome the excuse to continue their familiar practices (somewhat modified) in foreign relations, even if they should become increasingly subject to party control in other areas of policy.

PART THREE

*The Record of the Parties
in Foreign Affairs, 1939–50*

CHAPTER 7

The Impact of War

IN BRIEFEST OUTLINE the story of American political parties
in foreign affairs during the forties is an account of the rise
and decline of harmony between the parties. After the shock of
Pearl Harbor the previous strong partisanship abated, to be followed by a period in which mere acquiescence in the wartime decisions of the Commander in Chief gave way to active collaboration between party leaders in the establishment of the United Nations and then in the evolution of an anti-Soviet foreign policy.
There were fluctuations in this upward trend-line of cooperation,
but no general turn downward until after the 1948 election. Then
a number of forces came into play which so quickly weakened the
comfortable structure of "bipartisanship" as to call for a reappraisal of its earlier apparent strength and of its future potentialities under the American system of government.

This and succeeding chapters constitute an attempt to describe
and interpret these developments, to determine whether the historical record, like the congressional voting statistics, provides a
reasonable basis for expecting a workable compromise between the
harsh partisanship of 1941 and the "idyllic" bipartisanship of 1948.
This is a look at the role of American parties in foreign affairs in
the recent past in order to judge what it can be and should be in
the near future. No attempt will be made to provide a general
history of American foreign relations in this period, nor a full
account of all types of domestic political considerations which have

influenced foreign policy, e.g., pressure groups; it will even be necessary for the sake of space to omit some of the interesting episodes in which truly partisan considerations were important. But the major political developments will at least be surveyed for what they have to contribute to an understanding of the problem of party in contemporary American foreign relations and to the formulation of sensible conclusions regarding future possibilities.

PRE-PEARL HARBOR PARTISANSHIP

In Congress. Partisan conflict in Congress over foreign policy was strong in the years between the German invasion of Poland and the Japanese attack on Pearl Harbor. Members of the House of Representatives showed a considerably higher degree of partisanship than Senators, but in both chambers the successive legislative enactments sought by President Roosevelt to aid the allies had to be pushed through by Democratic majorities over strong Republican opposition. This was not merely a matter of beating down "crippling" amendments by party-line votes. It involved the final votes on entire pieces of basic legislation. To be sure, the rearmament of the United States itself, with the important exception of selective service, was not much of a party issue; moreover, there was very little conflict in the 1940 presidential campaign; and Republican leaders Knox and Stimson were included in the Democratic cabinet. But those developments should not be allowed to obscure the fact that party conflict in Congress persisted and in the House grew even more determined during 1941 until the country and the Republican leadership experienced the trauma of December 7.

The intensity of partisanship in this period is briefly indicated in the tables on page 131. In Table 6 the figures are based on the votes actually cast in the most important House roll calls dealing with preparedness and aid to the allies during the months between the outbreak of war in Europe and in the Pacific. They show the percentage of voting members of each major party who crossed party lines on a particular issue, it being understood that in these cases a majority of the Democrats always supported the administration and a majority of the Republicans opposed it.

TABLE 6. Percentage of Party Desertion on Foreign Policy Roll Calls
in the House of Representatives, 1939–41

	Dems.	Reps.
Repeal of arms embargo (11/2/39)	14%	12%
Selective service—60-day delay (9/7/40)	26	14
Selective service—enactment (9/7/40)	14	32
Lend-lease (2/8/41)	10	15
Ship seizures (5/7/41)	8	34
Extending service of inductees (8/12/41)	26	14
Arming American merchant ships (10/14/41)	9	26
Opening combat zones (11/13/41)	22	14

TABLE 7. Percentage of Party Desertion on Foreign Policy Roll Calls
in the Senate, 1939–41

	Dems.	Reps.
Repeal of arms embargo (10/27/39)	18%	35%
Selective service (8/28/40)	25	44
Lend-lease (3/8/41)	18	37
Ship seizures (5/15/41)	8	40
Transfer of seized ships to allies (5/15/41)	28	12
Extending service of inductees (8/7/41)	30	35
Opening combat zones (11/7/41)	26	19
Opening zones *and* arming merchantmen (11/7/41)	26	22

The two basic laws which made it possible for the United States to extend aid to the allies before Pearl Harbor were the repeal of the arms embargo in 1939 (permitting the allies to make cash-and-carry purchases) and lend-lease in 1941. They both went through the House by practically straight party-line votes. On other related issues there was solidarity in one party or the other but not in both. Depending on how drastic a particular Administration proposal appeared at the time, a quarter of one party would cross the lines while only about one-eighth of the other party would do so. If the administration's proposal was extreme, the Republicans were the more united (in opposition); if the administration's proposal was more widely acceptable, the Democrats showed the greater solidarity (in support). But the basic line-up was definitely partisan, and the House leaders of both parties were perfectly willing to use all their customary devices of authority to rally support for conflicting party stands.

Table 7 shows that in the Senate party lines broke more easily. Usually at least a third of the Republicans in the upper chamber supported the administration on critical roll calls. But as the country approached war the GOP Senators were, if anything, becoming more united in their *opposition* to the trend of administration policy. At least that was their reaction to the move to take a House bill which only *armed* American merchant ships and add to it permission for the ships to enter *combat zones.* So one month before Pearl Harbor, despite the seriousness of the English and Russian plight, less than a fifth of the Republicans in either house were willing to dispatch American ships with American crews to be torpedoed off the British Isles. Resistance in the Democratic party also was growing. In the critical roll calls during the summer and fall more than a quarter of all Democratic Senators deserted their party. Roosevelt could still rally his partisans, but the voting record reflected their doubts.

The 1940 Campaign. The record of strong partisanship which can so easily be traced on key issues in Congress during the "defense period" was not reflected to any comparable degree in the presidential election campaign of 1940, mainly because of the nomination of Wendell Willkie. In the circumstances of the Taft-Dewey deadlock, his appealing personality, highly "available" Hoosier farm and business background, and powerful support from lords of the mass media swept the Republican convention at the climax of an extraordinary campaign.

Willkie's lifelong devotion to Wilsonian internationalism—within the Democratic party until Roosevelt's administration—made it probable that he would wage no very bitter campaign against the President's foreign policy. After his nomination Willkie supported the draft bill, although a majority of those running with him in each house of Congress did not. He let it be known privately, through William Allen White of the Committee to Defend America by Aiding the Allies, that he favored releasing fifty reconditioned American destroyers to Britain, although he was unwilling to commit himself to a direct agreement with the President before the destroyers-for-bases deal was publicly announced.[1]

But in the last two weeks of the campaign, under the pressure of professional political advisers who were doubtless correct in appraising the balance of voting strength, Willkie turned toward sharp criticism of the "Third Term Candidate" whose promises to avoid war "could not be trusted for more than five months." Roosevelt was driven to give his famous "assurance . . . again and again and again: Your boys are not going to be sent into any foreign wars." Even Cordell Hull for the first and last time broke his resolve never to make frankly political speeches in the office of Secretary of State. Assaults on the administration's foreign policy, with which he was so closely connected, and fear of world developments during the interim between the election and inauguration of a new President persuaded him to make two important campaign speeches for Roosevelt in the first week of November. (This despite his own bitter disappointment over his failure to get the presidential nomination for himself. Roosevelt was not to forget Hull's assistance at this crucial juncture.) [2]

The unpleasantness of the last two weeks of the 1940 campaign in which both parties were grasping for the noninterventionist vote did not really offset the remarkable harmony which had obtained between the two presidential candidates during the first three months after the conventions, a period in which critically important steps in administration foreign policy had gone substantially unchallenged by the opposition candidate. Yet the fact remains that Willkie did not have a majority of the congressmen of his own party with him on the question of the draft during the campaign nor on the question of lend-lease immediately after inauguration. The wing of the party which *was* in sympathy with his views was not negligible; in the Senate it amounted to more

1. Walter Johnson, *The Battle against Isolation* (Chicago, University of Chicago, 1944), pp. 128–9. Robert E. Sherwood, *Roosevelt and Hopkins* (New York, Harper, 1948), pp. 174–6.

2. Cordell Hull, *Memoirs of Cordell Hull* (New York, Macmillan, 1948), *1*, 855–69, *passim*. Sherwood, *op. cit.*, p. 135. James Farley, *Jim Farley's Story* (New York, Whittlesey, 1948), p. 230–5, 244, 330–1. Sumner Welles, *Seven Decisions That Shaped History* (New York, Harper, 1951), p. 61.

than a third of the GOP members. But it was not a majority, and it was not much more disposed than the larger, noninterventionist faction to welcome his personal leadership after defeat. Personally Wendell Willkie probably swung few Republican votes in Congress during 1941. His contribution to American foreign relations had been to moderate what was potentially a very bitter election campaign at a very critical period in history. But even Willkie partly bowed to the forces of party conflict in the end, and thereafter, until Pearl Harbor, those forces retained mastery in his party, despite all of Willkie's activity.

Similarly, President Roosevelt's formation of a "coalition" cabinet immediately before the Republican National Convention of 1940 likewise failed—if it was even intended—to do more than to encourage that minority of the Republican party which was already disposed to go along with the Democratic administration, in measures increasingly less "short of war." To be sure, such encouragement was in itself of some value. But the timing of the Stimson and Knox appointments was so patently disruptive of the important GOP convention deliberations that it positively alienated many GOP leaders. The National chairman promptly proceeded to read the two "renegades" right out of the Grand Old Party. Their confirmation was strongly resisted by powerful Republicans in the Senate.[3] In the Cabinet Knox and Stimson were able to contribute their personal talents and play the symbolic role for the GOP minority which agreed with them. But like Wendell Willkie they were unable before Pearl Harbor to speak for a majority of their fellow partisans in collaboration with the administration.

The legislative record in 1941 demonstrated that in Congress the Republican party, as a party, especially in the House where stronger leadership is possible, was till the day of Pearl Harbor committed to opposing each successive interventionist proposal and offering as an alternative at each stage something so much weaker as basically to change the character of the policy. These were not simply exaggerated fights over the size of appropriations

3. Henry L. Stimson and McGeorge Bundy, *On Active Service in Peace and War* (New York, Harper, 1948), pp. 323–37, *passim*. Johnson, *op. cit.*, pp. 90–1.

or the form and personnel of administration. They really struck
to the roots of the developing policy of intervention in the European war. And by the middle of November 1941, when the Democratic party whip had again been required to force American con-
voys through to Liverpool and Murmansk, there seemed to be little
more that the administration could do except to resort to the
appalling expedient of trying to drive a declaration of world war
through Congress by the same partisan mechanisms.

THE COLLAPSE OF REPUBLICAN RESISTANCE

Of course Pearl Harbor solved the dilemma. At one stroke it cut
the whole ground from under the inflexible position which Republican congressional leaders had taken. It seemed to vindicate
the interventionist moves of Roosevelt and the few Republicans
who had stood with him and to confound the opposition. But by
the same stroke it turned American eyes away from these domestic
political struggles, and the largely discredited Republican leadership was able to take refuge in "all-out" support of the war effort—
silent or voluble, but in any case largely uncritical. This appears
to have been a fundamentally important result of the destruction
at Pearl Harbor of the Republican party's overextended lines of
opposition to administration foreign policy. Embarrassed GOP
leaders adopted a "wait-and-see" attitude, at the same time seeking
to cover their tracks with support of the war now in progress. If
they had had a less extreme record of foreign policy opposition
before Pearl Harbor, they might not have been so anxious to
make the public forget about it, and as a result more of them
might have dared to raise discriminating opposition to the President's conduct of foreign affairs during the war. Especially is this
true on the vital question of relations with Communist Russia and
the unconditional surrender of Germany. Powerful interests in the
Republican party (capitalist and German American) could probably have been counted on to offer substantial resistance to administration policy in these areas if leading party spokesmen had
not been so afraid of "rocking the boat"—not only of disturbing
the war effort but also of further jeopardizing their own positions

within the Republican party and, through consequent factionalism, the whole party's position before the nation.[4]

The extent to which the Republican leadership was shaken by Pearl Harbor was evident in the first meeting of the Republican National Committee at Chicago in mid-April 1942. Senators Robert Taft and Wayland Brooks of the isolationist hard core were found sponsoring resolutions on party policy which avoided any mention of foreign policy whatever, beyond urging vigorous prosecution of the war. This attitude of silent waiting, however, although it involved no reaffirmation of isolationism, was not nearly good enough for Wendell Willkie. He wanted the National Committee to register a pledge which began thus: "To undertake now and in the future whatever just and reasonable international responsibilities may be demanded in a modern world reduced in size and bound together by the airplane (etc.) . . ." The Republican leaders were not willing to go quite so far, but they did phrase a resolution which began thus: "We realize that after this war the responsibilities of the nation will not be circumscribed within the territorial limits of the United States; that our nation has an obligation to assist in bringing about understanding, comity, . . ." and then it continued with some of Willkie's language, minus the indicated (and significant) deletions:

> and cooperation among the nations of the world in order ~~that free institutions and a free way of life may be supported and encouraged in the rest of the world~~ that our own liberty may be preserved, and that the blighting and destructive processes of war may not again be forced upon us and upon the free and peace-loving peoples of the earth ~~by tyrannous aggressors, operating not by the rule of law but by the rule of force.~~

4. A good example of this attitude may be found in a private letter from the then isolationist Senator Vandenberg to Thomas Lamont, dated August 4, 1943: "Our Republican problem from a political point of view is—as you rightly indicate—complicated by the everlasting recurrence of the 'isolationist' theme . . . Speaking generally, it would be my observation that it is not the so-called isolationists who keep the issue alive, but it is the anti-isolationists who sometimes act as though they were afraid that they might lose their shibboleth." Arthur H. Vandenberg, Jr., ed., *The Private Papers of Senator Vandenberg* (Boston, Houghton Mifflin, 1952), p. 56.

The National Committee balked at "supporting the rest of the world" and at the international organization perhaps implied in "rule of law," but they did recognize an "obligation" on the United States to assist abroad. The statement was therefore regarded as a Willkie triumph, born of the reluctance of GOP leaders to risk a split with Willkie's supporters in an election year.[5]

Republican members of the House of Representatives, conscious of the election-year embarrassment of their pre-Pearl Harbor record, also managed to agree late in September on a brief campaign statement on foreign policy which began as strongly as the National Committee's but was hedged by a final sentence. The full text:

> We recognize that the United States has an obligation and responsibility to work with other nations to bring about a world understanding and cooperative spirit which will have for its supreme objective the continued maintenance of peace. In so doing we must not endanger our own independence, weaken our American way of life or our system of government.[6]

Certainly this was a noncommittal campaign platform, but it was something more than mere silence, and avoided the reaffirmation of unreconstructed isolationism.

5. *New York Times*, April 22 and 26, 1942, sec. 4, p. 10. For successive drafts of the resolution see *ibid.*, April 20 and 21, 1942.

To Senator Vandenberg the "advertised" Willkie victory was "sheer bunk." The whole fight had been "mere shadow-boxing with platitudes." His diary observed that "'isolationism' will be found very much alive (despite all these Willkie funeral orations) *when the time comes* to deal with the postwar world." The italics are Vandenberg's. Vandenberg, *op. cit.*, p. 30.

6. *New York Times*, September 23, 1942. The man who was to be the Republican candidate for President in 1944 and 1948 ran for re-election as Governor of New York in 1942 on a platform containing this plank, which he was in a position to dictate: "The United States must be prepared to undertake new obligations and responsibilities in the community of nations. We must cooperate with other nations to promote the wider international exchange of goods and services, to achieve monetary and economic stability, and thus discourage the growth of rampant nationalism and its spawn, economic and military aggression. As a further safeguard, we must join with other nations to secure the peace of the world."

During the summer of 1942 Governor Stassen of Minnesota, about to enter the navy, took the most advanced Republican position on international collaboration in a speech before the Governors' Conference on June 22, in which he called for a "world association." In succeeding months he developed his ideas with increasing emphasis on the "world legion" to enforce peace. Wendell Willkie undertook his famous "One World" flight around the globe in September and October, and although at the time his readiness to echo the complaints of each allied capital he visited disturbed the administration in Washington, there can be no doubt that the subsequent publication of his visionary account of his travels did much to confirm internationalist opinion in its unsuspicious appraisal of the Soviet Union and uncritical acceptance of the administration's policy of collaboration.[7] Willkie found that the administration's sponsorship of his trip antagonized other Republican leaders; so he felt prompted to criticize Roosevelt upon his return. At the end of the year Willkie's position in his party was still strong enough to enable him to find allies to block the nomination as National chairman of Werner Schroeder, Illinois National committeeman and candidate of the *Chicago Tribune.* Schroeder's backers had been confident of a majority before the National Committee met in St. Louis the first week in December 1942. But a "stop Schroeder" movement, quietly backed by Stassen and Dewey as well as by Willkie, forced the election of Harrison Spangler as a compromise candidate. Moreover, the National Committee reaffirmed its April resolution and endorsed the Republican Representatives' September statement.[8]

The Republican leaders were plainly unwilling to alienate any foreign policy faction of the party if it could possibly be avoided. Practically unable to unite on any positive policy themselves and reluctant to get out on a limb once more or to call attention to where the last one had been sawed off, they waited with extraordi-

7. Hull, *op. cit.,* 2, 1182–3. Sherwood, *op. cit.,* pp. 634–6. Accompanying Willkie were his backer, Gardner Cowles, and Joseph Barnes of the *Herald Tribune* and *PM.* The significant degree to which Willkie relied on Barnes's leftist advice is indicated in the biography by Mary Earhart Dillon, *Wendell Willkie* (Philadelphia, Lippincott, 1952), pp. 268–72, 280.

8. *New York Times,* December 13, 1942, sec. 4, p. 10.

narily uncritical passivity for the administration to take the initiative in framing American foreign policy.

EXECUTIVE PROCRASTINATION ON CONCRETE WAR AIMS

During 1942 and most of 1943 the administration was also unwilling to seek any long-range international settlements. The major reason for this reluctance to come to grips with issues of postwar international relations was of course the fear of antagonizing the Soviet Union to the point where she would make a separate peace with Hitler. Roosevelt was under constant pressure from the Joint Chiefs of Staff to avoid that danger. Another important consideration was domestic unity in the prosecution of war. It was clear that national solidarity went no further than a determination to punish Germany and Japan and to restore "Peace!" and that nationality and partisan controversies which could be kept silenced in the name of the "war effort" would almost certainly break out afresh if any attempt were made to define a consistent and feasible pattern of war objectives. Sumner Welles makes the additional observation that Roosevelt really did not feel "that to postpone discussion of these issues need seriously prejudice our hope of securing a good peace. For he had, and justly, great confidence in his own ability as a negotiator." [9]

The Beginnings of Postwar Planning. But Roosevelt was not unwilling to have the Department of State proceed forthwith to make studies and alternative plans for the postwar world, on the assumption that no controversial attempt would be made to implement them.[10] Accordingly, the rudimentary long-range plan-

9. Welles, *op. cit.,* pp. 133–5. Nor does the friction between Welles and Hull invalidate this further pertinent observation: "The Secretary of State was temperamentally disposed to put off dealing with controversial issues as long as possible. He preferred not to cross the proverbial bridge until he came to it. A remedial policy was to him preferable to a preventive policy. . . . If the [international] discussion of such exceedingly thorny problems as the Baltic states or Poland's eastern frontiers could be postponed until a peace conference, that was infinitely better than grasping the nettle now." *Ibid.,* p. 135.

10. "During the first part of 1942 it is quite true the President used frequently to say that he did not want to be drawn into the intensive studies of postwar

ning mechanisms in the Department of State were expanded and improved for this work.

The Advisory Committee. After a few false starts in the pre-Pearl Harbor period, serious preparatory study began on Lincoln's Birthday 1942 with the first meeting of the newly created Advisory Committee on Postwar Foreign Policy.[11] Its charter members included ten who were regarded as State Department regulars, five as representatives of the general public, two from the White House (Benjamin Cohen and David Niles), and one each from Treasury, Agriculture, and the Board of Economic Warfare. The initial public members were Isaiah Bowman of Johns Hopkins, Hamilton Fish Armstrong of *Foreign Affairs,* Anne O'Hare McCormick of the *New York Times,* Myron Taylor, and Norman Davis. James Shotwell of the Carnegie Endowment was added in June 1942 to the category of nonofficial and nonspecialized membership. None of these core members, be it observed, was a figure "in politics."

From the start the committee operated almost exclusively through subcommittees. Officially the main reason was to preserve secrecy. Public morale was thought to be endangered by talk of

---

settlements and world organization that were then already under way in the Department of State. This was primarily because he feared that if he did really get into them he would become so interested he might be tempted to devote less of his time and thought to the war effort itself. Also, I think, he wanted to keep an open mind regarding frontiers and other postwar problems, knowing that some compromises would be inevitable and that it would be unwise for him to become fixed in advance in his own convictions about the wisdom or justice of any particular solution.

"Throughout that year, when I would tell him of the work being accomplished by the various committees in the Department of State, he would say, 'What I expect you to do is to have prepared for me the necessary number of baskets and the necessary number of alternative solutions for each problem in the baskets, so that when the time comes all I have to do is reach into a basket and fish out a number of solutions that I am sure are sound and from which I can make my own choice.'" *Ibid.,* pp. 181–2.

11. The story of postwar planning is most fully told in the official State Department history, *Postwar Foreign Policy Preparation,* Department of State Publication 3580 (Washington, Government Printing Office, 1949). The book was written by Harley A. Notter (hereafter referred to as Notter) with the assistance of a departmental research staff. He himself for a long time held important posts in the postwar planning mechanism.

postwar planning. Another consideration was Hull's determination to restrict the work of the committee, insofar as possible, to very long-range planning.[12]

But if the Secretary's indecisiveness about bringing the work of his Advisory Committee to a head limited its ultimate effectiveness, his early determination that its operations should also include congressmen from both parties was surely a major contribution to whatever success the committee finally had.[13] As its membership began to proliferate, the first men invited, after representatives of the Secretaries of War and Navy, were Senators Connally and Austin of the Foreign Relations Committee. Austin was selected after consultation with other Republican leaders.[14] Both men were approved by the President, but Hull found him skeptical, then and later, that Hull "could achieve a non-partisan agreement with the Republicans which they would keep. . . . Nevertheless, he was not opposed to my making the non-partisan approach, and I accordingly went ahead." [15] On January 9, 1943, five more congressmen of long experience on foreign affairs committees joined the Hull Advisory Committee. They were Walter George and Elbert Thomas, Democratic Senators; Sol Bloom and Luther Johnson, Democratic Representatives; and Republican Congressman Eaton. And six weeks later GOP Senator Wallace White joined the group. Later in the year congressmen from other standing committees were brought in on the work of special subcommittees on communications and shipping: Democratic Senators Scott Lucas and Claude Pepper, Democratic Representatives Schuyler Otis Bland, Hardin Peterson, and Alfred Bulwinkle; and Republican Representatives Richard Welch and Charles Wolverton. And still others were enlisted in the preparatory work for specialized United Nations agencies which was carried on largely outside the Advisory Committee framework.

At the same time that Connally and Austin were brought into

12. Hull, *op. cit.*, 2, 1634. Notter, *op. cit.*, p. 93. Cf. p. 139, n. 9.

13. Welles, *op. cit.*, pp. 134–5. "My first concern was to make the membership of the committee absolutely non-partisan, and to give Republicans as well as Democrats adequate representation." Hull, *op. cit.*, 2, 1635.

14. Notter, *op. cit.*, p. 74.

15. Hull, *op. cit.*, 2, 1657.

the general work of the Advisory Committee, its political base was strengthened by the inclusion of Robert Watt from the AFL and Walter Reuther of the CIO for the study of economic problems. More formal representation of economic interests came early in April 1943, with the invitation of William Green, Philip Murray, and Eric Johnston to take part in economic deliberations. Percy Bidwell of the Council on Foreign Relations and Jacob Viner of the University of Chicago completed the list of fullfledged public members of the Advisory Committee. It should also be emphasized that extensive use was being made of studies prepared outside the government, especially by the Council on Foreign Relations and by the Federal Council of Churches.

However, the record of achievement of the various subcommittees through which the Advisory Committee operated during its first year and a half was not very commendable. A careful reading of Harley Notter's official history—hardly intended to deprecate the work of the department unduly—makes understandable Sumner Welles's reference to the committee's work as "a depressing story at best." [16] Jurisdictional disputes with other agencies, un-

16. Welles, *op. cit.,* p. 182.

These appear to be some of Harley Notter's most revealing observations about each of the subcommittees:

The Subcommittee on Political Problems—the only one which had congressional representation throughout: "That the Soviet Union would probably cooperate in regard to problems concerning ex-enemy countries, at least so far as military occupation was concerned, was a view early adopted. During the next year and a half of its activity, the subcommittee reached the further conclusion that Soviet cooperation on principal international problems would be essential, and as discussion proceeded, the assumption was accepted that such cooperation would be proffered because of the interests of the Soviet Union itself. Nevertheless, these were of necessity speculations. By March 1943 the conviction was reached that a definite answer to the basic question whether such cooperation would be forthcoming should be obtained as soon as practicable." (p. 102)

The Special Subcommittee on International Organization: "The definitive policy recommendations later adopted in this vital field were, however, not those formulated by this special subcommittee, and in various respects differed fundamentally, although in other respects the special subcommittee's views entered into the proposals ultimately advanced by this Government." (p. 114) The main difference was the emphasis in the early proposals on *regional* international organizations. This was later minimized for fear of rivalry between blocs, but it has finally become the main characteristic of international organization.

The Subcommittee on Territorial Problems: "A fixed conclusion of the sub-

reliable hypotheses for planning, and the lack of clear-cut objectives muddied much of the activity. By July 9, 1943, even Secretary Hull finally came to the conclusion that the time for exploratory thinking was past and that the need now was for position papers. Accordingly he adjourned the Advisory Committee. Research staffs under Pasvolsky's guidance proceeded to draw up policy summary papers on numerous problems, treated geographically and functionally.

Blueprinting Utopia. But it was most significant that during and after the period of the Advisory Committee emphasis was increasingly upon international organization as a cure-all for the world's problems. It would be difficult to overestimate the political importance of this development, both at home and abroad. For several months, in the name of United States and United Nations solidarity in the war effort, Americans had largely avoided public discussion of issues of postwar international relations. Now the

---

committee . . . was that the vital interests of the United States lay in following a 'diplomacy of principle'—of moral disinterestedness instead of power politics— and in continuing to adhere to the policy already enunciated by Secretary Hull that the United States must refrain from undertaking any commitment on territorial settlements until after the conclusion of hostilities." (p. 123)

The Subcommittee on Security Problems—the only one with military representation: "Practically from the opening of the discussion on overall security, emphasis was laid upon the necessity, as the most imperative basis for assurance of peace and security after the war, of a firm pact among the chief victor powers agreed upon prior to the conclusion of the war. A corollary of this conviction was that every effort should be made to come to an understanding with the Soviet Union and that a common policy with respect to future postwar settlements should be reached." (pp. 128-9)

The Subcommittee on Economic Reconstruction worked to construct UNRRA. The Subcommittee on Economic Policy graduated into the Myron Taylor Committee on Postwar Foreign Economic Policy and then into the Executive Committee for Foreign Economic Policy in 1944; but the Taylor Committee had no more than partially interlocking membership with Harry White's American Technical Committee which headed up in the Treasury to prepare for Bretton Woods, and when Roosevelt took a personal initiative to try out international organization in the noncontroversial area of food, arrangements for FAO were made outside the Advisory Committee structure.

The two other special subcommittees were that on Legal Problems (which drew up an international Bill of Rights, a plan for trying war criminals, and a revision of the Statute of the Hague Court) and the one on Problems of European Organization, which engaged in discussion and research but produced no report.

public was given some encouragement to look ahead to a world at peace, but in a frame of reference which diverted them as much as before from facing the really crucial questions of global power relationships. Through the intense and sustained efforts of many Americans in and out of the government, the domestic harmony on world affairs which was born from determination to avenge Pearl Harbor was in effect channeled toward visionary construction of elaborate designs for a postwar utopia. The preservation of harmony was a notable achievement. But it was accomplished by focusing public discussion of the postwar world overwhelmingly on mere mechanics of international organization.

Not only did friends of the administration's prewar foreign policy devote their attention to this cause, but even its bitterest critics to a remarkable degree exhausted themselves in attacking the designs of a heaven-on-earth which promised so much and demanded so little that few could oppose it for long. As an issue in American politics international relations came to be nearly synonymous with international organization, and as the months went by public figures and political leaders of both parties reached extraordinary consensus on that subject—while the decisions which really did most to shape the postwar world were made largely in private by the military, the President, and a few advisers who, for the most part, were leaders of neither political party.

What were the reasons for this overemphasis on the United Nations? There were several, of which these seem to be the most important: In the first place there were the considerations which had militated against any early precipitation of controversial postwar issues; international organization would at least be less disturbing than boundary settlements, both to our allies and to various factions at home, and it would not run afoul of the need for secrecy involved in high strategic considerations. It was convenient to discuss the United Nations at a time when we dared not raise such embarrassing issues as Russian claims in Eastern Europe. Most Americans seemed to find the emphasis on international organization not only convenient but eminently desirable. Their extraordinary eagerness appears to reflect a kind of powerful, pervasive guilt complex over the repudiation of the League of Nations—a sentiment assiduously fostered by those who had always been friends of the League. In a truly remarkable display of anachronism the American people between 1935 and 1945 first enacted the legislation which might have kept them out of World War I and then contritely accepted the international mechanisms which, of themselves, might have prevented World War II; but in the second case, as in the first, they seem to have been about two decades too late in apprehending the actual requirements of the contemporary situation.[17]

17. One other factor, still obscure but perhaps important, was the influence of far leftist opinion in and out of the Department of State in focusing on the forms of international organization the attention which should have been given to the realities of power politics.

CHAPTER 8

Organizing the United Nations

ONE IS STRUCK AGAIN AND AGAIN when reading the foreign policy debates in Congress and the press during the war by the preoccupation they show over avoiding the mistakes of 1919 and 1920. Wilson's old supporters felt vindicated but moved cautiously; many of his opponents were embarrassed and no longer adamant. For Secretary of State Cordell Hull, who well remembered the "Great Betrayal," "international organization in my thinking was always the central and decisive problem." [1] But he was determined not to jeopardize its successful attainment by any move smacking of Wilsonian partisanship or imperiousness. [2] The participation of congressmen and private citizens in the work of State's Advisory Committee on Postwar Foreign Policy during 1942 and early 1943 seemed an appropriate device for helping to develop a public opinion favorable to the idea of international organization. Outside the executive branch a movement was gathering momentum, with the aid of men in both parties, to avoid any repetition of America's refusal to approve the peace of Ver-

1. Hull, *Memoirs of Cordell Hull, 2*, 1637. Hull's authority to steer his department's activity in this idealistic direction was temporarily strengthened by the dismissal of Sumner Welles in August 1943. Thereafter Roosevelt had no intimate in the State Department on whom he could rely for top-level international *political* advice, while Hull devoted himself to building the United Nations.

2. "[It] was all-important to keep public opinion educated and stabilized up to date with respect to the hitherto controversial questions in foreign affairs. Otherwise Congress could not be expected to maintain any position it might take in the event public opinion should lapse or swerve in the wrong direction." Hull, *op. cit., 2*, 1261.

sailles and to join the League of Nations. All were deeply conscious of the problems posed by the two-thirds requirement for treaty ratification.

LAYING THE GROUNDWORK FOR ACTION

When the Seventy-eighth Congress convened in the winter of 1943, several resolutions were introduced in both houses of Congress relating to postwar international relations and proposing varying degrees of cooperation and organization. The State Department, however, was unwilling to precipitate any action. Hull's reply to a request from Sol Bloom for a line on one of the resolutions was exceedingly cautious: "What action the Congress wishes to take on this resolution is, of course, a matter for its own discretion. I may say, however, that the spirit of the resolution is entirely in accord with the foreign policy of this Administration." [3]

"B2H2." The administration's hand was not forced until the second week in March 1943, when a ringing appeal in Constitution Hall by Governor Stassen for an international organization with armed forces was followed by the publication of the Ball-Burton-Hatch-Hill Resolution in the Senate. Ball's close relationship to Stassen suggested that the timing of the resolution was not accidental, but its provisions were far less detailed than the Governor's. The most important section, however, was similar. It called for "an organization of the United Nations" with authority "to provide for the assembly and maintenance of a United Nations military force and to suppress by immediate use of such force any future attempt at military aggression by any nation." The resolution came from a two-party group *outside* the Foreign Relations Committee: two freshman Republicans, Ball and Burton, a veteran Democrat, Hatch, and Lister Hill, a first-term Democratic Senator with a substantial record in the House. They had shown their draft to about twenty-five Senators.[4]

The sudden publication was particularly embarrassing to the administration because the British Foreign Minister was then in

3. *Ibid.,* 2, 1260.
4. *New York Times,* March 15 and 16, 1943.

Washington for conversations. Hull explained to Anthony Eden
that a Senate resolution would indeed be "most desirable, assuming that the situation is first carefully canvassed to make sure that
any such proposal will receive an overwhelming vote—in any event
more than two-thirds of the vote."

> The task before us, therefore, I said, was to get detailed dis-
> cussion with all the Senators favorably inclined. We carefully
> had to work out during the next few weeks an agreement on
> every essential phase, so that there would be understanding
> and unity when the Senate took action. This preliminary
> step of full and detailed conference was an indispensable pre-
> requisite to any successful action by the Senate on a proposed
> resolution.[5]

Some concrete suggestion from the administration was needed.
Hull, however, cautioned department officials about the danger of
causing isolationists to run away "as fast as a wild stallion . . . at
the rustle of a leaf." The leaf was not allowed to crackle. The
State Department's modest proposal was that the Senate formally
advocate "participation by the United States in the creation and
maintenance of an international organization to insure permanent
peace." [6]

The B2H2 group was not satisfied. They wanted explicit reference to military force. At the opposite extreme were men in both
parties who opposed any international organization. On March
25 Connally set up a special subcommittee to go over the various
postwar policy resolutions. Its members were Connally, George,
Barkley, Thomas, and Gillette, Democrats; Vandenberg and White,
Republicans; and LaFollette, Progressive. Austin was not included
despite his contemporaneous service with Hull's Advisory Committee. The subcommittee made no progress in reconciling differences.

The Fulbright Resolution. It was not shaken into action in June
either, when the House Foreign Affairs Committee took the bull
by the horns and suddenly reported out the so-called Fulbright

5. Hull, *op. cit.,* 2, 1261.
6. *Ibid.,* 2, 1261–2.

Resolution. This was only partly Representative Fulbright's own resolution. His original had implied support for an international police force. Fulbright's name was attached to the committee's final product because, as a freshman Southern Democrat, he was a neutral figure on a committee which was tired of having Chairman Bloom take credit for every bill reported.[7] The resolution was devised without hearings. Bloom explained that this was because "agreement centered early in the discussions" on a draft which "did not involve commitment to any specific legislation."[8] The initiative really seems to have come from within the Congress.[9] (Even today men who worked closely on it continue to insist on that in private interviews.) The text was simple: "the Congress hereby expresses itself as favoring the creation of appropriate international machinery with power adequate to establish and to maintain a just and lasting peace among the nations of the world, and as favoring the participation of the United States therein." This received the cast vote in committee of every member, except for two absentees.[10] But some members of the Foreign Affairs Committee anticipated an opportunity to seek amendments on the floor.[11]

To symbolize two-party collaboration, Republican John Vorys was allowed to bring the Fulbright Resolution to the attention of the full House in a brief discussion, but no action was taken. The resolution was blocked by Chairman Sabath of the Rules Committee, after a formal meeting of the House leaders with Fulbright and Republican James Wadsworth. Wadsworth had appealed to Rayburn to give him a few weeks to work on the estimated fifty GOP Representatives who would vote against the Fulbright Resolution if it should be promptly brought to the floor; Wadsworth thought he could get the opposition down to a dozen. Secretary

7. Interview with a leading Republican on Foreign Affairs. (House rules do not permit joint sponsorship of legislation.)

8. *New York Times*, June 16, 1943.

9. See, for example, John Vorys, *Congressional Record*, June 16, 1943, p. 5943; and Luther Johnson, *Congressional Record*, September 20, 1943, p. 7664.

10. *New York Times*, June 16, 1943, quoting Chairman Bloom.

11. Statement of Robert Chiperfield, then the third-ranking Republican. *Congressional Record*, September 20, 1943, p. 7660.

Hull approved of the decision and justified it to Roosevelt, who had evidently favored prompt House action unless Senate sensibilities were too delicate.[12] So the postwar policy resolutions in both House and Senate were postponed till autumn. Hull accepts some responsibility: "Perhaps partly as a result of my insistence on thorough organization in the Senate and House so as to secure an overwhelming vote, the resolutions did not come to a head until some months later—but when they did they were handled in such a manner and passed with so stupendous a majority as to be eminently satisfactory." [13]

The Mackinac Conference. A major reason for delaying the vote in Congress in the late spring and summer of 1943 was the forthcoming Mackinac Island Conference of Republican officials to draft a declaration on postwar policy. It had become increasingly apparent to even the Old Guard in the Republican party that some positive statement of an attitude toward international relations would be required for the presidential campaign of 1944. The expectation that the war would be practically over by November 1944 was growing dim, and with it any hope that the GOP could simply ride to the White House on a tide of postwar frustration as in 1920 (and, *mutatis mutandis,* 1946). Virtual silence about controversial foreign policies had sufficed in 1942, but Wendell Willkie's persistent agitation and the wave of postwar planning in Congress made empty platitudes seem inadequate to hold the party together for victory in 1944, especially now that it appeared the war would still be going on and the voters would be reluctant to exchange "something" for "nothing" in midstream. Somehow the very real cleavage within the party would have to be bridged, and if a conspiracy of silence were not possible, it would be well to thrash out the issues sometime in advance of the National Convention, lest that crucial gathering prove fratricidal.

On May 31, 1943, Republican National Chairman Harrison Spangler announced the establishment of a Republican Postwar Advisory Council. It was to be composed of forty-nine party leaders

12. Hull, *op. cit.,* 2, 1262-3. Sabath took full responsibility for his action. *Congressional Record,* September 21, 1943, p. 7725.
13. Hull, *op. cit.,* 2, 1263.

who held "elective office," including some national committeemen as well as governors and congressmen, but pointedly excluding Wendell Willkie. ("Impartially" under the formula, Hoover and Landon were also omitted.) A conference was scheduled early in September on Mackinac Island to draw up a declaration of party policy.

The *congressional* party leadership intended to take charge of the conference. Spangler appointed Senator Taft to guide the drafting of domestic policy and Senator Vandenberg that of foreign policy. The membership of the Council's subcommittee on international relations would be hopelessly unbalanced unless the other congressional members should prove willing to stand up to the then noninterventionist Chairman Vandenberg. They were Senator Austin and Representatives Eaton and Bolton. Governors Green of Illinois and Martin of Pennsylvania were also on the subcommittee. Vandenberg came to Mackinac with a draft declaration based on a postwar policy resolution which he and Senator White had introduced in the Senate in July, acting as the two Republican members of Connally's Foreign Relations subcommittee on postwar international relations. The emphasis of the resolution was on avoiding detailed commitments long before the end of the war. The proposals went no further on the main point at issue than to advocate American participation "in postwar cooperation between sovereign nations to prevent [aggression] by any necessary means." [14] The broad phrase about means was largely canceled by the weasel words "cooperation" and "sovereign." The sentence did not go very much beyond the Republican National Committee's statement of December 1942—certainly not so far as the Fulbright Resolution, which had been reported out of committee in June 1943.[15]

Many of the gubernatorial delegates to Mackinac were dissatisfied, especially those from New England and the Far West. They were particularly offended by the Washingtonians' evident determination to obtain ratification of draft declarations quickly and without much amendment. Connecticut Governor Baldwin's reac-

14. *New York Times*, July 3 and September 6, 1943.
15. See pp. 136–8 and 149.

tion was snappy: "We think too." Not only did the governors have
some ideas; what was more important, they were likely to control national convention delegates in 1944, probably more effectively than
would members of Congress. Promptly the gubernatorial bloc
forced the conference subcommittees to open their doors for hearings at which all council members could freely present their views.
(The planned procedure had been to admit petitioning members
one by one into a locked committee room.) [16] New York's Governor
Dewey made the most startling proposal of the whole session at a
press conference on arrival. He said he favored an outright alliance
between Britain and the United States. But he made no effort to
press anything so specific on his fellow Republicans. Actually the
leadership of the insurgent bloc was in the hands of Baldwin, Earl
Warren, Governor Sewall of Maine, and, inside the drafting subcommittee, Austin and Eaton, their hands strengthened by the
revolt outside. Austin threatened to file a minority report if the
other leaders insisted on dodging the question of international
organization.[17]

Austin and his colleagues won their battle for explicit use of the
term "organization." That was as far as they got. Sovereignty was
retained at Vandenberg's insistence. The resulting key phrase was
"responsible participation by the United States in post-war cooperative organization among sovereign nations to prevent military
aggression and to attain permanent peace with organized justice in
a free world." Other language in the declaration hedged it further.[18] In the end it proved acceptable to all shades of Republican

16. *New York Times,* September 7, 1943.
17. The *New York Times* quoted him directly to that effect, September 9, 1943.
18. "(A) We must preserve and protect all our own national interests.

"(B) We must aid in restoring order and decent living in a distressed world.

"(C) We must do our full share in a program for permanent peace among nations.

"At this time a detailed program for the accomplishment of these great objectives will be impossible, and specific commitments of this council of the Republican party, or by the nation, would be unwise. We cannot know now what
situation may obtain at the war's end. But a specific program must be evolved in
the months to come, as events and relations unfold . . .

"We ground our judgment upon the belief that both the foreign policy and
domestic policy of every country are related to each other so closely that each member of the United Nations (or whatever co-operative organization perpetuating exist-

opinion from Colonel McCormick to Senator Austin. That of course was the main objective. And some advance had certainly been made over formal Republican pronouncements of the preceding year. Despite the absence of any explicit affirmation of the need for military power at the disposal of the international organization, the declaration could reasonably be said to imply such a need. At any rate there was no necessary conflict with the broad terminology of the Fulbright Resolution.[19] Presumably, Republican Representatives would feel encouraged to vote for it when they returned from vacation.

The UNRRA Agreement. In addition to the Mackinac Declaration one other development during the summer of 1943 was of particular importance for the evolution of a harmonious relationship between the major parties on questions of postwar foreign policy. That was the revision of the proposed UNRRA agreement.

On June 9, 1943, President Roosevelt at the White House informed the four top Democratic and Republican leaders in the House and Senate of his intention to proceed with the negotiation of a multilateral executive agreement to provide relief for war-devastated lands. When the proposed terms appeared in the form of a voluminous press release on June 11, Senator Vandenberg rebelled. He introduced a resolution calling for an investigation by

---

ing unity may be agreed upon) ought to consider both the immediate and remote consequences of every proposition with careful regard for:

    1. Its effect upon the vital interests of the nation.

    2. Its bearing upon the foreseeable international developments.

If there should be a conflict between the two, then the United States of America should adhere to the policy which will preserve its constitutionalism as expressed in the Declaration of Independence, the Constitution itself, and the Bill of Rights, as administered through our republican form of government. Constitutionalism should be adhered to in determining the substance of our policies and shall be followed in ways and means of making international commitments.

"In addition to these things, this council advises that peace and security ought to be ultimately established upon other sanctions than force. It recommends that we work toward a policy which will comprehend other means than war for the determination of international controversy, and the attainment of a peace that will prevail by virtue of its inherent reciprocal interests and its spiritual foundation, reached from time to time with the understanding of the peoples of the negotiating nations."

19. See p. 149.

the Foreign Relations Committee "to determine whether the draft agreement was of the nature of a treaty, and should be submitted to the Senate for ratification." Connally complied by establishing a subcommittee composed of himself, Elbert Thomas, Green, Vandenberg, and LaFollette. It was made perfectly clear to the State Department that extensive revisions in its plans were in order if the Senate were to be satisfied that its prerogatives had been properly protected. "Total disagreement" would have been Vandenberg's personal reaction to the UNRRA agreement if the State Department had refused to make concessions. Connally was also very angry.[20]

Nor did the State Department resist. Its assiduous compliance was impressive.

> I cannot emphasize too strongly that in the sixteen years I have been in this body, the greater part of it on the Committee on Foreign Relations, I have never had an experience like the present one in its total sympathetic, cooperative attitude on the part of the State Department and what appears to be the whole-hearted purpose to yield itself completely to the congressional intent and will in respect to this entire matter.[21]

Vandenberg and Green were the active members of the Foreign Relations subcommittee during the summer. They worked most closely with Francis Sayre, who was at that time Deputy Director of the Office of Foreign Relief and Rehabilitation Operations, the matrix of UNRRA in the State Department. Vandenberg "undertook to rewrite the draft agreement so as to eliminate from it those illimitable commitments which carried it into the realm of a treaty" and to bring it "back into what we thought was the realm of an agreement."

> We succeeded in rewriting it to a point where it is now literally nothing more than the authorization of appropriation, and there is no commitment in the text to anything except the expenditure of such moneys as are specifically appropriated

20. Vandenberg, *Congressional Record*, February 16, 1944, p. 1739. Tom Connally, *My Name Is Tom Connally* (New York, Crowell, 1954), p. 262.
21. Vandenberg, *Congressional Record*, February 17, 1944, p. 1808.

from time to time by Congress for this purpose. Furthermore, the agreement itself will be textually included within the measure providing for the authorization of the appropriations.[22]

At least the administration managed to avoid the two-thirds rule of formal treaty ratification. Moreover, Senator Vandenberg was mollified to a degree which was important when the Connally Resolution came to the floor in October and in retrospect even more important as a shadow of the future.

There was another aspect of these proceedings which had long-run political significance. At the preliminary policy-making stage members of the House Foreign Affairs Committee as well as the august personages of the upper chamber were consulted. And this was on a nonpartisan basis. Unlike the Senators, the Representatives made no important changes in the State Department's plans, but they did acquire some pride of participation. In the fall the House of Representatives authorized travel expenses for members of Foreign Affairs to attend as observers the Atlantic City Conference at which UNRRA was born. When the agreement came before the House in January of 1944, members of both parties in the corridors could point with pride to the i's they had dotted and the t's they had crossed. In retrospect key Republicans on the Foreign Affairs Committee regarded this as the first *legislative* expression of "bipartisanship," just as the Fulbright Resolution was for them the first *declaratory* action of that kind.[23]

THE FULBRIGHT AND CONNALLY RESOLUTIONS

Passage of the Fulbright Resolution. When members of Congress returned to the Capitol in September 1943 after their summer recess, the House leadership promptly decided that the groundwork was now adequate to permit a vote in the House on the Fulbright Resolution. But despite Mackinac the leaders were still not prepared to risk a procedure which would give opportunity for amending the resolution, even though the measure had been

22. *Ibid.*, October 27, 1943, p. 8802.
23. This paragraph is based on an interview with a key Republican on Foreign Affairs. See also Bloom's address, *Congressional Record,* January 20, 1944, p. 474.

reported unanimously from Foreign Affairs on the assumption that amendments would be in order. The decision was to bring up the bill under suspension of the rules, which would require a two-thirds vote but prohibit amendments, and to provide by special rule that under *this* suspension four hours' instead of the customary forty minutes' debate would be allowed.[24] (In the Senate, where there was no such neat procedure for blocking amendments, Connally's subcommittee on postwar resolutions showed no inclination to risk reporting one out even yet.)

In the House the *Republican* leadership also took a hand in the proceedings. Confronted with the Democratic ban on floor amendments, the Republican Steering Committee insisted that the Foreign Affairs Committee reassemble on the morning of the day the resolution was to come up and add the magic words "through its constitutional processes" to the brief Fulbright phrases about "participation of the United States" in "appropriate international machinery with power adequate" to keep peace.[25] With this bow to Mackinac and some assurance that the two-thirds rule in the Senate would probably protect any interests of the Republican party and prevent any extreme administration proposals for international organization, the House Republicans voted overwhelmingly for the Fulbright Resolution. In all, only 29 votes were cast against it on September 21, 1943, nearly all by GOP Representatives from the Midwest.

Over at the other end of the Capitol there was still no disposition to risk debate on a resolution. During the summer ten teams had been organized to tour the country on behalf of the far-reaching Ball-Burton-Hatch-Hill Resolution, each consisting of a Senator and a Representative of different parties; the success of the Vandenberg-Green-Sayre UNRRA negotiations, the Mackinac Declaration, and finally the Fulbright Resolution added flame to the fire the B2H2 groups were trying to build under Connally. But it was not until Secretary Hull's departure for a four-power

24. A. Sabath, *Congressional Record,* September 21, 1943, p. 7725.

25. John Robsion, a member of the Republican Steering Committee, *Congressional Record,* September 21, 1943, p. 7716; Representative Chiperfield, *Congressional Record,* September 20, 1943, p. 7660.

conference in Moscow made some immediate, symbolic Senate action appear vital that the Foreign Relations subcommittee suddenly decided to report a resolution on October 14, 1943. The full committee hastily approved it after three meetings, and in less than a week it was before the Senate.[26]

Many Senators were swayed by the thought of their old colleague who was now in Moscow, but not enough of them to match on the floor the final burst of speed which had been shown in committee.

> Last week we were told that unless we passed this resolution as it came from the Foreign Relations Committee, without amendment, we would not implement Mr. Hull in Moscow. We were told that if we would pass this resolution promptly, without amendment, he would have an immense force at his control with which to wring concessions to bring about agreement among the representatives of the participating nations. However, it develops that the agreement is *fait accompli,* and that the Senate is still debating the resolution.[27]

What Hull and Connally had long feared was now happening— a prolonged Senate debate on international organization—but what was surprising was that the filibuster was coming from the *internationalists*—from a fourteen-member bloc, led by Senator Pepper and the B2H2 group, which was fighting to replace the Connally Resolution with a "Pepper Resolution," along the lines of the old B2H2 Resolution.

The Connally Resolution on which Foreign Relations had finally been able to agree was no stronger than the Fulbright Resolution. Indeed the inclusion of the word "sovereign" perhaps made it weaker.

26. Senator Ball, *Congressional Record,* October 25, 1943, p. 8678.

Only Senator LaFollette dissented from the Foreign Relations Committee's decision to report the Connally Resolution. He wired Vandenberg: "With all due respect to other members of the committee I think a great mistake is being made by the committee in its present efforts to commit the United States to a future course in world relationship when the committee and the people of the United States are still in the dark as to the peace-table demands and the post-war policies of the other United Nations." *Congressional Record,* October 25, 1943, p. 8666.

27. Senator Danaher, *Congressional Record,* November 1, 1943, p. 8924.

> Resolved, That the war against all our enemies be waged until complete victory is achieved.
>
> That the United States co-operate with its comrades-in-arms in securing a just and honorable peace.
>
> That the United States, acting through its constitutional processes, join with free and sovereign nations in establishment and maintenance of international authority with power to prevent aggression and to preserve the peace of the world.

The B2H2 group was seeking to substitute language from the Pepper Resolution, especially (1) the words "international organization," instead of "international authority" or (à la Fulbright) "appropriate international machinery"; and (2) "power, including military force, to suppress military aggression and preserve the peace of the world."

For two weeks the Senators wrangled over terminology, most of the time being consumed by advocates of the stronger language. It became clear that they were filibustering to force a compromise.[28] The break finally came after the Four-Nation Declaration was signed in Moscow on October 30. Since the introduction of the Connally Resolution had from the beginning been intended largely as an assist to Hull at the Kremlin, it seemed appropriate (now that it was too late for that) at least to endorse part of what he had already done there. And this would provide a way out of the Senate's impasse. Accordingly, all the major factions agreed to add to the original language of the Connally Resolution Paragraph 4 of the Moscow Declaration, noting "that the Senate recognizes the necessity of there being established at the earliest practicable date a general international organization, based on the principle of the sovereign equality of all peace-loving states, and open to membership by all such states, large and small, for the maintenance of international peace and security." Vandenberg could derive satisfaction from the inclusion of sovereignty; the B2H2's, from "a general international organization." But the latter group failed to secure explicit reference to military force, and the qualms of

28. See, for example, *Congressional Record*, November 2, 1943, pp. 9016–17.

Vandenberg's associates were still further soothed by senatorial addition of one final paragraph observing that "constitutional processes" meant nothing less than Senate ratification; even the Mackinac Declaration and the GOP Representatives' forced amendment of the Fulbright Resolution had been less specific than that.

With nearly all factions thus appeased the Senate beat down, 70-15, a crippling amendment by Senator Danaher requiring that much of the Atlantic Charter be included in any future peace treaty, and on November 5 approved the resolution, 85-5.[29]

The size of the vote for the revised Connally Resolution and, to some extent, for the earlier Fulbright Resolution represented a strong vote of confidence in Secretary Hull and his cautious advance toward an international organization. On his return to Washington from Moscow Hull had the approval of the four powers as well as the United States Congress for the principle of international organization. So the department's planning became detailed—on the basis of a *global* structure, without the *regional* emphasis which had been favored during the months when Sumner Welles was a guiding hand in the old Advisory Committee.

EARLY CONSULTATION WITH CONGRESS ON THE UN BLUEPRINTS

On December 9, 1943, the Informal Political Agenda Group with Leo Pasvolsky as unofficial chairman, which had begun early in the year to try to bring the work of various subcommittees of the Advisory Committee into focus for the Secretary of State, began explicitly to concentrate on international organization.[30]

By March 1944 Hull had decided that the drafting work of the Informal Political Agenda Group had reached a point where explicit congressional advice should be sought in advance of detailed international negotiations. Another consideration in Hull's mind

29. Dissenters were Reynolds and Wheeler, Democrats; Hiram Johnson, Langer, and Shipstead, Republicans.

30. The "public" members were Norman Davis, Myron Taylor, and Isaiah Bowman. Other members were Under Secretary Stettinius, Leo Pasvolsky, Benjamin Cohen, James Dunn, Green Hackworth, Stanley Hornbeck, and Joseph Green. Not until the spring of 1944 was there regular military participation.

was the desirability of holding concrete bipartisan consultations before the presidential campaign began with its disruptive potential.[31]

Hull discussed the subject with Roosevelt, who did not disapprove his scheme, and then on March 22 he went before the Foreign Relations Committee to invite the chairman to name two or three Senators from each party to come to the State Department to review with him a draft of the international organization plan.

The process of selecting Senators took several weeks on Foreign Relations. Finally on April 25, 1944, a draft dated April 24 was submitted in strict confidence to three elder statesmen and to the Senators. The elder statesmen (not identified to the Senators) were a former presidential candidate from each party, Charles Evans Hughes and John W. Davis, and a former Republican governor of New York, Nathan L. Miller. The Senators, from the Foreign Relations Committee, included four who had served earlier on the Hull Advisory Committee—Democrats Connally and George, and Republicans Austin and White—and four new men from the "Connally Resolution" subcommittee—Barkley and Gillette, Democrats; Vandenberg, Republican; and LaFollette, Progressive. Elbert Thomas, the other regular Senate member of Hull's old Advisory Committee, was not available in Washington that spring, but he joined in consultations later in the summer.

The April 25 meeting with the Senators was little more than a briefing, but they did receive the basic documents. Hull emphasized "that this was an entirely informal meeting, and each one present could feel entirely free and easy, and no one would be requested to express an opinion, much less assume obligations, unless he wished." [32] Three subsequent sessions were held, during which the danger of perpetuating a possibly bad peace emerged as the main objection to early establishment of an international organization. The Senators were not disposed to insist on any particular changes in the existing draft plan prior to the initiation

31. Hull, *op. cit.*, 2, 1666. For considerable detail on the spring consultations see Hull, *op. cit.*, 2, 1656–70; Notter, *op. cit.*, pp. 259–70; and Vandenberg, *The Private Papers of Senator Vandenberg*, pp. 93–107.

32. Hull, *op. cit.*, 2, 1658.

of international negotiations. They were satisfied by assurances that ratification in treaty form would come later. But no public statement could be worked out commending the State Department draft to the attention of the allied powers. Vandenberg and La-Follette balked.

> Hull said: "If we postpone planning our League until after we get a Peace, everything will blow up." I [Vandenberg] said "You totally misunderstand me, Mr. Secretary: *I want you to go ahead with your League conversations at once and see what you can do;* but, with great respect, I do not think you have any right to expect this Senate Committee either to endorse your plans in advance or to agree that your League shall bind us regardless of whether the Peace satisfies the American conscience or not." [33]

The Secretary of State thereupon issued his own statement that the first phase of Senate consultations was over and international conversations were about to begin.

Senator Connally's reaction was that the Republican "tail wags the dog." [34] And Hull himself was not entirely satisfied with what he had accomplished with the Senators. Particularly disturbing was the possibility that a reservation regarding satisfactory peace treaties would be attached to ratification of the international organization charter. But at least the department's plan had received a very large measure of approval.

Consultation with members of the House of Representatives was delayed until the Senators had had their say. There was only one session before the Representatives departed for the national party conventions. It came on June 2 and apparently amounted only to a briefing session. Hull puts it very neatly: "With the Representatives the discussion did not become as involved as with the Senators." [35] Present from both parties were the Speaker, floor leaders, chief whips, and ranking members of the Foreign Affairs Commit-

---

33. Vandenberg, *op. cit.,* p. 105. The italics are Vandenberg's. The Senator was also unwilling to appear to commit his *party* in advance of the presidential campaign.

34. *Ibid.,* p. 106.

35. Hull, *op cit.,* 2, 1670.

tee. Each received a copy of the latest draft plan for the organization. Later that month, on June 22, Senators Ball, Burton, Hatch, and Hill received an interview they had requested with Hull and a briefing on the main points of the Foreign Relations Committee consultations, but again he was careful to protect the prerogatives of the Senate Committee by declining to give them copies of the draft plan, despite all they had done to promote the idea with the public.

On the night of June 13, with the national party conventions at last in the offing, Hull concluded that "the President, who had remained quiet on this subject for a long time, should himself say something, and say it emphatically." Accordingly State Department officials prepared a statement for Roosevelt to release explaining the current position of planning for a postwar international organization, emphasizing the nonpartisan character of the discussions which had been proceeding, and making it clear that "we are not thinking of a superstate with its own police forces and other paraphernalia of coercive power. We are seeking effective agreement and arrangements through which the nations would maintain, according to their capacities, adequate forces to meet the needs of preventing war and of making impossible deliberate preparation for war and to have such forces available for joint action when necessary." Roosevelt released the statement on June 15.[36] So there was available to the American people before the party conventions an authoritative though not a detailed outline of the project on which Secretary Hull and others had worked so long, so painstakingly, and so cautiously to unite the two parties.

PRESIDENTIAL NOMINATIONS AND PARTY PLATFORMS, 1944

The Republican Preconvention Campaign. During the winter and spring of 1944 the nomination of Thomas E. Dewey as Republican candidate for President had become assured. Skillful maneuvers based on his full control of the big New York delegation had established his predominant position in the party well in advance of the convention. In foreign policy he had set himself as slightly

36. *Ibid.*, 2, 1687-9.

more internationalist than the bulk of his party. He stood near the middle, between Bricker and Taft on the one hand and Willkie and Stassen on the other. By alternating a series of increasingly internationalist statements with long judicious silences he managed to avoid the total public commitment to one wing or the other which destroyed Willkie and gravely weakened Bricker.

Willkie, like Stassen, wanted nothing less than an international police force modeled on the wartime Combined Chiefs of Staff. And in seeking this far-reaching goal his tactics toward his fellow party leaders were those of an outside critic, scolding and threatening, not those of a sympathetic and cooperative associate, cajoling in private and praising in public.[37] He failed to seek support in grassroots Republican organizations; indeed he seemed to be deliberately bullying them. The payoff came in the Wisconsin presidential primary, April 4, 1944. Willkie rashly chose to make a personal campaign in that isolationist stronghold. He felt he had to show some strength in the Midwest. But it destroyed him. For thirteen days Willkie harangued the people of Wisconsin while Dewey sat silent in Albany, refusing to admit his candidacy and allowing Midwestern voters to forget the advanced proposal he had made six months before of an Anglo-American alliance. On primary day Dewey was the clear victor in a field of four which included Stassen and General MacArthur, with Willkie a miserable last.[38] He promptly bowed out of the race for the nomination.

Having thus won a vital primary as the leading "noninterventionist" candidate, Dewey broke a long silence on foreign policy by affirming his internationalism in a major address before the American Newspaper Publishers Association meeting in New York on April 27. He called upon the United States "to organize in cooperation with other nations a structure of peace backed by adequate force to prevent future wars."[39] This address turned away from his candidacy many Midwestern Republican leaders

37. Raymond Moley has given a discerning picture of Willkie's post-1940 position in the Republican party, in his 27 *Masters of Politics* (New York, Funk & Wagnalls, 1949), pp. 52–4.

38. For an inside account of the abortive MacArthur candidacy see Vandenberg, *op. cit.*, pp. 75–89.

39. *New York Times*, April 28, 1944.

who had backed him to stop Willkie. There was a last-minute attempt to build up Bricker.[40] (Taft had bowed out in favor of his fellow Ohioan for this round.) But the odds were all in favor of Dewey, since New York State appeared indispensable for Republican victory. At the convention Bricker was finally prevailed upon to accept second place on the ticket.

Foreign Policy in the GOP Platform. A bitter fight over the platform was successfully avoided at the convention, just as the party leaders had planned when they decided to gather at Mackinac nine months before. In the intervening months Assistant Secretary of State Breckinridge Long, Secretaries Stimson and Knox, Myron Taylor, Will Hays, and members of the Foreign Relations Committee with whom Hull had been conferring were among those who lent their influence to the drafting of planks in both party platforms which were satisfactory to the State Department.[41] The Roosevelt statement arranged by Hull on June 15 had been designed largely to prevent any misunderstanding from undoing their labors.

The Republican foreign policy plank was in fact based on the Mackinac Declaration and was presented to the Resolutions Committee of the National Convention in the name of the Mackinac subcommittee on foreign policy by Senator Vandenberg. He had consulted also with John Foster Dulles, representing Dewey, and with Senator Taft, representing Bricker.[42] The most important alteration made since Mackinac was explicit reference to the use of "peace forces," which Senator Austin, the other Mackinac leader, explained meant police forces in his part of the country. What they meant in Illinois was uncertain. At the convention, Austin was also named to head the Resolutions subcommittee on the foreign policy plank, and no important change was made from the language which he and Vandenberg had first submitted.[43] Opposition

40. *Ibid.,* June 18, 1944, sec. 4, p. 6.
41. Hull, *op. cit.,* 2, 1670.
42. Vandenberg, *op. cit.,* p. 87.

43. Wendell Willkie was not invited to address the convention, but he did submit a complete platform draft. On foreign policy its ringing tone was far different from the plank adopted, but actually, except for specificity about national quotas of armed forces for international use, it did not differ greatly in content. For the text see the *New York Times,* July 11, 1944.

which threatened to develop from Republican governors led by
Edge of New Jersey and Sewall of Maine was dissipated by the
assurance that the presidential candidate would be Dewey and
that he would make a satisfactorily internationalist interpretation
of the platform after his nomination.[44]

In the Democratic party the foreign policy plank for 1944 was
agreed upon by Hull and Connally. It was based on the Connally
Resolution of November 1943 and the Roosevelt statement of
June 15, 1944.

The Foreign Policy Planks. The major foreign policy planks of
both parties are here set side by side for convenient comparison.
The first sentence of the Democratic plank was from the Connally
Resolution; the second was from the June 15th statement. In the
Republican plank, the second and fourth sentences were from the
Mackinac Declaration; the others were added in the spring before
it was submitted to the Resolutions Committee. Brackets are used
to indicate major disputes in that committee over final terminology,
and any changes that were made: [45]

44. *New York Times,* June 28, 1944.
45. Other comparative planks are these:

Republicans	*Democrats*
"We shall develop Pan-American solidarity . . . through mutual agreement and without interference in the internal affairs of any nation . . . a genuine good neighbor policy commanding their respect and not one based on the reckless squandering of American funds by overlapping agencies."	"We shall uphold the Good Neighbor policy and extend the trade policies initiated by the present Administration."
"We shall seek, in our relations with other nations, conditions calculated to promote world-wide economic stability, not only for the sake of the world, but also to the end that our own people may enjoy a high level of employment in an increasingly prosperous world. [This was Dewey language from his April 27 speech.]	
"establish and maintain a fair protective tariff . . . primary obligation, which must be fulfilled, is to our own . . .	

Republicans	*Democrats*
We shall ["seek to" added] achieve such aims through organized international cooperation and not by joining a world state.	
We favor responsible participation by the United States in ["a" deleted] postwar cooperative organization among sovereign nations to prevent military aggression and to attain peace ["and" substituted for "with"] organized justice in a free world.	We pledge: To join with the other United Nations in the establishment of an international organization based on the principle of the sovereign equality of all peace-loving states, open to membership by all states, large and small, for the prevention of aggression and the maintenance of international peace and security.

"join with others in every cooperative effort to remove unnecessary and destructive barriers to international trade . . .
"tariffs . . . should be modified only by reciprocal bilateral trade agreements approved by Congress."

On Palestine:

"we call for the opening of Palestine to . . . unrestricted [Jewish] immigration and land ownership so that . . . Palestine may be constituted as a free and democratic commonwealth. We condemn the failure of the President to insist that the mandatory of Palestine carry out the provision of the Balfour Declaration and of the mandate while he pretends to support them."	"We favor the opening of Palestine to unrestricted Jewish immigration and colonization, and such a policy as to result in the establishment there of a free and democratic Jewish commonwealth."

The Republicans promised also to "keep the American people informed concerning all agreements with foreign nations" (a late change deleted Democrat Wilson's phrase about "open covenants openly arrived at"); "to sustain the Constitution of the United States in the attainment of our international aims" (this was essentially from the Mackinac Declaration, but, lest there be any doubt of its meaning, a late change added another sentence specifying Senate treaty ratification); and "we shall at all times protect the essential interests and resources of the nation."

Finally, there was advocacy of "the prompt extension of relief and emergency assistance to the peoples of liberated countries, . . . immediate feeding of the starving children of our Allies and friends in the Nazi-dominated countries, . . . [and] direct credits in reasonable amounts to liberated countries" to make essential purchases.

Republicans

Such organization should develop effective cooperative means to direct ["mobilize" rejected as "too military"; "recommend" rejected as "too weak"] peace forces ["adequate forces" rejected] to prevent or repel military aggression. Pending this we pledge continuing collaboration with the United Nations to assure these ultimate objectives.

Organized cooperation of the nations should concern itself with basic causes of world disorder . . . promote a world opinion . . . develop international law and maintain an international tribunal to deal with justiciable disputes.

We believe, however, that peace and security do not depend upon the sanction of force alone but should prevail by virtue of reciprocal interests and spiritual values, recognized in these security agreements.

The treaties of peace ["should" substituted for "ought to"] be just . . . sovereignty and self-government (for) victims of aggression ["*Axis* aggression" deleted in a last-minute change thought to be directed at the Soviet Union].[46]

Democrats

To make all necessary and effective agreements and arrangements through which the nations would maintain adequate forces to meet the needs of preventing war and of making impossible the preparation for war and which would have such forces available for joint action when necessary.

Such organization must be empowered to employ armed forces when necessary to prevent aggression and preserve peace.

We favor the maintenance of an international court of justice of which the United States shall be a member and the employment of diplomacy, conciliation, arbitration and other like methods where appropriate 'in the settlement of international disputes.

We pledge our support to the Atlantic Charter and the Four Freedoms, and the application of the principles enunciated therein to the United Nations and other peace-loving nations large and small.

The similarity of these planks in the platforms of both parties and the character of the candidates who would be interpreting them gave good assurance that the State Department would be safe in proceeding, even in the midst of an election campaign, to negotiate with foreign powers regarding a formal international

46. *Ibid.*, June 28, 1944. For the other changes here indicated in the draft of the plank see the *Times* editions of June 23 and 24, 1944.

organization. A conference was set to begin on August 21 at the Dumbarton Oaks mansion in Washington.

THE UNITED NATIONS IN THE 1944 CAMPAIGN

On July 1, 1944, Hull invited the general counsel of the Republican National Committee to accept a position as Special Adviser to the Secretary of State and in that capacity to serve as a member of the American delegation in the negotiations scheduled at the Dumbarton Oaks mansion in Washington. This appointment of Henry P. Fletcher was announced to the press on August 1, 1944. Fletcher had been a diplomat of wide experience, reaching the rank of Under Secretary of State at the beginning of Harding's administration. Later he had served on the Tariff Commission and become Republican National chairman during Roosevelt's first term. Especially in the absence of Myron Taylor, who had returned to the Vatican, Fletcher was expected to serve as at least a symbolic link to the Republican party.

On August 15, 1944, Hull telephoned Connally and Vandenberg that conversations about to begin at Dumbarton Oaks would not be at a top political level and that the British had already accepted the general principles of the American draft on which the Senators had been consulted. Neither Connally nor Vandenberg ventured to intrude himself on the conference itself, but Hull promised that they would be kept abreast of developments day by day. Speaker Rayburn was asked to pass the same information along to the House leaders who had been briefed on June 2.[47]

The Hull-Dulles Conversations. But the Republican presidential candidate was not disposed to let the State Department off so easily. The very next day, August 16, a press release from the Dewey camp appeared which expressed concern lest the Dumbarton Oaks Conference result in the subjection of small powers to a long-term military alliance of the Big Three. The moral contribution of little nations deserved more respectful attention, Dewey argued. Hull was very much disturbed at this intrusion of politics into his negotiations. In the evening he met with some department officials

47. Hull, *op. cit.,* 2, 1676.

at his apartment and directed them to prepare a reply. The Secretary cleared it at once with Connally and had it released before his press conference the next morning. At the conference he welcomed a suggestion that he talk with Dewey on international organization. Dewey replied by telegram the next day, August 18, pledging cooperation and designating his foreign policy adviser, John Foster Dulles, to engage in consultations.[48] Dewey's wire reached Hull at a cabinet meeting at the White House. Roosevelt was not impressed. Hull quotes him to this effect: "You'll see. They won't keep the agreement. They'll make a campaign out of foreign affairs." [49] But the President did allow Hull to enter into conversations with Dulles.[50]

Preparations for the conference were very elaborate on both sides, indicating due awareness of the importance of the occasion. Dulles consulted Dewey at Albany and invited Willkie to his home for an afternoon in New York. (Willkie had not committed himself to support Dewey's candidacy.) Further preliminary discussions were held in Washington with Republican members of Foreign Relations, including Vandenberg and Austin. Hull, for his part, reports he "seldom worked harder on any project than on the preparation for and conduct of the conversations with John Foster Dulles." [51] Both Dulles and Hull were besieged by professional politicians advising that two-party agreement would be im-

48. Dulles was chairman of the Commission on a Just and Durable Peace, of the Federal Council of Churches. Both Hull and Dulles have written accounts of their conversations. Hull, op. cit., 2, 1686–95. John Foster Dulles, War or Peace (New York, Macmillan, 1950), pp. 123–6. See also Notter, op. cit., 287–90.

49. Hull, op. cit., 2, 1657.

50. There was partisan controversy during the presidential campaigns of 1944 and 1948 as to who deserved the most credit for initiating "bipartisanship." For example, in the 1948 campaign Hull issued a statement (later said to have been drafted by Acheson) rebuking Dewey for claiming prime credit and observing: "If these competitive claims continue they will inject partisanship into the conduct of our affairs quite as effectively as though the debate were directed toward the substance of our policies." New York Times, October 16, 1948. It is interesting that Dulles shares this fear and emphasizes that "there is enough credit for all." Dulles, op. cit., pp. 179, 125. But if judgment must be rendered, Hull would surely seem to have the rightful claim to priority, though without Dewey's broad cooperation much of the Secretary's prolonged preliminary activity might have been in vain.

51. Hull, op. cit., 2, 1693.

possible, or at least would not be kept, and that real political advantage lay for the Democrats in taking exclusive credit for internationalism, or for the Republicans in trying to repeat the electoral success of Wilson's repudiation. But neither Dewey nor Roosevelt was prepared to take that risk, and Dulles and Hull seemed positively anxious to cooperate.

Nevertheless, their first meeting, on August 23, degenerated into hours of haggling over whether the approach to international organization which they were trying to work out was "nonpartisan" or "bipartisan." There really was a fundamental issue involved, but it seemed a little early to begin debating it. Basically the question was how much credit the Republicans would be accorded for cooperating with the Democratic administration. That was a problem which has ever since plagued "bipartisanship," but before the terms of any working agreement had been devised, either procedural or substantive, an argument over descriptive labeling was surely premature. Still, the terms in which the disputants phrased their differences deserve quotation, especially as revealing Hull's attitude in the important months when he was laying the groundwork for two-party cooperation.

> Dulles argued warmly for "bipartisan." His thought apparently was that his party would thereby be recognized as being equally involved in the formulation of the United Nations agreement and could obtain some political advantage thereby.
>
> I maintained, however, that, under our constitutional structure, we could not have both parties sharing the responsibility. The party in power had the responsibility for the execution of foreign policy. This responsibility could not be delegated. The opposition party, in my opinion, had the moral responsibility not to base its opposition, if any, to our proposals for the United Nations organization on partisan grounds.[52]

Dulles has implied a belief that Hull was under pressure: "He feared, or at least Mr. Roosevelt's political advisers feared, that the word 'bipartisan' might concede the Republicans an equal

52. *Ibid.*, 2, 1690.

status in a project that was now presumed to be politically profit-able." [53] Dulles' suspicions might seem to be confirmed by the sophistry of Hull's other argument against the term "bipartisan"— that sometimes there were third parties in America to be in-cluded. But actually the Secretary seems to have been thoroughly sincere and accurate in describing his own postwar planning efforts as nonpartisan rather than using any term implying that the elec-toral advantage of either or both parties was an important con-sideration.[54]

Hull seemed very stubborn to Dulles. The Secretary wanted to remove *all postwar* foreign policy problems from the campaign arena—not all *current* problems, but such developing issues as the future of Poland, as well as the United Nations organization. Dewey and Dulles were unwilling to subscribe to any agreement so broad. The statement finally issued was very cautious. It spoke of "agreement of views on numerous aspects" of international organization; actually the only change made in the American draft plan during these conversations was the addition of a sentence assuring constitutional processes of ratification for the later agree-ments *also,* whereby each member nation would place specific forces at the disposal of the United Nations. The press statement anticipated further Hull-Dulles conferences; Dulles had in fact won a promise that he would be kept fully informed of develop-ments at Dumbarton Oaks and have account taken of Dewey's sug-gestions and his own. The release concluded:

> The Secretary maintained the position that the American people consider the subject of peace as a nonpartisan subject which must be kept entirely out of politics.
>
> Mr. Dulles, on behalf of Governor Dewey, stated that the Governor shared this view on the understanding, however, that it did not preclude full public non-partisan discussion of

53. Dulles, *op. cit.,* p. 124.

54. It was Hull's own view that he did not "make a serious political speech during my stay at the State Department, with the exception of two last minute addresses in 1940. I was therefore severely criticized during political campaigns by some of the Democratic leaders; but I held fast to this policy, which time and experience have demonstrated to be the only sound course in the conduct of foreign affairs." Hull, *op. cit., 1,* 174.

the means of attaining a lasting peace. [The word "full" was Dewey's personal telephoned contribution.]

The question of whether there will be complete agreement on these two respective views and their carrying out will depend on future developments.

This extreme reserve was considerably relaxed the next day by a letter from Dewey expressing deep gratification. But it was more than a week before Hull got Roosevelt's approval for an equally enthusiastic reply and a proposal that both letters be made public. Dewey promptly telephoned Hull directly to give his consent. Hull quotes him as adding the cryptic observation that "he hoped he and I could carry on as we had done, regardless of the result of the election." [55]

Dulles and Dewey maintained contact with Hull during the next few weeks largely through former Ambassador Hugh Wilson, a Republican who had served under Roosevelt as well as Hoover. He was resident in Washington. James Dunn frequently channeled communications to him from the State Department for Dulles and Dewey.[56] But Dulles was dissatisfied with this circuitous procedure for bringing Republican suggestions before the Dumbarton Oaks Conference. Hull's sincere cooperation was not questioned, but Dulles came to the conclusion that there was no substitute for on-the-spot participation in the international negotiations themselves. "This experience made it clear to me that any bipartisan effort ought to give the opposition party member an opportunity to share in the formulation and development of policy." [57]

Dulles reports that he did "from time to time" make "certain suggestions, some of which were adopted." The official State Department history specifies only three. They can hardly be regarded as crucial.[58]

55. *Ibid.*, 2, 1694.
56. Notter, *op. cit.*, p. 316.
57. Dulles, *op. cit.*, pp. 125–6.
58. One was that nonmember as well as member states have the right to bring disputes to the attention of the United Nations. Another was that even disputes which threatened nothing worse than international "friction" be subject to inclusion on a UN agenda. Both points were accepted without objection by the other three powers in the final joint proposals. The third Dewey suggestion was that treaties

An Issue Emerges. The main issue which arose in the course of the domestic political consultations attendant upon Dumbarton Oaks was concerned with the machinery required for using American armed forces on behalf of the proposed United Nations organization. This was a topic which had arisen in the spring consultations; it particularly bothered the congressmen when Hull resumed his conversations with them on August 25, the last day of his meetings with Dulles. The senatorial group was urged by Hull to wait and decide this question when a formal agreement on the application of force reached the Senate for approval by "constitutional processes," as was being stipulated at Dulles' behest. The issue "was really domestic." [59] Vandenberg would not be put down so easily. In a long letter to the Secretary on August 29, he indicated willingness to let the President use armed forces under United Nations auspices inside the Western Hemisphere, but if world war were again needed to put down aggression Congress would have to give consent. On September 12, another meeting with the Senate group found Hull pleading that this emphasis on congressional control over military force must not be allowed to disillusion Russia about America's willingness to act promptly to support the United Nations against any threat to peace. Otherwise Russia might not join. The day before he had told Hugh Wilson that the movement under way to require congressional approval for each separate use of armed forces "might endanger the whole peace program if it were not nipped in the bud, and that it was up to the Republican leaders to do something about it before it was too late." [60]

The issue was brought to a focus at the end of the month by an announcement from Republican Senator Ball in Minnesota that Dewey "has not yet convinced me that his own convictions are so

---

be specified as reviewable when they caused disputes. Clearly involved was the fear of unjust peace settlements which had been previously expressed, notably by Republican Senators in consultation with Hull. But American and British delegates declined to press Dewey's specific provision in this regard.

Finally, when an impasse was reached on the UN "veto question" at Dumbarton Oaks, Dulles secured Hull's promise that "any concessions that would have to be made" would be "cleared with him." But this topic was not pursued further until after the election. Notter, *op. cit.,* pp. 326–7.

59. Hull, *op. cit.,* 2, 1696.

60. *Ibid.,* 2, 1695.

strong that he would fight vigorously for a foreign policy which will offer real hope of preventing World War III, against the inevitable opposition to such a policy." [61] Ball proceeded to catechize the candidates, promising to support the one who took the most unequivocal position (1) that international organization be established at the "earliest possible" time, before the conclusion of peace settlements; (2) that he would oppose treaty reservations "which would weaken the power of the organization to act to maintain peace and stop aggression"; (3) that the American delegate on the Security Council should have power to "commit an agreed-upon quota of our military forces to action ordered by the council to maintain peace without requiring further congressional approval." [62] That same week Wendell Willkie died, without having committed himself to the support of either candidate. Ball's choice therefore became particularly important for independent internationalist voters.

Dewey, however, was not willing to give assurance on Ball's third point. The Governor later told Defense Secretary Forrestal that he thought "he had a clear agreement with FDR not to bring the question of the use of force by the United Nations, and the American participation in the use of such force, into that campaign." [63] The Republican candidate's major foreign policy address on October 18 had only this to say: "The world organization must be enabled, through the use of force, when necessary, to prevent or repel military aggression." [64] But whatever the previous understanding with Dewey may have been, Roosevelt picked up Ball's challenge with less reservation in the famous "town council" analogy:

> A policeman would not be a very effective policeman if, when he saw a felon break into a house, he had to go to the town hall and call a town meeting to issue a warrant before the felon

61. *New York Times,* September 30, 1944.

62. *Ibid.,* October 3, 1944.

63. Walter Millis, ed., *The Forrestal Diaries* (New York, Viking, 1951), p. 348. The quotation is from the diary of December 13, 1947, and does not purport to be an exact transcription of Dewey's words.

64. *New York Times,* October 19, 1944.

could be arrested. So to my simple mind it is clear that, if the world organization is to have any reality at all, our American representative must be endowed in advance by the people themselves, by constitutional means through their representatives in Congress, with authority to act.[65]

There was some equivocation in Roosevelt's use of the word "act." But the context evidently satisfied Senator Ball, who promptly announced his support for Roosevelt. Dewey was thereby forced to be more specific than before. The following evening his first sentence on the subject was not really more equivocal than Roosevelt's. He explained that "of course" the organization "must not be subject to a reservation that would require our representative to return to Congress for authority every time he had to make a decision." But even after Ball's endorsement of Roosevelt, Dewey felt obliged, presumably for the sake of party unity, to add:

> Obviously Congress, and only Congress, has the constitutional power to determine what quota of force it will make available and what discretion it will give our representative to use that force.

However, that need not cause any fear, at least under a Republican President:

> I have not the slightest doubt that a Congress which is working in partnership with the President will achieve the result we all consider essential and grant adequate power for swift action to the American representative.[66]

---

65. *Ibid.*, October 22, 1944. In the same speech Roosevelt condemned the prewar record of the Republican party and asked: "Can any one really suppose that these isolationists have changed their minds about world affairs? That's a real question. Politicians who embraced the policy of isolationism—and who never raised their voices against it in our days of peril—I don't think they're reliable custodians of the future of America."

Considerable detail about the background of this speech and on the liaison between Roosevelt's speech writers and Senator Ball may be found in Samuel I. Rosenman, *Working with Roosevelt* (New York, Harper, 1952), pp. 480–2.

66. This slam at Roosevelt followed: "But those who would attempt to ride roughshod over the Congress and to dictate the course it should follow before it has even been acquainted with the facts are trifling with the peace of the world. They are deliberately, in my judgment, seeking to precipitate a hardening of minds.

w in this "a very ugly implication" and declared on
it he did "not think that the American people will
this policy of 'vote my way or I won't play.'" He
harge again on November 2, calling it "a threat to
party spite-fence between us and the peace." By this
des seemed to have dropped the original issue of how
ority the American delegate to the Security Council
would ... .[67] Neither Roosevelt nor Dewey returned directly to
that question in any major campaign speech after their initial
skirmish of October 21 and 23.[68] Thus the presidential campaign
ended without embroiling the United Nations organization, except to a very limited degree and even then in an "I can do it
better" spirit.

The "Conversion" of Senator Vandenberg. Not long after the election came an event of immense importance in assuring a continuation of the measure of interparty harmony on foreign affairs
which had been achieved during the campaign. This was the speech
which symbolized Senator Vandenberg's conversion to an interventionist foreign policy. Of course the transformation was actually a
slow process, extending back for many months, and by no means
complete on January 10, 1945. But the change was signalized on
that date to a public whose enthusiastic response startled even
Vandenberg.

The Senator's son has been at considerable pains to emphasize
the *gradualness* of his father's "conversion." [69] "The whole world
changed—the factors of time and space changed—with World War

If this stubborn course is pursued, it can only result once again as in 1919, in a
disastrous conflict between President and Congress." *New York Times,* October 25,
1944.

67. But Dewey long remained "very cynical about entering into 'gentlemen's
agreements'" after Roosevelt, in his view, had violated this one in the 1944 campaign. Millis, *The Forrestal Diaries,* p. 348.

68. Dewey's windup speech had only this to say: "We shall take the lead in the
formation of a world organization to prevent future wars. And we know that effort
can never be the work of one man or one nation. It can never be the product of
secret agreements worked out in secret conferences between two or three rulers. For
the United States, this great effort must have the support and understanding of all
our people. And it must, under our Constitution, have the support and approval of
the people's representatives in Congress." *New York Times,* November 5, 1944.

69. Vandenberg, *op cit.,* pp. 34–74, 90–139, *passim.*

II, and I changed with them." Vandenberg Junior declines to emphasize any particular motivating factor or great turning point in the wartime development of his father's thought. But James Reston, who became very close to the Senator, contends that it was the German rocket attacks on Britain in the summer of 1944 which shattered the old "isolationist's" confidence that it was geographically possible for America to maintain a policy of nonentanglement outside the Western Hemisphere. As Reston saw it, Vandenberg's mind, thus opened, became more amenable to suggestion in his frequent conversations with Dulles and the occasional State Department consultations in the fall of 1944. But only a day or two before it was given, the famous speech of January 10 was still primarily a mere assault on Soviet policy in Eastern Europe, calculated to please the Senator's Polish constituents in Detroit. Then some friends whose advice Vandenberg sought suggested that what was needed was a positive move to eliminate Russian fears (or excuses) that the West could not be trusted to prevent a renewal of German aggression. A four-power treaty of alliance against Germany should constitute adequate assurance, and who would appear better fitted to make the offer than a leading American "isolationist" like Vandenberg? The Senator cautiously tested this suggestion on other associates and decided to use it in his speech: [70]

> It would be a direct epilogue to the present war. . . . I know of no reason why a hard and fast treaty between the major allies should not be signed today to achieve this dependable end. We need not await the determination of our other postwar relationships. . . . Regardless of what our later decision may be in respect to the power that shall be delegated to the President to join our military forces with others in a new peace league—no matter what limitations may commend themselves to our ultimate judgments in this regard —I am sure that there should be no limitations when it comes to keeping the Axis out of piracy for keeps. I respectfully urge that we meet this problem now . . . having done so,

70. James Reston, "Events Spotlight Vandenberg's Dual Role," *New York Times Magazine*, March 28, 1948, p. 49.

most of the reasons given for controversial and unilateral actions by our allies will have disappeared; and then we shall be able, at least, to judge accurately whether we have found and cured the real hazard to our relationships.

The Senator's last words seemed to extend a hand to the administration:

I realize in such momentous problems how much easier it is to be critical than to be correct. I do not wish to meddle. I want only to help. I want to do my duty.[71]

Vandenberg was reassured beyond all expectation by the sensational public response his declaration aroused, even in a large segment of the isolationist Midwest press. He received more letters from a wider segment of the population than had ever come to him in a long public career, and as a shrewd and successful politician he was impressed.[72] Moreover, the administration grasped the hand Vandenberg had extended. Three weeks later he, and not the old reliable Senator Austin, was invited to join the American delegation to San Francisco. (Austin went to Chapultepec for a Pan-American Conference.) Participation in the work of the delegation speeded the education of Arthur Vandenberg.

THE ESTABLISHMENT OF THE UN

To describe the San Francisco delegation Roosevelt used Dulles' term rather than Hull's. He called it "in every sense of the word— bipartisan." [73] In addition to Vandenberg the members were Connally, Bloom, and Eaton from the Congress; Stettinius and Hull (inactive) from the State Department; and, from the public, Harold Stassen and Virginia Gildersleeve of Barnard College. The key staff figure was Leo Pasvolsky, who had directed State Department UN planning for many months. John Foster Dulles was at first omitted by Roosevelt, who, he observes, "then held a certain

71. The text of the speech may be found in *International Conciliation*, March 1945, pp. 211–22.
72. Reston, *op. cit.*, p. 49. See also Vandenberg, *op. cit.*, pp. 139–45.
73. *New York Times*, March 2, 1945.

rancour against Republicans who had been actively identified with the Dewey Presidential campaign." But Vandenberg and Stettinius wanted Dulles; so Roosevelt agreed that he be appointed on April 2 as a "principal adviser" to the delegation.[74]

The delegation held a dozen meetings in March and April before departing for San Francisco. Of particular concern was the problem of trusteeships, which had not been on the agenda at Dumbarton Oaks. The crux of the matter was how to avoid tying American hands with respect to the Japanese mandated islands for which we were fighting in the Pacific. The House Committee on Naval Affairs had indignantly appointed a subcommittee of investigation on January 23, 1945. There was political dynamite here which might even upset the treaty ratification in the United States Senate. The policy on which the delegation early agreed was that provision be made for "strategic trusteeships" whose administering (great) powers could protect themselves through the veto in the Security Council. And even then "subsequent agreement" would be required as to which territories would become trusteeships. At San Francisco there was a daily ritual in delegation meetings by which Connally and Vandenberg would demand reaffirmation of the "subsequent agreement" provision from Harold Stassen, who was responsible for these negotiations.[75]

Another issue on which politicians in the American delegation took a particularly strong position was the right of free debate in the General Assembly and the Security Council. For the General Assembly, it proved necessary to submit a virtual ultimatum to the Soviets, at the risk of breaking up the conference.[76] On the Security Council, agreement required special intervention by Harry Hopkins on a mission to Moscow, but he carried a firm message from Secretary Stettinius whose back was stiffened by his fellow delegates at San Francisco. At one point the Republicans had agreed privately "that we could no longer go along if there is any surrender to the Russians on this score." But later Stassen

74. Dulles, *op. cit.*, p. 126. The four ranking members of both parties on the House and Senate Appropriations subcommittees for the State Department were also invited to San Francisco, and some other Senators went on their own. Notter, *op. cit.*, p. 418.

75. Dulles, *op. cit.*, pp. 77–80.

76. *Ibid.*, pp. 37–8.

and others seemed about to "crack" just before Moscow fortunately accepted the American position. The Security Council veto would not apply to *discussion* of disputes, but it would apply to all forms of action including (and here is where Vandenberg remained dissatisfied) measures for *peaceful* settlement of disputes.[77]

The other question which most concerned the American political leaders at San Francisco was the preservation of regional associations, specifically the Pan-American system. Vandenberg was deeply involved as the American member of the conference subcommittee in this area. "I served notice on the [United States] Delegation, as a matter of good faith, that if this question is not specifically cleared up in the Charter, I shall expect to see a Reservation on the subject in the Senate and that I shall support it." In general Vandenberg found agreement on the part of Dulles, Congressmen Bloom and Eaton, and Nelson Rockefeller of the State Department.[78] He was opposed by Stassen and, vehemently, by Leo Pasvolsky who saw the risk that the projected international organization would return to "regionalism," away from the "universalism" toward which he had tried to steer it ever since Sumner Welles's departure from the State Department in 1943. Ultimately the defenders of Pan-Americanism won the substance of their battle in the form of the famous Article 51 on "collective self-defense," although the Western Hemisphere arrangements were not specifically authorized.

Vandenberg also succeeded in inserting in the charter various references to international "justice" about which he felt strongly.[79] But Dulles and he did not press to the end a demand for a specific *withdrawal* clause, which the former at least for a time regarded as a "must." On this point they settled for a formal conference declaration-of-interpretation, noting that it was "obvious" that

77. Vandenberg, *op. cit.*, pp. 195–6, 211, 203–4, 206–9. Vandenberg personally wanted the veto on *enforcement* action.

78. *Ibid.*, pp. 187–9.

79. *Ibid.*, pp. 173, 184. Connally was very skeptical about Vandenberg's "conversion," and very satirical about his insistence on "justice." "Actually, I [Connally] didn't meet anyone at the conference who objected to the inclusion of this word . . . [but Vandenberg] beamed like a knight who has just shattered the stout lance of a fierce opponent." Connally, *op. cit.*, p. 280.

"withdrawals or other forms of dissolution . . . would become inevitable if . . . the Organization was revealed to be unable to maintain peace or to do so only at the expense of law and justice." [80]

In general the American delegates were not pessimistic as they completed their work. And at long last the years of devoted effort by members of both parties were about to be rewarded in the Senate by virtually unanimous ratification of the Charter of the United Nations. In the United States Senate the week of debate at the end of July was a love feast which actually disturbed William Fulbright, recently elected to the upper chamber, because of its lack of realistic controversy.[81] There was still some uncertainty over what "constitutional processes" would be required to approve the prospective UN agreements regarding use of armed force. Connally declared his preference for the *treaty* method.[82] So did Vandenberg and, in the hearings, Dulles—both of whom asserted that the American delegation at San Francisco had assumed another treaty would be required. But none of them stood adamant against later approval by a simple congressional resolution.[83] And from Potsdam the day before charter ratification came a Truman letter clearly implying that that was what he intended to recommend. Only Senator Donnell objected at the time; [84] four months later he led a vain fight on behalf of treaty procedure when the Foreign Relations Committee by a large majority decided "to determine this question once and for all" by going out of its way in the United Nations Participation Act to authorize specifically the joint resolution method for approval of military agreements with the UN.[85]

80. Vandenberg, *op. cit.*, pp. 193–5.

81. *Congressional Record*, July 23, 1945, p. 7962.

82. *Ibid.*, July 24, 1945, pp. 7987 and 7990.

83. *Ibid.*, pp. 7990–91, July 25, 1945, pp. 8027–8. *Hearings* on the Charter of the United Nations before the Senate Foreign Relations Committee, July 1945, pp. 645–53, *passim*.

84. *Congressional Record*, July 28, 1945, pp. 8185–7.

85. Senate Report 717 (Foreign Relations Committee), November 8, 1945, p. 8. Ultimately, of course, the failure ever to conclude a military agreement rendered null the long months of dispute over this issue and enabled Truman to take matters into his own hands at the outbreak of hostilities in Korea.

On July 28, 1945, only the two Republican liberal isolationists Langer and Shipstead ventured to vote against the charter, while almost from his grave Hiram Johnson raised a lone voice in *absent* opposition. All the other "irreconcilables" had deserted them in the United States Senate. At the end of the year there was a little more active opposition to the United Nations Participation Act, but no important amendment was adopted on the floor of either chamber. All that were offered were decisively beaten. Only seven Senators were recorded against passage, of whom Taft and Wherry were the significant figures. In the House the bill was disposed of in one day, with only 14 Republicans and not a single Democrat voting in opposition.

Thus was successfully completed the full two-party collaboration which brought the United Nations organization into being during the war. It was a full bipartisan effort in the key respects that consultation was decidedly prior to decision and that the administration did not merely pick and choose amenable members of the opposition party but actually undertook on the whole to work with the recognized party leadership. To be sure, Hiram Johnson and Arthur Capper outranked Vandenberg on Foreign Relations. But their physical infirmities furnished a decent excuse for bypassing them; and who could have called Vandenberg a friend of the State Department when he was first appointed to the Foreign Relations Committee delegation with which Hull began his regular consultations in the spring of 1943? Thereafter, decent appreciation was shown for the services of the "Young Turks," Ball, Burton, Hatch, and Hill, but never at the expense of the prerogatives of the regular standing committee. And in the House the official leaders of both parties as well as the ranking members of Foreign Affairs were jointly consulted. Finally, the Dulles-Dewey relationship with the State Department during and after the 1944 campaign was explicitly bipartisan cooperation, between formally constituted party leaders, for which both sides sought electoral credit, whatever may have been Hull's initial intention.

The product was successful avoidance of the mistakes of 1919–20. But while public men in both parties outside the inner circle of the executive were devoting their attention to these laudable efforts, the basic decisions on America's political and military strategy—so far as they were known—were, on the whole, accepted uncritically, although many of the most important were being made without much participation by men from either party who had earned a status of political leadership in their own right rather than as mere protégés of the President.

CHAPTER 9

Getting Along with Russia

No ATTEMPT will be made in this study to trace the story of America's wartime diplomacy. What is important here is to observe the extent to which the policy domination exercised by the White House and the Joint Chiefs of Staff was *passively* accepted by the leaders of both political parties until the end of the war, when the resulting policy of conciliating our Russian allies was climaxed by a program of rapid demobilization for which politicians in both parties were *actively* responsible.

POLITICAL PASSIVITY TOWARD WARTIME STRATEGIC DIPLOMACY

One way to approach this subject is to take note of the personnel besides the President who held the topmost positions in the executive branch involved with foreign relations during the war. This would appear to be a minimum list: in the White House, Hopkins and Byrnes; in the Armed Services, the Joint Chiefs, Stimson, and Knox; in the State Department, Hull, Welles, and ultimately Stettinius; in the Treasury, Morgenthau and Harry White; and Vice-President Wallace. A recheck of these fourteen persons shows that only five of them were political leaders in their own right: Byrnes, Stimson, Knox, Hull, and Wallace. Of these five Byrnes was unquestionably a major figure in party politics and also a powerful man in the wartime administration, but his major concern was with the problems of the home front; Stimson and Knox had held positions of political leadership in the Republican party, but not actively for a number of years, and in the administration they were often by-passed by the Joint Chiefs' direct access to the President; Hull's position was politically so strong that Roosevelt could not let him go, but personally so weak that he was systematically ignored (ironically, Hull in the end used much of his political strength to destroy the only man in his department to whom the President did look regularly for over-all advice—Sumner Welles); Henry Wallace, finally, made himself the hero of the American left wing and for a time as head of the Board of Economic Warfare was in a position to influence foreign policy directly, but his public quarrel with Jesse Jones in June 1943 cost him that job and the following year he lost his vice-presidency, although he was retained in the administration as a symbol of liberalism.

Thus, even those top members of the wartime administration for foreign affairs who had achieved success on their own in politics were for various reasons less influential in foreign policy than their backgrounds might have led one to expect. A crude test of the actual situation may be found in reviewing the attendance record at the dozen major wartime international conferences. Outside the country, Stimson, Knox, and Wallace were never present, while Hull attended only the first Quebec Conference in August 1943 and the Moscow Conference in October of that year; Byrnes left the country only to go to Yalta. At the conferences in the United States the major available memoirs do not indicate that either Byrnes or Wallace was active, but Stimson and Knox often were, and Hull was sometimes included, though he was always kept carefully segregated (except of course at Dumbarton Oaks).[1]

1. "Prior to Pearl Harbor I had been a member of the War Council, composed of the President, the Secretaries of State, War, and the Navy, the [Army] Chief of Staff, and the Chief of Naval Operations, and I took part in its meetings. After Pearl Harbor I did not sit in on meetings concerned with military matters. This was because the President did not invite me to such meetings. I raised the question with him several times. . . . The President did not take me with him to the Casablanca, Cairo, or Tehran conferences . . . nor did I take part in his military discussions with Prime Minister Churchill in Washington, some of which had widespread diplomatic repercussions. I said to him: 'I'm not looking for increased responsibilities, but I do believe the Secretary of State should attend these meetings.' I referred

Who then did attend the conferences? The Joint Chiefs of Staff were at all the important ones, at home and abroad, except for the Hull mission to Moscow and those entirely on United Nations planning; and Harry Hopkins missed only these and the second Quebec Conference in September 1944. They were the key figures. (Other men of responsibility, not heretofore discussed, who received invitations more than once were Harriman and Welles; Morgenthau was active at the second Quebec Conference and at Bretton Woods; and Stettinius was present at Dumbarton Oaks, Yalta, and San Francisco.) [2] But it seems clear that the only Americans who were practically always, throughout the war, in a position to exercise determinant influence over the basic decisions in world strategy were the President, his personal confidant Harry Hopkins, and the Joint Chiefs of Staff. So strong was Roosevelt's public position and so great the people's respect for their military leaders that the President was thus able relatively to diminish the influence of other political leaders in foreign affairs without jeopardizing public support for his policies.

Not only the politicians but the civilian careerists in the State Department who had devoted years to the study of particular regions found that their influence was limited. Sumner Welles, for example, deplores Roosevelt's "deep-rooted prejudice against the members of the American Foreign Service and against the permanent officials of the Department of State. . . . It was very rare indeed that President Roosevelt could be persuaded to bring into White House conferences on foreign policy any of those State Department specialists." [3] State's authority in foreign affairs was further weakened by the proliferation of American war agencies operating overseas. The department's efforts to overrule conflicting foreign policies were often unsuccessful. It is true that despite these

---

to the British practice whereunder Foreign Secretary Anthony Eden participated in all war councils. The President's reply was that we had a different system here." Hull, *Memoirs of Cordell Hull*, 2, pp. 1109–10. Roosevelt's solution at Casablanca was to insist that Eden be excluded also. Sherwood, *Roosevelt and Hopkins*, pp. 661–2.

2. Potsdam, after Roosevelt's death, exhibited a markedly different line-up. Truman, of course, attended, with Admiral Leahy but minus the other Chiefs; and the new Secretary of State, James Byrnes, came strongly staffed from his department.

3. Welles, *Seven Decisions That Shaped History*, p. 216.

limitations the control of United States foreign relations during the war remained very largely careerist, while it ceased almost entirely to be partisan, bipartisan, or extrapartisan through the absence of decisive participation by politicians outside the White House. But fundamentally the policies which would determine the strategic settlement for the postwar world were not established through the channels of the civilian career service either. They were *executive* policies set by a Commander in Chief who gave great weight to the recommendations of his Chiefs of Staff and who had the skill to maintain general public support for the most far-reaching personal decisions.

How little criticism there was for the basic policy of alliance with Russia and postponement of strategic settlements till the end of the war can be summarily illustrated from debates in Congress and in the presidential campaign of 1944.

Lend-Lease Debates. Take, for example, the debates on successive renewals of the lend-lease program, where Congress could have directly influenced foreign policy by attaching conditions to grants of aid. When the program was first enacted, Russia was still allied with Germany, but the prospect that that would not long continue caused enemies of the bill in the Senate to propose an amendment to bar future use of the act to assist Communist Russia. Partly in view of the hypothetical nature of the question at the time, that amendment was defeated by about the same margin as all others, on March 7, 1941. During the summer, however, came the German invasion of Russia, and when the Congress next had a chance to pass on a related question, on October 7, 1941, the House with almost no discussion divided 69–25 against an amendment to an RFC bill designed to prohibit the use of any of its funds for loans to the Soviet Union. Lend-lease continued with no important foreign policy strings attached, and then the bill came up for its first renewal in the winter of 1943. After four weeks of study the House Foreign Affairs Committee reported it unanimously, and in the entire House debate only two speeches came to grips with the problems posed by the Soviet Union. Interestingly, those speeches were delivered not by Republican isolationists but by administration Democrats; significantly both men were Polish-Americans,

Lesinski of Michigan and Monkiewicz of Connecticut.[4] 'Actually, the isolationist Representatives in this March 1943 debate made only the most perfunctory criticisms of our allies, and in the Senate the entire lend-lease debate was wholly perfunctory, lasting about an hour on March 11. Twelve months later the Lend-Lease Act was again extended after a debate in both House and Senate which was devoid of significant discussion of foreign affairs, although an amendment was added providing that the act was not to be construed to authorize the President to assume any postwar foreign policy obligations on behalf of the United States.

General Foreign Policy in the 1944 Campaign. Since this was the presidential campaign year, it was to be expected that the votes of Americans of east European descent would be vigorously solicited at the very least by some strong innuendo regarding dangerous Soviet ambitions. There was a good deal of such talk in the "back door" Republican campaign. But what was significant was that neither the National Convention nor the candidate wished (or dared) to raise this problem very vigorously, even though Dewey had tied his hands through Dulles only with respect to international *organization.*

It may be recalled that the only intimation in the Republican platform of suspicion of America's major allies was a provision that "the treaties of peace should be just" and a last-minute deletion of the specification "Axis" from the pledge of "sovereignty and self-government" for the "victims of Axis aggression." During the campaign Dewey did not hit a great deal harder than that. The foreign policy declarations in the major Dewey-Roosevelt speeches (except on international organization, for which see pp. 173–6) may be summarized thus:

Dewey	*Roosevelt*
October 18, 1944:	*October 21, 1944:*
criticized personal diplomacy;	*criticized* the Republican preparedness record;
American failure to secure Soviet recognition of the London Polish regime;	*praised* his own record on preparedness;
the suffering of liberated Italy;	the Good Neighbor policy;

4. *Congressional Record,* March 8, 1943, pp. 1661–3.

Dewey	*Roosevelt*
the Morgenthau Plan at Quebec; Roosevelt's antipathy for DeGaulle.	Philippine independence; recognition of the USSR; *declared* "the great nations are committed to trust each other"; *promised* on Germany: no deal with Nazis; disarmament; stern punishment; no enslavement.
October 24, 1944: *criticized* Roosevelt's preparedness record; *included* a one sentence reminder about Poland, Italy, Scandinavia, "and the other small countries."	*October 27, 1944:* *praised* his own record on preparedness and especially as wartime commander in chief.

That was all Roosevelt had to say about the realities of foreign affairs during his campaign. On November 2 Dewey repeated his unspecified condemnation of secret diplomacy, and in his campaign windup on the 4th used strong language about the Morgenthau Plan.[5] But most interesting was Dewey's very cautious introduction of the Communist issue into the top-level campaign on November 1. He actually insisted on discussing it purely as a *domestic* question. This speech is really striking evidence of the unwillingness of responsible leaders of either party as late as November 1944 to face up to the real nature of the potential threat to America:

> In this campaign, the New Dealers attempt to smother discussion of their [domestic] Communist alliance. They smear any discussion of this major question of our day. They insinuate that Americans must love communism or offend our fighting ally, Russia. Not even the gullible believe that. . . . *No, the question of communism in our country has nothing whatsoever to do with our Allies* any more than it has to do with where a man was born. And I do not now propose to be silent when the New Deal through Mr. Roosevelt's political lieuten-

5. Dewey called it "as good as ten fresh German divisions . . . the blood of our fighting men is paying for this improvised meddling which is so much a part and parcel of the whole Roosevelt Administration . . . his own confused incompetence has thus prolonged the war." *New York Times,* November 5, 1944.

ant Hillman, strikes up a cynical alliance with Browder's Communists.[6]

But perish the thought that this "alliance" could have any *international* significance!

THE NOMINATION OF ROOSEVELT'S SUCCESSOR

Evidence of the operation of the alliance to which Dewey so cautiously referred was found by Republicans to reside in the Democratic National Convention of 1944. Certainly there, if anywhere, can be discerned a wartime domestic political struggle which was destined to have enormous effect on American foreign relations, whether or not Dewey chose to consider it in those terms. No study of the politics of American foreign relations in recent years would be complete without at least a brief reappraisal of the contest within the Democratic party for the succession to Franklin Delano Roosevelt in 1944—specifically for the vice-presidential nomination.

It would be easy in retrospect to overestimate the extent to which this was envisaged at the time as a foreign policy issue. Unquestionably Wallace's utterances during the early years of America's participation in the war had placed him in the forefront of those who increasingly idealized the *mariage de convenance* between the United States and the Soviet Union, and who pictured it as a true alliance of "peace-and-freedom-loving peoples." Wallace's classic utterance was the speech of May 8, 1942, which began, "This is a fight between a slave world and a free world," went on to talk of the "century of the common man," suggested that one object of the war was "to make sure that everybody in the world has the privilege of drinking a quart of milk a day," and proclaimed:

> The people, in their millennial and revolutionary march toward manifesting here on earth the dignity that is in every human soul, hold as their credo the Four Freedoms enunciated by President Roosevelt.

6. *Ibid.*, November 2, 1944. Italics added.

> These Four Freedoms are the very core of the revolution for
> which the United Nations have taken their stand. . . . The
> people's revolution is on the march, and the devil and all his
> angels cannot prevail against it. They cannot prevail for on
> the side of the people is the Lord.[7]

During the ensuing months the continuing radicalism of Wallace's
pronouncements was undoubtedly disturbing to important segments of conservative opinion with which the New Deal administration had perforce to work on close terms in wartime. In his
exceptional administrative position as head of the Board of Economic Warfare Wallace's speeches were bound to be examined
more seriously for their possible impact on policy than would most
vice-presidential utterances. In the spring of 1943 Roosevelt evidently decided that Wallace would be somewhat more useful as
a propagandist outside of Washington, and sent him on a good-will
tour of Latin America.[8] Upon his return to the capital Wallace
risked a direct appeal to public opinion to counteract the personal
weight which conservative Jesse Jones carried with key congressmen in the running fight between the BEW and RFC, over the
urgency and liberality of preclusive buying operations abroad to
keep products out of Axis hands. Roosevelt took advantage of the
opportunity to settle the dispute by the expedient (exceptional for
him) of firing both Wallace and Jones from their connection with
these operations, but he turned the job over to one who was regarded as a Jones man, Leo Crowley. Yet if all this signified any
rebuke to Wallace for his broad policy pronouncements or definite
evidence that Roosevelt would not support his renomination to the
vice-presidency, most of those who knew Roosevelt well remained
unconvinced.

Edwin Pauley (then treasurer of the Democratic National Committee) says he found only Edward J. Flynn, Charles Michelson,

---

7. Quoted in Dwight MacDonald, *Henry Wallace, the Man and the Myth* (New
York, Vanguard, 1948), pp. 65–9. At first only *PM* gave the speech full coverage, but
its build-up by liberals proceeded apace.

8. There seems to be no definite evidence that either this or the later "exile to
Siberia" immediately before the 1944 nominating conventions was against Wallace's
will.

George Allen (then secretary of the National Committee), and Pa
Watson prepared to work actively on the President to turn his
mind against Wallace.[9] Was it apprehension about Russia which
aroused them? Pauley's subsequent record on the Reparations
Commission (overburdening Germany and Japan) raises doubt
that farsightedness in *foreign* policy caused him to oppose Wallace's renomination. Flynn, for his part, has observed that Wallace
"seemed to have become the candidate of the radicals of the country," whose nomination would alienate "many conservatives who
were temporarily attracted to the President because of his foreign
policy," but he does not contend that fear of the Soviet Union
was a dominant consideration in their drawing a line between
Roosevelt and Wallace.[10] It seems rather to have been a more general revulsion against "radicalism," of the kind to which Dewey
later appealed while carefully avoiding attacks on our Russian ally.
And what still personally disturbed the party *professionals* was
Wallace's lack of *organization* experience. Despite all the incentive
to do so in retrospect, the men who have written of their participation in the choice of a successor to Henry Wallace as Vice-President
make little reference to *foreign* policy considerations as motivating
their actions.

But whatever their motives, they were certainly active. Pa Watson at the White House carefully steered potential convention
delegates to the President to describe how much of a drag Wallace
would be on the ticket, and Flynn conducted at Roosevelt's request a canvass which indicated that key industrial states would be
lost to the party if Wallace were the vice-presidential candidate,
despite the strength of the CIO in those areas and its voluble backing of Wallace.[11] In the spring of 1944 Roosevelt took a long vacation at Bernard Baruch's estate in South Carolina and sent Henry
Wallace on a mission to China and Soviet Asia timed to end just
before the Democratic National Convention in July. This mission
could be interpreted politically as propaganda of the deed, de-

9. Jonathan Daniels, *The Man of Independence* (New York and Philadelphia,
Lippincott, 1950), pp. 237–8.
10. Edward J. Flynn, *You're the Boss* (New York, Viking, 1947), p. 180.
11. *Ibid.*, p. 180.

signed to associate Wallace with world strategy preparatory to a
Roosevelt-Wallace wartime re-election campaign. Or it could have
been designed to get him out of the country while arrangements
were made to eliminate him. But most probably Roosevelt was
simply engaging in tired procrastination. Some time during this
period, however, if not before, the President was finally persuaded
that Wallace would be a net liability.

There is no definite indication in the participants' memoirs that
after Wallace himself had been ruled out, any consideration at all
was given to the foreign policies of alternate candidates. That is
hardly surprising in view of the fact that none of the men who
were most seriously considered was known to differ markedly with
the President's policy abroad. Flynn reports he went over a list of
alternate candidates with Roosevelt and concluded that Byrnes's
abandonment of the Catholic faith when he married would dis-
qualify him with a great many Catholic voters, and he would have
labor and Negro opposition; Rayburn's Southern background was
against him, and, worse yet, his Texas State delegation was split
and threatening to bolt from Roosevelt; other Senators were rejected; Truman "just dropped into the slot. It was agreed that Truman was the one who would hurt him least." Subsequently on
July 11, that decision appears to have been ratified, at least tentatively, at a White House dinner arranged by Flynn for high party
officials.[12]

Sidney Hillman and the CIO Political Action Committee may
be supposed to have been more concerned than the other Democratic political factions with the foreign policy of the vice-presidential candidate, in view of Hillman's definite commitment to accepting Communist support in the American Labor Party (after
Dubinsky quit on that issue late in 1943) and in the PAC. Perhaps
the Communists really took a strong hand in Hillman's decision
to accept Truman or Justice William O. Douglas and to reject
Byrnes, if it should be necessary to abandon Wallace. But Hillman's early death removed the best source of evidence on this.
And whatever the Communists' private expectations regarding

12. Flynn, *op. cit.*, pp. 180–1. Daniels, *op. cit.*, pp. 240–2. Rosenman, *Working with
Roosevelt*, pp. 444–5.

Russian-American relations under each of the candidates, they could hardly have found a public issue in foreign policy to dramatize between Truman, Douglas, and Byrnes in 1944. The backstage contest in the last few days before the nomination was therefore fought almost entirely on domestic grounds between backers of Truman and Byrnes, while out front Wallace's left-wing supporters made a colossal effort to stampede the delegates and were defeated by the firm hands of the city bosses.

Roosevelt himself, of course, had to make the final decision, either actively or by default. He delayed as long as possible and avoided unpleasantness by appearing to offer hope to all major contenders. Wallace received for his own use a Roosevelt letter announcing that "I personally would vote for [Wallace's] renomination if I were a delegate to the [National] Convention," but admonishing the convention to "give great consideration to the pros and cons of its choice." To National Chairman Hannegan went a Roosevelt note expressing satisfaction with "Truman or Douglas." [13] To Byrnes went such assurances that despite other contrary indications of the President's wishes he pressed his candidacy, and had actually secured the active personal support of Harry Truman. Truman says that Byrnes repeatedly told him that "Roosevelt would publicly say he was for [Byrnes] for Vice President." So Truman loyally cooperated.[14] But he could get nowhere with the labor leaders, especially Hillman. Roosevelt, traveling westward by train, occasionally phoned Chicago encouraging Democratic leaders to persuade Truman himself to run. But even a look at the Roosevelt-Hannegan note was not at first enough to induce Truman to become a candidate. Finally some of the big city bosses got the President himself on the phone from San Diego to tell Truman that the future of the Democratic party and the world depended upon his accepting the nomination.[15] The Senator yielded and went to break the news to Byrnes, who regarded it as

13. Rosenman, *op. cit.*, pp. 443, 449, 446–8. On the Hannegan letter cf. Daniels, *op. cit.*, pp. 249–50.

14. William Hillman, *Mr. President* (New York, Farrar, Straus & Young, 1952), p. 181.

15. Rosenman, *op. cit.*, pp. 447–51. Daniels, *op. cit.*, p. 245. Flynn, *op. cit.*, pp. 182–3. Hillman, *op. cit.*, pp. 181–2.

confirmed when he himself could not get the President to talk to him from California.[16] Byrnes then withdrew his candidacy "in deference to the wishes of the President."

On the following day the Wallace supporters had the run of the convention hall—to "give them their fling," said Mayor Kelly.[17] And the next day they were able to poll 429½ convention votes to Truman's 319½, with other votes scattered. But on the second ballot came the well-prepared wave of vote switches which clinched Truman's nomination.

All in all, in reappraisal ten years later, this political struggle which was so epic in its consequences seems strangely unreal. There can be little doubt that the decision to drop Wallace altered the course of history and shortened by years the period of postwar appeasement of the Soviet Union. And one may presume that the Communists in the PAC who fought so vigorously for Wallace's renomination did so with interests ulterior to those of the many liberals who stood with them—interests which must have centered on Soviet-American relations. Others who opposed Wallace were deeply disturbed by that very Communist support he was so clearly receiving. It was certainly one of the main reasons they did oppose him. But for them to proceed from that point to resist essential elements of Wallace's foreign policy for the reason that it was Communist supported—to press beyond the vague epithets of "mysticism," "radicalism," and "globaloney"—was very difficult because essentially his was also the administration's foreign policy and one which few politicians in either party were willing to oppose.

The situation, then, was for the most part one in which all that Wallace's supporters needed to say on foreign affairs was vehemently to affirm Roosevelt's policy; and Wallace's Democratic opponents were in no position to take issue with him directly on that score, even supposing they fully desired to do so, which seems most unlikely. They were therefore reduced to the epithets, to Wallace's controversial personality, and to some real issues in domestic politics which could be freely discussed. In this climate of opinion conservatives could beat Wallace with the "Communist" stick

16. Daniels, *op. cit.,* pp. 247-8.
17. *Ibid.,* pp. 251-2.

without much calling into question a pro-Russian foreign policy, in the same way that Dewey a few months later was able to make the same distinction (more explicitly) when attacking the whole Democratic party. The fact that the conservatives won, the fact that the struggle did have momentous foreign policy consequences, the fact that at least the Communists on one side in 1944 and some men on the other side anticipated some such consequences—none of these should be allowed to cloud recognition of the extent to which great issues in foreign policy were never defined in the process of removing Henry Wallace from succession to the presidency. And yet, until the coming of peace, this remained *the* domestic political controversy which actually had the most profound implications for the future of American foreign relations.

DEMOBILIZATION

Of course the basic decisions in America's wartime diplomacy were not *devoid* of public controversy; but it is not within the scope of this study to analyze the reception accorded various moves in Rooseveltian *Realpolitik*—so far as they were published—because they did not at the time become questions of *great* importance in domestic politics, as did international organization. Not until the last few months of the war was suspicion of the Soviet Union expressed openly by so many leading figures in public life that further concessions to the Russians threatened to become a major political issue. Even then there were developments to offset that tendency. The announcement of some of the Yalta agreements in February and March 1945 (especially the high-sounding Declaration on Liberated Europe), the decision of Marshal Tito to back down at Trieste in May and June, final agreement on the United Nations Charter and on a coalition government for Poland through Harry Hopkins' apparently successful mediation in Moscow during those months, the agreements at Potsdam and Russia's intervention on schedule (though unnecessarily) in the war with Japan—all these dampened the spreading fire of criticism of American policy toward the Soviets.

The Disintegration of Forces. During the summer and fall of 1945 suspicion of Soviet intentions was still not so widespread that political leaders of either party were willing to accept the onus of resisting rapid demobilization of American armed forces. In later years this came to be recognized as a momentous decision, ranking in its consequences with the wartime policies of conciliating Communist Russia and demanding unconditional surrender of the Axis. But where mere acquiescence had greeted much of the diplomacy of the "Grand Design," demobilization was promoted with positive enthusiasm in both parties, regardless of its effects on Soviet-American relations.

Plans for a gradual scaling down and redeployment of forces after the surrender of Germany were upset by the unexpectedly swift collapse of Japan. If Tokyo's surrender had been delayed, the supposed requirements of a continuing war in the Pacific would probably have furnished excuse and even justification for keeping forces in being which in fact might also have had some intimidating effect on the Soviet government. But with all the Axis now prostrate, it was necessary to be frank about needing large forces to overawe America's allies, and this the leaders of neither party were prepared to do against the public clamor to "bring the boys home." Quite the contrary. For at least two months after Japan's surrender those politicians who ventured to express themselves at all, practically without exception, sought to outbid one another with appeals for rapid demobilization.

To put this fateful development in fair perspective it should be observed that the mere existence of American forces would not have furnished any assurance that they would actually have been used in time to enforce a Western interpretation of such important wartime agreements as the Declaration on Liberated Europe or to exert pressure for further settlements favorable to the United States. The process of disillusionment in the American government was slow, and probably not until 1946 would even well-armed United States officials have cared to indulge in much show of force against the Soviets. But the psychological impact of non-Russian troops on the *scene* might have encouraged wavering

Europeans and delayed the most serious Soviet violations of war-time agreements until the time when growing realism permitted a more positive use of American strength.

For about a month after VJ day the administration managed to avoid authoritative announcements regarding the exact scope of the projected demobilization, while assuring the public that it would be swift. Until definite figures were cited, there was at least a possibility that the real troop requirements for "occupation duty" might be revised upward without implying a public challenge to the Soviet Union. This slim chance practically vanished on September 17 when General MacArthur proudly disclosed in Tokyo that within six months he would need only 200,000 troops, all volunteers. The War Department had indeed been planning on that basis but was embarrassed by the eager renewal of demobilization demands which this encouraging announcement produced. The Pentagon supported Under Secretary of State Acheson in a rebuke to MacArthur. But President Truman felt it was time for a basic policy statement:

> I think we should all be very clear about one thing. An impression has spread abroad that the speed of our demobilization is governed by our future needs for occupation and other forces. That is, of course, not true. . . . Carrying on our demobilization as rapidly as we can—which we are now doing —we shall not really face the problem of the size and make-up of the occupation forces until next spring. By that time we ought to know how many men we need for occupation and to what extent that need can be met through volunteers.[18]

Whatever logic this statement had was vitiated by the "point system" of demobilization. Developed in response to polled soldier opinion, then modified and speeded but not essentially changed by public and congressional criticism, this system focused attention on the hardship of the individual soldier rather than the efficiency of his unit. It hastened the return of the men who had served longest, had the largest families, etc., even though that meant stripping the military formations of key personnel. Even

18. *New York Times,* September 18, 19, and 20, 1945.

at the phenomenal demobilization rate of 1,000,000 men a month there were still millions of men in the armed forces for several months after the end of the war, but the system of discharge by points (usually without requiring replacements), rather than by units, produced helpless disorganization of the military machine. It remained adequate for police work but not for any stand against the Russians, as most Europeans could plainly see.

Not until mid-October 1945 did any prominent officeholder protest publicly against the demobilization program. Then Navy Secretary Forrestal spoke out, and at the end of the month General Marshall uttered very vigorous objections at a *Herald Tribune* forum.[19] Secretary of State Byrnes shared the concern which was felt by the heads of the armed services, but when Forrestal privately suggested that the President should undertake to resist the demand to bring the boys home by exposing Soviet-American differences, Byrnes demurred for fear of giving Russia grounds for claiming American provocation.[20] Unfortunately, it was probably true that by this time the momentum of demobilization was so great that it would have required a really dangerous crisis—real or manufactured—in Soviet-American relations to check the pace. In effect, the time was psychologically too late for half measures but too soon for harsh measures.

No Replacements. With the government decisively committed to the program of rapid demobilization, the problem of replacements threatened to become urgent. The army planners rested their hopes upon enactment of universal military training to provide reserves for swift mobilization to fill out a relatively small standing army. They envisaged cutbacks to about 500,000 men in the ground forces.[21] The air force would embrace 400,000. Navy planners wanted a half million men also, with an additional 100,000 for the Marine Corps.[22]

Selective service was still available to ensure that those levels

19. *Ibid.,* October 14 and 30, 1945.
20. Millis, *The Forrestal Diaries,* p. 102.
21. Secretary of War Patterson, *Hearings* on universal military training, before the House Military Affairs Committee, November 1945, *1,* 18.
22. Naval details were given in the *Annual Report of the Secretary of the Navy, Fiscal Year 1945,* 1946, pp. 1–14.

could be maintained, but it was scheduled to expire in May 1946. Renewal of a workable draft bill in that congressional election year proved to be very difficult. On two separate occasions during the complex legislative history of the draft renewal the House passed and sent to the Senate bills which would have deprived the army of the only substantial group of men who had not already been combed through by the wartime draft—the teen-agers. Ultimately the Conference Committee settled on 19 as the minimum age for inductions. But voting in the House had revealed grave Northern Democratic defections from the administration's program. Late in the summer, well in advance of the election, Truman halted all inductions, saying that voluntary recruiting was, for the time being, adequate.

In the process of securing this abortive renewal of the draft law, the administration abandoned any real drive for universal military training in 1946. Still another cornerstone of defense planning was not yet in place: the "unification" of the armed services. In this case the navy was responsible for blocking action for many months, during which integrated strategic planning, with coordinated assessment of military requirements and capabilities, was gravely impeded, whatever may be the long-run advantages of the loose "federal" defense structure for which the navy fought with general success.[23]

Atomic Stockpile. At least demobilization did not extend to atomic weapons. Here was a surviving remnant of American military power, but so terrible that it could not really be used as a threat in ordinary negotiations with the Russians. Only major Communist aggression could be deterred by the bomb. And even this American capability was jeopardized by the administration's plan for international atomic control divorced from restrictions on conventional armaments and military manpower. It may be fortunate that the Russians delayed accepting effective atomic control even at a time when the United States was not insisting that they dis-

23. Tracing the battle of unification through many pages of *The Forrestal Diaries,* Walter Millis actually asserts that "it is hardly too much to say that [it] delayed the nation for a year or two in grappling with the already dire state of world affairs" (p. 153). This seems extravagant, but the point deserves notice.

band their armies when she dismantled her bombs. Freedom to in-
spect the Soviet Union—a crack in the Iron Curtain—would have
been dubious compensation for performing the final act of unilateral American disarmament.

Congressmen were skeptical and refused to give the administration authority to implement an agreed international atomic
control plan without further legislative endorsements. Indeed,
when the Atomic Energy Act was before the House a bloc of Republicans and Southern Democrats strongly resisted any sharing of
atomic information abroad.[24] The administration took note of
these suspicions in the appointment of no less a public figure than
Bernard Baruch to handle atomic negotiations in the United Nations. No agreement was reached, and therefore the production of
atomic weapons could continue unchecked in the United States.

But among the major elements of military security at the end
of World War II, only atomic armaments can be said to have received special support from Republicans and conservative Democrats commensurate with their increasing criticism of the administration for "appeasing" the Soviet Union. On other national
defense issues—on demobilization, the draft, universal training,
speedy unification—the administration usually stood somewhat
ahead of Congress in security-mindedness. Upon Capitol Hill there
was little difference between the parties. The Republicans played
a valuable role in helping to impel a "get tough with Russia"
policy in 1945 and 1946, but in matters of national *defense* they
were generally not constructive on those occasions when they opposed administration proposals; their resistance served to impair
rather than to promote the strength which would be needed to get
really tough. Usually, however, no vigorous opposition was required. So widespread was the consensus in both parties regarding
the essential elements of demobilization policy that advocates of
cheap, voluntary forces rarely needed to fight hard for their objective.

24. *Congressional Record,* July 19, 1946, pp. 9471–9.
Vandenberg also was very active for several months in seeking to ensure security
of atomic information and some military participation in atomic development. Vandenberg, *The Private Papers of Senator Vandenberg,* pp. 227–30, 233–5, and ch. xiv,
passim.

Few politicians outside the heart of the White House and the Pentagon had borne much direct, active responsibility for the major decisions in American wartime diplomacy which determined the shape of the postwar strategic settlement. The party leaders stood accountable in that period only for failure to offer much resistance to policies with which they were not personally associated in the formative stages. But their active participation in hastening unilateral American demobilization at the end of hostilities deprived the leaders of both parties of a later opportunity to throw upon the late President Roosevelt all blame for facilitating Russian aggrandizement. The politicians' passive responsibility became an active responsibility, not to be forgotten in the rising din of demands for toughness toward the Soviets. Now to urge resistance while destroying weapons made little more sense than formerly to acquiesce in concessions while building armaments.

But at least the new attitudes showed a revived determination among party leaders to share in fundamental decisions of national security policy. It remained to be seen whether this would lead to a revival of prewar partisanship on basic foreign policy, perhaps destroying two-party harmony even in the specialized area of international organization. The end of hostilities brought an end to wartime adulation of a Commander in Chief and his Joint Chiefs of Staff, an end to idealization of allies, to much deceptive secrecy, to justifiable procrastination on controversial boundaries, and, apparently most important, an end to the clearly defined, formidable foreign enemy. What would remain to hold the parties together —beyond such "painless" notions as demobilization and international organization? The answer came in the gradual recognition of a new and terrible common enemy.

CHAPTER 10

Getting Tough with Russia

WITHIN a year and a half after the end of hostilities in World War II the American government, retaining the support of dominant segments of both political parties, was embarked on a costly policy of active resistance to the movements of her wartime ally, Soviet Russia. This represented a rapid about-face by the leaders of both parties, since neither group had offered much resistance to the optimistic executive policy of generous collaboration with Moscow during the war.

But for a number of reasons it was easier for Republicans to press for the change: the GOP had even less formal responsibility for the diplomacy of the Democratic administration than had Democratic politicians outside the White House circle; Republicans had done their "duty" by loyal support of the administration's all-out war effort, and now felt free to capitalize on the "failures" with which they had not been actively associated; moreover, resistance to Communist Russia had a special appeal for right-wing elements whose greatest strength was in the Republican party, and it might also win votes for the GOP among urban groups of Eastern European and Catholic background who would normally vote Democratic. Also, at first, when toughness with Russia merely meant halting aid to her and did not involve increasing aid to her potential enemies, it was easy for forces of economy-mindedness and "isolationism" to gird themselves in the shining armor of anticommunism; these forces were relatively strongest in the Republican party.

Most of the same forces, however, were present in the Southern right wing of the Democratic party, and similar pressures for a tough Russian policy came to bear upon the administration from that quarter. But they were counterbalanced by positively *pro-*Russian elements in the Democratic political alliance, which offered much more resistance than the "internationalists" in the GOP to a reversal of the trend of wartime diplomacy. In the end it proved impossible to develop a containment policy without causing the defection of this segment of Roosevelt's former coalition.

The emphasis in this chapter is on *domestic* political forces and their leaders, and how they expressed themselves and brought their weight to bear in a crucial period of transition. This was the context within which the diplomats manned the cables. Their professional efforts may be somewhat blurred by the political focus of this study; specific moves of the Russians may also be slighted; but it should be noted at the outset that there is no intention to minimize by this treatment the vital contribution which these other factors made to the development of American "patience with firmness" toward the Soviet Union.

REPUBLICANS PRESS FOR TOUGHNESS TOWARD RUSSIA

London and Moscow, 1945. At London in September 1945 American leaders for the first time allowed a high-level conference with the Russians to break down rather than make further concessions to the Russians. This was the initial meeting of the Council of Foreign Ministers to begin the drafting of peace treaties for Europe. Mindful of Wilson's experience with the Treaty of Versailles, Secretary of State Byrnes asked his former colleague Senator Vandenberg to suggest a Republican adviser to accompany him to the conference. (Byrnes did not then suppose that a Senator could himself be absent from Washington for months of treaty making.) Vandenberg nominated Dulles; Byrnes proffered the invitation; and Dulles accepted after further conferences with Vandenberg and Dewey.[1] Thus it happened that an outstanding Republican,

1. James F. Byrnes, *Speaking Frankly* (New York, Harper, 1947), p. 234. Dulles, *War or Peace,* p. 128.

who was closely associated with the titular head of his party and with the GOP leader of the Foreign Relations Committee, was on hand to share responsibility with the Democratic Secretary of State for a temporary collapse of negotiations with the Soviet Union.

Byrnes has taken full credit for the firmness which broke up the conference; in his book he does not even mention Dulles in this connection.[2] Dulles, for his part, concedes that the final decision was reached by Byrnes on his own, not as a part of joint conversations, but clearly implies that the Secretary's back was stiffened by the Republican's rejection of any compromise.

> Without my presence, Secretary Byrnes could not have known that he could come home with what, superficially, was a total failure without being subjected to criticism by the opposition. Because I was there, he knew that to make concessions would involve Republican attack, while not to make them would encourage Republican support. I made it clear that that was my own view, and that I believed it would also be the view of Dewey, Vandenberg, and other Republicans when I reported the circumstances to them.[3]

Dulles' interpretation of the London Conference is not incompatible with Byrnes's; they may be said to complement one another. But the events at Moscow three months later, where Byrnes went without Republican advice, lend some weight to Dulles' view of the importance of his own role at London. For at Moscow Byrnes threw away much of what he had fought for in London. The key London issues had been (1) whether the United States would recognize the governments of Romania and Bulgaria unless they were democratically broadened, and (2) whether the smaller powers, especially France and China, would have any effective voice in the drafting of peace treaties for the German satellites. Agreement was impossible. But then at Moscow, in a conference which Byrnes himself requested impulsively and without much preparation,[4] he accepted face-saving compromises on both points which

2. Byrnes, *op. cit.*, pp. 102–5.
3. Dulles, *op. cit.*, p. 127. There is an account of the conference on pp. 25–31.
4. Byrnes, *op. cit.*, p. 109.

preserved for the Russians the essentials of their position. (The details are not important here.) Probably Byrnes could have done nothing else if there was to be any early progress in drafting peace treaties. But this conciliation of the Soviets was undertaken by Byrnes and his diplomatic advisers entirely on his own responsibility as Secretary of State. It was not referred to President Truman (Byrnes blamed the State Department for this), and of course no Republican was in on the negotiations. Consequently Byrnes, on his return, was received very coldly at the White House and by GOP leaders.[5] He was widely accused of having "sold out" to the Russians.

Congressional Republicans in late '45. The Republicans in particular had publicly demonstrated on Capitol Hill a tougher attitude toward the Soviet Union during the fall of 1945. On his return from London Dulles had stirred GOP demands for more extensive consultation between the parties.[6] Then on November 1 all but two voting Republicans in the House supported a successful amendment to an UNRRA appropriations bill which would have barred the use of American funds in any country which impeded American newsmen reporting on UNRRA operations, i.e., any Russian satellite. The amendment was dropped by the Senate Appropriations Committee. But there was no mistaking the way in which widespread suspicion of Russia was multiplying the normal isolationist opposition to UNRRA;[7] nearly thirty Southern Democrats joined the House Republicans in this first clearly anti-Russian roll call at the Capitol.

5. In later years Truman was conveniently to date his break with Byrnes from the time of this December conference. "Byrnes lost his nerve at Moscow," quotes Jonathan Daniels in his semi-authorized biography of the President. And William Hillman in an authorized work presents a memo, dated January 5, 1946, which Truman says he read to Byrnes, complaining about not being kept informed and announcing "I'm tired babying the Soviets." The available evidence indicates that Admiral Leahy led the White House opposition to Byrnes's "appeasement" policy at Moscow. Leahy was personal Chief of Staff to the President, a daily military adviser, and an advocate of a tough line toward the Russians. Truman himself was especially offended by Byrnes's scheduling a radio report to the nation before making his report to the President. Daniels, *The Man of Independence,* pp. 309–11. Hillman, *Mr. President,* pp. 20–3. Byrnes, *op. cit.,* pp. 236–9.

6. *New York Times,* October 10, 1945.

7. *Congressional Record,* October 31 and November 1, 1945, pp. 10282–301, *passim.*

On December 5 a committee of Republican leaders of both houses reported a congressional party policy statement (looking toward the 1946 elections) which also included a rebuke—rather mild—for the administration's policy in Eastern Europe.

> We believe in fulfilling to the greatest possible degree our war pledges to small nations that they shall have the right to choose the form of government under which they will live and that sovereign rights and self-government shall be restored to those who have been forcibly deprived of them. We deplore any desertion of these principles.
>
> We will seek to find common policies with the other great powers. But we reject great power domination of the world and the thesis that world peace requires us to endorse alien doctrines or to abandon efforts to seek justice for the weaker peoples of the world.[8]

8. *New York Times*, December 6, 1945. The "Conference Committee" included Senators Taft, Vandenberg, and Millikin; and Representatives Martin, Halleck, Brown, and Wadsworth. The rest of the foreign policy text is:

"In foreign affairs we shall continue to strive to avoid partisanship. But we shall also seek to avoid secrecy, inefficiency, and drift.

"We support the United Nations organization for international peace. We look with particular hope to the General Assembly as the 'town meeting of the world' wherein the organized conscience of mankind shall find effective expression in behalf of peace with justice. We support the indispensable inter-American system as a regional part of the international organization.

"We will engage in essential international relief as a humanitarian obligation and to prevent chaos through misery. We demand sound management and protection against exploitation in this connection. We will assist other nations to rehabilitate themselves under arrangements consistent with intelligent American self-interest and overall limitations that shall not jeopardize our own economic recovery and stability.

"We advocate ultimate international agreements to stabilize military establishments. We demand open diplomacy, at home and abroad, and free communication throughout the world.

"We consider that the maintenance of a strong, solvent, free America is the basis of our greatest contribution to world order.

"We stand for a well trained and fully equipped Army, Navy, and Air Force adequate to meet any emergency under future conditions of warfare. It must be supported by the most modern scientific research, a strong industrial system, and adequate reserves of trained men with the best weapons and equipment."

[Revealing of intra-party conflict was the absence from the statement of any specific reference to universal military training or, even vaguely, to tariffs and reciprocal trade.]

But in general the Republican statement did not yet represent any serious break with the administration on foreign policy. (Indeed it was so moderate that the Republican National Committee endorsed it only after adding a stipulation that a noncongressional subcommittee be appointed to receive additional suggestions.) [9] The road was explicitly left open for further collaboration between the parties. But the going would be smooth only if the administration showed a firm hand at the wheel.

London, January 1946. That became doubly clear at the first meetings of the Security Council and General Assembly in London during January 1946. In keeping with the bipartisan precedent established in the creation of the United Nations organization, a distinguished delegation from both parties joined Byrnes as he rushed back to Europe after five days in Washington following the Moscow Conference. Present in London were Stettinius, Connally, Vandenberg, Mrs. Roosevelt, Dulles, Sol Bloom, Charles Eaton, Democratic politician Frank Walker, and Republican former Senator John Townsend. But there was friction in the delegation.

In the Security Council, where the major international issues arose, the American delegate was Stettinius, and the role of moderator which he played there was particularly dissatisfying to Republicans Vandenberg and Dulles. Stettinius did little more than to sit patiently by while Britain and Russia debated the presence of their respective forces in Iran, Greece, Indonesia, and the Levant, and then to offer an innocuous formula designed to remove each item from the agenda. Senator Vandenberg came back from London with a much more critical attitude toward the State Department than he had shown since 1944. He wanted greater boldness and more advance consultation in American foreign policy. The Republican leader felt Secretary Byrnes was "loitering around Munich." [10] In his report to the Senate he declared: "The situation calls for patience and good will; but not for vacillation. . . . There is a line beyond which compromise cannot go—even

9. *Ibid.,* December 9, 1945.

10. Personal letter to the editor of *Foreign Affairs,* April 2, 1946, quoted in part in Vandenberg, *The Private Papers of Senator Vandenberg,* p. 246.

if we once crossed that line under the pressures of the exigencies of war. But how can we expect our alien friends to know where that line is unless we re-establish the habit of saying only what we mean and meaning every word we say?" [11]

At a Cabinet luncheon at the end of January Secretary Byrnes chose to ascribe Vandenberg's critical attitude to a sense that his position was "unsatisfactory and [that he] was looking for a way out, mainly on the ground that he was being accused by his colleagues at home of having turned an appeaser . . . Vandenberg's —and for that matter Dulles'—activities from now on could be viewed as being conducted on a political and partisan basis." [12] Whatever measure of truth there may be in this accusation regarding Vandenberg could apply equally well to Byrnes himself, for now the Secretary of State was not to be outdone by the Senator in public demands for firmness toward the Soviet Union. He certainly took as hard a line as Vandenberg's in a radio report on February 28. Actually by that time there seems little reason to suspect that either of them was being driven by political expedience to espouse a policy much tougher than his personal convictions. Both men were moving with their times, not far ahead nor far behind. But Byrnes's comment about Vandenberg shows a recognition of the fact that in domestic politics it *was* the Republicans who were pressing most strongly for a hard line.

GOP Moves in Early '46. Their pressure took concrete voting form again on March 13, 1946, when the House rejected a GOP effort to cancel wartime lend-lease appropriations by an amount which would equal the value of goods still "in the pipeline" to Russia. This drive to halt the "windup" shipments to the Soviets was led by John Taber, John Vorys, Francis Case, Clare Hoffman, and Everett Dirksen. Every single voting Republican in the House supported them; like "UNRRA-free press" three months earlier, this was an issue on which economy-mindedness, isolationism, anti-communism, and diffidence before their fellow partisans on Appropriations all combined to reinforce GOP party loyalty. All but

11. *New York Times,* February 28, 1946.
12. Millis, *The Forrestal Diaries,* p. 132.

four Democrats finally rallied to resist what appeared to be mainly a Republican attempt to make political capital by a wholly unworkable gesture.

Then on April 1 a partisan GOP foreign policy plank emerged from the special subcommittee which the Republican National Committee had appointed in December to supplement the congressional GOP platform. The new statement condemned the "incoherence and inefficiency of administration handling of foreign affairs," and demanded:

> That the State Department be so reorganized that it may possess cohesion and unity of purpose; that only those persons who believe in the American way of life and are loyal to the American government shall be employed in the Department.
>
> That only Americans known for their devotion to our form of government be appointed to the various posts of representation in the UNO, and that they be given time and facility for study and the preparation of their positions. Let the United States act in the councils of the UNO in a manner commensurate with our world position and prestige, and give thereby direction, constructive purpose, and vitality to the UNO.
>
> That our administration leadership demonstrate through UNO in behalf of such nations as Poland the same zeal which is now so evident with respect to oil-rich Iran.
>
> That the President and the State Department demonstrate their trust in the UNO and in our own hemisphere organization, and consult with other states before acting in matters of interest to a number of states. [Latin-American sensibilities had been particularly offended.] [13]

The critical tone of this resolution was underscored by the fact that both leading candidates for the post of National chairman at this meeting of the Republican National Committee were conservative noninterventionists, Reece of Tennessee and Danaher of Connecticut. Their former isolationism was not held against them by the majority of the National Committee, but a progressive minority decided at the very last minute to demonstrate its strength

13. *New York Times,* April 2, 1946.

by giving support to John W. Hanes, a North Carolinian of prominent Democratic background who had served in Roosevelt's second
administration. Reece won the chairmanship, but notice had been
served on him of the suspicions of progressive and internationalist
elements in the party.[14] The strength of those elements still en-
sured that the tide of Republican criticism which had been rising
in foreign affairs during the winter of 1946, could yet be checked
by personal overtures from the administration and by a hardening
of its policy.

DEMOCRATS SPLIT OVER FIRMNESS
TOWARD RUSSIA

Both developments were already in process, and Republican
pressure deserves only part of the credit for the changes which took
place. Inside the administration itself there were major elements
working in the same anti-Soviet direction. Forrestal and Admiral
Leahy were particularly active, and from Moscow Ambassador
Harriman and his able adviser George Kennan were hammering
home to the State Department the importance of standing up to
the Russians.[15] The President himself had never been actively associated with the wartime foreign policy of his predecessor. Truman had no deep personal commitment to lead the country along
the lines of a "Grand Design," however great may have been his
sense of loyalty and humility on assuming the Roosevelt mantle.
He was open to new advice as the momentum of Roosevelt's ex-
periment waned at Potsdam and London. His Secretary of State
was a conservative Southerner and former Senator who could be
expected to respond more readily to criticism from the right than
from the left.[16]

Moreover, there was an immediate task in hand in Europe, the

14. Arthur Krock, *New York Times*, April 5, 1946.
15. For example, in February 1946 Forrestal entered in his diary an 8,000-word
cable from Kennan, requested by the State Department, in which he laid out the
essentials of the broad analysis which appeared in print the following year as Mr.
X's "Sources of Soviet Conduct." Millis, *The Forrestal Diaries*, pp. 135–40.
16. After all, Byrnes owed his presence in the State Department largely to his
prestige with conservative Senators, and his absence from the White House largely
to 1944 opposition from persons who later accused him of provoking the Russians.

drafting of peace treaties which would require Senate confirmation by a two-thirds majority. After the gratifying experience of the United Nations Charter, many State Department officials as well as their political superiors had learned the need for conciliating anti-administration Senators in both parties. And certainly, all politics aside, there was a growing intellectual conviction on the part of permanent officers of the department that Russia was dangerous and must be checked. (An illustration of this was the recall of George Kennan from Moscow in May 1946 to advise directly on Russian policy.) Thus the political pressures to "get tough" did not run counter to the trend of opinion in the State Department.

Leftist Counterattacks. Nevertheless, these pressures did run counter to rising protests from the left wing of the Democratic administration and its political allies, groups spearheaded by the CIO Political Action Committee which had won credit from practical politicians for a major contribution to Roosevelt's electoral victory in 1944. In the Cabinet Henry Wallace became the symbol of their views. They were heavily influenced by Communist infiltration, as was acknowledged later in the CIO's drive to purge itself.

Byrnes's concessions at Moscow and Stettinius' indecisiveness in the UN at London delayed any very vociferous cries of alarm from these groups until President Truman appeared to endorse a tougher policy by accompanying Churchill to Fulton, Mo., on March 5, 1946. Truman denied that he had seen the text of Churchill's appeal for Anglo-American partnership against Russia, but he has since verified the common assumption that Churchill had told him what he planned to say.[17] Truman's disclaimer of responsibility for Churchill sounded even less reassuring to leftist critics at the end of the month, when Byrnes in the UN pressed Russia to withdraw her troops from Iran, while putting no comparable pressure on Britain to get out of Greece.[18] Of course the

17. Truman insists, plausibly, that the Fulton engagement was arranged as a build-up for Westminster, the alma mater of his aide Harry Vaughn. Daniels, *op. cit.,* p. 312.

18. This was a famously successful stand against Russia, the first of its kind. But in retrospect it is worth noting that America and the UN did not at the time go so far as to protect Iran from the related Soviet demands to exploit its northern oil

cases were different. Russia's presence was unwelcome to the local government, and she had promised to leave; neither objection applied to Britain. But on April 4 Senator Claude Pepper keynoted a vehement left-wing assault on this policy of "ganging up on Russia," while letting other powers go scot free; the Communist-controlled executive board of the United Electrical Workers pulled out all the stops in denouncing "American imperialism" and "monopolists" dragging the country "on the road to war"; and on May 16 a giant Madison Square Garden rally heard Pepper exonerate Russia and blame Britain and America for delaying the peace treaties.[19]

More ominous yet was the announcement on May 11 of a campaign alliance between the CIO-PAC, the National Citizens PAC, and the Independent Citizens Committee of the Arts, Sciences, and Professions. The platform adopted by the new coordinating committee was very general, but the move signalized a consolidation of prominent liberal movements against the trend of American foreign policy, and promised to facilitate their domination by fellow travelers.[20]

Rapprochement with Vandenberg. Nevertheless, the administration moved ahead on the firmer line of policy it had demonstrated in the Iranian affair, and it actively sought to associate Arthur Vandenberg with its future policy. He and Connally were invited to accompany Byrnes to the next treaty-drafting meeting of the Foreign Ministers in Paris at the end of April. This was a step beyond two-party collaboration for the UN, though it was still related to the Senate's treaty prerogatives. Moreover, there were strong indications that no very vigorous Democratic campaign would be waged for Vandenberg's Senate seat in Michigan that November. His foremost potential opponent, former Governor Murray Van Wagoner, chose to seek gubernatorial office again,

---

through a "joint" company. That agreement fell through because many months later the Majlis dared to refuse to ratify it.

19. *New York Times,* April 5 and 8 and May 17, 1946.

20. Committee members from the CIO-PAC were Philip Murray, James Carey, and Sidney Hillman; from the NC-PAC, Elmer Benson, C. B. Baldwin, and Frank Kingdon; from ICCASP Jo Davidson, Harold Ickes, and its executive secretary, Hannah Dorner. *Ibid.,* May 12, 1946.

and only one Democrat ran for Senator in the April primary. He was James Lee, assistant corporation counsel of Detroit. Lee made no campaign at all against Vandenberg, delivered no speeches, and reported neither receiving nor spending one cent on the election.[21] A Democrat's chances against Vandenberg in Michigan that year were so slim anyway that this Democratic gesture was no great sacrifice, but it was thoughtful, especially since Connally was not being distracted by any substantial opposition in his Texas primary the same year.[22] Vandenberg, for his part, announced his support of the British loan agreement before leaving for Paris, although he had played no role in shaping it.[23] Then at Paris the extrapartisan delegation held firm on the major points at issue (Italian colonies and reparations, Trieste, and international control of the Danube); the result was a deadlock. On his return Vandenberg told the Senate he was "happy to say that this American delegation was a constant unit in thought and action. It had no differences." To Vandenberg this was "more important news" than the failure of negotiations.

> . . . the Council was a complete success in developing, at last, and in disclosing a positive, constructive, peace-seeking bipartisan foreign policy for the United States. It is based, at last, upon the moralities of the Atlantic and San Francisco charters. Yet it is based equally upon the practical necessities for Europe's rehabilitation. . . . I will support that sort of foreign policy under any administration; and I hope that any administration, whatever its political complexion, will stick to that sort of a foreign policy for keeps.[24]

The gradual renewal of harmony between the parties, on the recognized basis of a tougher foreign policy, was quickly reflected in Congress. During the deadlock at Paris about half the Republi-

21. *Ibid.*, April 24 and November 3, 1946.

22. Connally won his Texas primary (equivalent to election) with three times as many votes as his four opponents combined. *Ibid.*, July 29, 1946.

23. *Congressional Record*, April 22, 1946, pp. 4079–82. Like the Bretton Woods agreements, the British loan had gone to the Banking and Currency committees in both houses.

24. *Ibid.*, May 21, 1946, p. 5325.

cans in the Senate had joined Democrats in beating down crippling amendments and passing the British loan agreement. This
transfer of $3.75 billion ($4.4 billion if the lend-lease "windup"
be included) had originally been presented by the administration
almost entirely as a nonpolitical, businesslike investment.[25] Most
of the early debate centered around considerations of international
trade and currency transactions. But Vandenberg's pre-Paris endorsement of the loan was on frankly anti-Russian grounds; and
both Senate Majority Leader Barkley and House Speaker Rayburn, in their final pleas before the voting, used that same argument about keeping Britain out of "arms into which we do not
want her to be folded." [26] In the Senate only one more Republican
was recorded against the bill than for it, but in the House the GOP
opposed it 2 to 1. It was significantly evident that where anticommunism stood athwart economy-mindedness and isolationism instead of together with them, as it had been on "UNRRA-free
press" and postwar lend-lease to Russia, the Republican party's
unity disappeared. But the supporters of the loan did include both
Minority Leader Martin and the ranking GOP member of the
committee which handled the bill, Jesse Wolcott. No attempt was
being made even in the House to draw a party line against this
principal legislative expression of administration foreign policy in
1946.

There was more evidence in June and July of members of both
parties drawing together in foreign affairs. The team of Byrnes,
Vandenberg, and Connally was at work again in Paris at another
meeting of the Council of Foreign Ministers. And this time their
policy was successful in winning substantial Soviet concessions on
the Italian treaty (a free city at Trieste, the colonies to remain in
British hands pending later agreement, and a slight moderation of
the impact of reparations). The way was cleared for calling a larger
consultative peace conference. Returning home for a few days, the
American trio exchanged generous compliments in the Senate and

25. For example, Under Secretary of State Dean Acheson's presentation in the
Department of State Bulletin, February 10, 1946, pp. 185–9. He emphasized that
the loan was "not a reward for an ally."

26. *Congressional Record,* April 22, 1946, p. 4080, May 8, 1946, p. 4600 and July
13, 1946, p. 8915.

on the radio.[27] Meanwhile, another cooperative Republican Senator, Warren Austin, was appointed head of the permanent American mission to the United Nations when Stettinius resigned that post on May 31.[28] And another vestige of more credulous days was wiped away when the administration yielded on the Dirksen "UNRRA-free press" amendment, after the proposal had won the votes of almost half the Democrats and all but one Republican in the House on June 28.[29]

Showdown with Wallace. Within the Democratic party coalition, however, internal tension was mounting side by side with international tension. Secretary of Commerce Henry Wallace sent a long private memorandum to the President on July 23, 1946, condemning American militarism and advocating an American reconstruction loan to Russia and "collaboration with Russia in the industrial and economic development of areas in which we have joint interests, such as the Middle East" and the Balkans. He warned:

> It is certainly desirable that, as far as possible, we achieve unity on the home front with respect to our international relations; but unity on the basis of building up conflict abroad would prove to be . . . disastrous. I think there is some reason to fear that in our earnest efforts to achieve bipartisan unity in this country we may have given way too much to isolationism masquerading as tough realism in international affairs.[30]

Then on September 12, 1946, Wallace himself caused a showdown by his famous Madison Square Garden address.

It is interesting in retrospect to note that this speech was not wholly one sided. White House Counsel Clark Clifford has ex-

27. *New York Times,* July 16, and 17, 1946.

28. *Ibid.,* June 6, 1946. Byrnes takes credit for suggesting the appointment to Truman, who was "delighted" with the idea. Byrnes, *op. cit.,* p. 235.

29. This was very nearly the same as the amendment which the Senate had thrown out in December, but now, on July 16, the upper chamber was willing to modify it only slightly at the State Department's request. *Congressional Record,* July 16, 1946, p. 9069.

30. Text (released September 17, 1946), *United States News,* September 27, 1946, pp. 71–5.

plained that Wallace originally summarized the speech to Truman as "a sort of tough line with the Soviets," and that that is why Truman only thumbed it through. As Jonathan Daniels observes, Wallace probably really meant that.[31] Several times in his speech he repeated a demand that "we must insist on an open door for trade throughout the world," specifying the Balkans and China (under a Nationalist-Communist coalition). On the other hand, Wallace made a facile distinction between "economic" and "political":

> The real peace treaty we now need is between the United States and Russia. On our part we should recognize that we have no more business in the *political* affairs of Eastern Europe than Russia has in the *political* affairs of Latin America, Western Europe, and the United States . . . whether we like it or not, the Russians will try to socialize their sphere of influence just as we try to democratize our sphere of influence. This applies also to Germany and Japan. The Russians have no more business in stirring up native Communists to political activity in Western Europe, Latin America, and the United States than we have in interfering with the politics of Eastern Europe and Russia. . . .

But the Communists were showing no evidence of willingness to stick to even such a bargain as this, and Wallace opposed the use of force: "We are reckoning with a force which cannot be handled successfully by a 'get tough with Russia' policy. 'Getting tough' never brought anything real or lasting—whether for schoolyard bullies or businessmen or world powers. The tougher we get the tougher the Russians will get." America must not let "British balance-of-power manipulations" be the "key to our foreign policy. . . . We must not let the reactionary leadership of the Republican party force us into that position. . . . I am neither anti-British nor pro-British, neither anti-Russian nor pro-Russian. And just two days ago when President Truman read these words, he said they represented the policy of his Administration." [32]

31. Daniels, *op. cit.*, pp. 314–16.
32. Text, *United States News*, September 20, 1946, pp. 64–6.

Worse yet, Truman had also told a news conference that same afternoon that the whole speech was in accord with the policy Byrnes was pursuing in Paris. No one can be sure whether the President had read the text carefully enough to be justly accused of not *understanding* the new trend of American foreign policy. After all, Truman had good reason to temporize. This was the beginning of a congressional election campaign in which the Democrats would need every vote they could find. (Wallace's speech itself had been fired as the opening salvo of the party's campaign in New York City, at the heart of America's left.)

But Senator Vandenberg had no such political inhibitions as Truman. He was in Paris with Byrnes and Connally for the twenty-one-nation consultative peace conference on Italy and Eastern Europe and promptly announced he could cooperate with only one Secretary of State at a time. Byrnes delayed importuning the President for support until Wallace announced an agreement with Truman to keep silent on foreign policy only until after the peace conference. Then on September 18 Byrnes cabled his resignation unless Wallace as a Cabinet member were permanently muzzled on foreign affairs. The following day Byrnes went a little further and clearly implied a conviction that Wallace should be thrown out of the administration, although he was still not insisting on that. On the following day Truman cut the Gordian knot. Wallace left the government.[33]

Thus at the beginning of the election campaign the administration had been compelled to make a symbolic choice between its right and left wings. An attempt was made to gloss over the schism by the expedient, extraordinary in the Democratic party, of securing a statement from the National Committee on foreign policy, designed to suggest that Byrnes's methods would achieve Wallace's objectives.[34] Representative Vito Marcantonio took a different

33. Byrnes, *op. cit.*, pp. 239–43.

34. "America and the world are struggling to build a lasting peace, rooted in justice, fashioned by democratic processes, set firmly upon the rock of world organization and collective security, and dedicated to the gradual but steady advancement of the Four Freedoms throughout one interdependent world.

"Under the leadership of Presidents Roosevelt and Truman, America has forsaken isolationism and appeasement. Under Democratic administrations, America has

line; on behalf of the far left he raised a trial balloon for a third party.[35] He was premature. Henry Wallace actually did a little campaigning for West Coast Democrats in October.

Liberal Defeat and Division. Republicans were in a strong position to campaign by saying that the Democratic administration was trying to carry out a sound *GOP* foreign policy, but could not be trusted to do so because of dissension and Communist influence in its own ranks. The Democratic debacle which followed in the November elections was certainly the result mainly of domestic considerations, but it was bound to cause members of the non-Communist left to reflect on the vulnerability of the Democratic party as their political instrument unless the remaining ambiguity in its position on communism could be removed. Particularly the disastrous Democratic failure in New York State raised doubt of the value of continued alliance with the far left.

The CIO's National Convention in the middle of November took some notice of this controversy by restricting the activities of the local and state councils of CIO unions (which were often Communist strongholds) and adopting a resolution declaring: "we will not tolerate [Communist] interference . . . in the affairs of the CIO." This would have been more convincing, however, if it had not also been endorsed by Communist members of the executive board of the CIO when the board unanimously recommended its adoption; no debate was permitted on the floor; approval came by acclamation.[36] Philip Murray was plainly still unwilling to permit the breakup of the CIO over the issue of communism.

But the liberal intellectuals had finally come to a parting of the ways. At the turn of the year Americans for Democratic Action (ADA) and Progressive Citizens of America (PCA) were founded. The ADA announced: "We reject any association with Communists or sympathizers with communism in the United States." [37]

---

taken front rank in the creation of international organizations designed to insure political security, economic reconstruction, and social justice on a world basis.

"The American delegation at the Paris Peace Conference is struggling patiently and firmly for the advancement of these principles of peace—and the American people will back them to the limit." *New York Times,* September 27, 1946.

35. *Ibid.*
36. *Ibid.,* November 16, 18 and 19, 1946.
37. *Ibid.,* January 6, 1947.

PCA took no such position. It was a leftist offshoot of the alliance formed the preceding May by the CIO-PAC, the National Citizens PAC, and the Independent Citizens Committee of the Arts, Sciences, and Professions. It represented an outright consolidation of the latter two groups with eight other leftist fragments; the CIO-PAC was now maintaining a benevolent neutrality. Still aligned with the PCA elements were Philip Murray and Jack Kroll, director of CIO-PAC, but CIO Secretary-Treasurer James Carey and Walter Reuther of the Automobile Workers, among other CIO leaders, went with the anticommunist ADA.

THE PROMULGATION OF THE
CONTAINMENT POLICY

President Truman, for his part, issued a statement soon after Election Day praising the "national and not a party program" of the government in foreign affairs, "developed and executed on a bipartisan basis" (he had done his "best to strengthen and extend this practice"), and announcing that it would continue "so far as the Secretary of State and I are concerned." He asserted a firm belief "that our Republican colleagues who have worked intelligently and cooperatively in the past will do so in the future," but he was concerned "lest any in either party should seek in this field an opportunity to achieve personal notoriety or partisan advantage by exploitation of the sensational, or by the mere creation of controversy." [38] Privately, Truman made it clear to Forrestal that that was just what he was really expecting.[39]

Yet Vandenberg, at least, continued in full collaboration with Byrnes and Connally during November and December at the session of the Council of Foreign Ministers which completed the satellite peace treaties. When the task was finished, he announced that he expected to return from international negotiation to his duties in the Senate, but he still supported Byrnes "1000 per cent in what he is doing" and would "continue to do everything within [his] power to cooperate in maintaining the united American for-

38. *Ibid.*, November 12, 1946.
39. Millis, *The Forrestal Diaries,* p. 218.

eign policy which has been established in respect to [the United Nations and] the peace settlements in Europe." [40]

Soon after this, however, Truman accepted the resignation of Secretary Byrnes and appointed General Marshall to take his place in the State Department. Relations had long been strained between Truman and Byrnes; almost any President would have been galled by superior ability and prestige in a Secretary of State whose personal loyalty was at all questionable. In General Marshall Truman found fidelity coupled with ability and prestige. But Marshall did lack the intimacy with Senator Vandenberg which Byrnes had developed during the nine months they had worked so closely together. With the best of intentions on both sides, it would inevitably take time to re-establish close relations between Vandenberg and the Secretary of State.

The Truman Doctrine. There was no time to do so before the bombshell of the Truman Doctrine. Vandenberg and other GOP leaders were busy organizing the Eightieth Congress, Marshall was preparing himself for the March Foreign Ministers conference in Moscow on the German and Austrian treaties, and Truman was getting ready for a good-will visit to Mexico in the first week of March when, on February 24, 1947, the British Ambassador informed the State Department that in the new fiscal year starting April 1 his government could not afford to give further assistance to Greece or Turkey. When the Department of State had considered this possibility the previous autumn, it had evidently envisaged a smaller problem which could be handled by concealed American arms transfers via the British.[41] Now something bigger was obviously needed, and in a hurry if the British meant what they said about getting out in April. A week of hasty private briefings of the press and key congressmen followed. Vandenberg was certainly informed about the plans for Greece and Turkey, but it is not clear that he was much better prepared than others on March 12 for the grandiloquent scope of the "Truman Doctrine" in which the President enfolded this east Mediterranean police action: "I believe that it must be the foreign policy of the United

40. *New York Times,* December 18, 1946.
41. Millis, *The Forrestal Diaries,* p. 216.

States to support free peoples who are resisting attempted subjugation by armed minorities or by outside pressures."

By means of this breathtaking ascension of a trial balloon for the new "containment policy" which was being elaborated in the State Department with the aid of George Kennan the administration definitely recaptured the political initiative from the Republicans on the issue of anticommunism. It was revealing now to watch GOP congressmen recoil. Vandenberg himself was clearly resentful of the manner in which the Greek-Turk program had been presented to Congress—stupendous implied commitments, with little information, on short notice, and with a deadline.[42] Still he was prepared to cooperate.

But the Democrats pressed their advantage dangerously far. The Executive Director of the Democratic National Committee, Gael Sullivan, actually tried to make political capital by asking Republican Chairman Reece to add his signature to a joint statement, which would declare the "hearty accord" of both parties, not only on the Greek-Turk program but on the whole of the Truman Doctrine—"on the purpose and method of withstanding the spread of totalitarian aggression and enslavement wherever it may occur." [43] Sullivan published his own letter without giving Reece time to reply, and then later released with an air of triumph Reece's refusal to be put in the position of committing congressional Republicans.[44] The Democrats' crude injection of partisanship was generally embarrassing. Connally deplored it, and Vandenberg felt called upon to define to the Senate the conditions of his foreign policy leadership:

> Bipartisan foreign policy is not the result of political coercion, but of nonpolitical conviction. I never have even pretended to speak for my party in my foreign policy activities. I have relied upon the validity of my actions to command whatever support they may deserve. I have never made any semblance of a partisan demand for support and I never shall. . . . I expect every Republican, like every Democrat, to respond to

42. *New York Times*, March 14, 1947.
43. *Ibid.*, March 18, 1947.
44. Arthur Krock, *New York Times*, March 19, 1947.

his own conscience. I expect them all to act not as partisans but as Americans. I expect none of them to yield their judgments, at such an hour, to the political dictates of any party managers. On the latter basis, bipartisan foreign policy would die in revolt. I hope that we may avoid that tragedy.[45]

Vandenberg was apparently still feeling his way toward the pinnacle of semicoercive power he eventually reached in the Eightieth Congress. For the time being, he found himself in the embarrassing position for a GOP leader of having to "soften" an anti-Russian program of the Democratic administration to make it acceptable to a Republican-controlled Congress, without surrendering the anticommunist political label to Democrats. Despite its leftist wing the Democratic administration had dared to overtake and pass the isolationist-handicapped GOP on the road toward a really tough policy. But having released their trial balloon for world-wide containment of the Soviets, executive officials were content to concentrate on getting the Greek-Turk installment through Congress and refused to be drawn into details on future projects.[46] Such piecemeal tactics could not be acceptable much longer to a suspicious Congress, but at the time they seemed to imply some modification of the immeasurable Truman Doctrine, and hence probably simplified the task of altering the Greek-Turk program to fit the limits of tolerance of a Republican Congress anxious to reduce expenditures and taxes.

Getting Aid for Greece and Turkey. Vandenberg himself undertook the job of adaptation. His major accomplishment was to cut off the "neoisolationist" line of retreat into the United Nations.[47] In presenting the program to Congress the administration had

45. *Congressional Record,* March 18, 1947, p. 2167.

46. Acting Secretary of State Acheson explained that the situation in other countries was "utterly different, and what you can do in one case you cannot do in another case." *Hearings* on assistance to Greece and Turkey, before the Senate Foreign Relations Committee, March 1947, p. 30.

47. Vandenberg also sponsored a large-scale sales technique for the program in Congress by soliciting all the queries any member might care to raise and getting the State Department to answer them. The resulting 111 questions and answers were printed in *Hearings* on assistance to Greece and Turkey, before the House Foreign Affairs Committee, March-April 1947, pp. 341–86.

given the UN no role to play. On March 31 Vandenberg introduced amendments providing, most significantly, that the aid program could be stopped by request of the General Assembly or the
Security Council and that the United States would waive its veto
right on this subject.[48] This soothed the sensibilities of sincere
friends of the United Nations and opponents of the "get tough"
policy; in that respect it probably buttressed the administration's
case most in the Democratic party. But more important at the beginning of the Republican Eightieth Congress was the degree to
which it prevented noninterventionist congressmen from throwing
up an effective smoke screen of UN moralizing to cover their own
retreat from an expensive program of overseas action. In this
respect Vandenberg's amendments weakened the opposition particularly within his own party. Of course the "UN arguments"
continued to be used. But their limited impact in Congress among
sincere friends of collective security was indicated by the final roll
calls, which showed in the House that the 116 members voting or
paired against the bill included only 9 Northern Democrats (still
fewer Southerners) and only 25 Coastal Republicans (most of them
arch-conservatives from Pennsylvania); among the 23 names of
Senate opponents only Pepper, Taylor, and Murray stand out as
men with records such that they may reasonably be supposed to
have been swayed primarily by internationalism and/or leftism.

In the House the whole program nearly ran afoul of noninterventionist and economy sentiment in the Rules Committee. For
several days members from that wing of the Republican party
stalled action by holding open hearings on the bill. But the House
Republican leadership finally prevailed upon two of the Midwesterners to swing their votes and let the measure go to the floor,
while Speaker Martin gave assurances that GOP party loyalty
would not be invoked there to pass this "bipartisan" bill.[49] Despite
the soft pedaling of leadership activity more than half of the
House Republicans did finally vote for the bill, though far less
decisively than had their colleagues in the Senate.

48. Assistance was also to end upon the request of any government in Greece or
Turkey which represented a majority of the people of the country.
49. *New York Times*, May 3 and 4, 1947.

CONCLUDING OBSERVATIONS

The bulk of recorded opposition was plainly concentrated in the Midwest GOP. This group had been most vocal immediately after the war, when it had demanded toughness toward the Soviets at a time when toughness seemed to mean merely no further assistance and no diplomatic concessions. Later, the congressional voting record on the British loan in mid-1946 had seemed to reveal a basic penchant for economy and withdrawal underneath the verbal anticommunism of these Midwest Republicans; but the evidence is clouded because the immediate issue then was *economic* aid to England. Now in 1947 it was a matter of *military* aid to two small countries, Greece and Turkey, which had not aroused such antipathy as Britain among important segments of the American people—and which were immediately, critically threatened by Communist pressure.

Still, the Interior Republicans recoiled from this opportunity to implement their anticommunism. The attitude of many of them in later years was to be called "unilateral interventionism," as against the "multilateral interventionism" of the Truman administration; but here it was Truman who was intervening unilaterally, Vandenberg who was providing a tiny UN fig leaf, and the Interior Republicans who were simply being "old-fashioned" noninterventionists. Thus was shattered the superficial unity which the GOP had shown in the winter of 1945–46 on behalf of toughness toward Russia—a unity which had in fact played an important part in encouraging the administration to become "patient but firm." In succeeding years, on widely contrasting issues but generally along Coastal-Interior lines, a division would remain in the Republican party over what anticommunism really required. Initiative would normally lie with the Democratic administration. But it would at least find amenable to persuasion a third or more of the GOP congressmen, ready to consider giving extrapartisan support in foreign affairs.

The Democrats, for their part, had come through the fires of a reversal of policy toward Russia and the consequent defection of their far left wing with a surprising degree of unity persisting in the congressional party. Only 7 Democratic Senators and 13 Democratic Representatives voted against the Greek-Turk bill. Of course they now had the incentives of a minority party to stand together; and the battle against Henry Wallace still had many months to run, but the party was sufficiently united along the tough new line of policy to form a hard core on which the administration could rely while making overtures to cooperative Republicans to form the required majorities.

Thus the announcement of the Truman Doctrine brought into focus a general attitude (though not a detailed endorsement) which was sufficiently widespread in both parties to facilitate extra-partisan collaboration. Republican control of Congress made it essential. The development of this "bipartisanship" was rapid to the high point reached in the presidential election year of 1948.

CHAPTER 11

Palestine

WITH the principle of resistance to Russia well established, this seems an appropriate point to interrupt chronological sequence and consider two special areas of American foreign relations which came to have exceptional importance in party politics: Palestine and China.

Palestine is the classic case in recent years of the determination of American foreign policy by domestic political considerations. American Zionists showed themselves to be zealots, relentlessly determined to secure the intervention of the United States government on behalf of a Jewish state in Palestine. They had wealth to devote to the cause, and beyond that they had two peculiar advantages among the various pressure groups seeking to influence major American foreign policy. First, the Jewish population for which they claimed to speak was concentrated in urban centers in the big industrial states, especially New York, Pennsylvania, and California; these states were closely divided between the two political parties, and under the existing "general ticket" system of counting electoral votes for the presidency, Zionists appeared to be a dedicated group who might be able to swing *all* the many electoral votes of those key states to one party or the other and thus decide a national election; even state and local elections in these big states were of national importance for strengthening local party organizations which would be needed to help in national campaigns. Second and equally important, they were virtually unopposed by any other pressure group and faced an indifferent or

mildly sympathetic public. Anti-Semites, e.g., preferred to have
the remnants of European Jewry go to Palestine than come to New
York; American security interests in the Arab world were not
understood widely enough or felt strongly enough to create substantial political resistance to Zionism.

THE BREAKDOWN OF DIPLOMACY

In these circumstances leaders of both parties had nothing to lose
and everything to gain politically by competing for Zionist votes
and Zionist money. In the years 1939–45 the stakes in this game
grew much higher than before. Zionists developed a sense of great
urgency as a result of the decimation of the Jewish population of
Europe and the threat contained in the British White Paper of
1939 that no Jewish immigration would be permitted in Palestine
after 1945 (except with the unlikely consent of the Arabs). And
during the war the main center of world Zionism moved from
London to New York, where the politically strategic location of
millions of Jewish voters, plus coolly calculated contributions to
party campaign funds, were available to bring the pressure of the
American government to bear on Britain.

Anglo-American Negotiations. In 1944 both national party platforms carried planks strongly favoring the Jews.[1] Immediately
after the end of the war Truman accepted the suggestion of
Earl G. Harrison, United States Representative on the Intergov-
ernmental Committee on Refugees, that the American government ask England to grant the Jewish Agency's request for 100,000
immigrants to Palestine.[2] Britain replied with a stalling request
for a Joint Anglo-American Committee of Inquiry. Its establishment was announced on November 13, 1945.

However, the American Congress could not be put off so easily.
On December 12 the Senate Foreign Relations Committee reported out a resolution, cosponsored by such opposites as Taft
and Wagner, calling for American good offices to secure "free

1. See p. 166, n. 45.
2. Truman's letter to Attlee was dated August 31, 1945. Harrison's report to
Truman was published in the *New York Times,* September 30, 1945.

entry of Jews" into Palestine, "the Jewish national home." Only Chairman Connally ventured to vote against this resolution in committee.[3] In the Senate he pleaded for postponement till after the Inquiry Committee made a report, but Wagner sought immediate adoption of the resolution as a guide to its policy.[4] Former Adm. Thomas Hart (then in the Senate on gubernatorial appointment from Connecticut), reflected the views of the Navy Department when he offered a watered-down substitute frankly intended to mollify the Arabs. But he was drowned out in a *voice* vote which passed the Taft-Wagner Resolution.[5] In the House no one had to go on record either. New York Republican leader James Wadsworth did have the courage (slightly less remarkable, since he came from upstate) to move to recommit the whole resolution on forthright anti-Zionist grounds; on a standing vote he mustered 36 to 133 against recommittal. The resolution then went through by voice vote.[6]

When the Anglo-American Committee of Inquiry reported in April, it gave an endorsement of the 100,000 immigration figure but linked this with a recommendation that the British mandate be continued, with no objective of making Palestine into an Arab state *or* a Jewish state, or, by partition, one of each. Truman promptly endorsed some of the sections of the report to which Zionists were not opposed, but he offered Britain no American assistance in carrying it out. Attlee thereupon made it plain that his government was not going to enforce the report *alone,* or adopt merely the pro-Zionist parts of it; Foreign Secretary Bevin made matters worse by explaining publicly on June 12 that the reason Americans wanted to get Jews into Palestine was that "they did not want too many of them in New York." [7] This was a very hot issue when the British loan agreement came up in the House of Representatives in July. One-third of all the Democratic members who voted against that bill came from New York State.

In July another attempt was made to patch up a joint Anglo-

3. *New York Times,* December 13, 1945.
4. *Congressional Record,* December 17, 1945, pp. 12169–70, 12138.
5. *Ibid.,* pp. 12165–7, 12189.
6. *Ibid.,* December 19, 1945, pp. 12386, 12396.
7. *New York Times,* June 13, 1946.

American policy, with the appointment of Byrnes, Treasury Secretary Snyder, and War Secretary Patterson to a joint Cabinet Committee with the British. Henry F. Grady, a San Francisco businessman who had had some diplomatic experience, was chief of the negotiating deputies. Early in the fall their work also was aborted, when Zionist politics in New York again drove Truman to take a stand. It was a congressional election year. Lehman and Mead were being desperately hard pressed by Ives and Dewey for Senator and Governor respectively. The New York Democrats informed Truman that if he did not act, they would have to issue a statement on Palestine to forestall one from Dewey, and would then publicly call upon the President to endorse it. Bevin, forewarned, pled with Byrnes to block the move; the State Department's first draft was cautious. But on October 4 Truman's statement appeared. He still wanted 100,000 new immigrants in the Holy Land, and backed the Jewish Agency's proposal for "the creation of a viable Jewish state in control of its own immigration and economic policies in an adequate area of Palestine." That announcement torpedoed the current British negotiations with the Jews in London, which were based on the less generous "Morrison plan," outgrowth of the Grady committee's work. Bevin had regarded those discussions as very promising and was deeply incensed.[8]

The UN Partition Plan. On April 2, 1947, the British finally submitted the question of Palestine to the United Nations. A special session of the General Assembly was called, and with American support it voted to postpone debate on the merits of the issue until a special small-power committee could make an investigation and report. In September the majority of this committee recommended political partition of Palestine along "jigsaw" boundaries, with economic union, and with the interim admission of 150,000 Jews. A minority, composed of the members with substantial Moslem populations, dissented, asking for a *federal* state, which would probably have had the effect of assuring long-run Arab control.

President Truman consciously tried to avoid becoming per-

8. Kermit Roosevelt, "The Partition of Palestine, A Lesson in Pressure Politics," *Middle East Journal*, January 1948, pp. 12–13.

sonally embroiled once more, despite the urgent pleas of Robert Hannegan on behalf of the Democratic National Committee that very important campaign contributions depended on the administration's giving effective support to the Zionists.[9] After some delay the American government did announce its support for partition, but the State Department, wary of the Arabs, would not press other delegations to support it with sufficient vigor to satisfy the Zionists.[10] So the Zionists themselves did a job of international lobbying which was truly extraordinary in its scope. Certainly with the knowledge—Sumner Welles says at the instigation—of the White House, persons formerly or currently connected with the administration joined with congressmen and leading citizens in importuning the wavering delegates of small powers to vote for partition.[11]

Forrestal's Mediation. But no provision was made for enforcement. With the Arabs in rebellion against the plan and the British uncooperative to the point of obstructionism, this was an increasingly critical problem. James Forrestal, now Secretary of Defense, decided to play an active role in attempting to get leaders of both American parties to agree to remove Palestine from domestic politics, as the precondition for any settlement in the Middle East which would avoid permanent injury to American relations with the Moslem world. He secured Truman's permission to make an informal approach to Republican leaders.[12]

On December 10, 1947, Forrestal found Senator Vandenberg anxious to keep aloof from the matter, observing "that there was a feeling among most Republicans that the Democratic party had used the Palestine question politically, and the Republicans felt they were entitled to make similar use of the issue." Vandenberg, of course, was further able to extenuate his own obvious lack of

9. Millis, *The Forrestal Diaries*, pp. 304, 309, 323.
10. *Ibid.*, p. 345.
11. *Ibid.*, p. 346. Roosevelt, *op. cit.*, pp. 14–15. Sumner Welles, *We Need Not Fail* (Boston, Houghton Mifflin, 1948), p. 63. Daniels' semi-authorized biography says Truman "had a personal part behind the United States support of the resolution." Daniels, *The Man of Independence*, p. 317.
12. The story of these negotiations is told in Millis, *The Forrestal Diaries*, pp. 344–8 and 359–65.

eagerness to cooperate by the observation that Republicans should be in on the take-offs as well as the crash landings of foreign policy.[13] Three days later Governor Dewey said "he agreed in principle" with Forrestal "but that it was a difficult matter to get results on because of the intemperate attitude of the Jewish people who had taken Palestine as the emotional symbol" and "because the Democratic party would not be willing to relinquish the advantages of the Jewish vote." Vandenberg told Forrestal that Dewey was "responsive but skeptical." [14]

On January 21, 1948, Forrestal reported to Under Secretary of State Lovett on his conversations with Vandenberg and Dewey and wrote that he had found "complete agreement as to the desirability of the objective from various other Republicans, not in the leadership, such as John Taber, James W. Wadsworth, Dewey Short, and Everett Dirksen." Democrats had shown awareness "of the importance and danger of the situation," but concern also for campaign funds from Zionists seeking "a lien upon this part of our national policy." [15]

Forrestal himself, however, now wanted to turn over to the Secretary of State the burden of promoting further negotiations between Republican and Democratic leaders.[16] Forrestal was well aware (Bernard Baruch among others warned him) that he was becoming too closely identified with opposition to Zionism. It was politically unsafe. When Winthrop Aldrich of the Chase National Bank phoned him on February 3 that Dewey was now willing to consult on Palestine via Dulles and Secretary Marshall, a convenient opportunity appeared for Forrestal to bow out of his hazardous occupation.[17]

American Policy Reversals. Nothing important came of the Aldrich offer. But soon there did come, too late, a brief success for the "pro-Arab" group in the State and Defense Departments with whom Forrestal was generally identified—a Pyrrhic victory which merely destroyed whatever chance there may have been that Zion-

13. *Ibid.,* pp. 347–8.
14. *Ibid.,* p. 348.
15. *Ibid.,* pp. 359–60.
16. *Ibid.,* p. 361.
17. *Ibid.,* pp. 364–5.

ists would not seek revenge upon him, as they did so fiercely within a year.

The abortive anti-Zionist move was Ambassador Warren Austin's announcement to the UN Security Council on March 19, 1948, that *peaceful* partition was then impossible and that, therefore, the United States would favor a temporary trusteeship over all Palestine. Truman was caught unaware. He had just given the venerable Zionist Chaim Weizmann personal assurances that partition would be pushed.[18] But this was the height of the spring crisis of 1948—between the fall of Czechoslovakia and the Italian election—and the State and Defense Departments were acutely aware of the danger of enforcing partition by UN action; it would perhaps involve the admission of some Russian troops to help police Palestine, and would tie down slim American forces there.

Unfortunately, trusteeship at this late date promised to be equally expensive. Even the Arabs took the American policy shift as an encouragement not to lay down their arms but to press forward as the British withdrew. The Joint Chiefs of Staff estimated that 104,000 troops would be required to enforce trusteeship. America could scarcely spare one division.[19]

The United States delegation was having great difficulty getting support for its new plan in the UN, when another presidential initiative brought about another reversal of policy. This time it was the *de facto* American recognition of the new state of Israel on May 14, fifteen minutes after its independence had been proclaimed. Truman had deferred the day before to Secretary Marshall's objections; but when the State Department agreed to present the recognition plan to the British and French, White House aides Clark Clifford and David Niles, who for months had been active in the Zionist cause, successfully pressed Truman to insist on immediate recognition.[20]

18. Daniels, *op. cit.,* p. 318.
19. Millis, *The Forrestal Diaries,* p. 411.
20. Daniels, *op. cit.,* pp. 319–20.

LETTING ISRAEL WIN THE WAR

Zionism in the 1948 Platforms. War was now on in Palestine; teams of UN negotiators were trying to maintain the fragile truce agreements they were sometimes able to secure; and both parties in the American presidential campaign were as usual seeking to outdo each other in support for Israel. The full Resolutions Committee in each party convention made extraordinary pro-Zionist alterations in the Palestine plank presented to it by its drafting subcommittee. Their cuts and substitutions are indicated below: [21]

Republicans

~~We greet the new state of Israel and pledge it our friendly cooperation to the end that it may have a future commensurate with the proven greatness of its people who have suffered so much.~~

[Substituted]: We welcome Israel into the family of nations and take pride in the fact that the Republican party was the first to call for the establishment of a free and independent Jewish commonwealth. The vacillation of the Democratic administration on this question has undermined the prestige of the United Nations. Subject to the letter and spirit of the United Nations Charter, we pledge to Israel full recognition, with its boundaries as sanctioned by the United Nations, and aid in developing its economy.

Democrats

President Truman, by granting immediate recognition to Israel, led the world in extending friendship and welcome to a people who have long sought and justly deserve freedom and independence.

~~We look forward to extending full and prompt recognition to the permanent government of Israel as soon as it is established.~~ [Substituted]: We pledge full recognition to the State of Israel.

We affirm our pride that the United States, under the leadership of President Truman, played a leading role in the adoption of the resolution of November 29, 1947, by the United Nations General Assembly for the creation of a Jewish state. We approve the claims of the State of Israel to the boundaries set forth in the United Nations resolution of November 29 and consider that modifications thereof should be made only if fully acceptable to the State of Israel.

We look forward to the admission of the State of Israel to the United

21. *New York Times*, June 22 and 23, and July 13 and 14, 1948.

Republicans   *Democrats*

Nations and its full participation in the international community of nations. We pledge appropriate aid to the State of Israel in developing its economy and resources.

~~We recognize the right of the State of Israel to secure in the United States and elsewhere the arms and equipment necessary to defend itself, subject only to the decision of the United Nations. Subject thereto, we favor the lifting of the arms embargo to accord to the State of Israel the right to defend itself.~~ [Substituted]: We favor the revision of the arms embargo to accord to the State of Israel the right of self-defense. We pledge ourselves to work for the modification of any resolution of the United Nations to the extent that it may prevent such revision.

We continue to support, within the framework of the United Nations, the internationalization of Jerusalem and the protection of the holy places in Palestine. [This was for Christian voters, especially Catholics.]

Dooming the Bernadotte Plan. There could be little hope that the delicate problem of bringing peace to Palestine would not be further complicated by American election campaigning after the party conventions; in the event, all hope was dispelled in the Zionist drive to get both candidates, Truman and Dewey, to repudiate the Bernadotte peace plan in the early fall. Count Bernadotte, the UN mediator, was proposing that the Jews should give up their claim to the southern desert region, the Negeb, which had been assigned to them under the UN partition resolution of November 1947, and should receive in return western Galilee, which had not. At the UN General Assembly in Paris in September, Secretary Marshall had given general approval to this plan.[22] But the Jews were determined to have both regions. In mid-October their army began an offensive in the Negeb. And in America a series of Zionist advertisements called upon candidates to reaffirm support for the partition resolution's assignment of the Negeb to Israel.

Dewey acted first, on October 22, in a letter to one of his more surprising supporters, Dean Alfange, a founder of the Liberal party in New York and then chairman of the American Christian Palestine Committee. Truman replied with a statement the next day. (Neither candidate referred directly to the question of Israel's boundaries, except by reference to his party platform.) [23]

Dewey	*Truman*
As you know, I have always felt the Jewish people are entitled to a homeland in Palestine which would be politically and economically stable. My views have been clearly expressed over the years, and I did, indeed, approve the majority report of the United Nations Special Committee which recommended a partition of Palestine.	The Republican candidate for President has seen fit to release a statement with reference to Palestine . . . ten days before the election. I had hoped our foreign affairs could continue to be handled on a nonpartisan basis without being injected into the presidential campaign. The Republican candidate's statement, however, makes it necessary for me to reiterate my own position with respect to Palestine.
In my acceptance speech at Philadelphia I pledged my whole-hearted support of the Republican platform and that included the Palestine plank. My position today is the same.	I stand squarely on the provisions covering Israel in the Democratic platform. I approved the provisions on Israel at the time they were written. I reaffirm that approval now.
	[Quotes the Palestine plank.] When a permanent government is elected in Israel, it will promptly be given de jure recognition. [Spells out support of other provisions in the plank, calling the Bernadotte plan "a basis of negotiation."]

22. Dulles, who was in effect representing Dewey as a member of the American delegation at this UN session, absented himself from all meetings of his colleagues where Palestine was discussed, lest the Republicans be implicated in this partisan area of administration policy. Dulles, *War or Peace*, p. 50.

23. *New York Times*, October 23 and 25, 1948.

Truman returned to the attack in Madison Square Garden on October 28. Palestine was "a subject that has been of great interest to me as your President."

> Now this is a most important subject and must not be resolved as a matter of politics during a political campaign. I've refused consistently to play politics with that subject. I've refused, first, because it's my responsibility to see that our policy in Israel fits in with our foreign policy throughout the world; second, it is my desire to help build in Palestine a strong, prosperous, free and independent, democratic state.
>
> It must be large enough, free enough, and strong enough to make its people self-supporting and secure.

Truman then proceeded to trace his major pro-Zionist moves, reaffirmed the 1948 Democratic platform and called attention to the 1944 platform, "under which I have been trying to act. The platform of 1948 reiterates those provisions and goes a little further. And I'm glad it did go a little further." [24]

Dewey had nothing more to say about Palestine after the Alfange letter. But he did let his associate, Senator Ives, devote a large portion of a warm-up speech at their final campaign rally to a denunciation of Truman for "running out on every commitment he had made to the Jewish people," and for undermining the UN by policy shifts.[25]

At the United Nations in Paris the reaction to these Zionist eruptions in the American political scene was a decision to postpone all discussion of Palestine till the election campaign was over. That doomed the Bernadotte plan, for by November the advancing Israelis were deep into the Negeb, and the United Nations were clearly no more willing to *force* them back than the Jews were to withdraw voluntarily. The defeated Arab states were soon ready to accept armistice agreements which gave Israel territory far wider than the original UN partition resolution.

Thus Jewish military prowess and Arab incompetence solved the enforcement problem which had loomed so large in early dis-

24. *Ibid.,* October 29, 1948.
25. *Ibid.,* October 31, 1948.

cussion of the creation of a Jewish state in Palestine. American troops were not required. Thus conveniently was dispelled the immediate danger posed to the American people by the deep injection of Zionism into their politics. The financial drain on the United States Treasury for the support of the infant state of Israel and the Arab refugees from Palestine was counted in tens of millions in each succeeding year—not a very grave expense. But the cost in Arab good will remained imponderable. Undoubtedly it was very great.

ZIONISM AND THE AMERICAN SYSTEM

Clearly the exigencies of American politics were the foremost factor in permitting the birth of the new state of Israel. They furnished the womb which sheltered the infant till it was strong enough to fight for its own existence. Assuming what cannot yet be proved, that this was dangerously contrary to the interests of American national security, the question remains whether it was peculiarly the result of the present loosely organized party system in the United States or whether even tightly disciplined American parties would have behaved in similar fashion.

In the first place it can be asserted with confidence that under the present "general ticket" system of choosing presidential electors no practicable increase in responsible party discipline would stop the two parties from competing for Zionist voters. These voters are strategically located in states with huge electoral votes, and there is no comparably strong bloc of anti-Zionist votes, or even an anti-Zionist public opinion, on which party leaders could lean in resisting Zionist demands. It would be enormously difficult to promote a politically effective anti-Zionism without exacerbating anti-Semitism.

That difficulty would remain, in the second place, even if a constitutional amendment were to require a division of the electoral votes of each state between the candidates. But the geographical location of Zionist voters would then be less important in presidential elections, and therefore it would be at least possible for national party leaders to take a firmer stand against Zionism—if they were willing to risk the loss of state and local elections, e.g., New York in 1946. However, in New York or Pennsylvania even a state election is important to the future of the whole party, because each victory there helps to nourish a great many local party workers who are needed to get out the votes in *all* elections. Moreover, the requirements of party finance would still be important. On balance it seems probable that only the development of a substantial segment of public opinion which was actively aware of the dangers of Zionism to United States security would be able to counterbalance the fanatical determination of American Zionists, under any kind of party system. The establishment of Israel brought a respite but presumably not an end to this problem in United States relations with the Arab world.

CHAPTER 12

The Rediscovery of China

ON JANUARY 11, 1947, at the opening of the Republican Eightieth Congress, Senator Vandenberg delivered a major address on foreign policy before the Cleveland Council on World Affairs. His two major criticisms of current American foreign policy—mildly expressed—were on Latin America and China. The administration heeded Vandenberg's advice on Latin America that a settlement be reached with Perón in Argentina and that the long-postponed conference of American nations be held to formulate a mutual defense treaty. At Rio de Janeiro late in August the American delegation included Vandenberg, Connally, and former GOP Senator, then Ambassador, Warren Austin, who had negotiated with the Latins at Chapultepec two and a half years before. The treaty they produced was enthusiastically received by the Senate. Then Latin America dropped out of sight once more in American politics—partisan, bipartisan, and extrapartisan.

In contrast, the administration did not respond to Vandenberg's suggestion about China.[1] Republicans had been "waiting and seeing" there too, and they were allowed to go on doing just that. Rising GOP pressure for aid to Chiang received only the most grudging pretense of official compliance. Executive officers sought to pursue their own policy despite Congress. But unlike Latin America, this turned out to be a critical area at a time when it was too late to establish extrapartisan collaboration without its requiring the most drastic reversals of policy. The administration con-

1. See pp. 256–7.

tinued on its own, until near-debacle in Korea made its policy appear a failure. And then there were no Republicans around to share political responsibility.

For the purposes of this study the important questions about postwar China policy are why it became a party issue and what were the consequences of partisanship. Only incidentally are we concerned with the broader questions of why Chiang fell, whether the Communist victory could actually have been prevented, and, alternatively, whether early American support for Mao would have turned him Titoist. What was apparent five years after World War II was that America had failed to secure any kind of regime in China which was not actively hostile to the interests of the West. But the mere fact of this failure is not sufficient to explain why China policy became a party issue in the United States. The wartime policy of hopeful collaboration with Russia had also been a failure in all respects except the destruction of the Axis; the postwar policy of securing peace treaties with the German satellites was a failure in almost everything but form. Yet partisan recrimination over the loss of Eastern Europe was much less bitter than over the loss of China, despite the fact that millions of Americans are of Balkan descent while very few are of oriental origin. How is this to be explained?

ORIENTALISM IN THE GOP

Historical Background. One element, undoubtedly, was the long-term historical interest of Republicans in the Far East. This factor can easily be overestimated, but it was certainly of some importance. Partly it was a consequence of the trade potential of the Orient. During periods in which Republicans controlled the American government, shipping and mercantile interests on the Atlantic and Pacific seaboard sought rich profits in the China trade. At least as important was the activity of American missionaries. In the Bible belts of the Midwest, where the Republican party drew so much of its strength, the periodic visits and reports of missionaries aroused a sense of responsibility for the "heathen Chinee" which had political effects comparable to the commercial interests of influential men on the seaboard. In this connection it is not without significance that Walter Judd and John Vorys were the two congressmen who more than any others were responsible for pressing upon their GOP colleagues a large-scale program of aid to Chiang Kai-shek in the Eightieth Congress. Judd had been a medical missionary in China for several years before the war; Vorys had served with Yale-in-China.

Moreover, it was a historical fact that Republican presidents were in the White House during critical periods of American Pacific relations. It would be wrong to contend that the policies of Republicans when in power were consistently expansionist, or even activist, in the Far East. The Washington Naval Conference under Harding and especially Hoover's refusal to become deeply involved in Manchuria stand in marked contrast to much Republican activity under McKinley and Theodore Roosevelt. But events during their terms of office at least did force GOP leaders to take a responsible interest in the Far East—as events in Europe during the Wilson and Franklin Roosevelt administrations necessarily directed responsible Democratic attention in that direction. In a body whose leaders are men with as long seniority as in the United States Congress, the residues of interest thus aroused in young members can still influence their policy as leaders many years later. After Pearl Harbor many Republicans urged that the war against Japan be given priority over that against Germany. "We considered that the Republican war," remarked a Midwestern foreign affairs leader in Congress some years afterward. But he did not imply that he spoke for all his colleagues.[2]

MacArthur's Influence. The Asiatic orientation among some Republicans was reinforced to an important degree by the activity of Gen. Douglas MacArthur during and after the war. MacArthur had been President Hoover's Chief of Staff. He had won the exceptional confidence of wide sections of conservative opinion in America by his vigorous dispersal of the "insurrectionist" bonus marchers at the nation's capital in the depths of the depression. Then Franklin Roosevelt's replacement of MacArthur as Chief of Staff in 1935 and his prolonged self-exile in the Philippines per-

2. An interview in 1950.

mitted an aura of martyred mystery to begin to gather about the General. The outbreak of war with Japan, the heroic defense of Bataan, the American public's need for a hero in those desperate weeks, MacArthur's own eagerness to fill the role with histrionic skill and eloquence—all these established the General once more as a leader of American opinion, albeit leading indirectly. He was in frequent private correspondence with congressmen and other men of influence, advancing the usual arguments of a theater commander for more forces, but with the difference that for MacArthur his own Asiatic theater had taken on truly millennial importance (an attitude which may have dated back to his father's days of military glory as the pacifier of the Philippines).[3]

Now more than ever MacArthur could appear to have been martyred by the Democratic administration. Support for the General became an outlet for many Republican noninterventionists to vent their resentment against Roosevelt's political ascendancy after Pearl Harbor, without at the same time appearing to impede the war effort. Thus, for example, Senator Vandenberg, before his conversion, led an abortive MacArthur-for-President campaign in the spring of 1944.[4] But the size of this movement among Republicans should not be exaggerated, as was demonstrated by the speedy collapse of the General's candidacy in 1944. And it is important to note that much of whatever Republican interest there was in MacArthur was a reflection less of real concern for Asia than of hatred for Roosevelt and the search for any potentially good vote getter among America's military leaders who

3. MacArthur's philosophy in this period seems to have been very well expressed in a long memorandum which Bert Andrews of the *New York Herald Tribune* gave to Navy Secretary Forrestal in 1944, reporting on a visit to Leyte. Some excerpts of MacArthur's statements: "The Chinese situation is disastrous. It is the bitter fruit of our decision to concentrate our full strength against Germany. . . . We made the same old mistake of intervening in European quarrels which we can't hope to solve because they are insoluble. . . . Europe is a dying system. It is worn out and run down, and will become an economic and industrial hegemony of Soviet Russia. . . . The lands touching the Pacific with their billions of inhabitants will determine the course of history for the next ten thousand years. . . . If Chiang Kai-shek is overthrown, China will be thrown into utter confusion." Millis, *The Forrestal Diaries*, pp. 17–18.

4. This story is told at some length in Vandenberg, *The Private Papers of Senator Vandenberg*, pp. 75–89.

would be willing to oppose the Commander in Chief in time of war.

After the war, in lonely eminence in Tokyo, MacArthur managed a successful occupation of Japan with an absolute minimum of interference from Washington. But, correspondingly, his own influence over administration policy toward the other powers of the Western Pacific was slight. As danger to Chiang Kai-shek increased in China, MacArthur grew more urgent in his private expressions of concern to sympathetic congressmen and other leading citizens. There can be no doubt that the General's correspondence and interviews carried particular weight in the Republican party. Walter Judd, for example, used to quote him on behalf of Nationalist China in 1947, not by name in public but as "a great American out in the Far East"; [5] few informed persons were in doubt whom Judd meant. Periodically there was Republican agitation to bring MacArthur home to testify, notably when the China Aid bill was being considered early in 1948. But MacArthur's Delphi was Tokyo; he preferred to be consulted there. Perhaps if he had returned to America sooner he would have been even more successful in orienting the Republican party toward Asia. The experience of 1951 suggests that that is so. But he would have encountered great resistance in the Eastern wing of the party, and in other sections of the GOP as well when the expense of saving China was honestly computed.

As it was, MacArthur's known conservatism, his firm disagreements with Democratic administrations, his willingness to use and be used by noninterventionist elements of the GOP—as well as his unquestioned personal brilliance—all served to give him special prestige among Republicans, which helped to reinvigorate a special GOP interest in the Far East that commercial enterprise, missionary activity, and historical accident had in the past inculcated even among Republicans who took no comparable interest in Europe. When all this has been said, however, the dangerously attractive conclusion does *not* logically follow that the Republican party is the Asian party and the Democratic party the European

5. *Congressional Record*, July 18, 1950, p. 10554. Judd gives his version of the history of American policy in the Far East from V-J day to Korea, *ibid.*, pp. 10550–60.

party, and that the problem of finding a partisan cleavage in basic foreign policy has been solved. All that can wisely be concluded is that essentially noninterventionist elements in the Republican party have shown themselves to be somewhat less noninterventionist toward Asia than toward Europe, as they are likely to be somewhat less opposed to unilateral interventionism than to multilateral interventionism, and less opposed to interventionism in the form of military assistance than in the form of economic assistance. The relatively greater interest in the Far East is important. But foreign policy cleavages in the Republican party are too complex to be covered with a label of "orientalism." And too many special circumstances contributed to the GOP's gradual adoption of Far Eastern policy as a party issue in the late forties.

REPUBLICAN NONPARTICIPATION IN POSTWAR RELATIONS WITH CHINA

Stated in the simplest terms, the decisive factor in the situation was that the administration failed to associate prominent Republicans with its conduct of Chinese-American relations, on a basis either of "educational" indoctrination or of mutual compromise. There were a number of special reasons for this. One was the lack of any necessity to get legislative backing for what executive officials were trying to do in China immediately after the war; neither the administration nor the Republican leaders felt any urgency about formulating a program together. Another important consideration was General Marshall's attitude of independent, professional "nonpartisanship" when he was in control of American relations with China in 1946—relying on the *confidence* of politicians of both parties rather than their active cooperation—as contrasted with Secretary Byrnes's very personal bipartisan collaboration with Senator Vandenberg on the peace treaties in Europe that same year. Later a major consideration was the lack of any executive policy toward China which would be both clear cut and acceptable to leaders of both parties in Congress, and hence could furnish the basis for fruitful consultation. This factor and the others deserve further elaboration for an adequate understanding of the failure to establish extrapartisan collaboration in the years before China policy came to be regarded as "untouchable" by most shrewd politicians.

Nothing Urgent. Consider first the lack of any sense of urgency about securing active legislative support for American policy in China after the war. China simply did not appear to be a critical area in American foreign relations. As late as March 21, 1947, Under Secretary of State Acheson explained to Walter Judd (then almost alone in the vigor of his criticism): "The Chinese government is not in the position at the present time that the Greek government is in. It is not approaching collapse. It is not threatened by defeat by the Communists. The war with the Communists is going on much as it has for the last 20 years." [6] In this frame of mind, which was general in both parties, it seemed safe to leave Chinese-American relations up to the experts—especially, and this was another important point—since the few American experts there were on China appeared predominantly to be agreed that a satisfactory policy was being pursued. Notably, the publications of the Institute of Pacific Relations in the postwar years, and those to which its outstanding members gave their authoritative stamp of approval in reviews, etc. rarely presented any vigorous defense of Chiang Kai-shek or suggested a forceful alternative to the administration's policy of peaceful unification of China or mere drift. [7] Whether or

6. *Hearings* on assistance to Greece and Turkey, before the House Foreign Affairs Committee, March 1947, p. 17.

7. Of importance, but outside our focus of concern here, is the question of direct Communist influence in the IPR, which was commonly regarded in those years as the authoritative organization for research and publication on the Far East. No brief summary here can do justice to the massive weight of evidence accumulated by the McCarran Committee during its long investigation in 1951 and 1952. By the standards reasonably applicable to congressional probes, this one was conscientious and productive. Its 5,000 pages of testimony, with extensive and orderly documentation, deserve more respectful attention than they have received from most liberal critics, many of whom have not even bothered to read the committee's 200-page report. Unfortunately, there is room here only to state a personal conclusion: that a Communist solution for Asia was favored by a large enough proportion of the active participants in the American IPR to affect substantially the content of its publications and the character of its public relations work and contacts with government. See the *Hearings* on the Institute of Pacific Relations, before the Internal Security Subcommittee of the Senate Judiciary Committee, 1951–52. Senate Report 2050 (Internal Security Subcommittee), 82d Congress, July 2, 1952.

not a contrary policy was in fact feasible and desirable, it was not being presented by any large number of those whom the well informed citizen and congressmen had been taught to regard as experts on China. In an area about which so few Americans had any personal basis for challenging the experts (unlike Europe, for example) it is small wonder that public criticism was slow to develop.[8]

Another reason for the lack of a sense of urgency about China in 1946 and early 1947 was undoubtedly General Marshall's enormous personal prestige. After Marshall returned from China in January 1947 to become Secretary of State, Senator Vandenberg voiced these sentiments:

> In my opinion no Communist ever entered a coalition for any purpose except to destroy it. Therefore, in that aspect, I have not been in step with some phases of the China policy during the last year or two. Nevertheless, one of the greatest and ablest men of this nation, gifted not only with a military sense but with a high sense of statesmanship, has spent a year —one of the best years of his life—in China, trying to work out a policy for this nation; and so far as I am concerned, I have been quite willing that he should have the opportunity to see whether it could be done.[9]

The GOP Deliberately Stands Apart. This last statement by Vandenberg suggests another element, less certain, in the lack of urgent Republican demands to have a say on China in the early postwar years. This is the strong possibility that the Republican leadership, even Vandenberg, secretly welcomed the excuse the administration's inactivity gave them to remain mere "sidewalk superin-

8. This is a danger in any little known area of the world. Gabriel Almond has stated it succinctly: "If only a handful of experts are informed and concerned and there is no real policy competition before the 'attentive public,' there is a grave danger that the merits of a problem will not receive adequate attention and that accidental elite biases will obscure significant security interests." Almond, *The American People and Foreign Policy,* p. 85.

9. *Congressional Record,* April 16, 1947, p. 3474. The Senator's son observes, "The first major indication in Vandenberg's papers that he was gravely concerned about Chinese developments" came at the end of 1946. (This was when Marshall gave up his mission in China.) Vandenberg, *op. cit.,* p. 521.

tendents" of the administration's conduct of affairs in the Far East. Executive officials concerned with China were obviously not particularly interested in GOP advice. Republicans could wait and see what happened, periodically calling public attention to the fact that they were not being consulted and hence were not responsible. If something should go wrong, they could make political capital out of it; for men like Wherry that opportunity in itself might have been enough; others like Vandenberg could reassure themselves that nothing *really* dangerous to American national security was likely to happen in China anyway. James Reston remembers Vandenberg himself explaining this attitude toward consultation early in 1946.[10] Late in 1947 the Senator publicly indicated he was not really interested in extending his extrapartisan collaboration to China policy:

> I do not believe that the Senate Foreign Relations Committee has been consulted in any substantial degree regarding Asiatic policy during the past year or two. We have not had the China problem before us in any detail whatever . . .
>
> Let us have no doubt on the subject. I have never found the Secretary of State unwilling to express complete candor at any time I have talked to him. Unfortunately it is a pretty big world at the moment, and so far as the chairman of the committee [Vandenberg himself] has been concerned, he has had his hands pretty full with the immediate problems under his authority.[11]

By 1948 Vandenberg and Dulles had been privately won over to the State Department's view of the hopelessness of American intervention on behalf of Chiang Kai-shek in China, far more than had other leading Republicans who were supporting the Greek-Turk program and the Marshall Plan in Europe (men like Dewey, Bridges, Vorys, and Judd).[12] Thus it became particularly conven-

10. Reston, "Memorandum to General MacArthur," *New York Times Magazine*, April 22, 1951, p. 61.

11. *Congressional Record*, November 24, 1947, pp. 10708-9.

12. Dulles' 1948 view was given in an interview in July 1950. On Vandenberg's unwillingness to go to great lengths to save China, see Vandenberg, *op. cit.*, pp. 523-9, *passim*.

ient for Vandenberg, in order to preserve the confidence of party colleagues who generally accepted his leadership in foreign policy, not to be closely associated with a China policy of which they disapproved; [13] he was still able, unostentatiously, to modify their China projects and thus render them a little more palatable to the State Department.[14]

Thus, on the Republican side, it can be said in summary that the factors working in 1945–47 to prevent any serious GOP attempt to participate in China policy were unfounded optimism about the situation in China, general agreement among the supposed experts, confidence in General Marshall, a probable desire to leave some of the apparently less dangerous areas free from "bipartisan" collaboration for possible party advantage, and later, as China became a real issue, the desire to preserve party harmony by soft-pedaling any agreement with the administration. But the absence of Republicans did not mean that Democrats were actively in control of China policy. In the State Department and advising General Marshall in China were the experts themselves, in close touch with the other experts outside the government who supported them. It was the policy of these men in the Far Eastern Division which was being followed, insofar as it was supported by Marshall, and to call it the considered policy of the Democratic party would be a distortion. The Democrats in general were simply reposing personal confidence in George Marshall, or at least they felt reliant that his tremendous prestige would protect his decisions

13. Observe, for example, the double talk in this letter from Vandenberg to Senator Knowland, dated December 11, 1948, commenting on criticism from Alfred Landon, 1936 Republican candidate for President: "Mr. Landon may be of the opinion that we 'gulled' ['bipartisan'] Republicans should have yelled our heads off about China and the Generalissimo during the past year or two, but in my opinion it would only have precipitated and underscored a discussion of Chiang's weaknesses and would have nullified any remnant of his prestige. It is easy to sympathize with Chiang—to respect him . . . —as I always have and still do. But it is quite a different thing to plan resultful aid short of armed American intervention with American combat troops (which I have never favored and probably never shall). I think our China policy was wrong (and always said so) in striving to force a Communist coalition on Chiang . . . I am afraid I totally miss Mr. Landon's point when he volunteers to take Republican responsibility for these Democratic decisions which never were, and are not now, any part of the bipartisan liaison." *Ibid.*, p. 527.

14. See pp. 262–3 and 265–6; also p. 261, n. 37.

politically in 1946 and 1947. The State Department personnel in this area were glad thus to avoid having politicians mixed up in their conduct of foreign affairs; conveniently they were not under compulsion like their colleagues in the European Division to seek congressional support for legislation. Republicans, it appeared, could be safely ignored.

THE POLICY OF PEACEFUL CHINESE UNIFICATION

Foreign Service Crusaders. The chief of the Far Eastern Division was John Carter Vincent. He had been elevated to that post on the recommendation of Dean Acheson immediately after Acheson became Under Secretary of State to Byrnes in the summer of 1945. The move seems largely to have been designed to favor the "China hands" over the Japanese specialists in postwar Pacific planning; but as late as the spring of 1947 Acheson still backed Vincent enthusiastically as a man of "the finest intellectual quality," with whom "I have worked intimately." [15] Actually, Vincent, by his own admission, was so ignorant of communism in his own special field that as late as 1952 he had never bothered to read any book by a Chinese Red leader. He had spent many years in China as a Foreign Service officer and preferred to rely on his own observations.[16] Accordingly he did not believe until the middle of 1946 that the Chinese Communists were accepting guidance from Moscow.[17] Earlier he had reached the conviction, "correctly or incorrectly, [that] the worst that could happen in China in those days was the all-out civil war." [18] This was in harmony with a very widespread attitude among the China hands. Many critics have labeled this attitude procommunism; undoubtedly it did lead some of them at

15. Acheson's letter to Senator Walter George, April 18, 1947 (containing a long private memorandum defending Vincent, point by point, against most of the accusations which have since become public)—reprinted in the *Hearings* on the Institute of Pacific Relations, before the Internal Security Subcommittee of the Senate Judiciary Committee, April 8, 1952, pp. 4540–6.

16. Vincent testimony, *ibid.*, pp. 1705, 1745–6, 1783, 1949.

17. *Ibid.*, pp. 1708–10.

18. *Ibid.*, p. 1709. Vincent repeated this thought three more times in the next seven pages of testimony.

some times to regard Chinese communism as a lesser evil than the Kuomintang. But more fundamentally their fatal flaw seems to have been an extreme missionary humanitarianism, a virtue dangerously excessive for the framers of a nation's foreign policy. Herbert Feis in his masterly study of wartime diplomacy makes this observation: "[They] were moved by a longing that since China was their cause . . . it should be a worthy cause. They did not think or write solely as American officials . . . indifferent to the plight of the people of China. They wanted China to become a well-governed and well-cared-for country as well as a strong ally." [19] If Chinese well-being seemed to require a peaceful, "democratic" coalition between the Nationalists and the Communists, American policy should adjust to that situation and promote the negotiations. The thinking of *some* of the China hands went further: If the survival of Chiang Kai-shek's regime would necessitate a protracted civil war in addition to the Kuomintang's other evils, the United States should not encourage him but rather should adjust to a Communist victory.

Partly influenced by this kind of thinking—and even more, at first, by the desire to have strong Chinese assistance in the war against Japan—American policy since the middle of World War II had acquired a settled objective: the peaceful unification of the warring Chinese factions. Whoever went as chief of mission to China at the end of 1945 would be expected to pursue some variant of this established policy. But it is important to note that the Democratic administration had not *intended* to leave the experts unchaperoned by politicians. It was the understanding of both President Truman and Secretary of State Byrnes that Herbert Hoover's old Secretary of War, Patrick J. Hurley, an active Republican, would return as American Ambassador to China after convalescence in the United States in the fall of 1945. During Hurley's previous mission to China, from late 1944 to late 1945, he had shown considerably more interest than had the State Department's

19. Herbert Feis, *The China Tangle* (Princeton, Princeton University, 1953), pp. 90–1, 210–14, 270–4. The colder realities of American national interest may be subject to similar distortions in the future, especially in backward areas where the number of United States experts is very small and where human misery is so great as to arouse their *intense* sympathy.

China hands in assuring that Chiang Kai-shek's regime would be preserved in the unification which they were attempting to promote with the Communists.[20] There seems good reason to believe that these futile negotiations would have broken down sooner if Hurley had returned to China instead of General Marshall. Possibly the resulting impasse would have hastened by several months the demand for a strong pro-Chiang policy. As it was, such pressure did not arise until late in 1947, when the Nationalist position in China had already begun to sag.

The Hurley Resignation. Hurley had a chance to force the issue in December 1945, but he bungled it then, and thereafter for more than a year Marshall's prestige held full sway. Before his dramatic resignation Hurley's suspicions had been deepening regarding the State Department personnel who he thought were undercutting him; some of them seemed *too* eager to promote unity between the Nationalists and the Communists, even at the cost of the Kuomintang regime. Hurley also felt unsure of his support from the President and Secretary Byrnes. Suddenly on November 27, 1945, he submitted an angry, vituperative letter of resignation.[21] The administration was wholly unprepared; a hasty search began for a replacement with sufficient standing to repair the political damage. Within a few hours Truman's advisers had prevailed upon him to call in General Marshall. Truman, reluctant, thought the General deserved some rest, but Marshall accepted the post.[22] This was the curious combination of circumstances by which the unimpeachable George C. Marshall became a buffer for the China hands in the State Department and was put in a position to acquire those strong personal convictions about China which came to play such an important part in the domestic as well as the international politics of Chinese-American relations.

20. *Ibid.,* pp. 255–74, and *passim.*
21. The story of Hurley's resignation is well summarized in Feis, pp. 406–12. Primary source material may be found in the Hurley resignation *Hearings* of the Senate Foreign Relations Committee ("Investigation of Far Eastern Policy," mimeo., December 1945); and in Hurley's testimony at the MacArthur dismissal *Hearings* of the Senate Armed Services and Foreign Relations Committees ("Military Situation in the Far East," June 1951), pp. 2936–7.
22. Millis, *The Forrestal Diaries,* p. 113.

Patrick J. Hurley had his hearing before the Senate Foreign Relations Committee. In retrospect it is clear that his performance and Secretary Byrnes's rebuttal were of great importance, constituting until 1947 the *only* hot political battle over the State Department's conduct of relations with China. And the department appeared to win this skirmish hands down. It is tantalizing now to recognize how much validity there was in the charges Hurley was making about the attitude of Foreign Service officers—but at the same time to see how confused and unconvincing was his presentation.[23] There were a number of reasons for Hurley's failure. One was the uninformed character of the questioning to which he was subjected by the Senators. Another was his inability to secure the release of documents to support his case.[24] Hurley himself weakened his own position by hopping about from issue to issue in a virtually incoherent fashion. He clouded it further by dragging in attacks on British imperialism and conflicts in Iran. But above all, Hurley's testimony failed to win converts because his China policy was never clearly differentiated from the administration's. He still continued to advocate unification of the Nationalists and the Communists, and was able merely to allege that certain middle-level State Department personnel were undermining this official American policy in order to benefit the Chinese Reds. Hurley never seemed to recognize that the unification policy itself might be intrinsically advantageous to the Communists, that only some determined American support of Chiang's armies in civil war would suffice to preserve the foundations of the central govern-

23. *Hearings* in an investigation of Far Eastern policy, before the Senate Foreign Relations Committee, December 1945. These hearings were held in public but were never printed. Consequently, except for the relatively few specialists who have been able to consult the transcript at the committee office, the interested public has had to rely on sketchy press reports for coverage.

24. One which Hurley particularly wanted to exhibit was a Foreign Service memo which was described to the Senators by Secretary Byrnes as merely "written in rather forceful language and the conclusions it drew were rather drastic." *Ibid.*, mimeo. transcript, December 7, 1945, p. 197. Actually, the memo contained conclusions like this: "Any new [Chinese] government under any other than the present reactionary control will be more cooperative [with the United States] and better able to mobilize the country." John Stewart Service, October 10, 1944; reprinted in *Hearings* in the State Department loyalty investigation (the "Tydings-McCarthy hearings"), 1950, p. 1988.

ment. Perhaps if Hurley had gone to China in 1946 he would have come around to that view; but he made no such argument in December 1945. And without his lead there was no important Republican critic of the administration who was disposed to promote a change of official *policy* after Secretary Byrnes promised a private investigation of the personnel problem.[25] The Foreign Relations Committee voted to discontinue hearings and dispense with a report. Even Senator Bridges, who had led the GOP attackers, agreed the time was not yet ripe for a fuller investigation of the State Department.[26]

The Marshall Mission. Thus Marshall went to China with no serious congressional opposition to his mission from either party. That is important. Moreover, when he returned in March 1946 to report on his progress in secret hearings of the Foreign Relations Committee, he "got the impression" that he was "being supported," although there was "no formal expression of opinion." [27] Although of course no congressmen or other politicians actually participated in the Marshall mission, it is hard to escape the conclusion that the General was correct in his estimate of American opinion. The prevalent attitude was decidedly one of passive acquiescence. In 1946 American public discussion of the Marshall policy in China was at an absolute minimum. And what little criticism there was was pressed as vociferously from the left as from the right, even in Congress.[28]

Much has been made of the question of the authorship of the directive Marshall carried with him to China and of the influence that General Stilwell's contempt for Chiang Kai-shek may have had in prejudicing Marshall against the Generalissimo.[29] Actually

25. A superficial and ineffectual probe was conducted by the State Department's Legal Adviser. Feis, *op. cit.,* pp. 411–2.

26. *New York Times,* December 12, 1945.

27. Marshall testimony, *Hearings* on the military situation in the Far East, before the Senate Armed Services and Foreign Relations Committees, May 1951, p. 570. This statement by the General was not challenged elsewhere in the "MacArthur hearings."

28. A characteristic sortie from the left may be found in the *Congressional Record,* July 26, 1946, pp. 10223–8.

29. The drafting of the instructions is reviewed in detail in Feis, *op. cit.,* chs. xxxv and xxxvii. This record shows that the influence of Marshall and his military

it seems more important to remember that Marshall was in China for a whole year, trying to mediate between the Nationalists and the Communists to secure a government and an army in which both would participate. He had already been there eight months when in August he arranged an embargo against the shipment of combat equipment to China, in order to conciliate the Communists. And he remained in China four months after that without seeking a redefinition of his mission from Washington. In October he temporarily recommended his own recall from China on the ground that "this is the only way to halt the military campaign and to dispel the evident belief of the Government generals that they can drag along the United States while carrying out their campaign of force." Marshall went on to suggest that Truman write Chiang that he was being recalled because "there must be no question regarding the integrity of his position and actions which represent the intention and high purpose of the United States Government." [30] Surely during the months he spent in China General Marshall, however dependent upon State Department advice he may have been at the beginning, must have become sufficiently well informed about the country to bear full responsibility for persisting in the role of impartial mediator. Any recommendation from Marshall for a change in United States policy would have carried the greatest weight in Washington. American Marines were still on the scene in China; American military supplies were still coming in during most of 1946. If the policy which had been set in late 1945 had been reversed when it clearly began to break down in mid-1946, the six-month interval would probably not of itself have fatally altered the balance of forces. And by that time Marshall certainly understood what he was doing. But neither then nor later as Secretary of State did he recommend a policy decisively favoring the Nationalists *or* the Communists. The importance of that fact for the purposes of this study is that it further reduces whatever small responsibility the Democrats as a party can

aides was thrown slightly more in favor of Chiang Kai-shek's regime than the policy which was currently being promoted through the State Department by John Carter Vincent. See esp. pp. 404, 413–15, 418–20.

30. Department of State, *United States Relations with China* [the "White Paper"] (Washington, Government Printing Office, 1949), p. 192.

realistically be said to have had for China policy in the first two years after the war. Secretary Byrnes and President Truman did look in on the Far Eastern Division of the State Department late in 1945. But thereafter, with General Marshall out in front by personal conviction, the China hands in the department were almost as little troubled by Democratic as by Republican intruders.

THE STATE DEPARTMENT TRIES TO
KEEP A FREE HAND

By 1947 the period in which nothing that happened in China seemed very urgent had passed. The period in which General Marshall controlled China policy like a proconsul ten thousand miles from Washington had also passed. But still there was no move from the State Department to associate Republicans with a policy toward China. The trouble now was that the department had no policy, or, if it had, it was not a policy which officials dared to publicize.

Senator Vandenberg made this pronouncement about China at Cleveland on January 11, 1947:

> While recognizing the Nationalist government of Chiang Kai-shek, we have—through a year's mission headed by our distinguished General Marshall—been impartially urging that it produce unity with a rival armed party, the Chinese Communists.
>
> Under the determined leadership of Chiang Kai-shek, a National Assembly has just produced a new constitution and the government is being reorganized with a coalition of non-Communist parties. We can hope that this Nanking charter, with its first great national election promised before next Christmas, will weld together a strong and competent China.
>
> It is my own view that our Far Eastern policy might well now shift its emphasis. While still recommending unity, it might well encourage those who have so heroically set their feet upon this road, and discourage those who make the road precarious. Our marines, having finished their task, are coming home. But there will never be a minute when China's

destiny is not of acute concern to the United States and to a healthy world.

Surely that is not a statement which demanded *heavy* American intervention in China as the price of Republican cooperation. Vandenberg did indicate a desire for *some* intervention. Now, it may be true that Chiang could have been saved only by very large-scale intervention by the United States "beyond the reasonable limits of its capabilities" (as Acheson asserted in the 1949 White Paper).[31] But it seems to be carrying logic in the conduct of foreign affairs to self-defeating extremes to make that belief a justification for at-

31. Department of State, *op. cit.*, p. xvi.

General Marshall's explanation on this point in the 1951 MacArthur hearings is so frank that it deserves quoting at length, especially as it argues authoritatively a viewpoint which differs considerably from the one here adopted:

"The issue in my mind, as Secretary of State, was to what extent this government could commit itself to a possible involvement of a very heavy nature in regard to operations in China itself.

"The situation, the conditions as I understood them, and having been out there some time, and having officers under me pretty much all over North China reporting to me with frequency, the situation was such that we would literally have to take over control of the country in order to insure that the armies functioned with efficiency. We would have to make a very considerable initial contribution, and we would be involved in the possibility of very extensive continuing responsibilities in a very large area.

"At that time, our own military position was extraordinarily weak. I think . . . we had one and a third divisions in the entire United States. As I recall General Wedemeyer's estimates, about 10,000 officers and others would be necessary to oversee and direct those various operations. In view of our general world situation, our own military weakness, the global reaction to this situation, and my own knowledge out of that brief contact of mine in China, we could not afford to commit this government to such a procedure.

. . .

"I knew of my own knowledge the very doubtful basis on which [the Nationalist] operations and their governmental procedure rested. I knew the difficulties they would have in maintaining morale, and in maintaining their military force with any degree of fighting efficiency; and I had very decided professional military doubts as to the competence of the leadership that would have to undertake these operations.

"Now those were the problems I was struggling with personally, while I was Secretary of State, rather than the feeling on the one side of bolstering up, we will say, the Communist procedure, and the feeling on the other side, in regard to the Nationalist forces."

Hearings on the military situation in the Far East, before the Senate Armed Services and Foreign Relations Committees, May 1951, pp. 465–6.

tempting to block *all* substantial aid, in order to cut American losses. By spending expeditiously a few hundred million more on military aid, as the GOP requested, and by sending as many military advisers as could possibly be spared, the State Department in 1947 could probably still have forced the Republicans to share public responsibility for any later decision to cut the losses. In a public debate commensurate with the true importance of China, the American people would have had a chance to weigh the alternatives—to measure their national interest in Chiang's survival against the empirically demonstrated costs in United States troops and dollars. If then the American public had shown a willingness to press on, the rewards of victory or even of stalemate would have been vastly greater than was eventually the case in Korea. If, on the other hand, there was unmistakable public unwillingness to continue the costly involvement, the development of a new policy could have proceeded without the paralysis of partisan recrimination which did come in 1949 and 1950 because the responsibility for Chiang's downfall had *not* been clearly shared. Even granting the legitimate priority of an expensive build-up of Western Europe, it was politically foolhardy to allow a country as important as China to slide into unfriendly hands without any public showing of understanding and acceptance from leaders of both American parties. For the State Department—even for General Marshall— to "go it alone" was sure to invite a frustrating governmental deadlock over any future "salvage" policy in the Far East.

Suppose the State Department wanted a free hand, not because it had *no* active policy toward China in 1947–48 (on the ground that an active policy would be intolerably expensive) but because its Chinese specialists were not really much disturbed by the prospect of Chiang's collapse and were already working to promote "titoism" in China. If, in fact, that was the attitude of some of the subordinate personnel, it would again betray a failure to submit to the limitations which American democracy imposes upon the choice of foreign policies. For there was not much more prospect that a pro-Mao policy would work unless it were very actively pursued than that a pro-Chiang policy would work unless *it* were very actively pursued; and the American people could hardly have been persuaded to embrace Communist Mao at the same time they were being convinced of the wisdom of the Truman Doctrine. To be sure, pro-Mao passivity or secret activity would have stood a somewhat better chance of success than a similar private attitude toward Chiang. Tito himself was not won by active wooing. But to frame a *secret pro-Mao* policy on that hope would have been to gamble against its being paralyzed later by the predictable hardening of public opposition which would follow the failure of the *publicly* declared *pro-Chiang* policy. It seems exceedingly unlikely that such machiavellianism could succeed in the conduct of American foreign relations toward a country as important as China. And there is no convincing evidence that that is what the State Department was actually plotting in 1947 and 1948. More likely on the part of most key officials there was merely underestimation of the potential power of a Communist regime in China, and hence of its potential danger to the West—[32] coupled with an honest desire to avoid incurring further losses by seriously supporting Chiang, especially at a time when so much would also have to be spent to restore a respectable defense posture in industrial Europe. Such thinking led the State Department to avoid collaboration on China policy with Republicans during the Eightieth Congress, the last time there was much chance of bringing in the GOP before the "crash landing."

CONGRESS ACTS ON BEHALF OF CHIANG

Pressure from some Republicans for a more positive government policy in support of Chiang Kai-shek finally began early in 1947, but it cannot be said to have reached any serious proportions before Congress adjourned for the summer. The State Department

32. Along this line see George Kennan's remarks before an expert panel at the State Department, October 6, 1949, reprinted in *Hearings* on the Institute of Pacific Relations, before the Internal Security Subcommittee of the Senate Judiciary Committee, 1951, pp. 1556–65. For example, "It has been my own thought that the Russians are perhaps the people least able to combine with the Chinese in developing the resources of China and producing anything which in a physical sense would be dangerous to us." Also David Rowe's recollection of Kennan's views at the beginning of 1949, *ibid.*, pp. 3986–7.

made only three apparent concessions. One was the removal of
John Carter Vincent to Switzerland (his four-year tour of duty in
Washington was expiring anyway).[33] Another was the lifting of the
arms embargo, which enabled Nationalist China to buy weapons
in the United States if she could afford the prices. The third "concession" was the decision of Marshall, who had become Secretary
of State, to send his old protégé General Wedemeyer, in the summer of 1947, to make another up-to-date survey with recommendations on China.[34]

The Wedemeyer Report. Republican Congressman Walter Judd,
pursuing his crusade for Nationalist China, instigated the Wedemeyer mission in 1947. At least that is the view of both Wedemeyer
and Judd himself.[35] Certainly Secretary Marshall and the State
Department's Far East officials showed little interest in the report
after it was submitted, except to delete offensive portions and then
try to get Wedemeyer to sign an expurgated version for publication. Failing that, they suppressed the entire document with a
top-secret classification.[36] Like their antagonist Judd, the China
hands were apparently more interested in the domestic propaganda
value of a report from Wedemeyer than in getting a fresh appraisal
of facts. Probably they had had real hope that the wisdom of a
noninterventionist policy toward China would now reveal itself
to Wedemeyer, especially in view of his close personal relationship with Marshall. But when Wedemeyer came back emphatically
interventionist, they were not disposed to abet Walter Judd by

33. Vincent's account of the transfer is in *Hearings* on the Institute of Pacific Relations, before the Internal Security Subcommittee of the Senate Judiciary Committee, January 26, 1952, p. 1894.

34. Wedemeyer had worked very closely with Marshall in the Army General Staff
during World War II until his assignment to the Far East theater late in the war,
where he soon replaced Stilwell as Chiang's Chief of Staff. His relations with Chiang
were much better than Stilwell's. Wedemeyer returned to the United States in May
1946.

35. Wedemeyer testimony, *Hearings* on the military situation in the Far East,
before the Senate Armed Services and Foreign Relations Committees, June 1951,
pp. 2296, 2312. Interview with a source close to Judd.

36. Upon his return to Washington Wedemeyer had a talk with Marshall about
the report, but other officials of the State Department failed to consult any of the
members of the mission about the philosophy behind the recommendations. Wedemeyer testimony, *ibid.*, pp. 2365–7.

letting the report be published, even with official disclaimers and for the information of Congress.[37]

But the existence of the report was known, and its suppression aroused widespread suspicion—not, however, equal, in all probability, to the stir which friends of Nationalist China could have made if Wedemeyer's text had been available to them as a Bible. They had to rely on lesser prophets and on *indirect* communications from the greatest of them all, General MacArthur, who was still in Tokyo. Surely of the prophets who were publicly recognized to be such the one who made the first great impact on American opinion was William Bullitt. Bullitt's famous "Report on China" which was featured in *Life* in mid-October 1947 (about a month after Wedemeyer made his suppressed report) can be said to be the opening gun in the long-delayed great assault on the administration's conduct of relations with China.[38] Thereafter Henry Luce, moved undoubtedly by his long family ties with China as well as by his anticommunism, kept his publishing empire up in the vanguard of American supporters of Nationalist China. His influence in Republican party circles, especially in the

37. Senator Vandenberg's position on this China aid issue was typically ambiguous. "I never actually saw the Wedemeyer Report. But I listened to a complete paraphrase of it from General Marshall [no date indicated] and I was satisfied that its release would have been a serious blow to Chinese-American relations. It is my opinion that some of his recommendations would have gotten us into serious trouble—even the fact of their proposal." Confidential letter to Senator Knowland, December 11, 1948. Vandenberg, *op. cit.*, pp. 527–8.

38. On the key problem of military aid to Chiang, Bullitt called for American military advisers in training and operations, the immediate release of "certain stocks of munitions" by the United States, with rush delivery to Manchuria, and *direct* American military control of the Nationalist army's services of supply, but not of its army in the field. Munitions costs would be a matter of bookkeeping, but if in effect arms were given away from existing American stocks, the current costs of the operation could probably be kept under $200 million a year for three years. William Bullitt, "A Report to the American People on China," *Life,* October 13, 1947, pp. 152–4.

Wedemeyer's suppressed report had similarly urged munitions supply and American training and advisory missions down to the tactical level (for troops not currently in combat areas); he had not recommended American management of Chinese logistics, but he had recommended the potentially costly venture of a "Big 5 guardianship" over Manchuria, under the UN, to save it from the Communists. Department of State, *op. cit.*, Annex 135, pp. 810–14.

Northeast, was considerable. Here, even for those in the GOP who knew nothing about China, was a loudly anti-Communist issue which Republicans, happily uninvolved, could raise against Truman without the inhibitions which "bipartisanship" then produced regarding the Marshall Plan for Europe.[39] Governor Dewey took up the cry in two November speeches.

"Interim Aid" for China. In Congress the Republicans in the *lower* chamber were most ready to raise the new issue. President Truman had been obliged to summon a special session of Congress to meet in November to pass emergency aid legislation for Europe, prior to consideration of the full Marshall Plan. This was the so-called "interim aid" bill. Walter Judd, who had spent his vacation in the Far East and talked with MacArthur, was now determined to include China in this aid bill and in the forthcoming Marshall aid legislation. He was joined by John Vorys, but Republican leaders were divided.

Secretary Marshall tried to head off the immediate pressure by promising the Senate Foreign Relations Committee that the administration would soon submit to Congress a $300 million economic assistance program for China, to last for fifteen months.[40] That was on the same annual scale as the economic part of the aid that Bullitt was recommending. Vandenberg and his fellow Senators were willing to wait. But leading members of the House Foreign Affairs Committee were impatient. They and their colleagues reported out an interim aid bill which authorized approximately the same total as the Senate bill but added China to the list of countries to which grants could be made by immediate appropriations as soon as Marshall had formulated his program.[41]

39. There were of course also at work a few missionary and church groups and a vast variety of business interests, American and Chinese, some very probably having access to American government money once given to Chiang—all making whatever contacts they could by different techniques with different members of Congress. This has been called the "China lobby." But the fragmentary evidence available does not reveal much coordinated effort, at least before 1950. For a sensational exposé see *The Reporter*, April 15 and 29, 1952.

40. *Hearings* on interim aid to Europe, before the Senate Foreign Relations Committee, November 1947, p. 43.

41. House Report 1152 (Foreign Affairs Committee) 80th Congress, December 2, 1947, p. 14. *Congressional Record*, December 11, 1947, pp. 11296–7.

This gesture was obviously still rather tentative, and it aroused little opposition in the House. An isolationist Republican move to limit Chinese aid to $100 [*sic*] was rejected by a voice vote with little debate. In the Senate Vandenberg did not want thus to burden the European relief funds with Chinese demands. But Vorys privately pleaded with him that it was necessary in order to build up the low prestige of the House Foreign Affairs Committee, with Marshall Plan legislation in view, and that the House would be impressed if its committee succeeded in putting over a proposal which the administration was resisting and which Vandenberg did not favor.[42] Vandenberg yielded to the extent of permitting China to be included among the potential recipients of aid under the bill. But he undertook to give the appropriations committees leeway to adjust this grant to China, by providing in the final act that if China were aided under any other legislation its share of the interim aid funds could be transferred to Europe.[43]

The House Foreign Affairs Committee thus managed to get a China aid authorization, in vague terms, but no China aid appropriations came from the House Appropriations Committee to implement it. In the continued absence of a definite plan from Marshall, Chairman John Taber's committee simply omitted China from the money bill. Taber's lack of enthusiasm for spending in China, like Vandenberg's, was here visible on interim aid as it was the following year on the larger China aid bill. Similarly, Styles Bridges' stronger interest in Nationalist China was revealed on both occasions. The Senate Appropriations Committee, of which he was chairman, earmarked $20 million for China. At Vandenberg's suggestion this was changed on the Senate floor to $18 million so that it would fit the "post-UNRRA" authorization and could be used in furtherance of that specific program.[44] Here at least was a plan, without waiting for Marshall's. It was accepted

42. This is the report of a man who worked closely with the Foreign Affairs Committee.

43. *Congressional Record*, December 15, 1947, p. 11346. This was a bid for $18 million of funds authorized under the "post-UNRRA" aid bill of the preceding spring (P.L. 84), but never appropriated because the House Appropriations Committee had lost interest in granting funds to Communist Poland and Hungary.

44. *Ibid.*, December 19, 1947, pp. 11679–80.

by the House conferees. But of course it involved only minuscule economic assistance. The rapidly developing controversy was over large-scale military aid for China.

The China Aid Act of 1948. Not until mid-February 1948 did the Marshall proposals for a China aid program reach Capitol Hill, and even then they did not include any provision for military aid. But Chiang's military requirements—or at least the political pressures on his behalf in the United States—had not been entirely ignored. The $300 million figure which Marshall (and in effect Bullitt) had used in discussing economic aid in November had now been upped to a request for $570 million for fifteen months of economic assistance. This increase of $270 million almost exactly equaled the $274 million in dollar and sterling exchange which China held at the end of 1947. The idea was to enable China to use her own resources for "purchasing things for their military effort if they wished to do so." [45] But the United States government would not be thereby increasing its own military commitment in China.

Some increase in the American military commitment was, however, precisely what Chiang's congressional supporters were after. Their technique was to try to transform some of the economic aid into military aid and then to have it administered in a manner somewhat like the Greek-Turk program, i.e., with expanded American military missions, though the increasing involvement of American officers in the supervision of smaller and smaller Greek units precluded the use of any single clear model by the China bloc. The House Foreign Affairs Committee reported its China aid bill as part of an omnibus foreign aid bill which had the European recovery program as its core; the recommendation was to earmark $150 million for military aid to China under the provisions of the 1947 Greek-Turk law—leaving $420 million for economic aid, but part of that might also be diverted toward the military. The military aid provision encountered no serious opposition in the House from either party. It went through unaltered, as did the economic aid section.

45. Marshall testimony, *Hearings* on the postwar recovery program, before the House Foreign Affairs Committee, February 1948, p. 1569.

The State Department plan succeeded more easily, however, with the Senate Foreign Relations Committee. There, only executive hearings were held; on re-reading the secret transcripts in 1951 Senator McMahon reported without contradiction that "the discussion showed a complete, unanimous agreement in the committee that the Chinese situation was just hopeless." [46] The State Department's view was so prevalent that when the Foreign Relations Committee reported a separate China aid bill, the report which went to the floor with the bill was bitterly critical of Chiang Kai-shek. Chagrined at the oversight, Vandenberg ordered a more diplomatic substitute prepared the next day.[47] But the bill itself was scaled down to twelve months, unlike the fifteen for Europe, and the House's $150 million military aid fund, reduced to $100 million, was deprived of its formal military designation and made available, upon appropriation, "to the President for additional aid to China through grants, on such terms as the President may determine." [48] "On its own option and responsibility" China could use this money for military supplies, explained the revised report.[49] On behalf of the Foreign Relations Committee Vandenberg insisted, "as a matter of elementary prudence, that this process must be completely clear of any implication that we are underwriting the military campaign of the Nationalist government. No matter what our heart's desire might be, any such implication would be impossible over such a vast area." [50] Senators did not dispute the view. In the upper chamber the only vocal opposition came from a few members who thought even Vandenberg's bill went too far.

In conference the Senators prevailed on the essential points: the twelve-month program, $463 million total, lack of specifications for the "military" aid. The figure for this unrestricted grant to the President was set at $125 million—halfway between the Senate version and the House's former figure of $150 million (which was

46. *Hearings* on the military situation in the Far East, before the Senate Armed Services and Foreign Relations Committees, June 1951, p. 1903.

47. *New York Times*, March 28, 1948.

48. Senate bill 2393, 80th Congress, Section 3b.

49. Senate report 1026 (Foreign Relations Committee), 80th Congress, March 25, 1948, p. 9.

50. *Congressional Record*, March 30, 1948, p. 3668.

to have been for avowed military aid). Assistant Secretary of State Willard Thorp indicated to the House Appropriations Committee that the administration felt no responsibility for initiating, and very little for supervising, grants of aid to China under this section.[51]

House Republicans made one more effort to pin down the administration on military assistance. The House Appropriations Committee slashed the total of aid to China a bit more ruthlessly even than it did the European Recovery Program—by a rate of practically 30 per cent a month. But the $125 million military component was left relatively intact. (It would have to run for fifteen months.) Taber's drastic cut was made more palatable to the China bloc by a stipulation in the bill that the $125 million must be administered "consistent with the general objectives and limitations of the act providing for assistance to Greece and Turkey."

The administration compromised to the extent of promising the Senate Appropriations Committee that the American government would supervise Chinese military *procurement* under the $125 million section.[52] In return the Greek-Turk stipulation was removed from the appropriations bill by the Senate committee. The Senators appropriated almost exactly the full sum which had been authorized for aid to China. But in conference with the House they allowed $60 million to be slashed (a monthly rate of 13 per cent), while salvaging the $125 million special fund, now available within the shorter span of twelve months. In return, however, for the total cut, Taber's conferees gave up the Greek-Turk stipulation and accepted the vague language of the authorizing bill.

THE MALADMINISTRATION OF CHINA AID

In effect this last deal was a double victory for an administration seeking to cut losses in China. And it was a deal made by Republi-

51. *Hearings* on foreign aid appropriations, before the House Appropriations Committee, May 1948, 2, 412–13.
52. Secretary of the Army Kenneth Royall, *Hearings* on foreign aid appropriations, before the Senate Appropriations Committee, June 1948, pp. 470–1.

can leaders, especially by leaders outside the Foreign Relations Committee, where State Department seduction could more easily have been alleged. Now at last the GOP was definitely involved in a China aid policy which in all probability would prove to be too little, too late. If the administration had thereupon shown vigor and determination in administering what little Congress had provided, it might still have been possible at least to minimize the paralyzing effects of rigidly partisan recrimination when Chiang fell.[53]

But the will to make any such effort was lacking in the administration. There was no substantial expansion of the American military advisory function in China, and little effort was made to expedite arms shipments. The record of similar bureaucratic delays in the implementation of other military assistance programs to Europe and Asia in later years cautions against accusation that the administration was deliberately slowing up an unwanted program of military aid to Chiang. It is enough that the situation in China had become so desperate that if it were not treated with urgent priority, even a *show* of American effort would be nullified. But not until the end of July were the agencies agreed on a *procedure* to facilitate Chinese procurement from their own stocks. Then it was thought necessary to make availability studies. The United States was insisting on charging China full replacement costs for many kinds of equipment; so the Chinese and their American advisers had to budget carefully. Finally, a commitment was obtained to transport material free in American naval vessels; so a whole new shopping list had to be prepared in September to get utmost value from the extra funds that would now be available for the equipment itself. Not until November were substantial shipments moving.[54] During the months of delay, Chinese Communists, now

53. Actually the Republican platform adopted in that month of June 1948 contained only this polite bow toward China: "We will foster and cherish our historic policy of friendship with China and assert our deep interest in the maintenance of its integrity and freedom." Governor Dewey in his campaign spoke only vaguely of "bringing an end to the tragic neglect" of China. *New York Times,* June 23, and October 1, 16, and 28, 1948.

54. Admiral Badger, General Barr, and Senator Knowland, *Hearings* on the military situation in the Far East, before the Senate Armed Services and Foreign Relations Committees, June 1951, pp. 2749–50, 3037–8, 3043–4.

at last on the general offensive, had conquered Manchuria and placed themselves in position to begin their southward march in China, which proceeded rapidly in 1949.

By indifference if not by intention the administration had utterly bungled its chance to show that an aid program of "GOP proportions" could not save Chiang. It would still be possible for Republicans to claim that they had done their best to save China but that the Democratic administration had sabotaged their efforts. Even State Department-minded Republicans were hardly likely to offer any public defense of this failure to implement effectively the delicate compromise they had effected on China aid to placate both Walter Judd and General Marshall.

"In the years between '47 and '49 there was not a single, solitary suggestion made for the formation of policy, change of policy, or disagreement with policy [on China] by any member of this [Senate Foreign Relations] committee" in its executive sessions.[55] Content with this passive acquiescence from these few key Senators, the State Department allowed the Democratic administration to be left to take whatever public blame was America's for Chiang's eventual defeat. Long having failed to associate sympathetic men from either party *directly* with its policies of mediation or non-intervention in China, the State Department now permitted a still more divisive doubt to grow concerning the administration's good faith in carrying out the semi-interventionist program on which congressmen of both parties had compromised. Nor did the department manage by its "self-sufficiency" to preserve a free hand to frame a new policy for a new China. For in this atmosphere of mutual suspicion between the Far Eastern Division and the congressmen, especially Republicans, the collapse of all Nationalist China in 1949 brought a wave of partisan bitterness which paralyzed American policy toward China, until American troops found themselves at war with hundreds of thousands of Chinese Communists in Korea.

55. That is the statement made "without fear of contradiction" by Senator McMahon after re-reading the secret transcripts on China in those years. *Ibid.*, p. 1906.

CHAPTER 13

European Recovery and the Eightieth Congress

It is now in order to direct attention back from Palestine and China to the focal area of American foreign relations in the Eightieth Congress, which of course was Europe. The outstanding constructive developments in United States foreign policy in the two years after the enunciation of the Truman Doctrine in March 1947 were the establishment of the European Recovery Program and the beginnings of a defense structure for the Atlantic community.

The thrust of these projects was decidedly anti-Communist and anti-Russian.[1] That fact greatly facilitated the extrapartisan cooperation which would be absolutely necessary if costly action were to be taken when the GOP was in control of both houses of Congress. But the great expense of these programs and the fact that they involved extensive American commitments in Europe went against the grain of a very large section of the Republican party (a section which was glad to join in the cheers for mere anti-Communist speeches and low-priced diplomacy). Another major section of the Republican party—concentrated on the Coasts—was

---

1. Exception might be made of the brief month of June 1947 when the State Department made the gesture, hopeful or cynical, of inviting Russia to participate at the inception of the European Recovery Program. But even then Marshall's statement of his plan at Harvard was implicitly anti-Communist if not necessarily anti-Soviet. He said it was directed against "hunger, poverty, desperation, and chaos." *New York Times*, June 6, 1947.

prepared to go along with the basic proposals of the Democratic administration regarding Europe. As a result it was exceedingly difficult to achieve unity in the GOP either on a basis of resistance to, or collaboration with, the administration's programs for Europe.

The administration had a much more reliable foundation in the Democratic party in Congress. The left-wing defection of which Henry Wallace became the leader did not retain many adherents in the legislature. Therefore the Democrats had a sound basis from which to work even in a Republican-controlled Congress, if they could find eminent members of the GOP who were willing to collaborate.

In the important respect that such cooperation was usually not sought until after basic policy decisions had been reached by executive officials, the collaboration which obtained in the Eightieth Congress was usually not fully bipartisan; it was extrapartisan, with the important exception of the Vandenberg Resolution. But in the other key respect, that the administration was able to work with the officially recognized leader on foreign affairs of the opposition party in Congress, the collaboration was bipartisan. In sum, the prevailing relationship between the parties on European affairs in the Eightieth Congress was extrapartisan, but it seems to have been as close to bipartisan as is necessary or desirable. That was thanks mainly to Arthur Vandenberg.

VANDENBERG AND THE GOP LEADERSHIP IN HOUSE AND SENATE

Beyond all doubt the most important single phenomenon in the domestic politics of American foreign relations during the Eightieth Congress was the leadership of Senator Arthur Vandenberg. Essential elements of that leadership have already been reviewed,[2] and there is no need to restate them here. Suffice it to observe in summary (1) that Vandenberg was a man of vanity and ambition who found in collaboration with administration foreign policies a degree of popularity, press adulation, and "inside" influence

2. See pp. 117–19.

such as few men can ever hope to attain (much of this was the shrewd gift of the administration and especially of sympathetic publicists); (2) he possessed personal qualities of leadership, skills of compromise, great seniority, the rank of President pro tempore of the Senate, and a record of party regularity which had even included isolationism (in the GOP even the bitterest opponents of his latter-day foreign policy found it difficult to deny that he was "one of us"); (3) after 1944, and especially after 1946, there was a rapid snowballing effect whereby the prestige which he won by "unpartisan" leadership (as he liked to call it) magnified his political importance in his own party, and then in turn this partisan authority strengthened his hand for "unpartisan" national leadership.

As long as Vandenberg refrained from irrevocably committing himself on his willingness to accept the Republican presidential nomination in 1948, there was always a margin of doubt as to what strength he might command in the convention and to whom it might be thrown if he finally withdrew; yet he would not at once become a marked man whom other Republican leaders knew they would have to tackle offensively and destroy in order to secure the nomination for themselves. The most important consequence of this was Senator Taft's decision that discretion was the better part of valor in relations with Vandenberg on foreign policy. Taft resigned himself to Senate party leadership on domestic matters and rarely assumed the foremost position among the bloc of noninterventionist and economy-minded Republican congressmen who would have welcomed his abilities as their leader. That left Majority Leader Wherry as Vandenberg's most prominent GOP antagonist in the Senate. But Wherry's extremism and obvious ignorance in foreign affairs left him no match for Vandenberg in debate.

In the House there was no Republican of a prominence comparable to Vandenberg's who wanted to assume leadership on behalf of administration foreign policies. Indeed, for the first half of the Eightieth Congress, the central House leadership chose to take the position—convenient in a divided party—that a "bipartisan" foreign policy meant that party leaders should simply keep their hands off foreign policy issues. It would be left to the Foreign Affairs Committee to defend its own measures, without any formal assistance or opposition from the Republican party leadership.

But in the Senate Vandenberg was getting a majority of his fellow Republicans to go along with important foreign affairs legislation of the Democratic administration. That meant that a hands-off attitude on the part of House leaders would probably enable Democrats and their extrapartisan collaborators from among GOP Representatives to prevail in the end against the recorded opposition of a majority of the House Republicans. That was embarrassing in a Congress which was supposed to be Republican controlled.

One solution would be for the central House leadership to corral votes in *support* of Vandenberg's general position; the other would be to rally House votes *against* it, in the hope that Vandenberg ultimately would yield. If final Republican agreement between the houses could be achieved on either basis, it would at least clarify the whole party's position. House leaders in 1948 tried both devices, prudently acting in each case in response to the wishes of the standing committee immediately concerned. All went well when the House leaders supported a Foreign Affairs Committee which in turn was in general agreement with Vandenberg— on the first *authorization* for the European recovery program. But the House leaders were finally forced to withdraw in ignominious defeat when they supported an Appropriations Committee which was in fundamental disagreement with Vandenberg—on the first *appropriation* for the European recovery program. That was just before the National Convention and Vandenberg, at the zenith of his power, secured the support of all the major candidates as he enforced his policy against the will of the House leaders.

It is impossible here to show the impact of Vandenberg's leadership on all the important questions of foreign policy in the Eightieth Congress. The moderating effects of his influence on GOP China policy have been discussed (Ch. 12) and something has been said of the "peril points" compromise which he and Millikin worked out on the tariff question.[3] This chapter is primarily con-

3. See pp. 63–4.

cerned with the evolution in the Eightieth Congress of Republican collaboration on European affairs, after the Greek-Turk program set a precedent for costly aid programs to contain communism.

The "post-UNRRA" relief bill of 1947 (P.L. 84) was the last important piece of legislation on which the administration laid itself open to assault by including assistance to countries within the Russian sphere. The proposal was to spend $350 million for continuing relief requirements, estimated by UNRRA, in Austria, Greece, Italy, Hungary, Poland, and China. There was to be unilateral American supervision of expenditures, and provision was made for avoiding other features of UNRRA which Congress had found most objectionable. Nevertheless, a firm stand by Senator Vandenberg was required to save the essentials of the program, and Poland and Hungary were dropped before the program was implemented.

In the House of Representatives the authorization was cut almost in half on April 30, 1947. The Republican majority voted more than five to one to reduce the grant to $200 million. (Nearly four out of five recorded Democrats opposed the cut.) GOP members of the Foreign Affairs Committee itself were almost evenly divided; those with seniority were predominantly in favor of the reduction. In general, Republican leadership was lacking both inside and outside the committee to resist the House economizers.

In the Senate, however, Vandenberg held out firmly against any reduction. He did promise that so far as he knew there would be no more foreign relief measures in that session of Congress.[4] After such assurance so effective was Vandenberg's leadership that even Senator Taft voted against a motion to duplicate the House's cut to $200 million. Only twelve Republican Senators were recorded as favoring the cut. Nearly three times as many opposed it.

For Republicans in the House of Representatives this was a bitter pill to swallow. Most of the House managers accepted the full $350 million figure—but not John Vorys. His refusal to sign

4. *Congressional Record,* May 14, 1947, p. 5242.

the conference report precipitated another floor fight in the House on May 21. But this time three dozen members of the GOP switched sides on the issue. Their votes sufficed to enable a predominantly Democratic majority to defeat a recommittal motion which was favored by two-thirds of the House Republicans.

Certainly a major factor in this reversal was the reluctance of leading House Republicans to become publicly embroiled in a long conference battle with Vandenberg. John Taber's Appropriations Committee similarly proceeded to cut only $18 million, all of which could be assessed against Poland and Hungary; [5] this "compromise" was accepted in the Senate. But House GOP leaders in their Eightieth Congress naturally suffered some embarrassment at the Democratic "victory" on a key provision to which Republican Representatives had been overwhelmingly opposed. The experience suggested a need to reconsider the "hands-off" attitude of GOP leader Martin on foreign policy.

It also showed once more the continuing power of economy-mindedness and noninterventionism, especially when there was any possibility of dressing them in anti-Communist robes of virtue. Grants of aid to Communist countries, even when combined with much larger grants to anti-Communist nations, would furnish a talking point for the opposition in Congress and thereby multiply its effectiveness. The administration would have to avoid these ambiguities about communism if its foreign policies were to secure the support of a very large segment of the GOP in the House as well as in the Senate.

THE MARSHALL PLAN

Inventory and Organization. Surely the State Department was aware of this situation in Congress when it took the calculated risk of offering to let Russia share in the grand project for European recovery which Secretary Marshall publicized at Harvard on June 5. Probably department officials felt confident that the Soviets themselves would choose not to join any cooperative international

5. *Ibid.,* July 18, 1947, p. 9334. House Report 990 (Appropriations Committee), 80th Congress, July 18, 1947, p. 5.

venture which would breach the wall of secrecy surrounding their economy, even if it did not subject them to American financial pressure. There *was* some risk that the Russians might involve themselves in European "cooperation" just far enough to be obstructionist, but fortunately for the future of the Marshall Plan in America Molotov stood so rigidly on the principle of economic sovereignty that the foreign ministers of France and Britain did not feel obliged to prolong the effort at collaboration.

Vandenberg and other congressmen did not share in the preliminary departmental discussions which evolved the Marshall idea. The State Department under Marshall had grown quite careless, compared with the Byrnes era, about acknowledging its indebtedness to Vandenberg. Due respect, through the fostering of private consultations, was not paid till after Vandenberg had saved the "post-UNRRA" authorization late in May.[6] But in any case the repeated pleas of congressmen for "a look at the whole picture" were undoubtedly a factor in promoting the "omnibus package" aspect of the Marshall Plan in the State Department's thinking about foreign aid.

Vandenberg himself reacted sympathetically to Marshall's proposal that the European countries jointly evolve a recovery program and together submit their agreed request for American aid in implementing it. The Senator welcomed this "overall basis instead of dealing with unanticipated crises one by one." But he also offered the suggestion that there be a "sound, overall inventory of our own resources to determine the latitudes within which we may consider these foreign needs. . . . The situation invites the prompt creation of a special bipartisan advisory council at the highest attainable level as a center of coordination and as a further source of advice to both the executive and the Congress."[7]

The administration recognized that such a device would make it possible to secure the interested involvement of numerous prominent citizens, together with a mass of reports and documentation which, even if never read in Congress, would furnish physical evidence to doubters that appropriated billions were not going to be

6. James Reston, *New York Times*, June 8, 1947, sec. 4, p. 3.
7. *New York Times*, June 14, 1947.

put into the hands of ignorant bureaucrats who were just starting
from scratch to decide how to throw the money away. About a week
after Vandenberg's shrewd suggestion the President announced
the appointment of three major committees to investigate different
aspects of the aid program. The Krug Committee, under the chairmanship of the Secretary of Interior, was to consider the capacity
of American resources for large-scale foreign aid—and dispose of
the argument that the physical costs would be too great. The President's Council of Economic Advisers would study the impact of
the program on the domestic economy and demonstrate that the
economy could stand it, perhaps with some controls required. The
third and most important of the committees, that headed by Secretary of Commerce Harriman, was a nongovernmental committee
of distinguished private citizens from different fields of economic
and academic endeavor. They were to make an independent over-
all survey in order to advise the President on the proper limits of
the aid program—and incidentally become convinced themselves
and convince their influential business associates of the merits of
the scheme.

Of course suspicion was widespread that these investigations—
even that of the "independent" Harriman Committee—would
amount to mere whitewash of the State Department's program.
Among Republicans in the House of Representatives particularly
there was sentiment for a more fully independent congressional
investigation of the whole project. At the same time there was a
complementary desire on the part of some friends of the Marshall
Plan to promote better understanding of the enterprise among a
broad cross section of leading Representatives, not just among
members of the weak Foreign Affairs Committee; perhaps some
of the doubters might be won over and some adversaries be muted.
Moreover, there was the added appeal to all sides in the House
that such a committee, if it really mastered the facts on foreign aid,
would be better able than the House Foreign Affairs Committee
alone to stand up to the august Senate Foreign Relations Committee—and perhaps through it to the State Department.

These arguments, especially the anti-administration demand for a double check, persuaded the GOP House leadership to put through a resolution from the Rules Committee on July 22 establishing a Select Committee on Foreign Aid. Its investigative mandate was broad, it was given plenty of money, and it acquired a good staff for its overseas task forces as well as for the major research job in Washington. Nineteen members were appointed by the Speaker and the Minority Leader so as to secure able and influential representation from the major standing committees—but not, at least on the Republican side, in such a way as to favor any large foreign aid program.

The Herter Committee's recommendations came out in a series of interim reports. The most important—at least from the viewpoint of domestic politics and administration—was unquestionably that which called for the administration of Marshall aid, especially in the form of food, fuel, and fertilizer, through an independent government corporation, to be newly established under the title of Emergency Foreign Reconstruction Authority. The corporation would have a bipartisan board of directors appointed by the President and confirmed by the Senate; one of them would be designated as chairman and chief executive officer.[8] It was thought that this device would attract expert business leadership to the control and operation of the big aid program. Businessmen would be tough minded toward foreigners, creative activists in philosophy (rather than utopian exponents of nineteenth-century "free trade") and be free of diplomatic restraints on agents out in the field. In short they would be what the reconstruction job demanded and the Foreign Service could not supply. Of course it was no accident in this Republican proposal that the administration of billions of dollars would be removed as far as possible from the Democratic President and his Secretary of State. In October and November Governor Dewey and his financial backer Winthrop Aldrich of the Chase National Bank offered similar proposals.[9]

The State Department and the Budget Bureau, however, naturally protested that this would be bad administrative practice,

8. *Ibid.*, November 8, 1947.
9. *Ibid.*, October 1 and November 6, 1947.

that, in Marshall's famous phrase, "there cannot be two Secretaries of State." [10] Inside the congressional Republican party, too, there were specialized objections. The corporate device would probably by-pass the appropriations committees and deprive them of their normal "second look" at spending proposals; the mere authorization of capital would be sufficient to keep the aid business running. Neither Vandenberg nor Eaton wanted to alienate appropriations chairmen Bridges and Taber by sponsoring such a proposal, and House leaders Martin and Halleck tried to discourage Herter from making this and other recommendations.[11]

Vandenberg hit upon the happy expedient of commissioning the eminently respectable Brookings Institution to devise a compromise administrative scheme.[12] Late in January Brookings recommended an agency separate from the State Department but noncorporate in form, under a single administrator of Cabinet rank. The Secretary of State would have the right of appeal to the President when he and the administrator were unable to agree on matters of mutual concern.[13] Vandenberg was satisfied with this compromise, and its timing helped to weaken an incipient "revisionist" GOP bloc in the Senate, which was just getting organized to present Vandenberg with agreed, drastic amendments to the whole recovery program, and would appeal to him to support the changes for the sake of party unity.[14] These opposition Senators continued their fight on other grounds, but less powerfully than had been feared. Secretary Marshall promptly accepted the new administrative plan, and it was approved by Herter within two weeks.[15] The dispute over organizational plans soon subsided, though there were still some later adjustments in detail.

By calling in the Brookings Institution, as by suggesting the two-party Harriman Committee, Vandenberg had skillfully moved to

10. *Hearings* on the European Recovery Program, before the Senate Foreign Relations Committee, January 1948, p. 9.
11. Interviews with leading members of the Herter Committee and its staff. Martin's coolness to the corporation plan is also indicated in the *New York Times*, November 8, 1947.
12. *Ibid.*, January 3, 1948.
13. *Ibid.*, January 25, 1948.
14. *Ibid.*, January 27, 1948.
15. *Ibid.*, January 29 and February 11, 1948.

forestall opposition to the European Recovery Program as a whole by nullifying in advance the criticisms easiest to answer. In April he further bolstered the standing of the Economic Cooperation Administration for the arduous appropriations battle which was still to come by securing the appointment of liberal businessman Paul Hoffman as chief of the fledgling agency.[16]

Getting the Money Authorized. The foremost struggle over the European Recovery Program came, as was to be expected, on the question of money—how much aid was to be given. Whatever particular objections might be offered to special aspects of the enterprise, the primary goal of critical congressmen was to cut the total.[17] That seemed especially important to a Republican Congress whose members were determined to carry out their pre-election promises to cut taxes while still balancing the budget. Even though the government was running a large surplus at existing tax rates, a very expensive foreign aid program would jeopardize the plan to reduce revenue. But in spite of this strong incentive no serious reduction was made by the Republican Congress in the administration's projected spending for European recovery. In producing this result Senator Vandenberg's leadership reached its highest point. He was aided of course by the war scare of early 1948, by the plainly anti-Communist character of the Marshall Plan as it developed at the end of 1947, by the absence of any conspicuous

16. Vandenberg, *The Private Papers of Senator Vandenberg*, pp. 393–4.

17. An issue which attracted particular attention from the Republicans during the European recovery debates was the revival of Germany. This was mainly a consequence of the existence of large German-American voting groups in the Republican Central States, and of the appeal of the economy argument to "get Germany off the American taxpayer's back" and restore German productiveness "for the sake of European prosperity." It also undoubtedly reflected pure humanitarian compassion for the horrifying conditions in occupied Germany before 1948. As the months went by there was also an increasing interest expressed by business and military men who sought profits and allies in Western Germany.

But even the Republicans were not united on German recovery. John Foster Dulles came to be regarded as a "France-firster" and thereby came into some conflict with General Clay in Germany. Dulles' position was closer to the State Department's, and Senator Vandenberg generally shared their cautious concern for the opinion of other European countries. But the Republican Appropriations Committees became pro-German strongholds; there the nationality influences from the Midwest were especially potent.

major failure in American foreign policy for which the administration could be blamed exclusively, and by the continuing Coast-Interior cleavage in the GOP which gave him a bloc of Coastal Republican votes on which he could rely when soliciting other support in his party.

The first major engagement came on the Interim Aid legislation in the late fall of 1947. On the appeal of the State Department —Vandenberg refusing to take an initiative—Truman had been persuaded to call the "second worst Congress in American history" back into session. The President struck a note which Republicans at least regarded as partisan when he appealed for the passage of an anti-inflation program of controls legislation. But the main objective of the special session was to secure emergency aid funds for France, Italy, and Austria to meet their balance-of-payments difficulties by keeping the "pipelines" full of relief goods until Congress could study and approve the grandiose Marshall Plan.

The Senate Foreign Relations Committee promptly voted out a bill which seconded the State Department's major requests. On the floor Vandenberg spoke very strongly for the full $597 million figure, but both he and Connally commented that the Appropriations Committee would later have a chance to screen it further.[18] A group of noninterventionist Republican Senators sponsored an amendment to cut the total authorization to $400 million. None of these men was a leader in the upper chamber, but they had the support of Senator Taft, even though he did not go so far as to co-sponsor this vital amendment to which Vandenberg was opposed. The proposed reduction was defeated, 56-30, with the recorded Republicans voting 27-20 against it.

The House Foreign Affairs Committee waited until the day after Senate approval of the bill and then reported an authorization of $590 million, which was to include China.[19]

In the House Representative Vorys, who was managing the interim bill, privately appealed to Speaker Martin for the assistance of the House leadership. The embarrassment of the "post-UNRRA" bill in May was not repeated. With the assistance of the

18. *Congressional Record*, November 26, 1947, p. 10907.
19. See p. 262.

leaders it was possible to dispose of every amendment and then pass the bill without a single record vote being taken. Whatever might finally be decided in conference and by the Appropriations Committees, no Representative would endure the shame of having to change his vote in public. When the Conference Committee reported back the Senate figure of $597 million (China now included) [20] the House of Representatives finally went on record. The report was approved, 313-82, with Republicans recorded more than 2 to 1 in its favor. (Democrats were nearly unanimous.)

The appropriations hurdle was still to be faced. Taber's committee cut the total to $509 million. On the original theory of the House Foreign Affairs Committee that $60 million should go to China out of their House-approved recommendation of $590 million, Taber's cut represented only $21 million less than Europe "deserved" (in the continued absence of a specific administration program for China). But this House of Representatives theory had not been endorsed in the vague language about China which came out of conference with Vandenberg and his fellow Senators. Nevertheless, Foreign Affairs Committee members now tried only to raise Taber's appropriation by $26 million. They failed even in that attempt, by a voice vote. [21]

The Senate Appropriations Committee upped the European aid grant to $550 million and threw in $20 million more for China. Vandenberg did not resist the reduction which this still represented from the original authorization of $597 million. Nor did any Senator wage a floor battle when Bridges yielded more than half way to Taber in conference over the European appropriation ($522 million agreed), in order to secure immediately $18 million for China. [22]

Ultimately Vandenberg and the administration may be said to have prevailed anyway, for in the crisis atmosphere of March 1948 the House Appropriations Committee agreed to appropriate $55 million more of interim aid funds. The full House and the upper

20. See pp. 263-4.
21. *Congressional Record*, December 17, 1947, p. 11543.
22. The conference report was accepted without Senate debate or record vote in an adjournment rush on December 19, 1947.

chamber promptly followed suit. That brought the total for Europe back to $577 million. Only the grant which went to China separated this sum from what the State Department had originally requested in November 1947.

Immediately after passage of the main Interim Aid appropriation late in December 1947, the administration submitted its plans for the Marshall Plan of European recovery. The initial request was for a four-year authorization of $17 billion. Executive officials were soon persuaded to drop the specific figure from the long-range authorization.[23] But Vandenberg and the rest of the Foreign Relations Committee did not insist on abandonment of the four-year "continuing authorization," provided that no specific sums were authorized beyond the first year of the program. Thereafter, unless special new legislation should be introduced, the Appropriations Committees would have full charge of financing the Marshall Plan. This arrangement proved acceptable to the Senate and was not challenged by proposed amendments on the floor.

In the House, however, resistance to the concept of a four-year program was greater. Herbert Hoover had protested formally on January 21 against "even a moral commitment" to four years of the Marshall Plan.[24] In the Foreign Affairs Committee Republican leader John Vorys was an enthusiastic supporter of the integrated, long-term approach, as contrasted with "New Deal muddling," but he and his fellow committeemen had special reasons also for wanting to avoid a direct four-year authorization, even though the sum was to be left indefinite. The Foreign Affairs Committee was frankly afraid that the Appropriations Committee, acting in secret, would assume full control of the program after the first year.[25] Vandenberg's powerful Foreign Relations Committee could perhaps afford to take that risk, but not their weak counterpart in the House. Therefore the Foreign Affairs Committee struck a compromise in its own interest. The four-year concept was retained in an expression of "congressional intention," but there would have

23. *New York Times*, December 20, 1947 and January 6, 1948.
24. *Ibid.*, January 22, 1948.
25. Representative Mundt, *Congressional Record*, March 31, 1948, p. 3834.

to be a new authorization bill as well as a new appropriations bill for each of the four years of the program.[26]

This modification of the four-year principle was not sufficient to satisfy all members of the House. On the floor Lawrence Smith, isolationist member of Foreign Affairs, sponsored an extra sentence declaring that the act placed no "legal or moral obligation upon any succeeding Congress to continue the present aid program beyond twelve months." This move was defeated by the close teller vote of 127-117.[27] The attitude of the House and especially of its self-conscious Foreign Affairs Committee was so clearly in favor of *some* modification of the Senate's straight four-year authorization that Vandenberg yielded in conference and accepted the Representatives' language on this point. There would be annual authorizations as well as appropriations during the four-year period.[28]

Removal of the $17 billion figure and adjustment of the authorization period were only two of the changes in Marshall Plan financing which Republican friends of the program developed in order to save the essentials. Others included a budgetary trick sponsored by Chairman Millikin of the Finance Committee; its effect was to shift the fiscal year a little so as to conceal the impact of Marshall Plan expenditures.[29] And GOP members of the House Foreign Affairs Committee prescribed that $1 billion of the authorization should be handled as a public debt transaction—not by appropriations in the regular budget.[30] This was another useful palliative. But there was also a frontal attack to be faced.

Organization of the opposition to the Marshall Plan in the Republican party began early in January. It took the form in the Senate of "revisionism," not die-hard resistance, but the revisions

26. *Congressional Record*, March 31, 1948, p. 3829. House Report 1585 (Foreign Affairs Committee), 80th Congress, March 20, 1948, p. 95.

27. *Ibid.*, March 31, 1948, pp. 3828–32.

28. Vandenberg, *Congressional Record*, April 2, 1948, p. 4034. House Report 1655 (Conference Committee), 80th Congress, April 1, 1948, pp. 15, 31.

29. *New York Times*, February 18, 1948.

30. House Report 1585 (Foreign Affairs Committee), 80th Congress, March 20, 1948, p. 36.

which were sought cut to the heart of the program. Numerous specific alterations were demanded; some of them were ultimately accepted. The major objective of the opposition was to reduce expenditures. The press noted the first meeting of about twenty "revisionist" Senators on January 13. They definitely constituted the familiar bloc of Republicans whose noninterventionism and economy-mindedness had long been recognized. The conspicuous exceptions to this rule were Joseph Ball of Minnesota and William Knowland of California. Majority Leader Wherry associated himself frankly with the "revisionists," but Taft remained cautiously on the sidelines until the crucial Senate debate on reduction of the authorization.

Vandenberg promptly stole much revisionist thunder by his Brookings compromise on administration of the European Recovery Program, but the opposition bloc was buttressed on January 21, when Herbert Hoover appealed for reduction of the administration's projected $6.8 billion for *fifteen* months to just $4 billion for the same period.[31] More gains were made on January 26 when Senator Bridges, chairman of the Appropriations Committee, protested vehemently against the administration's request for $6.8 billion. He noted that the official figures showed that only $4.5 billion were actually to be spent on ERP during the first fifteen months. Why was an additional $2.3 billion needed just to permit advance contracts for the following year?[32]

That seemed a strong argument. The very next day, however, Foreign Relations Committee members informally raised a trial balloon to dodge Bridges' criticism. They began to talk of revising the administration's fifteen-month specific authorization to an equivalent specific authorization for twelve months.[33] That would mean that the whole program could be reviewed promptly after the presidential election. It could easily be altered if the new administration and Congress (presumably Republican) should then wish to reject all the masses of evidence which the various Truman committees had accumulated to support the current estimates. In

31. *New York Times*, January 22, 1948.
32. *Ibid.*, January 27, 1948.
33. *Ibid.*, January 28, 1948.

the meantime Democrats would not be able to pin a label of "too little, too late" on Republicans. Vandenberg later explained to the Senate:

> If it fails, let the responsibility rest elsewhere. I say again, as I have said so many times before, these recommended figures are not sacred. But in the light of the powerful credentials they possess, unless the Appropriations Committee can strongly prove them wrong, let us give them the benefit of any doubts for the time being. Next January is not long to wait for the accounting with so much at stake.[34]

On February 13 the Foreign Relations Committee voted unanimously to recommend a specific authorization of $5.3 billion for twelve months instead of $6.8 billion for fifteen months. This was a reduction in dollars of a little more than the one-fifth reduction in time, but it did accurately reflect what the administration had actually planned to use for spending and advance contracts in the first twelve months of a program which would be mounting in tempo thereafter.[35] No real reduction had been made, only another bit of tailoring.

The great test in the Senate came on March 12. Taft himself emerged to do battle against Vandenberg's cohorts. In a long speech he defended his own amendment to cut the twelve-month authorization to $4 billion. His objective, he said, was to hold all foreign expenditures within the existing total rate of $5 billion a year. Projected ERP spending would drive the total much higher unless reductions were made.[36] Friends of the program replied that an increase now would bring recovery, not just relief, to Europe, and permit real reductions in later years. On the roll call Vandenberg prevailed. Taft's amendment was defeated, 56-31, but so close was the division in the Senate GOP that only one more Republican voted against it than voted for it. The careful groundwork which Vandenberg had laid was really needed.

Under the circumstances, prospects for the full authorization in

---

34. *Congressional Record,* March 1, 1948, p. 1919.
35. *Ibid. New York Times,* February 14, 1948.
36. *Congressional Record,* March 12, 1948, pp. 2641–50.

the House could hardly be regarded as favorable. The country had been deeply shocked by the Communist seizure of Czechoslovakia at the end of February 1948, and there was growing awareness of the importance of the Italian election scheduled for April. But even extensive leaks from the Pentagon had not yet conveyed very widely the extreme apprehension which stirred administration circles when General Clay cabled from Germany early in March that "a new tenseness in every Soviet individual with whom we have official relations . . . gives me a feeling that [war] may come with dramatic suddenness." [37] Not until March 16 was the Central Intelligence Agency able to give President Truman a brief estimate from the armed services and the State Department that war was unlikely within the next sixty days. [38]

A couple of days before, without warning to congressional leaders, Truman had arranged to address a joint session of House and Senate on March 17. [39] The President struck a note of crisis and asked for speedy enactment of selective service, universal military training, and the European recovery program.

In this crisis atmosphere the House leadership was stirred to vigorous action on behalf of ERP. At least, foreign aid was less objectionable than UMT and the draft. Vorys and Eaton and other Foreign Affairs Committee members had been in frequent consultation with Speaker Martin and Majority Leader Halleck. Now it was decided to hasten action on the recovery program. On March 19, two days after Truman's speech, the Foreign Affairs Committee approved its bill. There would be $4.3 billion in appropriations and another $1 billion in borrowed money for Europe —a total of $5.3 for twelve months, the Senate figure. There would also be other money for China, Greece, Turkey, and the International Children's Emergency Fund. On straight party lines the Foreign Affairs Committee thus decided to "package" almost all foreign aid. [40] House Republicans felt that more votes would be gained than lost by associating the military aid programs with the economic aid programs for Europe. Vandenberg and the State De-

37. Millis, *The Forrestal Diaries*, p. 387.
38. *Ibid.*, p. 395. Not until April 2 did CIA extend its no-war prediction beyond sixty days and even then the air force was unwilling to go along. *Ibid.*, p. 409.
39. *New York Times*, March 16, 1948.
40. *Ibid.*, March 20, 1948.

partment resisted this move, but it prevailed, and it did help ERP in the House. After a meeting of the Republican Policy Committee the Rules Committee on March 22 scheduled almost a week of House debate on foreign aid—the votes to be taken after the Easter week end, so that Representatives might have a chance to consult their constituents.[41]

Herbert Hoover entered into the new spirit of the occasion by writing a letter to Speaker Martin, which floor manager Vorys read to the House early in the debate. It contained an endorsement of the full $5.3 billion total authorization for ERP as "a major dam to Russian aggression." (The effect of this was somewhat qualified by Hoover's explicit emphasis on later review by the Appropriations Committee.) [42]

The amendment to reduce the authorization came to a vote on March 31 and was disposed of without a roll call; a standing vote of 112-61 blocked a cut equivalent to the one which Taft had vainly pushed in the Senate. Then the "package" authorization for foreign aid went through on a roll call, 329-74. Republicans voted almost three to one in its favor, Democrats almost unanimously.

With the assistance of Vandenberg and other Republican leaders the administration had finally secured an authorization for European recovery which was essentially the equivalent of its original request. A major battle had been won, but the climactic engagement —on appropriations—was still to come.

Getting the Money Appropriated. By the end of May 1948 international tension had greatly subsided. On June 3 John Taber's committee dared to report a foreign aid appropriations bill which had the effect of reducing ERP funds by almost as large a margin as the cuts which had been rejected by both Senate and House when they were making the authorization. This was accomplished by complex devices; the major features were extension of the period in which funds were to be spent to fifteen months (without of course increasing the funds), and a requirement that Japanese recovery be financed out of the same appropriation.

The central House leadership which had supported the Foreign Affairs Committee in March now supported the very different

41. *Ibid.*, March 23, 1948.
42. *Congressional Record*, March 24, 1948, pp. 3435–6.

recommendations of the Appropriations Committee. In a single day, without a single record vote, the money bill was put through the House. The test came on an amendment sponsored by Dirksen, who was a member of the Appropriations Committee, to restore the twelve-month period, so that funds would not have to be stretched through fifteen months. Dirksen was defeated on a standing vote, 148-113. When the Committee of the Whole had risen and record votes were in order, Clarence Cannon, ranking Democratic member of the Appropriations Committee, asked for the yeas and nays on a motion to recommit the bill, with the object of securing a larger appropriation, but not even one-fifth of the congressmen present were willing to support his request; hence there was no record vote at all.[43] Such a result would hardly have been possible without active intervention by the leaders of both parties —the Democrats presumably preferring to take their chances in conference with the Senate under conditions where Taber's bill had not been "nailed down" through a record vote; the Republican leaders wishing to avoid explicit advertisement of the continuing division on foreign policy in GOP House ranks. Since the powerful Appropriations Committee would have the support of a *majority* of the Republican Representatives, the strategy of Martin and Halleck was evidently to minimize and then to hide the faction in their own party which opposed Taber's foreign aid reduction.

But Martin and Halleck had to pay a price for promoting superficial party unity in the House by supporting Taber. The price was to find themselves aligned with Taber in an all-out struggle with Vandenberg where ultimately every major Republican candidate for the impending presidential nomination took a stand on the other side. For in the Senate Vandenberg determined to make a fight to restore the ERP funds, even though it would place him in direct conflict with the GOP House leadership just before the Republican National Convention. He was more aggressive on this issue than he had indicated in March he would be.[44] That embittered many of his opponents in both chambers.

43. *Ibid.,* June 4, 1948, p. 7213.
44. Vandenberg had given Chairman Bridges of the Senate Appropriations Committee this assurance and warning when the Taft amendment was before the Senate

Vandenberg asked Bridges' permission to make a personal appearance before an open session of the Senate Appropriations Committee to protest the House cut. He received his opportunity on June 9. As spectacular political drama it was probably the climax of Vandenberg's career. Two days earlier two leading presidential candidates had endorsed his position in advance, condemning the House cut. They were Dewey and Stassen. Taft had not ventured to approve Taber's action. Vandenberg's immediate objective was mainly to reinstate a *twelve*-month period for the expenditure of the reduced funds. His chief argument was that drastic general reductions between authorizations and appropriations would upset programs in European countries which had been undertaken on the basis of the earlier expectations.

The Senate Appropriations Committee under Chairman Bridges agreed to adopt the twelve-month period and proceeded to restore enough of the specific cuts to make the committee's action an emphatic victory for Vandenberg's position. He pressed it home on the Senate floor by demanding a record vote to affirm the restoration of the twelve-month period. Only ten Republicans voted against him. Both Taft and Wherry cast their votes on Vandenberg's side.[45]

Taber was not so easily moved. Even though he had no record vote in the House to sustain him on the time question, as the Senators had, he held out for nearly five days of conferences. The Republican National Convention was about to begin, and Taber doubtless hoped that the Senators would ultimately make major concessions in a rush to get away. Senator Taft finally destroyed

---

in March: "The Senator from New Hampshire [Bridges] is asking me about the function of the Appropriations Committee. . . . I consider that the committee has not only a freedom to act but a responsibility to act. When the committee acts, if the Senator from New Hampshire and I disagree about the ultimate figure, it will be a legitimate subject again of debate; and I am sure the Senator from New Hampshire will concede that. But there will be no recrimination from the Chairman of the Foreign Relations Committee . . . if the figure is changed, although of course I must emphasize that in the opinion of the Chairman of the Foreign Relations Committee the figure of $5,300,000,000 is essential, up to at least the time when the next Congress can audit the whole enterprise in January of 1949." *Ibid.,* March 12, 1948, p. 2707.

45. *Ibid.,* June 15, 1948, pp. 8309–10.

this hope. He announced on June 18 that he was willing to hold
Congress in session as long as was necessary to sustain the original
"moral commitment" on ERP.[46] Taft went even further: Vandenberg's diary records a Taft "statement to me" about this time
"that he would wish me to be his Secretary of State." [47] Taft
aligned himself as vigorously as he could at that late date in support of Vandenberg's position on European recovery appropriations. All the other major presidential candidates had already taken
their places in the same line-up on that issue. Taber finally yielded
to the pressure. He was granted a face-saving "compromise" that
the new President would have to make a special determination
that there was need to spend the money in twelve months instead
of fifteen; a Republican President might decide that it could be
made to last longer. Taber, further, withdrew from his inclusion
of Japan under the European appropriations; other funds were
found for her.

The House approved the conference report on June 20 by a roll
call vote of 318-62. Republicans voted more than three to one in
its favor. As the Senate approved the report by a voice vote, Vandenberg observed: "The conferees have done a splendid piece of
constructive work which maintains the full spirit of this great
enterprise." He paid a special compliment to Appropriations
Chairman Senator Bridges "for what I know has been his stalwart
loyalty to a great ideal." [48]

It was clear that during the many months of work on ERP not
only Bridges but numerous other Republicans had contributed
assistance and suggestions which facilitated the ultimate passage
of virtually the full European Recovery Program. The initiative
had been the administration's, but the defense was mainly in the
hands of friendly Republicans. And Vandenberg himself was
surely the decisive figure among them. Without his powerful efforts
the outcome could hardly have been so favorable to the administration.

46. *New York Times,* June 19, 1948.
47. Vandenberg, *op. cit.,* p. 438.
48. *Congressional Record,* June 19, 1948, p. 9123.

THE VANDENBERG RESOLUTION

Vandenberg finally had a chance to receive full credit for a major piece of foreign affairs legislation with the passage of the "Vandenberg Resolution" on June 11, 1948. This may fairly be called a bipartisan rather than merely an extrapartisan enterprise in foreign policy. Vandenberg was certainly the recognized leader of his party on foreign affairs in Congress, in form as well as in fact, and Dulles was the foreign policy confidant of Thomas E. Dewey, titular head of the Republican party and active candidate for renomination. Both men were formally and seriously consulted before the administration committed itself by public pronouncements or by diplomatic exchanges to any formal association with a West European defense pact. Moreover, the shape of the initial commitment when it did come was established in consultation with Vandenberg and other members of the Senate Foreign Relations Committee, and unanimously sponsored by them.

It is true that before Vandenberg was brought into the enterprise the administration had already decided to take some action, but apparently no irrevocable commitment had been made; so the Republicans were really in a position to influence policy privately in advance, not merely to offer assistance at a price after the administration had already taken a plunge. In that important respect the Vandenberg Resolution, foreshadowing the Atlantic Pact, differed from the ERP and even more from other postwar foreign aid programs, resembling, rather, the preparation for the United Nations Charter. However, there were also some differences between the UN planning and the Atlantic Treaty planning—notably the failure to bring in the House of Representatives at the congressional resolution stage and later the suspension of negotiations during an election campaign, followed by a long delay in resumption of bipartisan collaboration while the international discussions proceeded to an advanced stage. In organizing the UN more continuous care was taken to preserve and foster bipartisan collaboration.

The development of the North Atlantic Treaty began with the organization of the five-power West European defense pact in the winter of 1948. At first it was composed of Britain, France, and the Low Countries, but by March 12 British Foreign Secretary Ernest Bevin was urgently proposing to Marshall the development of an Atlantic security arrangement.[49] In succeeding weeks the Canadians pressed as hard as the British for some form of Atlantic alliance which would include the United States.

During Senate consideration of the ERP bill Arthur Vandenberg vigorously and successfully resisted the inclusion there of any proposals for new international political organizations. However, he spoke of the possibility of new regional arrangements like the Rio Treaty, and described as an "inevitable responsibility" the development of "reorganized, stabilized, and vitalized mechanisms of an instrumentality for international security which will deliver the goods." [50]

In his crisis address to Congress on March 17 President Truman referred to the "great significance" of the five-power pact signed in Brussels that same day; he expressed confidence that America would, "by appropriate means, extend to the free nations the support which the situation requires . . . I am sure that the determination of the free countries of Europe to protect themselves will be matched by an equal determination on our part to help them to do so." Staff men from the State Department and Senate Foreign Relations Committee went to work privately to produce a draft resolution. Under Secretary of State Lovett worked intimately with Vandenberg, formulating plans and making revisions, at the Senator's home as well as his office.[51] By April 22 Lovett was able to report to the National Security Council that the Senate and the President would be asked for "a statement that we were willing to consider, under Article 51 of the United Nations, steps looking

49. Millis, *The Forrestal Diaries*, p. 392.
50. *Congressional Record*, March 3, 1948, pp. 2025-9 and March 13, 1948, p. 2747.
51. Vandenberg, *op. cit.*, pp. 404-6.
Robert Lovett's importance in extrapartisan consultations in the 80th Congress was very great. He got along well with Vandenberg and was a frequent visitor at the Senator's apartment. He was widely respected by other members of Congress, where his conservative background as a Wall Street banker was a political advantage in this period. At the State Department Lovett usually exerted great influence on Marshall's policies and was himself Acting Secretary of State during Marshall's long absences at international conferences.

to the construction of a regional agreement, if it proves to be in the interests of the security of the United States." Forrestal's diary note on this continued: "The tactics would be to have this action initiated by the Republicans and to have the ball picked up immediately by the President, who would state his interest in the plan and make some further appropriate comments." [52]

Formal implementation of this tactical plan included the summoning of John Foster Dulles from his vacation hideout to join Vandenberg, Lovett, and Secretary Marshall at an important Blair House conference on April 27. There Lovett explained his view that the rising tide of fear in Europe could best be halted by a regional pact modeled on the Rio Treaty. Vandenberg generally concurred and produced the draft of a Senate resolution on which he had been working with the Under Secretary. Dulles "was at first doubtful about so formal a treatment of the situation. I knew that it would be difficult to draw the line for inclusion within, and exclusion from, the pact and thought at first that it might be better to start our European commitment by a Presidential Declaration like that of President Monroe. It could perhaps be formalized later." [53] But the State Department already had Vandenberg's approval for the broad concept of regional association; so consultation with other members of the Foreign Relations Committee could proceed on that basis.

The members agreed to lay the congressional groundwork for an Atlantic regional arrangement in the same Senate resolution which would soothe some strong agitation for revision of the United Nations Charter. On May 19 the Foreign Relations Committee unanimously reported out the "Vandenberg Resolution." Most of it dealt with the United Nations and consisted of little more than pious hopes. But the crucial paragraphs declared that

52. Millis, *The Forrestal Diaries*, p. 423. Lovett explained privately to Forrestal the next day that the United States was not yet deeply committed. "The whole point of the conversations" then in progress with the European powers was "to make it clear that we were not willing to become bound to an unequivocal contract to come to their assistance unless and until they manifested a desire to help themselves." If they did, Lovett envisaged military lend-lease of "not less than $3 billion." *Ibid.*, p. 425.

53. Dulles, *War or Peace*, p. 96. Vandenberg, *op. cit.*, p. 406.

the American government should foster "the progressive development of regional and other collective arrangements for individual and collective self-defense in accordance with the purposes, principles, and provisions of the Charter," and should promote "association of the United States, by constitutional process, with such regional and other collective arrangements as are based on continuous and effective self-help and mutual aid, and as affect its national security." The committee's report emphasized that each of these last phrases constituted an important condition which would limit American commitments.[54]

When the resolution came up in the Senate on June 11 the isolationist members who might have been expected to oppose it did not do so. For the most part they simply abstained, both from the debate and from the roll calls—thereby paying their respects to Vandenberg on a measure which would have no *legal* effect anyway. Claude Pepper was left to conduct most of the opposition; he was attacking from a left-wing position which by that time was almost idiosyncratic in the Senate. Only six members were recorded in favor of his amendment to delete the key sections on regional arrangements. Only six went on record against final passage. Wherry supported the resolution, but Taft and other Midwestern Republicans were notably absent. Seventy-nine Senators, however, stood with Vandenberg when the votes were cast or announced. That was certainly an impressive victory to climax the first stage of bipartisan collaboration in building a North Atlantic defense organization.

SUMMARY

Thus at the end of the Eightieth Congress the extrapartisan collaboration on European affairs which had been developing since the administration agreed to "get tough with Russia" culminated

54. Senate Report 1361 (Foreign Relations Committee), 80th Congress, May 19, 1948, p. 6. In addition to whatever power might accrue from new regional arrangements there was an immediate warning to the Russians that they could not expect to nullify resistance to their aggression by using their Security Council veto. The American government was to make "clear its determination to exercise the right of individual or collective self-defense under Article 51 should any armed attack occur affecting its national security."

in bipartisan initiation of formal steps toward some kind of American alliance with Western Europe. The two-party agreement which made this possible had been spurred on by a shared sense of urgency regarding Communist pressure in Europe which was far more widespread than the contemporaneous concern over events in the Far East. Collaboration was also easier because the Truman administration could not yet be charged with exclusive blame for any major defeat in American foreign relations and was undeniably seeking to forge real weapons against the agreed enemy in Europe, whether or not those weapons were the best ones. In the Republican party there was still no unity on behalf of expensive programs of aid for Europe, but there was a very large minority readily prepared to support them—a minority of the GOP which could be turned into a working majority by able and vigorous leadership. Such leadership was uncertain in the House, but in the Senate it was consistently and powerfully exercised by Senator Arthur Vandenberg. His imposing personality, compromise skills, seniority, regularity—and especially his possible availability for the presidency—enabled him to make decisive contributions when he chose to collaborate with the administration. The State Department had sought and secured his assistance on European affairs— rather late in the development of the Marshall Plan, very early on the organization of European defense. In each case he and other cooperating members of both parties worked out palliative modifications of the administration's programs but fought vigorously to preserve the essentials of the measures, which had become in part their own creations.

The Republican nominating Convention of 1948 would furnish the crucial test of whether elements in the party who, with Vandenberg, favored "bipartisan" collaboration would hold the upper hand. By forcing the issue on behalf of the full ERP appropriation and by securing adoption of the Vandenberg Resolution just before the convention, the Senator helped to "nail down" a Republican platform declaration which endorsed his line of policy. Because the nominee was Dewey, a high degree of bipartisanship continued during the presidential election campaign of 1948.

CHAPTER 14

Foreign Affairs in the Presidential Election Campaign of 1948

BIPARTISANSHIP in recent American foreign policy reached its peak in the 1948 presidential election campaign. To an extraordinary degree the nominees of the two major parties avoided mutual criticism on foreign affairs until the last week of the campaign, when it was too late to cause any momentous controversy. They even spared each other attacks on past performance in areas where the parties had not been cooperating. During most of the campaign there were formal, fully bipartisan arrangements on foreign affairs. This was more than extrapartisanship. The designated "Secretaries of State" of both candidates were in constant collaboration on most issues of foreign policy and were jointly conducting general negotiations with representatives of almost all the nations of the world. Indeed they went so far as to agree on plans for facilitating the accession to power of the Republican contender with a minimum of dangerous governmental weakness during the interregnum —if his expected victory materialized.

But despite the close relationship between the major party candidates, foreign policy was made a strong issue in the election campaign as a whole by reason of the presence of a third party, which was founded precisely to challenge the "bipartisan" foreign policy. It proved to be impossible for the Democrats to accomplish the transition from Roosevelt's Grand Design to the Truman Doctrine without quickly precipitating a split in their party, which expressed itself in the organized Wallacite opposition in the election campaign. This opposition presented such a grave threat to Truman's prospects that shortly before the election he made a few desperate moves, the result of which was to bring about a quarrel on foreign policy even between himself and Dewey. Thus a strain was put upon bipartisanship which was only exacerbated by Dewey's final defeat. But during the campaign as a whole the area of expressed disagreement between the major parties was so small and the collaborative mechanisms so elaborate as to constitute a landmark in American foreign relations—a landmark which exhibited political weaknesses as well as strengths in full bipartisanship.

THE RENOMINATION OF THOMAS E. DEWEY

Foreign policy played a remarkably small part in the preconvention primary campaign of Republican candidates for the presidency in 1948. The leading contenders were Dewey, Stassen, and Taft. Of them only Taft could properly be regarded as opposed to the essentials of administration foreign policy, and even he moderated his criticism rather than repudiate Vandenberg and alienate Eastern Republican leaders. Dewey in particular did frequently use China as an issue; but China had usually been outside the scope of two-party collaboration anyway, and Dewey did not use the Far Eastern situation as grounds for any general assault on administration foreign policy.

The effect of the preconvention primary battles was to produce the prospect of a deadlock in the Republican Convention. Stassen had been conducting an extraordinary open campaign for the nomination literally for years. At the end of April 1948 he was definitely the front runner, after winning votes from Dewey in the latter's Eastern preserve of New Hampshire and scoring decisive victories in Wisconsin and Nebraska. But his supposed liberalism antagonized the Old Guard, and they were further alienated when he took on Taft in the latter's home state of Ohio. The indecisive result of that primary early in May weakened both Taft and Stassen. Stassen moved to protect himself on the right and got into an intense stumping contest with Dewey in Oregon on the issue of outlawing the Communist party in America. Dewey took the liberal side of the argument and won every Oregon delegate. Thus by convention time each candidate had demonstrated both strength and weakness in the primaries.

That was the situation which made Vandenberg's position as a potential compromise candidate seem so strong, and made the various other candidates so wary of alienating him. But Vandenberg was unwilling to seek the nomination actively. He would go no further than to indicate his availability in case of a genuine "draft" movement. He was content to use his strategic position to secure a satisfactory foreign policy plank in the platform.[1]

There could be no draft for Vandenberg unless the convention became totally deadlocked and each faction regarded him as less objectionable than the other. That proved not to be the case. The Dewey forces had the largest single bloc of votes; their various opponents were unable to agree on anyone else. On June 12 isolationist Colonel McCormick wooed Stassen into a "stop-Dewey" alliance with Taft. The apparent incongruity of this combination weakened Stassen even further and deprived Taft of any sizable accession of strength from Stassen's original supporters. (The failure of the Taft-Stassen alliance was signalized in a Credentials Committee fight over Southern delegates, which Dewey's supporters won.)[2] Dewey's own bid for a right-wing alliance was more successful. The high-tariff Grundy organization in Pennsylvania threw its convention support to him. Then Grundy's rival for control of the GOP in Pennsylvania, Governor Duff, failed to persuade Midwestern Republican leaders to take the Taft strength, along with Stassen's remnants, and turn it over to Vandenberg in a final bid to stop Dewey. In the view of men like Colonel McCormick, Vandenberg was even more objectionable than Dewey. Dewey therefore emerged the victor among his divided opponents

1. Vandenberg's role in maneuvers before and during the 1948 convention is extensively detailed in Vandenberg, *The Private Papers of Senator Vandenberg,* ch. xxii, "On Not Running for President."

2. Vandenberg's *Papers* record (pp. 437–8) that Stassen "came to me at the last moment and was prepared to give me his full support"; apparently this move came after the failure of the alliance with Taft.

and was not even obliged to take as a vice-presidential candidate a man with an "isolationist" record like House floor leader Halleck (who had been prominently mentioned in the Dewey camp for second place on the ticket when Indiana went to the New Yorker). Instead, the vice-presidential nomination went to Governor Warren of California, who like Dewey stood in general on Vandenberg's side of the party fence on foreign policy.[3]

It seems clear that at this Republican Convention of 1948 foreign policy did play a part in the battle over nominations. Obviously it did so in regard to the vice-presidency, but the presidency was also affected, at least to the extent that candidate Dewey may have made some concessions on tariff policy to secure the crucial support of the Grundy faction and that Vandenberg's potentialities as a "stop-Dewey" candidate (in the absence of activity on his own part) were in the end decisively weakened by the fact that he now stood with the extreme "internationalist" section of the party. But Vandenberg's very "extremism" had contributed mightily toward precipitating early approval by the various candidates of the concept of a strong platform plank on foreign policy. And the final nominee, Dewey, was not a candidate who would seek to water down many of the principles for which Vandenberg had taken his stand in the Eightieth Congress, including "unpartisanship" on European affairs.

THE MAJOR-PARTY PLATFORMS OF 1948

Vandenberg himself supplied the basic draft of the Republican foreign policy plank of 1948; it was slightly doctored by Dulles. For the rest of the story Vandenberg's diary note seems worth quoting. It carries an emotional quality as well as the facts:

> Before he presented the working paper to his [Resolutions] Committee, [the Chairman] Senator Lodge . . . added four or five . . . extreme ["internationalist"] statements . . . for

3. Vandenberg himself was active in the "smoke-filled room" where the Vice-President was selected. "I argued that we could not go to the country with a ticket which did no more than personify the split on [international cooperation] among Republicans in Congress. I recommended either Stassen or Warren." *Ibid.*, p. 440.

the express purpose of giving the little coterie of isolationists on his Committee something to knock out. One was a tacit condemnation of the House Republicans for having voted for European relief and then against necessary appropriations for it. In due course, the "extras" were knocked down, just as Lodge had planned, and he emerged with what I consider to be a miraculous performance . . .

Thus *my* platform was adopted by the Convention *unanimously*—which means that the Chicago Colonel [McCormick of the *Tribune*] and many of my bitter Congressional foes who were Delegates must have voted for it. Life *does* have its amusing consolations. I did not need the nomination in order to be vindicated.[4]

The language of the two party planks on foreign aid and other issues is compared below. It will be observed that the differences in 1948 were rarely fundamental, although the tone of the Democratic phraseology was rather strongly partisan. (Also indicated are changes made *at the convention* in the evolution of the Republican platform.)[5]

| *Republicans* | *Democrats* |

Foreign Aid:

We dedicate our foreign policy to the preservation of a free America in a free world of free men. With neither malice nor desire for conquest, we shall strive for a just peace with all nations.

America is deeply interested in the stability, security, and liberty of other independent peoples. Within the prudent limits of our economic welfare, we shall cooperate on a basis of self-help and mutual aid to assist other

Under the leadership of a Democratic President, the United States has demonstrated its friendship for other peace-loving nations and its support of their freedom and independence. Under the Truman Doctrine vital aid has been extended to China, to Greece, and to Turkey. Under the Marshall Plan generous sums have been provided for the relief and rehabilitation of European nations striving to rebuild their economy and

---

4. *Ibid.,* p. 429.

5. Changes in the evolution of some key paragraphs from Vandenberg's original *preconvention* draft may be found in Vandenberg, *op. cit.,* pp. 429–30.

Republicans

peace-loving nations to restore their economic independence and ~~to pre-serve and perpetuate~~ the human rights and fundamental freedoms for which we fought two wars and upon which dependable peace must build. ~~We will implement with appropria-tions any commitment made by leg-islative enactment.~~

We ["guarantee" *changed to* "shall insist on"] business-like and efficient administration of all foreign aid.

Democrats

to secure and strengthen their safety and freedom.

The Republican leadership in the House of Representatives, by its votes in the Eightieth Congress, has shown its reluctance to provide funds to support this program, the greatest move for peace and recovery made since the end of World War II.

We pledge a sound, humanitarian administration of the Marshall Plan.

We pledge support not only for these principles—we pledge further that we will not withhold necessary funds by which these principles can be achieved. Therefore we pledge that we will implement with appropriations the commitments which are made in this nation's foreign programs.

Appeasement:

We shall erect our foreign policy on the basis of friendly firmness which welcomes cooperation but spurns appeasement. We shall pursue a consistent foreign policy which invites steadiness and reliance and which thus avoids the misunderstandings from which wars result. We shall protect the future against the errors of the Democrat administration, which has too often lacked clarity, competence, or consistency in our vital international relationships and has too often abandoned justice.

The United States has traditionally been in sympathy with the efforts of subjugated countries to attain their independence, and to establish a democratic form of government. Poland is an outstanding example. After a century and a half of subjugation, it was resurrected after the first World War by our great Democratic President Woodrow Wilson. We look forward to the development of these countries as prosperous, free, and democratic fellow members of the United Nations.

Ex-Enemy States:

We shall seek to restore autonomy and self-sufficiency as rapidly as possible in our postwar occupied areas,

We pledge our best endeavors to conclude treaties of peace with our former enemies. Already treaties have

Republicans

guarding always against any rebirth of aggression.

United Nations:

We believe in collective security against aggression and in behalf of justice and freedom. We shall support the United Nations as the world's best hope in this direction, striving to strengthen it and promote its effective evolution and use. The United Nations should progressively establish international law, ~~control atomic energy,~~ be freed of any veto in the peaceful settlement of international disputes, and be provided with the armed forces contemplated by the Charter. [*Senator Brooks of Illinois led a noninterventionist bloc in the full Resolutions Committee which sought to delete this entire last sentence, but they succeeded only in getting rid of international atomic control.*]

Regional Arrangements:

We particularly commend the value of regional arrangements as prescribed by the Charter; and we cite

Democrats

been made with Italy, Hungary, Bulgaria, and Rumania. We shall strive to conclude treaties with the remaining enemy states, based on justice and with guaranties against the revival of aggression and for the preservation of peace.

We support the United Nations fully and we pledge our wholehearted aid toward its growth and development. We will continue to lead the way toward curtailment of the use of the veto. We shall favor such amendments and modifications of the Charter as experience may justify. We will continue our efforts toward the establishment of an international armed force to aid its authority.

We advocate the grant of a loan to the United Nations, recommended by the President but denied by the Republican Congress, for the construction of the United Nations headquarters in this country.

We believe the primary step toward the achievement of worldwide freedom is access by all peoples to the facts and the truth. To that end we will encourage the greatest possible vigor on the part of the United Nations Commission on Human Rights and the United Nations Economic and Social Council to establish the foundations on which freedom can exist in every nation.

A great Democratic President established the Good Neighbor policy toward the nations of the Western

Republicans

the Western Hemispheric Defense Pact as a useful model.

We shall nourish these Pan-American agreements in the new spirit of cooperation which implements the Monroe Doctrine.

Democrats

Hemisphere. The Act of Chapultepec was negotiated at Mexico City under Democratic leadership. It was carried forward in the Western Hemisphere defense pact concluded at Rio de Janeiro, which implemented the Monroe Doctrine and united the Western Hemisphere in behalf of peace.

We pledge continued economic cooperation with the countries of the Western Hemisphere. We pledge continued support of regional arrangements within the United Nations Charter, such as the Inter-American Regional Pact and the developing Western European Union.

Defense:

We propose . . . the maintenance of armed services for air, land, and sea to a degree which will insure our national security; and the achievement of effective unity in the Department of National Defense so as to insure maximum economy in money and manpower, and maximum effectiveness in case of war. We favor sustained effective action to procure sufficient manpower for the services, recognizing the American principle that every citizen has an obligation of service to his country.

We recognize that the United States has become the principal protector of the free world. The free peoples of the world look to us for support in maintaining their freedoms. If we falter in our leadership, we may endanger the peace of the world—and we shall surely endanger the welfare of our own nation.

For these reasons it is imperative that we maintain our military strength until world peace with justice is secure. Under the leadership of President Truman, our military departments have been united and our government organization for the national defense greatly strengthened.

We pledge to maintain adequate military strength, based on these improvements, sufficient to fulfill our responsibilities in occupation zones, defend our national interests, and to bolster those free nations resisting Communist aggression.

Republicans   *Democrats*

Disarmament:

We shall relentlessly pursue our aims for the universal limitation and control of arms and implements of war on a basis of reliable disciplines against bad faith.

We advocate the maintenance of an adequate army, navy, and air force to protect the nation's vital interests and to assure our security against aggression.

We advocate the effective international control of weapons of mass destruction, including the atomic bomb, and we approve continued and vigorous efforts within the United Nations to bring about the successful consummation of the proposals which our government has advanced.

The adoption of those proposals would be a vital and most important step toward safe and effective world disarmament and world peace under a strengthened United Nations which would then truly constitute a more effective parliament of the world's peoples. [*This plank was worked out by the drafting subcommittee after considerable effective agitation by internationalist and peace groups at the convention.*]

Trade and Tariffs:

At all times safeguarding our own industry and agriculture and under ["reasonable" *changed to* "efficient"] administrative procedures for the legitimate consideration of domestic needs, we shall support the ["reciprocal trade agreements" *changed to* "system of reciprocal trade"] and encourage international commerce. [*Chairman Millikin of the Senate Finance Committee pressed successfully for these changes by the full*

We pledge ourselves to restore the reciprocal trade agreements program formulated in 1934 by Secretary of State Cordell Hull and operated successfully for fourteen years—until crippled by the Republican Eightieth Congress. Further, we strongly endorse our country's adherence to the International Trade Organization.

Republicans   *Democrats*

Resolutions Committee, as well as
securing the deletion of all reference
to reciprocal trade and tariffs from
the preamble of the platform.] [6]

6. *The Republican plank on China may be found on p. 267, n. 53. The two party planks on Palestine are on pp. 234–5.*
The Republican preamble included these words about foreign policy:
"Our foreign policy is dedicated to preserving a free America in a free world of free men. This calls for strengthening the United Nations and primary recognition of America's self-interest in the liberty of other peoples. Prudently conserving our own resources, we shall cooperate on a self-help basis with other peace-loving nations. ~~"With necessary regard for domestic needs we favor reciprocal trade agreements and the encouragement of international commerce.~~ [*This was included by the drafting subcommittee but was deleted in the full Resolutions Committee on the insistence of Chairman Millikin of the Senate Finance Committee.*]
"Our common defense must be strengthened and unified."
Here is some later Republican language of a general character:
"We pledge that under a Republican administration all foreign commitments shall be made public and subject to constitutional ratification. We shall say what we mean and mean what we say. In all of these things we shall primarily consult the national security and welfare of our own United States. In all of these things we shall welcome the world's cooperation. But in none of these things shall we surrender our ideals or our free institutions.
"We are proud of the part that the Republicans have taken in those limited areas of foreign policy in which they have been permitted to participate. We shall invite the minority party to join us under the next Republican administration in stopping partisan politics at the water's edge."
The Democratic preamble referred to the bipartisan principle only to take exclusive credit for it:
"Ours is the party which first proclaimed that the actions and policies of this nation in the foreign field are matters of national and not just party concern. We shall go forward on the course charted by President Roosevelt and President Truman and the other leaders of democracy."
The rest of the Democratic preamble struck the same highly partisan note:
"Ours is the party under which the framework of the world organization for peace and justice was formulated and created. Ours is the party under which were conceived the instruments for resisting Communist aggression and for rebuilding the economic strength of the democratic countries of Europe and Asia—the Truman Doctrine and the Marshall Plan. They are the materials with which we must build the peace." *The preamble went on to monopolize for the Democrats full credit for victory in World War II and for the establishment of the UN. It was, as Vandenberg said, "amazingly impertinent" under the existing circumstances. New York Times, October 5, 1948. State Department officials had protested in vain that Republicans should receive some credit in the Democratic platform for their contribution to the "bipartisan" policy. James Reston, New York Times, July 14, 1948.*

BIPARTISANSHIP IN THE 1948 PRESIDENTIAL CAMPAIGN

Dewey Campaigns for "Unity." The climate of the Republican Convention, the nature of the platform, and the character of the nominees gave assurance that foreign policy would not be an *outstanding* issue in the campaign between the two major parties in 1948, unless by chance the Democrats should precipitate a quarrel. But foreign policy might still have been *something* of an issue in Dewey's campaign. The Democratic administration could have been attacked vigorously on the record of its wartime diplomacy and postwar Far Eastern diplomacy, to both of which Republicans had shown mere passive acquiescence or outright opposition. There were special reasons for the extreme moderation of Dewey's campaign, especially on foreign affairs.

Number one was the sublime overconfidence of the Republican strategists. Considering the public opinion polls, the disintegration of the Democratic party (on its right as well as on its left), and the obviously superior *personal* ability of the GOP nominee, Dewey's associates became so certain of victory that they planned a campaign based on the principle that the problem was not to get elected but to avoid antagonisms which would impede effective Republican government after the election had been won. That end would be most easily attained if Dewey confined himself to thoroughly reasonable and responsible utterances and avoided any suspicion of demagoguery. This view was endorsed with extreme vigor by Senator Vandenberg, who shared the nearly universal expectation of easy Republican victory. He himself wanted to avoid an active campaign on Dewey's behalf if it were not really necessary, lest he impair the smooth relations he had established on foreign policy with Senate Democrats; such relations would help to oil the wheels for Dewey's foreign policy in 1949.[7]

7. Vandenberg, *op. cit.,* pp. 446–50. Dewey did not press Vandenberg very hard to do more than to make one radio address—from Washington where he would not even become involved in a Senate race. In this report to the nation on October 4, Vandenberg explained the meaning of "bipartisanship," the Republican contributions to it, the areas in which it had not prevailed (which were merely cited), the declarations of Republican leaders' willingness to pursue "bipartisanship," and

The other major reason for the extreme moderation of Dewey's campaign on foreign policy—apart from his own views and the circumstances under which he was nominated—was the renewal of the European crisis of 1948. In the winter and spring of the year tension had centered around Czechoslovakia, Italy, and, less publicly, Scandinavia. In the late spring there came a notable relaxation in cold-war hostilities. But just at the time of the Republican National Convention in June, the Russians imposed their blockade of Berlin, and for several months thereafter the explosive possibilities of that situation were a cause for great concern. The fact was that America's legal right of access to Berlin was in some doubt as the result of official negligence during and after the war, and executive officers were particularly anxious that these mistakes should not be used as partisan ammunition against Truman in the campaign. Such arguments coming from Americans would strengthen the Russians' hand in negotiations and in propaganda regarding the future of Berlin.[8] Even more disastrous in its effects upon Berliners and other worried Europeans would be a decision by Dewey in his campaign to oppose the continuation of a holding operation in Berlin which promised to be both expensive and dangerous.

Remembering the generally successful bipartisan consultative relationship regarding the UN during the 1944 campaign, State Department officials conferred with Vandenberg and partly at his urging called Dulles into the confidential conferences at which plans for Berlin were under discussion. Dulles, to his satisfaction, was much closer to the center of decision than he had been in 1944. Vandenberg, back in Michigan, was kept informed by telephone. They both joined Dewey at his New York farm on July 24

---

presented some statements from the platform and from Dewey on general foreign policy. It was a very sober, sincere, honest, and thoroughly respectable report to the nation, not a "campaign speech." But for the public to which it was directed—attentive to foreign affairs—it must have been an effective campaign document.

President Truman, however, was not much disturbed by such "kid-glove" campaigning. He actually called Vandenberg secretly to the White House and in the course of conversation expressed appreciation for the moderation of this "grand speech." *Ibid.,* pp. 452, 457-8.

8. Arthur Krock, *New York Times,* August 5, 1948.

and reviewed the situation.[9] The strategy of great moderation on foreign affairs in the GOP presidential campaign was clearly indicated in the statement which Dewey issued after their meeting: "The present duty of Americans is not to be divided by past lapses, but to unite to surmount present dangers. We shall not allow domestic partisan irritations to divert us from this indispensable unity . . . In Berlin we must not surrender our rights under duress." [10]

Dewey did embarrass the administration in mid-August when he publicly urged that Italy be given control of her former colonies under UN trusteeship. This produced a secret rebuke from Vandenberg too, and a polite rejoinder from Dulles pleading that Vandenberg "be tolerant of the exigencies of the campaign and of political influence." [11] Again on September 22, 1948, the Republican Governor created a stir by declaring that the United States had a "magnificent opportunity to use our [Marshall Plan] aid to bring about . . . a federation" of Western Europe. The explicit use of the word "federation" gave rather startling emphasis to the idea of European "unity" on which both Dewey and Dulles had concentrated during the ERP debate of the preceding winter. Also on September 24 Dewey set as one of his objectives "a mighty worldwide counter-offensive . . . of truth . . . of hope"; he would "tell our magnificent story of freedom." But all this foreshadowed no major change in American foreign policy, as Dewey's major foreign policy address made clear.[12]

The speech was delivered at Salt Lake City on September 30 and included these nine points (all in Dewey's own words):

(1) Unstinting support to the United Nations.

(2) All reasonable aid to friendly and like-minded nations.

(3) Use it . . . for pushing and . . . prodding . . . toward European Union.

9. Dulles, *War or Peace*, pp. 130–1.

10. *New York Times*, July 25, 1948.

11. Vandenberg, *op. cit.*, pp. 447–8.

12. *New York Times*, September 23 and October 1, 1948. Dewey's address of February 12, 1948, in the *Commercial and Financial Chronicle*, February 19, 1948, p. 827. Dulles testimony, *Hearings* on the European Recovery Program, before the Senate Foreign Relations Committee, January 1948, pp. 588–9. Also Dulles, *op. cit.*, pp. 108–9.

(4) Bring a demilitarized Ruhr to life . . . under international control.

(5) Bring an end to the tragic neglect of China.

(6) Remain strong and grow stronger.

(7) [Make Latin America] full partners . . . against aggression [and] in developing our material and spiritual resources.

(8) Tell the . . . story of America.

(9) Enlist the spiritual resources of mankind in a great moral awakening.

Equally important to the preservation of harmony on foreign affairs was Dewey's brief observation that "it serves no useful purpose to review" the diplomatic defeats "in that long series of secret conferences culminating in Potsdam." He did mention, in passing, Eastern Europe and the Far East, especially Manchuria and North China, but wholly without the vigorous denunciation which would have been required to establish even these retrospective questions as sharp issues between the parties in the 1948 campaign. Barring a sudden move by Truman, Dewey had made it clear by the end of September that there would be an extreme soft-pedaling of controversial foreign policy in his campaign.

Dulles as "Co-Secretary of State." Close bipartisan relations on foreign policy reached a new height in September, when Dulles accompanied Secretary Marshall to the meeting of the United Nations General Assembly in Paris. Dulles was quite obviously Dewey's personal representative. The State Department provided him with a special "telecom" arrangement whereby he conferred almost daily with Dewey through his brother Allen Dulles, who was with the Governor on his campaign train. Most of the foreign ministers of the world were in Paris, and nearly all expected that Dulles would officially be one of them after the first of the year. He was treated, and behaved, very much like a Secretary of State already. At Paris and on week-end missions to Vienna, Berlin, Copenhagen, and Stockholm, "I sought to reaffirm at those exposed points my confidence in a continuity of the strong European policy that had developed under bipartisan auspices of the past, and to reassure those who might be wavering." [13] In dangerous Berlin Dulles made a special effort to demonstrate publicly his solidarity with General Clay despite their well known past disagreements. Dulles sent Eric Johnston (liberal businessman, formerly of the Chamber of Commerce and then of the Motion Picture Association) to act as a kind of personal "ambassador at large," visiting capitals like Belgrade and Madrid where it would have been bad form (and bad politics) for Dulles to have gone himself.[14]

The intimate understanding which developed between the State Department and Dulles extended ultimately to the formulation of plans for the delicate transition period between the "Republican victory" in November and "Dewey's inauguration" in January. Dulles explains:

> The result was that Governor Dewey was in a position such that, if elected, he could have helped to assure a transition from Democratic to Republican Administration without damage to our international position or collapse of the cooperation of free nations under United States leadership. The contingency we prepared for did not happen. But in view of the then estimate of probabilities it would have been almost criminal not to have had plans to meet that eventuality.[15]

But while Secretary Marshall in Paris was arranging with Dulles for the "interregnum"—presumably with Truman's consent if not his active interest—the President himself was in no mood to concede defeat. He had secured renomination for the presidency over the opposition of most factions of the Democratic party. In the weeks immediately preceding Truman's nomination the intra-party controversy had turned almost exclusively on domestic questions. But that was only because the faction which was strongly opposed to his foreign policy had already broken away to form a third party. The challenge from Henry Wallace was focused directly on foreign affairs. It posed a grave threat to Truman, and near the end of

13. Dulles, *op. cit.*, pp. 131–5.
14. C. L. Sulzberger, *New York Times*, November 8, 1948.
15. Dulles, *op. cit.*, p. 135.

the campaign this caused some skirmishing on foreign policy even between Truman and Dewey.

THE WALLACE PARTY

In order to establish the background of these developments it is necessary to retrace our steps and sketch briefly the evolution of the Wallace party.

Left-right Split in the CIO. Our last previous look at the left wing of the old Rooseveltian domestic coalition was in December 1946, when the liberal intellectuals split formally over the issue of anti-communism into the ADA (Americans for Democratic Action) and the PCA (Progressive Citizens of America). The Democratic party in Congress showed remarkably little defection toward the left; only nine Northern Democrats in the House and three liberal Democrats in the Senate went on record against the Greek-Turk program (including its military features) in the spring of 1947. The very fact that their party was now in the minority in Congress helped to promote its solidarity. Politically the most important organization which was still abstaining from support of the tough trend of administration foreign policy was the CIO. If that organization should be half hearted in its support of Democratic candidates in the 1948 election, the party's prospects would be seriously impaired. But the "middle-of-the-road" CIO leaders like President Philip Murray wanted to avoid any drastic commitment which would destroy the unity of their organization. All-out endorsement of "militarist" programs like that in Greece and Turkey would surely have had that effect. Nor did the left wing in the CIO wish to force a break as long as it could forestall decisive pronouncements contrary to Russian policy.

But fence sitting in the CIO could not continue indefinitely. Quietly a fight was under way in individual unions to eliminate Communist influence. By October 1947 at a National Convention of the CIO the best terms which the left wing unions could secure were a resolution against "warmongering," an unequivocal declaration against all compulsory forms of military service, and some

possibly ambiguous language in a resolution which did endorse
the Marshall Plan. Communist as well as anti-Communist elements
in the CIO supported the foreign policy resolution at the convention. But the left-wingers were disturbed by the trend against
them, which included the threat to their position posed by the
non-Communist affidavit requirement in the Taft-Hartley Act,
passed in June. In mid-November 1947, after the CIO National
Convention, leftists were ousted from power in the executive board
of the mighty Automobile Workers Union.[16] The Communists decided to take the bull by the horns and work for the third-party
candidacy of Henry Wallace for President—even if the majority
of the CIO executive board could not be persuaded to subscribe
to this strategy for putting pressure on the Democrats and the
result should be to split the CIO itself.

On December 29, 1947—just a year after the ADA-PCA split—
Henry Wallace announced that he would campaign for the presidency as leader of "a new party to fight these warmongers." The
Democrats, he declared, had become a "party of war and depression." Within a week CIO President Murray had announced plans
to fight the Wallace candidacy.[17] Two weeks later the CIO executive board formally refused to give the third party an endorsement;
the CIO-PAC would not be available to assist Henry Wallace's
campaign. For non-Communist CIO leaders the Wallace candidacy
was a direct challenge which had to be met, both to preserve their
own position with rank-and-file members and, if possible, to protect the Democratic party in order to bring about a relaxation of
the Taft-Hartley Act. Undoubtedly also the spring crisis of 1948
facilitated a hardening of the union leaders' attitude toward the
Communist minority among them. Late in April Philip Murray
castigated the Wallace movement before a convention of the Tex-
tile Workers, charging formally that "the Communist party is
directly responsible for the organization of a third party in
the United States." [18] During the succeeding months Communist
penetration of the CIO was combated so vigorously that in Sep-

16. *New York Times,* November 12 and 14, 1947.
17. *Ibid.,* January 8, 1948.
18. *Ibid.,* April 29, 1948.

tember President Albert Fitzgerald of the United Electrical Workers, the largest union generally considered to be Communist controlled, did not even venture to submit Wallace's candidacy to his union's convention. Fitzgerald was co-chairman of Wallace's Progressive party and could have obtained an endorsement for it from the UE convention—but admittedly only at the risk of precipitating a deeper division in a union which the leftists controlled.[19] Wallace's Communist supporters were now so much on the defensive that they would not run that further risk for his sake. Truman's re-election in spite of Wallace was the last straw. The November CIO Convention produced the long-awaited showdown debate between left and right—and the adoption of a foreign policy resolution frankly denouncing Soviet Russia for its opposition to the Marshall Plan and its abuse of the Security Council veto.[20]

Wallace and the Communists. The Communists had overplayed their hand in the Wallace movement. Probably Wallace's own refusal to dissociate himself from them in any emphatic way encouraged them to move in too brazenly, without decent disguises. At any rate it certainly hastened the departure of non-Communist members of the PCA who would have been willing to assist a third-party candidacy which was less flagrantly Communist.

At the National Convention of the Progressive party in July 1948 long standing, well known fellow travelers were bluntly given the key positions out front, not just behind the scenes. Albert Fitzgerald was chairman of the convention; Congressman Vito Marcantonio headed the Rules Committee; Lee Pressman was secretary of the Platform Committee. When three Vermont delegates tried to strengthen the plank on Soviet-American relations by adding just the assurance that "it is not our intention to give blanket endorsement to the foreign policy of any nation," some party liners on the floor objected that this "would be an insinuation against a friendly ally of the United States." The Platform Committee with Communist assent would go no further than to insert a provision that peace was a "joint responsibility" of the

19. *Ibid.,* September 8, 1948.
20. *Ibid.,* November 23 and 24, 1948.

United States and the USSR. When a curious delegate inquired why a plank supporting a "unified homeland" for the Macedonians had been deleted at the last moment, he was given elaborate "explanations," which failed to include the fact that the recent defection of Tito's Yugoslavia made a unified Macedonia no longer attractive to the Stalinists.[21] In his acceptance speech Wallace himself announced, not just that America's position in blockaded Berlin was untenable, but that "we can't lose anything by giving it up militarily in a search for peace." [22]

In all probability Wallace was truly infused with missionary zeal on behalf of the cause of peace and had allowed himself to be persuaded that any kind of political vehicle would be acceptable which would help him to reach a wide audience and bring pressure to bear on the administration to moderate its policy toward Russia. It may well have been true that only the long-prepared, far-reaching structure of the Communist party and its affiliates could have provided him with a framework adequate to build a national third party within just a few months, on behalf of a cause which could so easily be labeled pro-Russian. But if Communist organization was essential for Wallace's peace crusade, it seems equally probable that the name of Wallace was essential to the Communists for whatever ulterior purposes they sought. The guess may be hazarded that the Communists' organizing ability would have been forthcoming on behalf of Wallace even if he had shown more coolness toward them and had resisted their most brazen advances. But Wallace became so carried away by his mission to build a new party for peace that he made little effort to restrain the Communists in order to preserve liberal support. Actually it was his leftist associates, against his wishes, who decided late in the campaign to try to halt the decline of liberal support for him by withdrawing third-party candidates in numerous congressional races where their presence on the ballot would defeat liberal Democrats and elect Republicans. Wallace publicly rebuked his campaign manager C. B. Baldwin when this was announced, protesting that it would prevent the building of a party for 1952. "We've got to build a

21. *Ibid.*, July 26, 1948.
22. *Ibid.*, July 25, 1948.

party, Beanie; we've got to build a party." [23] But the more reasonable decision of his campaign managers stood. [24]

Wallace's Impact on the Election Results. Henry Wallace, however, remained in the campaign for the presidency despite the withdrawal of Progressive party candidates for many lesser offices. He posed a great threat to the Democrats which, coupled with the Dixiecrat defection on the right, seemed doomed to defeat Truman. The nature of that threat was demonstrated in concrete terms by the final results of the election; for the sake of specificity they will be presented here, out of the chronological sequence of the general discussion.

Contrary to all expectations, Truman did win the election. But the results showed that Dewey won the states of New York, Michigan, and Maryland (a total of 74 electoral votes) by pluralities which were smaller than the number of votes cast for Wallace in those respective states. On the reasonable assumption that the vast majority of Progressive party votes would have gone to the Democrats if there had been no third party in the race, it may safely be asserted that Wallace deprived Truman of 74 electoral votes. Furthermore, Illinois, which Truman won with a plurality of only 34,000 votes, would certainly have gone Republican if the Wallace party had been allowed to appear on the ballot. [25] Truman would have barely won the electoral votes required for re-election even if an "honest" ballot in Illinois had deprived him of that state's electoral votes, but he could not have survived also the loss of either California or Ohio—states in which Wallace came desperately close to causing Truman's defeat. [26] If any two of the three states of California, Illinois, and Ohio had gone Republican

23. *Ibid.,* September 22, 1948.

24. To the leftists it was probably also of some importance that the liberal Democrats concerned, if elected, would at least be more likely than their Republican opponents to resist drastic Communist-control measures at home and *military* programs of resistance to communism abroad.

25. In the last days of the campaign the Republican organization in Illinois tried desperately to facilitate Progressive party efforts to get legalized. But court action all the way up to the United States Supreme Court failed to secure that result.

26. In California, where Wallace won 190,000 votes, Truman was left with a plurality of only 18,000. In Ohio Wallace received 38,000, Truman's plurality was just 7,000.

as the result of Wallace's intervention, Truman would have lost the election. All of them *very* nearly did.[27]

On the other hand, Dewey would have had to win all three of those states to have secured outright electoral victory. If he had won only two of them, thanks to Wallace, the election would have been thrown into the House of Representatives. There a Republican–Southern Democratic coalition might well have left the Wallacites entrenched among the liberal remnants of the Democratic party as an element apparently indispensable to victory in a presidential election. An *outright* Dewey victory probably would have produced a somewhat longer dispute in Democratic ranks as to whether the Progressives or the Dixiecrats were more responsible for Truman's defeat and hence more nearly indispensable to future Democratic victories; but both groups would probably have been able to argue that the choice had to be made.

Truman's outstanding contribution was to make the contrary demonstration in 1948: that by concentrating his campaign on mobilizing beneath the regular Democratic standard those major elements of Wallace's potential strength which were far more interested in racial equality and economic security than in foreign affairs, it was still barely possible for a Democratic candidate to win the presidency without making important concessions either to the "states' rights" demands of the Dixiecrats or to the foreign policy demands of the Progressives.

PARTISANSHIP IN THE 1948
PRESIDENTIAL CAMPAIGN

Truman's political advisers did concoct plans for one major sortie and several minor ones directed toward undermining the attractiveness of Wallace's foreign policy position by positive professions of peaceful intentions toward Russia as well as by negative

27. Considered from the other point of view, in addition to the three states (New York, Michigan, and Maryland) which did go Republican because of Wallace, there were five states (Connecticut, Delaware, Indiana, Nevada, and Oregon) in which the Wallace vote very nearly equaled the GOP margin of victory. The Republicans would probably have won the 33 electoral votes of these states even if Wallace had not been in the running—but by perilously small pluralities.

attacks on communism in the Progressive party. These moves put a definite strain on bipartisan relationships, but Dewey chose not to take them as justification for a serious break until very late in the campaign, when it was too late for criticism to penetrate very deeply.

The Vinson Mission. The major Truman project was the abortive Vinson mission to Moscow. This idea originated with two of Truman's speech writers, David Noyes and Albert Z. Carr.[28] The latter at least was undoubtedly sympathetic toward much of the Wallace case against the trend of American foreign policy. It was his view that "one of the possible by-products of the campaign might be a reduction of the mounting war fever in the United States."[29] Others of Truman's advisers were more interested in the purely political advantage to be gained from a visit to Stalin by Chief Justice Vinson to emphasize the peaceful intentions of the American people and the Truman administration; for one thing, it would be a useful counter to Wallace's repeated offer to make a mission to Moscow. What Truman's personal view of the matter was, it is impossible to say. He did allow preparations to go to the point where his agents were arranging for free radio time just thirty-six hours before he wanted to go on the air to announce Vinson's mission—without yet having told the State Department about the project, to say nothing of the Republican leaders.[30]

Truman did at that late hour submit the proposal to Secretary Marshall in Paris. The teletyped protest came back swift and vigorous. A visit to Stalin by Truman's personal friend and envoy would be interpreted by other Western delegations at the UN as an effort to by-pass them in unilateral negotiations, especially on the Berlin blockade; that quarrel had just been submitted to the Security Council and was a matter of truly desperate concern to unarmed Western Europe. Under Secretary Lovett seconded

28. Daniels, *The Man of Independence,* p. 361.

29. Albert Z. Carr, *Truman, Stalin, and Peace* (Garden City, Doubleday, 1950), pp. 106–10. This book contains the fullest available account of the Vinson mission, pp. 111–20.

30. Daniels, *op. cit.,* p. 361. Carr, *op. cit.,* p. 118. Arthur Krock, *New York Times,* October 10, 1948.

Marshall's objections. Truman promptly agreed to postpone action and summoned Marshall home for consultations. Connally and Vandenberg were invited to a secret meeting with the President, evidently so that he could inform them of the projected mission; but Connally arrived first and his reaction was so negative that Truman never directly raised the issue with Vandenberg.[31] Very soon, however, some radio network officials let the press know of the abortive plan, and State Department officers proceeded to leak copiously regarding the evil consequences of the President's "political gesture." [32] Newspapers were howling their protests as Marshall arrived. After he talked for a few hours with Truman, a formal White House communiqué announced that the project was dead.

Probably if the simple idea of a "good-will" mission to Russia by the supposedly nonpolitical Chief Justice, with no intent to negotiate specific issues, had been carefully cleared with the State Department, with Dulles and Vandenberg, and with Britain and France, no decisive objection would have been met. Such clearances might conceivably have contributed something to the peace of the world by making possible a successful Vinson mission—though a successful mission seems most unlikely. From a political standpoint, however, the clearances would have destroyed whatever advantage was to be gained for Truman by his making the announcement suddenly, dramatically, and unilaterally. As it was, Truman must have lost some votes by the demonstration of ineptitude and confusion in his administration, but he may have gained even more from the lingering memory that he had at least tried to "do something for peace."

Secretary Marshall conferred with Vandenberg in Washington during his visit home; Dulles conferred by telecom with Dewey;

31. Tom Connally, *My Name Is Tom Connally*, p. 331. Vandenberg, *op. cit.*, pp. 457–8.

32. For their anonymous observations, see Arthur Krock, *New York Times*, October 10, 1948. Joseph Harsch listened more skeptically: "We had a feeling, sitting around after the conference, that we were watching an interregnum operate. Harry Truman is still titular President of the United States. But at the State Department his views and wishes were regarded as an obstacle to be overcome, not as authority to be obeyed." *Christian Science Monitor*, October 14, 1948.

and the initial Dewey strategy was to place himself ostentatiously on a plane of national responsibility far above Truman by declining to take the opportunity in public speeches for an all-out attack on the President's "incompetence" in foreign affairs. GOP leaders did explain privately to reporters in Albany their view that the Vinson project had been disastrous and their own reluctance to weaken still further the American position in Paris by making a public issue of Truman's abortive scheme.[33] The President, for his part, made two more partisan jabs at Republicans on foreign affairs in the early weeks of his campaign, but his major foreign policy address on October 18 was statesmanlike.[34] On October 23 he sent a personal wire to reassure Vandenberg that no new move resembling the Vinson mission would be made without consulting the Senator.[35] And on the Republican side Governor Dewey's speeches on foreign relations showed that he was continuing to ignore partisan provocation.[36]

Truman "Gives 'em Hell." In the last week of the campaign, however, Truman's strategy became more desperately hard hitting, and one effect was to raise a foreign policy issue. The President moved bluntly to mobilize the votes of racial and religious minorities in the big Northern cities where Wallace's strength lay. On October 25 Truman's speech in Chicago was designed to imply

33. James Reston, *New York Times,* October 17, 1948, sec. 4, p. 3.

34. *Truman's jabs:* (September 27) "The Republicans killed the international wheat agreement. That is the kind of treatment the farmer has been getting from the Republican party." (October 13) "The American people should consider the risk of entrusting their destiny to recent converts who now come along and say 'Me too, but I can do it better'" [pointing to prewar Republican isolationism]. *Truman's "statesmanship":* (October 18) "All three together—world peace, world economic recovery, and the welfare of our nation"; conciliation, but firmness and not appeasement; (in defense of the Vinson mission) "whenever an appropriate opportunity arises I shall act to further the interests of peace within the framework of our relations with our allies and the work of the United Nations." *New York Times,* September 28, October 14 and 19, 1948.

35. Vandenberg, *op. cit.,* pp. 459–60.

36. *Dewey:* (October 12) "Bipartisanship" hailed, Republican contributions cited, as in Vandenberg's radio address. (October 15) Repetition of main points of Salt Lake City speech. (October 20) "Let us act decisively to arouse and strengthen and solidify the free world so that the forces making for peace will be more powerful than the forces making for war. We can once again lead from strength and not from weakness." *New York Times,* October 13, 16, and 21, 1948.

that Dewey was a "front man" for "a few men [who] get control of the economy of a nation," like Hitler, Mussolini, and Tojo, each of whose cases was cited. Truman carried the fascist analogy further:

> Demagogues have even dared to raise the voices of religious prejudice in the Eightieth Congress. We need only remember the shocking Displaced Persons Bill passed in the second session of the Eightieth Congress which cruelly discriminated against Catholics and Jews.[37]

In using such arguments Truman carefully distinguished himself from the Communists and Henry Wallace, emphasizing rather that *Dewey* was the beneficiary of Communist activity (October 26):

> The Communists count on a reactionary Republican administration making all the mistakes that ignorance and greed can inspire, and they expect that a Republican administration will reduce the American people to another Hoover depression that will undermine the Marshall Plan and pave the way for world revolution.[38]

The President used the same argument in greater detail at Boston on October 27. Citing each major achievement in postwar American policy toward Europe, he chorused: "The Communists will never forgive me for that." [39]

Dewey now felt free to hit back about the Vinson mission and about Russian gains since the war. On October 27 he condemned divisive appeals to prejudice as echoes of the Communist party line, and declared:

> We shall not achieve peace by conducting these desperately important matters on a "happy-thought" basis, or by jovially remarking that we "like good old Joe."
>
> In a little more than three years the Soviet has extended its sway nearly halfway around the world, and it now rules more than 500 million human beings.[40]

37. *Ibid.,* October 26, 1948.
38. *Ibid.,* October 27, 1948.
39. *Ibid.,* October 28, 1948.
40. *Ibid.*

Dewey went on to present some examples of Communist advance.

Truman made his reply with exuberant unrestraint in a full-fledged partisan speech on foreign affairs October 29. The President put all the blame on Dewey for introducing foreign policy issues into the campaign: "He has torn off his mask of bipartisanship and revealed the ugly partisan passion underneath." Truman paid brief tribute to the contributions of "certain Republicans in recent years" but emphasized, by the record, that "the Republican party, as a party, is a late convert to the cause of international good will and cooperation."

> Mr. Grundy . . . masterminded the choice of the Republican candidate. . . . Do you want to return to Grundyism? . . . [The Republicans] simply crippled the [reciprocal trade] act and extended it for one year instead of the customary three, thinking that next year . . . they will be able to finish the job . . .
>
> When the European recovery program was before the Senate the isolationist forces in the Republican party rose behind Senator Taft in an attempt to slash that program and change it from one of world reconstruction to one of hand-out relief. . . . If it had not been for the experience and wisdom of the Democratic party in international affairs, the European recovery program would have been mutilated before it was launched . . .
>
> These are some of the reasons which lead me to believe that our foreign policy is safer in Democratic than in Republican hands.

Truman also had a new twist on the Communist argument:

> The Communists have real reason to hope that Republican isolationism will exert its pressure within the Republican party and, in a period of time, they can take over nation after nation in the world.[41]

It was too late for Dewey, even if he so desired, to make a full counterattack. It was the last night of his campaign and there were

41. *Ibid.*, October 30, 1948.

other subjects to cover. Dewey was content to limit his criticism on foreign affairs to an attempt to turn back on Truman the peace argument which the President had been emphasizing to protect himself from Wallace:

> By [the administration's] daily shifts in policy our friends at the world council tables for peace are being left stunned and the work for peace is paralyzed. In this grave hour a party that cannot keep the peace within itself cannot be entrusted with the solemn task of uniting our country or of keeping peace in the world.[42]

CONCLUDING OBSERVATIONS

Thus at the very end of the 1948 campaign the presence of Wallace's third party produced a situation in which the Republican and Democratic candidates did express bluntly the *negative* arguments in foreign affairs for their respective candidacies. But it was too late for the criticism to penetrate deeply. *Positive* arguments had been given often before and had revealed that there was little to choose between the intended policies of the candidates, but negative arguments had been avoided ("What's wrong with my opponent that makes me better"). They had been avoided because of Dewey's sublime overconfidence, because of the critical Berlin blockade situation, and because of the widespread belief among leaders in both parties that the necessary foreign affairs collaboration between them could not survive an extensive partisan debate —even a debate on subjects which had heretofore been handled almost exclusively by executive officials, like wartime strategic diplomacy and postwar relations with China.

It may possibly be true that the extraordinarily close relationship between Dulles and Marshall in the 1948 campaign was in fact dependent on Dewey's pulling his punches on Poland and China. If that *is* true, it is natural that Dewey's ultimate defeat should cause future campaigners—shunning his overconfidence— to demand evidence of a much graver international situation than existed in 1948 before going to such extreme lengths to avoid

42. *Ibid.,* October 31, 1948.

foreign policy controversies. Collaboration on the Marshall-Dulles pattern—with all its international advantages—cannot be expected to require the opposition to soft-pedal issues on which no extra-partisan collaboration has previously been established. Dewey overextended the scope of his bipartisanship on foreign affairs to areas where he had no "duty" to do so. Thereby he weakened his own campaign, and hence the future political attractiveness of *any* form of "bipartisanship." [43]

As for Henry Wallace's Progressive party, its presence on the ballot in 46 states did give voters a chance to express emphatic disapproval of the trend of foreign policy on which major-party leaders had reached such close agreement. The result was to demonstrate with unexpected clarity how little strong opposition existed in America to the general tough trend of policy toward Russia. Wallace received only 1,157,100 votes out of the 48,690,416 cast for President in 1948. Even if he had been on the ballot in Illinois, it is hardly conceivable that he would have received more than 3 per cent of all the votes which were cast in the election. In consequence, Wallace was unable to precipitate Truman's defeat and hence unable to claim indispensability in future Democratic campaigns. He was not even able to force Truman to make heavy foreign policy concessions during the campaign. The Vinson mission itself, if handled with less haste and partisanship, would probably not have seemed so grave an undertaking.

Nevertheless, it was true that Wallace's few votes were so strategically located in the biggest states that, coupled with the Southern Democratic defection, they did come very close to defeating Truman. Probably Wallace impaired his own potential by allowing his very useful Communist supporters to become too blatantly dominant in the Progressive party organization. That gave Truman an opportunity to protect the regular Democratic ticket by pointing to its anti-communist purity (the "purity" of a widow

43. This was a lesson which the Eisenhower campaign managers in 1952 seem to have taken to heart. In an atmosphere of deep public dissatisfaction over the Korean War, Eisenhower's own pre-election statements showed a rather subtle awareness of the degree of criticism in which he could indulge as a presidential candidate without gravely upsetting international relations or his future relations with friendly Democrats.

more than of a virgin) and thereby offset some of his potential losses to the Communists.

There was another important reason for the success of Truman's response to the Wallacite challenge on his left. He put extreme emphasis on his own *domestic* radicalism—at the same time he refused to make similar concessions to the Progressives on *foreign* policy. By this strategy the President succeeded in mobilizing support from urbanites who would otherwise have voted for Wallace or simply stayed home. But as a secondary consequence he found himself committed at the beginning of his new term of office to press for the Fair Deal with unwonted vigor, although the costs of major domestic projects could not easily be met except at the expense of national defense and foreign aid. Thus the Wallacite pressure, which failed to produce direct modifications of foreign policy in 1948, was an indirect cause for budgetary developments in 1949 which did seem to foreshadow important modifications of foreign policy. This caused new strain in the Democratic party and contributed to a gradual decline of "bipartisanship" in the Eighty-first Congress.

CHAPTER 15

The Downturn of Extrapartisanship

THE MOST IMPORTANT general tendency in the politics of American foreign relations in the remaining months before the Korean War was the rise of partisanship. This development was most pronounced in Far Eastern affairs, as will be shown in the next chapter. Here we are concerned with other factors in the first session of the Eighty-first Congress which contributed to the deterioration of extrapartisanship.

The defeat of Thomas E. Dewey had naturally been a profound shock to Republican leaders, especially since it shattered a nearly universal expectation of his victory. Inevitably the outcome caused re-examination of GOP behavior. There was a school of liberal Republicans who argued in effect that on domestic affairs Dewey had not been "me-tooish" enough—mainly because he could not frankly repudiate the record of the Eightieth Congress. There was another school which condemned his moderate campaigning as soporific to regular Republican voters; what was needed was an all-out anti-Truman offensive to rouse the regulars—and forget about the independents. This view was likely to include a denunciation of the political consequences for the GOP of excessive "bipartisanship" in foreign affairs. Some conservative Republicans went so far as to despair of ever winning a presidential election against the party of the "hand-out state," except by uninhibited attacks from every angle on every unpopular element in its *foreign* policy.

The obvious disparity between the extreme lengths to which

Dewey had gone to avoid partisan issues in foreign affairs and the comparatively moderate lengths to which Truman had gone for that same purpose was inevitably a special source of bitterness among Republicans. GOP leaders who supported "bipartisanship" tended to condemn Truman for having violated its spirit; those who detested the idea (especially the isolationists) derided Dewey as a fool for having allowed himself to be "taken in." Both denunciations could of course be combined, even by people who had less far-reaching views of what "bipartisanship" really required of political candidates. It could reasonably be argued that Republicans were benefiting politically by being identified with successful administration policies in Europe but failed to take full advantage of their free hand to condemn American foreign relations in other areas where the administration had acted alone with much less marked success.

INDEPENDENT MOVES BY THE DEMOCRATS

Mounting Republican doubts about the advantage of collaboration with administration foreign policies were deepened at the beginning of the Eighty-first Congress by an apparent tendency of Democrats to assert their independence of Republicans. GOP leaders who were eager to do away with "bipartisanship" exaggerated the evidence in order to put the blame on the Democrats, but there was some real substance to their complaint.

"Packing" the Foreign Relations Committee. The first conspicuous irritation was the decision of the Democratic majority in the Senate early in January to change the party ratio on the Foreign Relations Committee from 7-6 to 8-5. This was intended to satisfy Senator Fulbright's long ambition for membership.[1] But coupled with Connally's well known jealousy of Vandenberg for the unique prestige he had won in their joint enterprises, it seemed to be a deliberate slap at the former GOP majority—especially since Vandenberg's candidate was a Republican Senator who had fully cooperated with the administration, Wayne Morse of Oregon.[2]

1. Fulbright had gained fame in the House through his connection with the Foreign Affairs Committee's resolution which foreshadowed the UN.
2. *New York Times,* January 6, 1949.

Actually Connally had very little use for Fulbright and made that abundantly clear. But the fact remained that the Democratic Committee on Committees had changed the party composition of Foreign Relations just to satisfy one of their colleagues. Vandenberg's Republican critics could ask: "Was it for this that you worked to secure unanimity in the Committee on nearly every measure of the Eightieth Congress?"

Dean Acheson. Within a week there followed the appointment of Dean Acheson as Secretary of State. Republicans had not been consulted. They were not enthusiastic.[3] To be sure, Acheson had had an amount of diplomatic experience which was unusual in appointees to the office of Secretary of State. He had been Under Secretary to Byrnes and (for a few months) to Marshall. During a large part of that period he had been Acting Secretary while his superior was abroad at conferences. But Acheson was also known to be a thoroughly partisan Truman Democrat, who had even opposed the preconvention efforts of most factions of the Democratic party to unseat the President in 1948. During the campaign Acheson had been active on Truman's behalf.[4] Yet Acheson was not a professional politician, and he had no personal following among politicians of either party. Unless and until he could secure such a following, he would be dependent for support in Congress upon President Truman, upon the agreed merit of his policies, and upon his personal skills of advocacy.

In the following months Acheson undertook to preserve the support of the White House by such exaggerated formal deference to Truman as to impair his own chances, already very slim, of establishing himself as a national leader whose domestic political power would command respect from party leaders. He was in fact exercising wider personal authority in foreign affairs than even Byrnes and Marshall—by reason of his wider experience and Truman's support; but Acheson avoided the dramatized missions and frequent radio reports which had helped those men to stand on their own despite Truman's political weakness. Moreover, in the view

3. Vandenberg, *The Private Papers of Senator Vandenberg,* pp. 469–70.
4. James Reston, "Secretary Acheson: A First Year Audit," *New York Times Magazine,* January 22, 1950, p. 8. For an example, see above, p. 169, n. 50.

of Vandenberg and others, it was largely loyalty to Truman which kept Acheson from seeking to establish a fruitful "Lovett-type" relationship with the Republican leader.[5] Such intimacy might well have compromised Acheson's position at the White House; the Secretary of State was rigidly determined to let nothing come between him and the President, who under the Constitution bore formal responsibility for the conduct of foreign relations.

Politically Acheson began as Truman's creature and never rose much above that status. In January 1949 the "miraculously" elected President may have seemed strong enough to sustain a hand-picked diplomatic specialist in the role of Secretary of State, but Truman's decision to make the attempt was bound to irritate Republicans and anti-administration Democrats from the very beginning; by the following year doubts of its wisdom were far more widespread. Truman and Acheson were so closely linked that in their growing political weakness they seemed to undermine one another. Truman contributed to this outcome not only because of his lack of great popularity and respect in Congress but even more because of his indifferent *public* advocacy of his administration's conduct of foreign relations. For some reason the President's *active* defense of the State Department was only spasmodic.

With Truman such a weak reed to lean upon, Acheson was in fact left largely dependent upon his capacity to frame wise and successful policies which would command sufficient support on their merits, and upon his own recognized personal skills as an advocate. But the collapse of Nationalist China in 1949 made the State Department's policies more widely suspect than they had been since the war. As for Acheson's advocacy, Congress was already familiar with it from his several years in the upper echelon of the State Department. His presentation possessed a technical brilliance which was intellectually overwhelming—but often not inwardly reassuring. In voice, manner, dress, and suspected sympathies he was far too "English." He found it difficult to restrain himself from demolishing the arguments of congressional opponents with a swift incisiveness which seemed insulting. Even for many congressmen of moderate disposition, Acheson was often just

5. Vandenberg, *op. cit.*, pp. 506, 500–1.

too smooth and "cagey" to inspire full confidence. As long as he had appeared to be acting as advocate for other men's policies, many of these traits were forgiven him. But after he was plainly on his own, as Secretary of State for a trusting President, the uneasiness in Congress increased. Acheson's famous remark about Alger Hiss in January 1950 finally supplied an argument—however far fetched—which could be used in public explanations of the suspicions and antipathies.

It is not enough to protest that these suspicions were the unworthy products of prejudice and were exaggerated by Republicans for partisan purposes. Acheson's initial appointment had certainly also involved considerations of (Democratic) partisanship and loyalty to the Democratic President. The trouble was that Truman had appointed a partisan individual who had no party following. He was too partisan to be entirely welcome even to would-be collaborators in the *opposition* party; and yet he had been too far removed from active politics to have powerful and determined supporters in his *own* party—outside the White House, which, however, itself supported him in international diplomacy far more steadily than in domestic politics. Especially after the Hiss episode it was possible to make attacks on Acheson without their producing full-fledged Democratic counterattacks in his defense. Under such circumstances the temptation to attack was tremendous. Lacking a firm foundation in his own party, Acheson was in a poor position to overcome the handicaps of his "Trumanism" and his personality in preserving extrapartisan collaboration with Republican leaders. He was a target so vulnerable that it was often easier to stand aside and let the arrows fly. The fault was Truman's as much as anyone's for having so presumed upon his own enduring prestige as to appoint a brilliant diplomat instead of a national or political leader to the post of Secretary of State in 1949.

"Point Four." In addition to the Acheson appointment and the change in party ratio on Foreign Relations, the insertion of the then inchoate "Point Four" concept in Truman's inaugural address seemed to betoken a self-confident determination on the part of the President and other Democrats to assert their independence

of Republicans in the control of foreign affairs early in 1949. Truman's special counsel Clark Clifford, preparing the inaugural for January 20, asked the State Department for "a noble concept that was challenging and inspiring." Back came the notion of fostering the development of backward areas by American technical assistance and government guarantees for private investment.[6] There was some precedent for the idea in the work of the Institute of Inter-American Affairs and the Export-Import Bank, but the administration had no agreed plan or policy for large-scale expansion of efforts in this field until several months later. Even after that, a few more months were required to work out extrapartisan modifications of the scheme with Representative Herter and Senator Saltonstall. Yet Truman went right ahead in his inaugural address to announce a "bold new program" which he called "Point Four" of American foreign policy (after the UN, ERP, and defense assistance). And for years the administration refused to drop from the program the odd label "Point Four," which by its very obscurity required frequently reiterated explanations—referring always to the inaugural address of President Harry Truman. This was hardly calculated to facilitate its consideration in a nonpartisan atmosphere.

THE ATLANTIC PACT: LATE FLOWERING OF BIPARTISANSHIP

The Point Four presentation, the Acheson appointment, the change in party ratio on Foreign Relations—all these rasped Republican sensibilities in early 1949, though not sharply enough to endanger the fruition of the one great pending bipartisan project, the North Atlantic Treaty. This fully collaborative effort, which had begun with the Vandenberg Resolution the year before, is evidence enough that the decline in extrapartisanship was not a swift development. This one tale of harmony may help to give perspective to the examples of friction in other areas of American foreign relations during the Eighty-first Congress.

Soon after the election secret international negotiations for the

6. Arthur Krock, *New York Times,* January 28, 1949.

North Atlantic Treaty were resumed by Under Secretary of State Lovett. The work had been largely in abeyance since September because Dulles had requested that no definitive action be taken during the presidential campaign. There was some further delay in resuming systematic bipartisan negotiations because of the post-election congressional "rest period" and the change of personnel at the top of the State Department. But after the beginning of February Vandenberg and Connally were consulted nearly every other day.

The "Lovett draft" of the treaty, which Acheson had inherited, included the two basic principles (1) that an armed attack upon one of the treaty partners should be regarded as an armed attack upon all, and (2) that each nation should then "take military or other action forthwith." Exactly what form of action was required would remain within the discretion of each state. Vandenberg and Connally, noting this language, asked that "military" should not be mentioned explicitly. The State Department bowed tentatively to the phrase "take action forthwith," and the two Senators assured their colleagues on February 14 that the United States would not be morally or legally bound to fight.[7] This created a storm of protest in Europe and even in the United States sufficient to indicate that two-thirds of the Senate could be persuaded to swallow something stronger. Acheson thereupon went before the full Foreign Relations Committee in executive session on February 18 and obtained a consensus that there might be explicit treaty reference to a possible choice by the United States to use military measures against the aggressor.[8] The language soon agreed upon for this key paragraph referred to "taking forthwith, individually and in concert with the other parties, such action as [each state] deems necessary, including the use of armed force, to restore and maintain the security of the North Atlantic area."

Other minor changes in the treaty draft were made at the behest of the Foreign Relations Committee. In a further effort to achieve the widest possible measure of Senate agreement on the treaty, Connally consented to allow two "outsiders"—Senators

7. *Congressional Record*, February 14, 1949, pp. 1164–8.
8. James Reston, *New York Times*, February 19, 1949.

Watkins and Donnell—to sit in on the hearings of the Foreign Relations Committee and question witnesses directly.[9] Their unfriendly, probing questions helped to elucidate obscure sections
of the pact and created greater confidence in the Senate that the
Foreign Relations Committee was not simply rubber-stamping a
project to which it had long since become committed by direct participation. But unfortunately Connally's temper frayed, and Watkins withdrew in a huff.[10]

The Foreign Relations Committee reported the treaty unanimously, without reservations or crippling interpretations. On the
Senate floor the chief opposition came from Senator Taft. With
Wherry and Watkins he attempted to add a "declaration" to the
effect that "the United States ratifies this treaty with the understanding that Article 3 commits none of the parties thereto, morally
or legally, to furnish or supply arms . . ." Taft was concentrating
his fire against the peacetime military assistance program on which
the Senate would act after ratification of the treaty. Vandenberg
fought against him to prevent a Senate vote which would appear
to be an advance rejection of that program. The prejudicial "declaration" was defeated 74-21 on the key roll call, July 21. Eighteen
Republicans voted with Taft, 25 with Vandenberg, on this clear
test of foreign policy leadership in mid-1949. Only three Democrats voted against the administration. Later two other reservations, more drastic, received only half as much support as had Taft,
Wherry, and Watkins. The treaty was ratified unchanged by a vote
of 82-13. Republicans were recorded three to one in its favor. The
result was a fitting climax to an impressive achievement in bipartisanship.

INTERNATIONAL "CALM" AND THE
MILITARY BUDGET DISPUTE

For the most part, however, it remains true that cooperative relations in the Eighty-first Congress were extrapartisan, with a trend
toward real partisanship. As was to be expected, this tendency was

9. Arthur Krock, *New York Times*, May 6, 1949.
10. *New York Times*, May 10, 1949.

most conspicuous in Far Eastern affairs, and therefore the next chapter will be devoted to that subject. But here it is first important to emphasize that in addition to the evidence—real and exaggerated—that the administration was disposed to act more independently of Republicans in foreign affairs than in the Eightieth Congress, an important factor weakening extrapartisan ties in 1949 was the absence of a sense of general crisis. If the administration had wished, the collapse of Nationalist China could certainly have been used to develop a crisis atmosphere comparable to that obtaining in the spring of 1948, but the administration had no such desire. With the liquidation of the Berlin blockade in the spring of 1949 after a notable American psychological-warfare victory through the airlift, the prevailing expectation was a period of relative peace between Russia and the West. A vitally important effect of this complacency was to increase the popularity of budgetary economy, even on defense expenditures, and to make highly unpopular any serious attempt to restore the taxes which the Eightieth Congress had cut despite Truman's veto. Yet the President would have to find new money somewhere for the Fair Deal programs for which he had campaigned so vigorously. Thus a sharp conflict developed between the administration's welfare and fiscal policy on the one hand and its foreign and defense policy on the other. How combine the Fair Deal, plus a budget balanced without new taxes, plus foreign aid, plus an adequate military establishment? No satisfactory solution was really possible, but makeshift settlements had to be found when budgets were prepared and appropriations voted. These tended to divide both parties, but especially the Democrats, until the Korean War for a time greatly relaxed the budgetary inhibitions.[11]

The Beginnings of Rearmament. To gain perspective on the disputes over the defense budget in 1949, it is desirable to go back to the Eightieth Congress and to the rearmament program which was stimulated by the spring crisis of 1948.

As a result of the demobilization program after World War II, defense expenditures had fallen from $45 billion in the fiscal year

11. The beginnings of a similar corrosive trend may perhaps be discerned in the experience of the Eisenhower administration after the cease-fire in Korea.

ending June 30, 1946, to $14.3 billion in fiscal 1947 and stood at approximately $11 billion in 1948 and in the budget estimates for 1949.[12] This figure included stockpiling costs.

At the beginning of 1948 President Truman's Air Policy Commission under Thomas Finletter provided a sounding board for the air force to request a basic strength of seventy groups, to be achieved by increasing the defense budget by about $1.5 billion each year for at least two years and probably for five. At this rate the total would pass $18 billion a year by 1952, even if the army were not increased at all.[13] Early in March a select committee of both houses (called the Congressional Aviation Policy Board) issued a report which avoided outright endorsement of the seventy-group program but suggested no other alternative. It called upon the President to recommend alterations in the defense budget then before Congress.[14]

The popularity of these recommendations grew rapidly in the crisis atmosphere of that month, especially after Truman's speech to Congress on March 17, in which he asked for the draft and universal military training. Air power seemed to offer a less painful substitute. Defense Secretary Forrestal, however, was determined to effect a balanced increase in the forces of all three services; he had "substantial misgivings" at that time about the air force's capacity to strike deep into Russia.[15] By March 25 he was ready to present recommendations to Congress for an increase of $3 billion in the budget estimate of $11 billion. But the air force chiefs made plain their dissatisfaction with their share of this increase. They pressed the House of Representatives into voting $822 million additional toward a seventy-group air force. Riding the spending wave, John Taber did manage to insert (in the floor amendment by which he sponsored the increase) a "hooker" which left the money available for an extra year at the President's discretion.

12. Millis, *The Forrestal Diaries*, pp. 352–3.

13. *Survival in the Air Age,* a report of the President's Air Policy Commission, January 1, 1948, pp. 31–6.

14. Senate Report 949 (Congressional Aviation Policy Board), 80th Congress, March 1, 1948, pp. 6–10.

15. Millis, *The Forrestal Diaries*, p. 538.

It would not have to be spent until 1950; presumably Taber intended that it should not be.[16]

If more money was thus to be made available, Forrestal wanted its expenditure better balanced. He got the Joint Chiefs of Staff to agree to expand the original $3 billion special program by $481 million (but not by the $822 million which the House had voted). Truman allowed this new compromise recommendation to be presented to Congress on April 21. However, between the Italian election and the Berlin blockade the international tension relaxed markedly. The Budget Bureau took a firm hand in the proceedings. Its calculations showed that the projects represented by the Defense Department's final agreed request would lead to a military budget of more than $18 billion in 1952, even without the seventy-group air force. The Budget therefore took the tentatively accepted total additional defense request for fiscal 1949 and cut it from $3,481 million to about $3,100 million. The Bureau further sought to establish the principle that defense appropriations in fiscal 1950 should not exceed $15 billion. In other words the cost of the military establishment would go from about $11 billion in 1948 to about $15 billion in fiscal 1950 but would level off there and go no higher.

Forrestal strongly protested this decision, but he was not well supported by General Marshall as Secretary of State. Marshall was more interested in getting universal military training and in avoiding the dislocations which would result from starting projects grander than Congress would be willing to sustain in later years. The President's decision, strongly influenced by Budget Director Webb, was to delay spending the extra $822 million which Congress did vote and to direct the defense chiefs to hold the pace of rearmament under their other special appropriations to a level which would not require more than about $15 billion in 1950. Thus a $15 billion ceiling on the American military establishment was formally, if tentatively, set by Truman as early as May 13, 1948.[17]

16. *Ibid.*, pp. 412–17.
17. *Ibid.*, pp. 418–19, 429–33, 435–8.

Preparation of the budget for fiscal 1950 began within a few weeks at the Pentagon. Forrestal was still aiming to breach the President's ceiling. The Defense Secretary prevailed upon the Joint Chiefs of Staff to limit their agreed official request to $17.5 billion, and then he secured George Marshall's formal endorsement of this figure, though Marshall's new special interest was in speeding arms to Western Europe.[18] However, when Forrestal renewed his negotiations with the Budget Bureau and the President, it was made clear to him that the $15 billion ceiling still stood in principle. The best compromise that the Defense Department was able to obtain was that the $822 million which had been set aside from Congress' extra appropriations for fiscal 1949 would not be deducted from the President's budget request for fiscal 1950. It would be spent after all in addition to the new $15 billion.

Forrestal's own position was gravely weakened after the President's re-election. The Defense Secretary had taken no active part in the campaign; he had made no speeches. Forrestal argued that his post, like that of the Secretary of State, should be free of partisan responsibilities. Apparently Forrestal assumed, furthermore, that Dewey would win.[19] Critics suspected that he was hoping to stay in high office as an example of "bipartisanship" after the Republican victory. Democratic politicians resented his absence from the fray. Apostles of air power chafed at his efforts to assure balanced forces even at their expense. Labor and liberal groups were suspicious of his Wall Street connections and his "militarism." Jewish interests were indignant about his anti-Zionism; Walter Winchell and Drew Pearson turned their most powerful guns against him. Finally, there was a very well-deserving Democrat who wanted a job—Louis Johnson. He had excellent connections in the American Legion and three years' respectable experience as Assistant Secretary of War just before World War II—and he had rescued Truman's campaign finances at a very bleak moment. Truman did not actually request Forrestal's resignation until March 1, 1949, but the combined assaults and predictions of his imminent departure had weakened the Defense Secretary's capacity

18. *Ibid.*, pp. 500–2, 508–10, 536.
19. *Ibid.*, pp. 473, 494–5.

for leadership several weeks before that. The appointment of his old opponent at the Budget Bureau, James Webb, to be Under Secretary of State replacing Forrestal's good friend Lovett also seemed to signal that the rearmament program which had begun in the spring crisis of 1948 would not survive the milder international climate of 1949.

Congress and the Defense Budget, 1949. When the limited defense budget for fiscal 1950 reached Capitol Hill at the beginning of the Eighty-first Congress, the House Appropriations Committee acted as a vehicle for air power advocates. Small cuts were made in army and navy funds, but the air force received $787 million more than Truman had requested. The only fight in the House came on an attempt by the Armed Services Committee to get $300 million more for *naval* air power. This was a fight between committees, across party lines. Cannon and Taber, ranking Democrat and Republican on Appropriations, stood against members of both parties on Armed Services. The Appropriations Committee was the decisive victor. The navy amendment was defeated on a standing vote, 125-63, and then the bill was passed unchanged, with only Marcantonio appearing against it.

In the Senate effective economy sentiment was far stronger. Indeed that is probably a major reason why House members were willing to vote the money so freely. The Senate Appropriations Committee voted to cut the House bill by $1.1 billion—leaving about $500 million less than even the administration had first requested for the military establishment. In addition, $275 million which Truman wanted for stockpiling was ordered cut back from an earlier appropriations act. The extra money which the House had voted for air was entirely removed from the Senate bill.

When the bill reached the Senate floor, the Democrats showed considerable division. Republicans were nearly solid in support of the committee's decision to hold the air force at the 48 groups which Truman was requesting rather than go up to 58 as the House had done. A sizable contingent of liberal Democrats from the South and Northeast wanted to spend the larger sum, but the majority of the Democratic party also, in all sections, was against them. Three amendments were offered aiming to cut the appro-

priation even further. They failed, but all received the support of
the vast majority of Republicans and several Democrats, including
Northerners.

These roll calls gave the Senate managers about as strong a mandate for defense economy as the House managers had for heavy expenditures, in the month-long Conference Committee sessions
which began late in September. On October 10 the House conferees undertook to reinforce their position by securing roll calls
of 306-1 and 306-0 respectively to support their insistence on 58
air groups and on full stockpiling funds. Truman then called in a
delegation of leading Senators and told them he still wanted the
stockpiling money but not the air force funds. Still the Senate
voted unanimously to continue to hold out against the House, even
on stockpiling. Finally on October 17 the conferees agreed in effect
to pass the buck to the President. The stockpiling funds desired by
the administration were cut by only $100 million; the extra air
money went into the bill, but with a tacit understanding that it
need not be spent. Both houses approved the compromise by voice
vote. The President promptly impounded the "surplus" appropriation.[20]

The "Louis Johnson Budget." The optimistic White House view
of the situation was simultaneously being reflected in plans for the
military budget for fiscal 1951. General Eisenhower had been
brought in by Forrestal shortly before Louis Johnson's arrival to
assist in preparations for a budget in the neighborhood of $15
billion. The President's ceiling would stand, it was now assumed.
But it was going to be very hard to make it stick while continuing
to build up the navy and air force simultaneously. One of Johnson's first acts in office was to secure the views of the Joint Chiefs
of Staff about the building of the navy's superaircraft carrier which
was about to begin. The air and army chiefs recommended against
it. Johnson proceeded to secure the agreement of Eisenhower and
the chairmen of the Senate and House Armed Services Commit-

20. The sum actually impounded by presidential letter dated November 8, 1949,
was approximately $736 million. *Hearings* on the military situation in the Far East,
before the Senate Armed Services and Foreign Relations Committees, June 1951, p.
2650.

tees. Truman then assented to prompt cancellation of the carrier.[21]

In the Executive Office of the President, Chairman Edwin G. Nourse of the Council of Economic Advisers was particularly anti-militarist in his outlook, and contended that "a program of military expenditures at any level much above the present [about $15 billion a year] would force us out of the free market procedures of a peacetime economy and drive us to the acceptance of a number of direct controls." [22] In his later book about his experiences on the CEA, Nourse consistently minimizes the effective influence of the Council, but he did note in his diary, on August 26, 1949, that the new Budget Director Frank Pace "seems quite sympathetic with the points of view which I have expressed" about the budget then in preparation.[23] Nourse believes that it was Pace who secured an invitation for him to participate in staff meetings of the National Security Council during the spring and summer of 1949.[24]

On July 1, at a top-level White House meeting, Pace informed the defense chiefs that the ceiling for the regular military establishment in fiscal 1951 would be $13 billion instead of the $14.6 billion on which they had agreed with Eisenhower's assistance. Thus in fiscal 1951 the projected additional military assistance to West European countries would not much increase the total national budget (and any further growth in military aid in later years could simply be dovetailed with expected reductions in economic assistance under ERP). CEA Chairman Nourse had publicly pressed for a similar telescoping as early as April 1949,[25] but Defense Secretary Louis Johnson was opposed to this further cut in his department's regular appropriations and protested vigorously

21. Johnson testimony, *ibid.*, pp. 2636–7.

22. Edwin G. Nourse, *Economics in the Public Service* (New York, Harcourt, Brace, 1953), p. 493 (in reprint of speech at an official orientation conference for the military establishment, November 10, 1948). This and a later orientation speech in a similar vein created considerable public controversy about the future of the administration's rearmament policy (*New York Times*, April 7 and 8, 1949), but Nourse in his book gives assurance that both speeches were officially cleared by the White House—the second by Treasury Secretary Snyder, Budget Director Pace, and President Truman himself (p. 405).

23. Nourse, *op. cit.*, p. 283.

24. *Ibid.*, p. 249.

25. *New York Times*, April 7 and 8, 1949.

to Pace and Truman. He managed to secure their approval for adding the $500 million of projected stockpiling money to the proposed $13 billion ceiling, making a new ceiling of $13.5 billion for fiscal 1951—a net reduction of about $1 billion instead of about $1.5 billion from previous plans.[26] (Also ultimately available in the new budget was most of the money which Truman would not allow to be spent under the congressional appropriations for fiscal 1950.)

Johnson considered resigning but decided to stay and do his best within the new limitation. Of course he thereby accepted responsibility for it, just as he had accepted responsibility for the earlier ceiling by taking the office of Defense Secretary after a limitation had been well established by the President. But in realistic terms it is important to recognize that the ceilings, both old and new, were set over the Defense Department by the Budget Bureau with the approval of the President and on the recommendation of the chairman of the Council of Economic Advisers. Louis Johnson took most of the blame, but the basic decisions were made in the White House by presidential advisers who were struggling in a relatively peaceful international climate to balance defense and foreign aid requirements against politically profitable welfare measures without raising taxes or seriously unbalancing the budget.

This time the President's economy-mindedness was not opposed by the House of Representatives. The House Appropriations Committee voted the defense budget virtually as requested in the spring of 1950. There was a token cut of $200 million. Chairman Carl Vinson of the Armed Services Committee sparked a campaign to get $583 million more for air, including naval air. Dwight Eisenhower appeared before the Senate Appropriations Committee and asked $500 million more than the House Committee was recommending. This pressure did induce Cannon's committee to add $385 million by amendment to its own bill on the floor. The

26. Johnson testimony, *Hearings* on the military situation in the Far East, before the Senate Armed Services and Foreign Relations Committees, June 1951, pp. 2597–9, 2606–8, 3246.

increase was unopposed on May 9, 1950, but it still did not much alter the President's recommendation.

Before the Senate Appropriations Committee could act, the Korean War began.

SUMMARY OBSERVATIONS

Louis Johnson became the scapegoat for the administration's failure to achieve a higher level of preparedness before Korea. No doubt a Democratic scapegoat was needed, for actually the party had had a relatively free hand in working out the strictly military budget, within a discretionary range of a few billion dollars. Republicans were not disposed to offer important political resistance to defense expenditures of the size requested or less—or probably even to considerably greater military spending if the administration were willing to emphasize the dangerous international situation and minimize the Fair Deal. That was the crux of the matter. What was essentially at issue between the parties and within the Democratic party was *domestic* policy, fiscal and welfare. Taxation, deficit financing, and the Fair Deal were the centers of controversy. In turn they impinged upon foreign policy through limitations on the size of the total budget, especially as these were permitted to affect the largest item, military expenditures. The Republican tax cut in the Eightieth Congress had sharply reduced the area of discretion open to Democratic budget planners in the Eighty-first. Within the remaining area the administration had to balance foreign and domestic demands. An easy way out for Truman would have been to mount a "crisis," on the basis of the Far Eastern situation and the Russian A-bomb. But aside from unpleasant international consequences, such a solution would have required also the postponement of Fair Deal legislation. The 1948 election results argued against such a strategy.

But as long as the administration was unwilling to jeopardize its domestic program, an unreal atmosphere of optimism had to be allowed to prevail about foreign and defense requirements. The administration itself took care of the slicing of *military* estimates in accordance with the mood it was encouraging; Republican critics were then generally reluctant to sponsor further heavy reductions on defense. Party-line conflict was avoided for the most part; the Fair Deal's chances had not been deliberately destroyed; the international consequences were comfortingly unpredictable; but the administration did not seem to be reducing its foreign aid programs on the same drastic scale. Those congressmen, especially in the GOP, who had been reluctant to support foreign aid even during the spring crisis of 1948 now felt encouraged to attack vigorously this surviving "extravagance" in the administration's total national security budget. It was mainly in this foreign aid sector that the peaceful atmosphere which the administration was allowing to persist contributed to a loosening of cooperative ties between the parties before the outbreak of war in Korea.

Still it is not to be thought that the extrapartisan collaboration on European affairs which had reached such a high point in the Eightieth Congress was destroyed or even very rapidly weakened in the Eighty-first by budgetary considerations in a mild international climate—nor by the developments which seemed to indicate a growing sense of independence on the part of some leading Democrats, developments like Point Four, the Acheson appointment, and the reconstitution of the Foreign Relations Committee. These factors did indeed contribute in 1949 to a gradual decline in the closeness of extrapartisan relations. But no stalemate barrier arose between the parties until the beginning of 1950—and then it appeared primarily on Far Eastern affairs, where the record of active cooperation in the past had been very small indeed.

CHAPTER 16

China Post Mortem

WITH THE COLLAPSE of Nationalist China in 1949 there developed a higher, more sustained level of partisan friction than had arisen regarding the conduct of American relations with any major area of the world since before World War II.

Here was a tremendous Communist victory in which Republicans were not involved. As periodically they had rather smugly reminded the public, their active cooperation had not been sought in the years when Chiang's vulnerability was in the making. Then, before it was *obviously* too late to save him, many members of the GOP had gone on record for substantially more assistance than the administration was prepared to give. And finally even the minimal and presumably inadequate aid program which the Eightieth Congress did vote had not been implemented by the administration with sufficient expedition to remove suspicion that bad faith was being shown to the members of both parties who had compromised on that modest gesture of support for Chiang. Clearly the Republicans did not need to muffle their criticism of the administration for fear of an obvious inconsistency with their own past record, and they were free to continue to propose any kind of aid program for Chiang which was not on its face ludicrously unfeasible or shockingly expensive. (Noninterventionist and economy-minded Republicans could reassure themselves with the almost certain knowledge that the administration itself would ultimately block *any* heavy aid program.)

Congressional Democrats, at the beginning of 1949, were virtually as much entitled to criticize the State Department as were the Republicans. Neither group had been much involved in the administration's conduct of Far Eastern affairs. But most of the Democrats were naturally reluctant to embarrass their fellow partisan in the White House at the beginning of his second term, and all of them, even the Southerners, had less incentive than Republicans to be inattentive to considerations of expense and feasibility when weighing proposals for new assistance to Nationalist China.

The administration itself still had the choice of cooperating in further gestures of support for Chiang or of ending them as promptly as possible. Now at least it was too late to suppose that substantial grants of assistance to Nationalist China could do much to temper partisan criticism in America. Nationalist China was disintegrating and the Democratic administration would not be able to diffuse its political responsibility for America's role in the antecedent events. More than ever, therefore, the temptation was to seek complete disentanglement and a free hand, from the Kuomintang abroad and from the China bloc at home. The first step was to put increased reliance on the Democratic party majorities in House and Senate to act—though perhaps with reluctance and indifference—to resist the pressure for new commitments in China, while the State Department reconsidered the whole problem of the Far East.

But the longer the department delayed in formulating a tentative new policy, the longer the period before it could be unveiled, even privately, for the advice and consent of congressmen of either party who might be sympathetically disposed; and the more difficult it would be for even the most moderate members of the opposition party to wait patiently by while officials wiped from their eyes the dust of the disintegrating Kuomintang. Yet the atmosphere of mutual suspicion which for years had been allowed to develop between the Far Eastern Division and Congress was such that the State Department knew it would appear still more unreliable if it tried to begin extensive consultations on a new Asian policy before it had anything concrete to suggest. And the most vital factor in the new Far Eastern situation—the power of Red China and the closeness of its relations with Russia—could not quickly be assessed. So the State Department had new reasons for continuing its familiar practice of not seeking close contact with Congress on Asia. Thus the department reacted with such deliberation to the shockingly swift collapse of Nationalist China that more and more Republicans declined to hold their fire while the suspect Far Eastern Division devised a new policy without much congressional participation.[1]

Democratic party lines also grew gradually tighter in Congress as members came to the conclusion that Republicans were simply making political capital out of a situation which by this time had become irreparable. In the summer of 1949 the legislative history of the Mutual Defense Assistance Act showed that the growing China partisanship could endanger other foreign aid programs, but also that compromise was still possible. At the beginning of 1950, however, the cleavage became very sharp regarding the defense of Formosa. The administration's flexibility in the conduct of Far Eastern relations was severely limited. And many Republicans in their partisan bitterness became amenable to the demagogic tactics of Senator McCarthy.

THE CONTRACTION OF AID
TO NATIONALIST CHINA

The military collapse of Nationalist China began in full scale in Manchuria in September 1948. By the end of January 1949 all of Manchuria and much of North China, including Peiping, was in Communist hands. The prompt reaction of the China section of the State Department was to recommend "going to the American public now [late November 1948] to explain the inadequacies of the Chiang Kai-shek government." Secretary Marshall, with Truman's approval, rejected this extreme measure. Forrestal noted

1. The consultations which were held in 1949 are summarized in a letter by Ambassador-at-Large Philip Jessup, dated December 8, 1949, printed in *Hearings* on the nomination of Philip Jessup, before a subcommittee of the Senate Foreign Relations Committee, October 1951, p. 885.

that Marshall "felt that this would administer the final *coup de grâce* to Chiang's government, and this, he felt, we could not do." [2]

Acheson, however, was determined to cut loose from the sinking ship as swiftly and abruptly as possible. Within two weeks after he became Secretary of State, the National Security Council recommended that Truman halt shipment of $60 million of military materiel which still remained out of the Eightieth Congress' $125 million "additional aid" fund for China. The NSC advice was certainly approved by Acheson and most probably originated in the State Department, though officers in the Defense Department were also disturbed by the prospect of more weapons falling into Communist hands.

The White House moved to forestall new congressional criticism by calling a private conference on February 5, 1949, including the President and Vice-President, Acheson, Vandenberg, Connally, Eaton, and Bloom. Vandenberg, whose diary records this episode, has identified only his own views and those of Vice-President Barkley. The Republican Senator strongly resisted the proposed action. His arguments were interesting:

> There is something here vastly more important than what happens to $60 million worth of supplies . . .
> Regardless of the justification of previous charges that our American policy has been largely responsible for China's fate [parenthetically at another point Vandenberg noted that "this charge is only partially justified up to date"], if we take *this* step at *this* fatefully inept moment, we shall never be able to shake the charge that we are the ones who gave poor China the final push into disaster. Millions of our own people will be shocked; and we shall seriously lose prestige throughout the world. I decline any part of any such responsibility. I beg of you, at the very least, to postpone any such decision for a few more weeks until the China question is settled *by China* and *in China* and not by the *American government in Washington.* This blood must not be on *our* hands . . .
> I make it plain that I have little or no hope for stopping

2. Millis, *The Forrestal Diaries,* p. 534.

the immediate Communist conquest. That is beside the point. I decline to be responsible for the *last push* which makes it possible.[3]

In effect, Senator Vandenberg at this date was urging the policy to which Owen Lattimore later gave a notorious label: "letting China fall without making it appear we pushed it." But the State Department was reluctant to continue to make even that limited concession to domestic political expediency.

In this instance Truman and Barkley supported Vandenberg, and some shipments were allowed to continue. But the State Department would not permit any further aid programs of substantial proportions for Nationalist China.

Thumbs Down on the China Bloc. On February 7, 1949, fifty-one Republican Representatives addressed a letter to President Truman inquiring urgently about plans for support of non-Communist China. Acheson's reply came in a special meeting with the GOP congressmen in which he made the famous remark that he could not foresee the outcome in China "until the dust settled." [4] The following day, February 25, Senator McCarran, antiadministration Democrat from Nevada, introduced a bill to provide $1.5 billion in loans for Nationalist China for economic and military purposes; American officers were to direct Chinese troops in the field; and the customs at Chinese ports would be pledged as collateral for the loans. On March 10 fifty Senators, half of them Republicans, half Democrats, issued a public appeal to Chairman Connally to allow the Foreign Relations Committee to give the measure full consideration and hearings. Signers did not necessarily endorse McCarran's bill, but they did seek "an affirmative policy for the United States with respect to Asia through providing effective assistance to the Government of China on a realistic basis." [5]

3. Vandenberg, *The Private Papers of Senator Vandenberg,* pp. 530–2. The italics are Senator Vandenberg's.

4. Acheson's explanation of his remark may be found in *Hearings* on the military situation in the Far East, before the Senate Armed Services and Foreign Relations Committees, June 1951, pp. 1765–6.

5. *New York Times,* March 11, 1949.

By this time Communist forces were poised along the Yangtze and within five weeks they would sweep across the river virtually unopposed and begin their uninterrupted push southward to Canton. Acheson turned thumbs down on the Senators' proposal in a letter to Connally:

> To furnish solely military materiel and advice would only prolong hostilities and the suffering of the Chinese people and would arouse in them deep resentment against the United States. Yet, to furnish the military means for bringing about a reversal of the present deterioration and for providing some prospect of successful military resistance would require the use of an unpredictably large American armed force in actual combat . . . contrary to . . . the interests of this country.[6]

But the second year's authorization for the European Recovery Program was about to come to a vote in Congress. To protect that bill from partisan assault, if for no other reason, there would have to be at least a nod in Chiang's direction. It can hardly be called a bow. State Department officials made it plain that they wanted Congress to go no further than to allow what still was left of the 1948 China aid appropriation to be spent the following year.[7] It was said to be a matter of $54 million.

Republicans on the House Foreign Affairs Committee were particularly ill satisfied. Democrats on the Committee in 1949 even refused to combine China aid with ERP in one bill as had been done in the Eightieth Congress; but the very day after the ERP bill had been reported to the House speedy action began on the "$54 million" China measure which the State Department was suggesting. It was approved almost immediately by the committee and scheduled for passage in the House ahead of the ERP bill. But all the Republican members of Foreign Affairs registered their protests about China policy in minority statements published on March 30.[8] When the "$54 million" China bill came up in the House on April 4, vociferous objections by Vorys and Judd led

6. Department of State, *United States Relations with China* [the "White Paper"], Annex 186, p. 1053.

7. *Ibid.*, p. 1054.

8. House Report 323, Part II (Foreign Affairs Committee), 81st Congress, March 30, 1949.

the Democratic managers to abandon a clause which would have given the President full discretion to dispense the funds without regard to the provisions of the China Aid Act of 1948.[9] Then the bill was passed on a roll call of 279-70. Forty Democrats and 29 Republicans voted against the measure. Most of them were Southerners or Interior members of the GOP, but there was also heavy absenteeism in the New York delegation, especially among Democrats.

In the Senate, action on China came the same day. There Connally was offering to amend the ERP bill on the floor to include the "$54 million" for China. But, as in the House, he was under pressure, especially from Republicans led by Knowland of California, to limit the President's discretion in the expenditure of the funds. Senator Knowland did not press, as did his China-bloc colleagues in the House, for a reaffirmation of the principles of the 1948 act, but he did want to make certain that the President would be free to spend the money only "in areas of China which he may deem to be not under Communist domination." Connally for a time argued that mere relief funds should not necessarily be barred from individual Chinamen because they were Communists. But he bowed to Knowland's phraseology, which was adopted by voice vote in the Senate.[10] The Conference Committee retained most of the Knowland amendment, giving the President discretion in the use of the balance of the China Aid Act appropriations in *noncommunist* areas of China.[11] (Actually there was more left to administer than the $54 million which had been loosely cited in discussion of the new bill.)

The renewal of this small grant, however, was hardly calculated

9. *Congressional Record*, April 4, 1949, p. 3828.
10. *Ibid.*, April 2, 1949, pp. 3768-71 and April 4, 1949, p. 3787.
11. House managers' statement, *ibid.*, April 14, 1949, p. 4632. On the authorization for a second year of the European Recovery Program itself, friction between the parties was still at a low level, comparable to the 80th Congress. The authorization of funds emerged from conference exactly as requested by the administration.

It should be noted that this strong continuing support in both parties for the Economic Cooperation Administration was due in large measure to the assiduous efforts of its chief, Paul Hoffman, to cultivate Congress. He had, of course, excellent Republican connections, and he acted decisively to halt Democratic sniping by ruling himself out as a candidate for the GOP presidential nomination in 1952. For example, *New York Times*, May 19, 1950.

to satisfy Chiang's congressional supporters. What they wanted was action on the McCarran bill. Then on April 14 Acheson's earlier letter to Connally flatly opposing the measure was published. Connally announced that the Foreign Relations Committee would hold no hearings on the bill, despite the previous appeal from twenty-five Senators of each party. In Senate debate on April 15 Republican Styles Bridges called for a full-scale congressional investigation of the administration's China policy. His attack was strongly supported by McCarran and Knowland, and Wayne Morse and Walter George were also critical of Acheson's position. Knowland introduced a formal resolution on April 21 asking for a joint House-Senate investigation of China policy. Such a move would have brought in Foreign Affairs Committee critics from the House, to offset the supposed "whitewashing" tendencies of the Foreign Relations Committee, but of course the resolution itself was buried in the Senate group.

That same week, however, the Chinese Communists swept across the Yangtze, and the Nationalist government moved to Canton. On April 28 Truman invited Bridges and Wherry to come with Acheson to the White House for a private explanation of the situation in China. Wherry was visibly sobered after the meeting, and Bridges said Congress should know what they had been told.[12] The swift and unresisted advance of the Communists in China was temporarily muffling many of their most vociferous enemies in the United States. McCarran and Knowland did provide General Chennault with two committee platforms on May 3 to air an appeal for $700 million a year for non-Communist elements in South China, but his program as described in public session was vague.[13] Acheson dismissed it on May 4 with a curt declaration that American policy was unchanged.[14]

WAITING FOR THE DUST TO SETTLE

For the next few weeks there was a lull in agitation by the China bloc while future possibilities were re-examined. But increasingly

12. *Ibid.*, April 29, 1949.
13. *Ibid.*, May 4, 1949.
14. *Ibid.*, May 5, 1949.

the State Department's continued unwillingness to offer any positive policy in the disintegrating situation tended to undermine even the links of passive acquiescence which had existed between some leading Republicans (notably Vandenberg) and the operating officials in the Far Eastern Division.

In negotiations beginning on May 6, the department arranged that the Western powers at least consult before recognizing a new Communist government in China.[15] But the State Department was also getting ready to free itself of most past entanglements with the Nationalists. Officials were busy in the spring of 1949 preparing a documentary defense of the conduct of American relations with China in the years preceding Chiang's collapse. This was the project which Marshall had rejected as a *coup de grâce* in November 1948, but Acheson now approved it. Late in June Philip Jessup was put to work editing the material which the China hands had collected.[16]

The Butterworth Confirmation Fight. With the State Department busily engaged on an apologia and waiting for the dust to settle before presenting a new policy even for purposes of consultation, Republicans were even freer than before to condemn the China disaster. For their part the Democrats, who in March and April had still been willing to make the political gesture of registering sympathy with McCarran's aid bill, now felt reluctantly compelled by political necessity to offer partisan protection to the administration against the Republicans' partisan attacks.

The pivotal Senator was Arthur Vandenberg. Privately he had a new reason for delaying the showdown as long as possible. His personal friendship with General Marshall had ripened to the point where "I hate to have any part of [the China quarrel] because I dislike to say *anything,* however indirectly, which reflects

15. *Hearings* on the nomination of Philip Jessup, before a subcommittee of the Senate Foreign Relations Committee, October 1951, p. 615.

16. *Ibid.,* pp. 813, 936. Jessup was a Columbia professor of international law who had served as chairman of the Institute of Pacific Relations in 1939–40 and also as chairman of its Research Advisory Committee in 1943–44. He had then been an American representative at various international gatherings, including the spring meeting of the Foreign Ministers Council in 1949, at which the Berlin blockade was lifted.

on anything that George Marshall ever did." But finally "Acheson precipitated [an] issue," and "I *had* to get into it—couldn't stave it off any longer." [17]

The issue was the confirmation of Walton Butterworth to be Assistant Secretary of State for Far Eastern Affairs. He had been filling much the same job with a lesser title since September 1947, when he replaced John Carter Vincent. Now the Hoover Commission reorganization of the State Department required that the Senate confirm Butterworth in his new rank if he were to continue to hold the position. On the Senate floor, June 24, 1949, Vandenberg protested that the appointment—in effect the reappointment—was a "very great mistake" because it signified the "continuation of a regime which inevitably is connected with a very tragic failure" in the Far East. Vandenberg conceded Butterworth's ability but thought it a "mistake in public policy . . . not to bring a fresh point of view to the assignment." [18] Bridges and Knowland struck more vigorously at the State Department's conduct of China policy. Connally hit back with the question "whether there is any member of the Senate who would have voted to send a United States Army to try to settle the controversy between the Chinese factions in China?" [19] But the Senate passed over Butterworth's appointment and likewise refused to approve it on thirteen later occasions, until on September 27 confirmation came on a highly partisan roll call in which only five Republicans and not a single Democrat crossed party lines. Vandenberg himself was ill in Michigan.

Immediately after Vandenberg had gone so far as to clash publicly with Connally over an aspect of China policy (June 24), 16 Republicans and 5 Democrats released a letter to Truman requesting assurance that the United States would not recognize Communist China. Knowland circulated the message for signatures, but by not requesting Vandenberg to sign he avoided putting him on the spot.[20] For publicity purposes it was enough to have the

17. Vandenberg, *op. cit.*, p. 534. In this and succeeding letters to his wife, the Senator showed deep concern that an apparent coolness on Marshall's part might in fact have resulted from the intensified debate on China policy (pp. 533–6, 563).
18. *Congressional Record*, June 24, 1949, pp. 8292–3.
19. *Ibid.*, p. 8296.
20. *New York Times*, June 25, 1949.

letter appear the same day as the Vandenberg-Connally debate. Acheson replied with a letter to Connally on July 1, giving assurances that the Foreign Relations Committee would be consulted before any decision was reached to recognize Communist China.[21] The recognition question could still be postponed for a time because the Chinese Communists did not even establish a formal government until October.

Skirmishes in the Lower House. In June the House Foreign Affairs Committee also became involved in a showdown fight over Far Eastern policy along party lines. There it was the administration's proposed economic aid program for Korea which was tinder for the smoldering China dispute, as the Butterworth nomination was in the Senate. Hearings on the Korean bill began on June 7 before the House Committee. They were used by Republican members, led by Judd and Vorys, to secure in executive session what they regarded as a very damaging picture of State Department inconsistency: economic aid on a large scale for Korea, requested at the very moment that the last American occupation troops were being withdrawn from the peninsula; no policy for the great adjacent power, China—which had already demonstrated the inadequacy of economic aid programs.

> Members of our committee practically begged representatives of Defense and State to keep American forces in Korea for another year or two—even if only a battalion as the symbol of American power and determined interest. . . . If the Russians were to make an all-out attack, we would be no worse off than we would be in Berlin—and our presence certainly would be the strongest deterrent to attack.[22]

But on June 30 the army announced the withdrawal of all American troops except a training mission. That same day a sharply divided Foreign Affairs Committee, after personal face-to-face appeals from both Truman and Acheson, approved the economic aid authorization for Korea.[23]

---

21. *Hearings* on the nomination of Philip Jessup, before a subcommittee of the Senate Foreign Relations Committee, October 1951, p. 615.
22. Judd, *Congressional Record*, July 18, 1950, p. 10557.
23. *New York Times*, June 21 and July 1 and 2, 1949.

The China bloc on Foreign Affairs, however, was not yet ready to abandon its fight. Feelings were further exacerbated when the State Department, on grounds of "irrelevancy," took the record of the executive session hearings on Korea and deleted most of the Representatives' critical probing of Far Eastern policy in general.[24] Vorys has described later moves, succinctly:

> I appeared before the Rules Committee with a group of my colleagues and urged that no rule be granted. I said: "If this bill comes to the floor, it will be defeated, but in order to explain it some things must be said that will hurt Korea and the prestige of the United States in Asia."
>
> I asked for an executive session of the Rules Committee and got it, and explained what we had learned. The Rules Committee held up the bill until September 27, and the House leadership never let the bill come to the floor until January 19, 1950. On that day, as I had predicted, this $385 million economic plan was defeated.[25]

The circumstances of the bill's defeat and final passage will be discussed later in this chapter. But it should be mentioned here that the campaign was clearly in Vorys' hands after the Korean aid bill passed the Foreign Affairs Committee. Judd, for all his dissatisfaction with Far Eastern policy, preferred half a loaf to nothing at all. That was also the attitude of Senator Knowland, whose succinct endorsement enabled the bill to pass the Senate after just fifteen minutes' discussion on October 12. The vote was 48-13, 7 Democrats and 6 Republicans being recorded in opposition.

The White Paper. During July 1949 the finishing touches were put on the State Department's White Paper on China. Defense Secretary Johnson protested the political advisability of issuing the report. He secured a few factual alterations but was overruled by the President on the main issue.[26]

The White Paper was released on August 5 with a summary

24. Vorys, *Congressional Record*, January 19, 1950, pp. 634–6.
25. *Ibid.*, July 18, 1950, p. 10530.
26. Johnson testimony, *Hearings* on the military situation in the Far East, before the Senate Armed Services and Foreign Relations Committees, June 1951, pp. 2668–9, 2679.

cover letter signed by Dean Acheson, which was all that was widely read of the 400 pages of history and 600 pages of documents. Acheson's conclusion:

> The unfortunate but inescapable fact is that the ominous result of the civil war in China was beyond the control of the government of the United States. Nothing that this country did or could have done within the reasonable limits of its capabilities could have changed that result; nothing that was left undone by this country contributed to it. It was the product of internal Chinese forces, forces which this country tried to influence but could not. A decision was arrived at within China, if only a decision by default.[27]

The key phrase of course was "reasonable limits of its capabilities." Elsewhere in the cover letter these were defined in frankly political terms—what the American people would have accepted.[28] With "capabilities" thus defined and "result" denoting ultimate Communist victory, the statement may well be perfectly accurate. But the public had not been given a direct chance to make that harsh choice of sacrifices, and the State Department had imprudently failed to identify leaders of both parties with *its* estimate of what the public would stand, at the times when momentous decisions were being made to limit American commitments in China.

It is, however, a profitless enterprise to pick apart the language of this apologia. For future policy (beyond the Open Door shibboleths) Acheson had little more than a firm threat to Communist China against violating the UN Charter by external aggression, and a belief that "ultimately the profound civilization and the democratic individualism of China will reassert themselves and she will throw off the foreign yoke."

> I consider that we should encourage all developments in China which now and in the future work toward this end. . . . The implementation of our historic policy of friendship for China . . . will necessarily be influenced by the degree to which the Chinese people come to recognize that the Com-

27. Department of State, *op. cit.*, p. xvi.
28. *Ibid.*, pp. x, xvi.

munist regime serves not their interests but those of Soviet Russia and the manner in which, having become aware of the facts, they react to this foreign domination.[29]

This clearly suggested that the dust had settled enough for Acheson to envisage a China policy which would be decidedly anti-*Russian* and anti-*Stalinist;* at the same time there was not much indication of hope that Mao's regime *as such* would turn *Titoist.* With that combination of principles, there could not be much early hope for the American China policy either. Thus it is interesting that Acheson focused his attention on "areas not now under Communist control in Asia" when on July 18, 1949, he appointed Philip Jessup to direct a new survey of Far Eastern policies and programs.[30]

Military Assistance for the "General Area" of China. As members of the China bloc found time to digest the White Paper, their criticism mounted. The climax came on August 21 in a bitter memorandum signed by Bridges, Knowland, Wherry, and McCarran, which called the White Paper "a 1,054-page whitewash of a wishful, do-nothing policy which has succeeded only in placing Asia in danger of Soviet conquest." [31]

The China bloc had agreed upon a new immediate objective. This was to incorporate military aid for non-Communist China in the general military assistance bill which was pending before Congress. The bill was commonly regarded as implementation of the Atlantic Pact; it also contained grants for the continuation of programs in Greece, Turkey, Iran, Korea, and the Philippines—but not China. On August 4—the day before publication of the

29. *Ibid.,* pp. xvi–xvii.

30. Secret memorandum from Acheson to Jessup dated July 18, 1949, made public in *Hearings* on the nomination of Philip Jessup, before a subcommittee of the Senate Foreign Relations Committee, October 1951, p. 603.

The State Department also undertook to provide itself with a little political protection and perhaps some sound advice by associating with the Jessup survey the respected head of the Rockefeller Foundation, Raymond Fosdick, and Everett Case, former General Electric officer, then President of Colgate University. There was no pretense that either of them was well informed about the Far East; they would act "more or less as judges or a jury." *Ibid.,* pp. 603–4.

31. *New York Times,* August 22, 1949.

White Paper—Knowland and eleven other Senators, nearly all of them Republicans, had introduced a proposed amendment to commit $175 million of the military assistance to non-Communist China, with provision for an American advisory mission. In the House a similar move was made by Republicans Lodge and Vorys and Democrat Walter of Pennsylvania, an ardent anti-Communist. The amendment failed in the Foreign Affairs Committee by a vote of 11-7.[32] It was also defeated when offered on the floor August 18; there the tellers counted 164-94 against it.

In the Senate the proposal had better prospects, largely because the military assistance bill was being handled jointly by the Foreign Relations and Armed Services Committees. The administration favored this combination, both in order to mitigate a possibly damaging jurisdictional quarrel and in the hope that a large number of Senators would become sympathetically familiar with the measure. But Bridges and Knowland were both prominent members of Armed Services; that meant that China would get a better hearing than was likely on Foreign Relations alone.

Connally was serving as chairman of the combined committees; he stalled consideration of the China aid question till near the end of six weeks of elaborate extrapartisan negotiation and compromise over the terms of the military assistance bill. Great efforts were being made to secure a heavy two-party majority in favor of reporting the bill to the floor.[33] Ultimately the issue of China had to be faced.

It was brought to a head in bitter floor debate between Knowland and Connally on September 7 and by testimony offered to the committees the following day by Admiral Badger, American fleet commander in Far Eastern waters. Badger's statement

32. *Ibid.*, August 16, 1949.

33. Vandenberg had not been consulted in advance about the terms of this measure. The administration draft *first* submitted was withdrawn from Congress and largely rewritten, after protests which were sparked by Republicans and fully supported by many Democrats. Then Vandenberg and Dulles worked closely together to secure further amendments from the combined committees.

Dulles himself had just been given an interim appointment as Senator by Governor Dewey. He had secured formal membership only on minor Senate committees, but devoted his attention to assisting Vandenberg on the aid bill.

strengthened the China bloc, but Connally stood with the State
Department in offering an amendment which went no further
than to give the President total discretion to spend or not to spend,
without any detailed accounting to Congress, $75 million any-
where in "China and the Far East." On September 9 this amendment was adopted on absolutely straight party lines in the combined committees by a vote of 11-9. Vandenberg went along with
the other Republicans who regarded the move as the merest gesture; every Democrat followed Connally and the State Department.
The gravity of this outbreak of partisanship was underscored by
the committee's vote later that same day on a move by Senator
George to cut the *European* authorization from $1 billion to $300
million. Several interventionist members of the China bloc voted
in favor of the cut in order to demonstrate their irreconcilability;
it was rejected by a margin of only 13-10.[34]

At this point Vandenberg stepped in to heal the breach. After
a couple days of negotiation he secured a large measure of agreement for a change in the geographical limitation of the President's
discretion from "China and the Far East"—which the State Department seemed disposed to read as just "the Far East"—to the
"general area" of China. The President would still have a very
free hand in secret expenditures and could avoid China proper
and Chiang Kai-shek entirely. But at least Knowland would feel
he was getting a little closer to his goal. Every voting Republican
on the committees approved the new amendment on September
12. Five Democrats held out against it; three of them were economy-minded Southern leaders who later recorded the only opposition to reporting the whole bill to the floor; the other two,
Thomas of Utah and Green of Rhode Island, were presumably still
following the basic State Department line against further Chinese
entanglements.[35]

Thus in September 1949 it proved still to be possible to compromise the China question between the parties, but it was significant of the increasing deterioration of relations in this field that

34. *New York Times*, September 10, 1949.
35. *Ibid.*, September 13, 1949.

compromise came only as a recoil from concrete evidence that rigid partisanship on a China issue had spread even to the Foreign Relations Committee and that it was seriously jeopardizing another almost unrelated program which both sides agreed to be vital. Vandenberg's formula was not challenged on the Senate floor and it survived the Conference Committee, but the phraseology was obviously so ambiguous that only heavy concessions in its interpretation—either by the State Department or by the China bloc— would be able to establish any real harmony between Democrats and Republicans over its implementation.[36]

RECOGNIZE RED CHINA?

In the subsequent months before the Korean War there were two main questions in China policy which agitated American politicians. One was whether Communist China should be recognized; the other was whether to aid the Nationalists in the defense of Formosa.

During the congressional hearings on Philip Jessup's nomination as delegate to the UN in the fall of 1951, an intensive effort was made to elucidate the recognition issue. Republicans tried very hard to confirm the suspicions, which had been very general in the autumn of 1949, that the United States would soon recognize the "People's Republic of China," but the evidence which was developed did not prove that the Truman administration or even the top levels of the State Department had ever been committed to recognition. Jessup himself was disturbingly weasel worded in much of his testimony on this subject, although he did make what seems to be a fair summary of the evidence adduced:

> I think the essential fact which is documented in the statement I made, supported by the documents you have seen, is

36. Although the increasing partisan friction over China is the most interesting aspect of the Mutual Defense Assistance Act of 1949 for the purposes of this study, it would be a distortion of legislative history on this measure to omit mention of the other major issue which concerned the House even more vitally than did China. That was the unification of North Atlantic defense planning, for which Vorys and Richards fought with special vigor and general success.

that the Department of State did not at any point reach the conclusion, if I may put it this way, that recognition was just around the corner. They never reached the conclusion that if the British, Indian, and other governments recognized, that we would need to follow.[37]

Dean Acheson at a news conference on October 12, 1949, had repeated the American criteria on recognition of a new government: (1) that it control the country it claimed to control; (2) that it recognize its international obligations; and (3) that it rule with the acquiescence of the people who were ruled. On none of these points did the Communist regime qualify when it announced its existence on October 1, 1949,[38] and as for the second point, its unrecognizability was intensified on October 24 when the Communists climaxed nearly a year of house arrest for the American consular staff in Mukden (Manchuria) by slapping them into jail for a month.

In November and December 1949 Great Britain made it clear in diplomatic correspondence that *she* intended soon to recognize the People's Republic of China. The memoranda on the subject which were then exchanged between Whitehall and the State Department were shown to Foreign Relations Senators in 1951.[39] John Sparkman concluded that this evidence showed "we were fighting recognition by telling them we would not go along." Smith of New Jersey, a most respected Republican critic, commented:

> I think that is probably a fair statement to make. While the documents do take this position, they indicate that very often you will find the [Acheson points]. The condition will be dependent on these conditions: one, two, three. It looks as though we were implying that if those conditions were complied with we might again think of recognition. That was the only impression I got from reading the documents.[40]

37. Jessup, *Hearings* on the nomination of Philip Jessup, before a subcommittee of the Senate Foreign Relations Committee, October 1951, p. 659.

38. *Ibid.*, pp. 615–16.

39. *Ibid.*, pp. 650, 654.

40. Sparkman and Smith, *ibid.*, p. 657.

Acheson gave a similar impression in executive session testimony before the Senate Foreign Relations Committee on January 10, 1950.[41]

It does appear to be true that on the vital top level of decision making in the State Department early recognition of Communist China was not so favorably considered as was generally believed at the time. It seems exceedingly unlikely, however, that any such widespread opinion would ever have formed if lower levels of the department were not privately guiding the press to anticipate recognition. Even Senator Connally showed that somehow he, like others, had been led to expect it. He found in Acheson's very cautious testimony of January 10 an implication that the Secretary was fulfilling his obligation to consult Foreign Relations before acting on recognition, "but very likely he will consult us again before the final action," which would not come "in a hurry." [42] In the same climate of opinion Senator Vandenberg wrote on January 9: "I am opposed to recognition of the Communist regime in China at this immediate moment—although realities may force an early abandonment of this position." [43] Other congressmen and interested citizens found other evidence to substantiate a belief that recognition was to be expected. Given the existing partisan suspicion about China policy, such an important area of uncertainty was bound to provide a focus for recrimination, even if the secret facts did not yet justify it.

Moreover, there certainly seemed to be a chance that the Communist government would somewhat mend its international manners. If so, the sham issue of recognition would become a very real one in the United States. What would Acheson and Truman regard as behavior satisfactory to meet their criteria? The administration's decision to leave the Nationalist Chinese on Formosa to the mercy of Communists from the mainland seemed to foreshadow ultimate recognition of the People's Republic. As long as Formosa was supported, such recognition would hardly be possible. The most reliable way to keep the administration's hands tied

41. Reproduced, *ibid.*, pp. 791-3.
42. *New York Times,* January 11, 1950.
43. Vandenberg, *op. cit.,* p. 538.

on recognition would be to get it committed to the defense of Formosa. And the strategic utility of the island would constitute a uniquely potent argument for this China-bloc policy.

DEFEND FORMOSA?

The Democrats Take Their Stand. Since late in 1948 the administration's Formosa policy had been that the United States did not have sufficient armed forces to commit any of them to the defense of Formosa, despite its admitted strategic importance. The island was to be defended as long as possible by *diplomatic* and *economic* means.[44] On August 4, 1949, Acheson circulated a memorandum predicting that Formosa would fall to the Communists because economic and diplomatic weapons were no longer reliable. The Joint Chiefs of Staff met on August 16 and "reaffirmed their previous views that overt United States military action to deny Communist domination of Formosa would not be justified."[45] In September the Joint Chiefs considered the advisability of sending a military mission to Formosa to investigate the situation; they decided against it.[46] On October 12 representatives of the three services and the State Department completed a new survey of prospects and unanimously agreed that Formosa would fall in 1950.[47]

Late in October Senator Alexander Smith returned from a tour of the Far East pleading against recognition of the Communists and in favor of American occupation of Formosa if necessary to save it from Mao. Smith's agreement with the China bloc was particularly important, for he had been a stout supporter of Vandenberg and sincerely believed in "bipartisan" collaboration. Moreover he was a hard-working member of Foreign Relations, a regular Republican, and a modestly impressive gentleman. Smith gave his views to Acheson in a letter dated November 4 and in a later interview. He elaborated them in a report to the Foreign Rela-

44. Acheson testimony, *Hearings* on the military situation in the Far East, before the Senate Armed Services and Foreign Relations Committees, June 1951, pp. 1671–2.
45. Memorandum by Wedemeyer (then Deputy Chief of Staff of the Army) dated August 26, 1949, included *ibid.*, p. 2371.
46. Louis Johnson testimony, *ibid.*, pp. 2577, 2664, 2678–9.
47. Acheson testimony, *ibid.*, pp. 1770–1.

tions Committee and made his conclusions public in a press conference on December 1.[48]

A week later the Chinese Nationalist government abandoned the mainland and announced the establishment of a temporary capital on Formosa. The following day, December 9, the National Security Council met and reconsidered the Formosa situation. The State Department briefed the press that same day with all the arguments, political and military, against any change in the "firm" American policy not to use armed forces to defend Formosa.[49] But the Joint Chiefs were wavering, and Secretary Johnson begged them to make a military recommendation without regard to political considerations. They agreed to recommend that a military fact-finding mission be dispatched to Formosa.[50] Johnson's memorandum with supporting data was received by the President at Key West on December 17. But the State Department resisted:

> We took the attitude that since the very statement of our problem indicated that this could not be successful and that only the interposition of armed forces of the United States could save the island, what we would be doing would be making an effort here which was by hypothesis ineffective, and we would involve ourselves with further damage to our prestige and to our whole position in the Far East.[51]

Louis Johnson learned at lunch with the President on December 22 "that I had lost my fight on Formosa . . . I was told . . . that he wasn't going to argue with me about the military considerations but that on political grounds he would decide with the State Department." [52]

The decision was not formally reached until a meeting of the National Security Council on December 29, but it was so clear within the administration what Truman intended to say that as

48. The text of Smith's letter to Acheson and his report is included, *ibid.,* pp. 3315–26.

49. Ferdinand Kuhn, *Washington Post,* December 10, 1949.

50. Johnson testimony, *Hearings* on the military situation in the Far East, before the Senate Armed Services and Foreign Relations Committees, June 1951, p. 2665.

51. Acheson testimony, *ibid.,* pp. 1674–5.

52. Johnson testimony, *ibid.,* pp. 2577–8.

early as December 19 the State Department began sending out information guidance papers to its missions throughout the world —and to department officials dealing with the domestic press— advising them to minimize the importance of Formosa, since its fall "is widely anticipated." [53] By a curious coincidence this document leaked to the press through General MacArthur's command in Tokyo on January 3—the very day after Herbert Hoover took the headlines to advocate an American naval defense of Formosa. Hoover's recommendation was promptly endorsed by Taft; but Vandenberg kept his silence, Lodge expressed "very grave doubts," and even Judd for the time being wanted only a large American mission as in Greece. Knowland, however, had arranged for Hoover's statement and was immediately able to seize upon the leaked guidance paper to strengthen the China bloc's hand by vehement denunciation.[54] Alexander Smith joined Knowland in demanding that the document be produced for public inspection. Even Charles Eaton deserted the State Department to support American military action to hold Formosa.[55]

Acheson on January 4 arranged an appointment a few days later with the Foreign Relations Committee to discuss Far Eastern affairs. But the administration decided not to wait so long before declaring its position. On January 5 President Truman himself announced unequivocally:

> The United States government will not pursue a course which will lead to involvement in the civil conflict in China. Similarly, the United States government will not provide military aid or advice to Chinese forces on Formosa.

This statement constituted a showdown rejection of new commitments. The administration was fighting loose from entanglements, and the immediate reaction was sure to be an angry one. The failure to consult moderate Republicans before the precipitate declaration caused an additional widening of the breach between the parties. Vandenberg himself formally deplored the an-

53. Text of the guidance paper, *ibid.*, pp. 1667–9.
54. *Washington Post*, January 3, 1950. *New York Times*, January 4, 1950.
55. *Ibid.*, January 5, 1950.

nouncement of conclusions before congressional consultations, though he still wanted to avoid "active American military preparation" for the defense of Formosa.[56]

On the Democratic side Senator Connally slashed with uninhibited vigor at those Republicans who were seriously advocating a military defense of Formosa. He warned on January 9:

> I am going to review this matter from time to time. Whenever this subject is brought up again, I am going to want to know who the Senators are who want to plunge this country into war—not directly to do so but to risk doing so—in the name of bitter attacks on the President and the Secretary of State.[57]

Connally and a few other administration Democrats sustained this "peace offensive" against the Republicans. It struck a responsive chord in public opinion. The presence of the customary non-interventionists Hoover and Taft in the front ranks of the China bloc, urging extreme military measures, was giving an appearance of pure partisanship to its demands regarding Formosa. This appearance, enhanced by the disassociation of Vandenberg and Lodge, constituted a handicap to sincere members of the China bloc, for it tended to solidify Democratic resistance. Then on January 12 the attack was turned back against the Republicans by an impressive full-length survey of Far Eastern affairs which Acheson delivered before the National Press Club in Washington. His central theme was that the interests of China and Soviet Russia conflicted and "we must not undertake to deflect from the Russians to ourselves the righteous anger, and the wrath, and the hatred of the Chinese people which must develop." [58]

Acheson's presentation seemed at the time enormously effective. As press and public reaction grew increasingly unfavorable to "adventures" in Asia, the Democratic Senators became more confident that pure partisanship was at the heart of the weakening Republican campaign for Formosa. On January 17 it was possible

56. *Ibid.*, January 6, 1950.
57. *Ibid.*, January 10, 1950.
58. *Department of State Bulletin*, January 23, 1950, p. 115.

to hold a "rebuttal" meeting of the Senate Democratic conference and secure "consensus [in the words of floor leader Lucas] that the President and the State Department are handling this matter in the right fashion and that intervention in Formosa might lead ultimately to war." Lucas declared that to the best of his knowledge every Democratic Senator was ready to go to the end with the President on the general decision against intervention, though there might be disagreement on details.[59] It was the first such partisan conference on foreign policy which Senate Democrats had held in many months. Thus finally the party-line cleavage on China policy which had long been developing was formally crystallized.

GOP Retaliation in the House. The reaction of *House* Republicans to the administration's decision on Formosa was to carry through their threat to defeat the Korean aid bill. Without consulting any GOP Senators, Representative Vorys led the attack when the Democratic House leadership finally ventured to bring the bill to the floor on January 19, 1950. Republicans opposed it six to one. The House Democrats showed no comparable solidarity in its favor; only about three out of four of them supported the bill. It survived a recommittal motion by just four votes and then went down to defeat by the margin of a single vote. Many members of both parties took the attitude that if Formosa was not of vital importance neither was Korea. Economy-minded and noninterventionist Republicans and Southern Democrats were glad to be able to vote against one expensive "rat-hole" program on the pretext that not enough was being spent in another nearby area. Resentment was also rife against the State Department for having expurgated criticism from the hearings on the bill held the previous June. A handful of Republicans (including notably Judd, Herter, and Eaton) made "half-a-loaf" arguments in *favor* of the bill, but their party was overwhelmingly against them, and so were a quarter of the Democrats (nearly all of them Southerners).

Senate Republicans, however, including the China bloc, regarded this as a highly irresponsible tactical blunder, intruding in the middle of their campaign for Formosa. The Senators had not been consulted by House GOP leaders, and they immediately

59. *New York Times,* January 18, 1950. See also pp. 109–10.

made public their desire that a new Korean aid bill be passed.[60] The administration had to make a small concession, however, to accomplish this result in the House. It agreed to an extension of the period in which previously appropriated economic aid funds for China would be spent—in *Formosa*. The extension ran only till the end of June; but it showed already how difficult it would be for the administration to rely on Democratic partisanship to prevent further involvements with Nationalist China.

When the revised bill came before the House on February 8, Vorys supported it unenthusiastically. Five out of seven Republicans still opposed it, but Democratic solidarity had increased to the point where five out of six Democrats voted for the bill. On February 10 the Senate approved the new measure by a voice vote without debate.

Partisan Deadlock. American China policy had now reached deadlock. The administration had for the time being sufficient constitutional and political power to prevent the China bloc from forcing it into a heavy military commitment in Formosa. On the other hand, the friends of Nationalist China had demonstrated the capacity to upset other administration programs for the Far East if Chiang Kai-shek were rejected completely. The newly announced State Department policy was officially aimed at turning Chinese hostility against the Russians. Whatever might otherwise be the chances of such a policy, it could hardly make much progress until Mao had overcome his domestic enemies on Formosa, but until the very moment of Mao's invasion, the United States would perforce have to remain to *some* extent identified with his Nationalist enemies—yet not strongly enough even to demand advantageous terms of the Communists. This was a Gordian knot which only a speedy and successful Red conquest of Formosa could cut. Actually it was expected to do so within the year. Yet because such an outcome would further embitter partisan recrimination in an American election year, the general policy stalemate was sure to continue at least into 1951.

The Democrats had taken a firm stand that they would do very

60. *New York Times*, January 21, 1950. Also an interview with a man then close to the Senate Republican leadership.

little *more* for Chiang; the Republican position was equally firm
that at least they should do no *less*. There was a dual irony in this
situation.

On the one hand, the political stalemate was in effect contributing to a continuation of the "wait-and-see," "do-nothing" conduct
of American relations with China for which the administration
had long been condemned. To be sure, there still was—as there
had been before—a serious argument, from the standpoint purely
of prudent diplomacy, for thus "waiting for the dust to settle" a
little more; the true strength and character of Red China might
yet be revealed with greater clarity. But the fact remained grave
that the years of accumulated partisan suspicion had virtually destroyed all freedom of choice to move in *any* direction.

The irony on the other side was that the administration now
found itself caught in a trap between Republican and·Democratic
party commitments—for the very reason (in large measure) that it
had endeavored for so long to behave *independently*.

Dénouement. The Democrats temporarily emerged from the Formosa debate of January 1950 with considerable partisan advantage
for their "peace" stand; [61] but the Alger Hiss conviction, Acheson's sympathetic comment on it, and the Klaus Fuchs and Judith
Coplon espionage cases that winter all encouraged the more rabid
and embittered Republicans, especially members of the China bloc,
to seek to undermine the entire structure of administration policy
in the Far East through charges that it was being made by Communists for Communists. Democratic party lines, which had formed
fairly tightly on the specific issue of Formosa in January, did not
sustain much active resistance to this more generalized assault. More
than ever the administration was doomed to continue relations
with Chiang on Formosa, even if it should desire to break loose
entirely.

That fact was confirmed in new legislation during the spring.
The renewal of the ECA authorization for the third year contained
a provision continuing the authorization to spend previously appropriated China aid funds (now estimated in the neighborhood
of $100 million). The act stipulated: "So long as the President

61. Arthur Krock, *New York Times*, January 15, 1950, sec. 4, p. 3.

deems it practicable, not less than $40 million of such funds shall be available only for assistance in areas in China (including Formosa)." The House managers explained they had "informal assurances of the intention of the Secretary of State that the funds should be reserved for such purpose as long as there is practicable access to any portion of China, such as Formosa, remaining free of Communist control." [62]

Clearly in *Washington* the passage of time was not bringing the administration any closer to securing a free hand to pursue a new Far Eastern policy. Most people still believed, however, that in *Asia* the day was drawing near when the problem of Chiang Kai-shek would be wiped away by a Communist invasion of Formosa.

The actual event was quite the contrary. The invasion came in Korea, and under its impact the administration's policy toward Formosa crumbled rapidly.[63] Even if strategic considerations had not then dictated a coupling of the defense of Formosa with the defense of Korea, the need for home-front unity in America would almost certainly have done so.[64] The State Department had little practical choice but to abandon for an indeterminate period the policy of nonintervention in Formosa. It was just six months since the showdown which had cemented this policy in America. For that short period, by partisan defense against partisan attack, the administration had barely been able to maintain a mere "free hand to do nothing." Now even that was lost, whether or not it could ever have been worth what it cost in party warfare. Such was the culmination of long years of noncooperation at home regarding America's relations with the great subcontinent of China.

62. *Congressional Record,* May 23, 1950, p. 7526.

63. On January 5, 1950, Acheson had qualified the President's announced decision not to defend Formosa by observing that "in the unlikely and unhappy event that our forces might be attacked in the Far East, the United States must be completely free to take whatever action in whatever area is necessary for its own security." It certainly is not obvious that the Communist attack on South Korea was an attack on "our forces" within the original meaning of Acheson's statement. The quotation is from the *Department of State Bulletin,* January 16, 1950, p. 81.

64. In July 1950 this was the view expressed in an interview by a House Republican (among others) who was himself in a position to cause a great deal of trouble for the administration if Formosa had still been undefended.

CHAPTER 17

Contention over Partisanship Within the GOP

THE MONTHS of 1950 before the Korean War were a period of heightened controversy within the GOP as well as between the parties. The very principle of two-party cooperation on foreign affairs came under heavy public attack by important Republicans.[1] And the breakdown in practice proceeded from the Formosan dispute to the McCarthy denunciations. But many prominent members of the GOP resisted the tendency and managed to preserve a substantial measure of extrapartisanship in policy areas outside Asia.

THE EMERGENCE OF MCCARTHYISM

There were some immediate, special reasons for the forthright challenge to "bipartisanship" in the Republican party at the end of 1949, in addition to the more general deteriorating factors which had been at work since the 1948 election—the mild international climate, traces of Democratic independence, and the China situation.

1. The best criticism from an orthodox Republican standpoint is an article by George H. E. Smith entitled "Bipartisan Foreign Policy in Partisan Politics," *American Perspective,* Spring 1950, pp. 157–69. Smith had been staff director of the Senate Republican Policy Committee. It seems only fair to add that Smith's article is the best writing that has appeared on the subject of "bipartisanship" from *any* viewpoint, although it disagrees with most of the thesis of this book.

The Weakening of Vandenberg and Dulles. One important new element was the breakdown of Vandenberg's health. Age alone would have disqualified him for the GOP presidential nomination in 1952, and hence he never had in the Eighty-first Congress the tacit threat of command of National Convention delegates to use as a weapon in behalf of his policies. Still his great prestige could not be discounted by rival party leaders like Taft and Wherry as long as he was physically able to exercise authority. But in the summer of 1949 his doctors urged him to withdraw from his Senate activities for a prolonged examination and possible operation on his lung. He postponed this move until after the Senate passed the military assistance bill in September.[2] During that period he was heavily dependent on the new Senator Dulles for advice and assistance in reshaping the legislation to forestall the attacks of other Republicans. Then in the autumn Vandenberg had a serious operation which was only partially and temporarily successful, and Dulles was defeated in a special New York election for his seat in the Senate. Both these developments helped to undermine the authority of the wing of the GOP which favored two-party collaboration on foreign affairs.

The circumstances of Dulles' defeat in themselves constituted a special pretext for hostile Republicans to attack "bipartisanship." Dulles had chosen to wage a vigorously conservative campaign on domestic issues against the Democratic candidate Lehman. Presumably this decision was compounded of different elements: personal conviction, the desire to enhance his reputation for party regularity and thus to strengthen his position for "bipartisan" leadership in the Senate, and the belief that a hard-hitting campaign would get regular Republicans to the polls while his "bipartisan" experience would preserve independent votes. President Truman reacted to the strong challenge to his *domestic* policy with a vigorous series of endorsements of Lehman's candidacy, despite the contributions Dulles had made to the President's *foreign* policy. Only the most extreme interpretations of the requirements of "bipartisanship" in foreign affairs would have insisted that Truman do otherwise, but the extraordinary silencing

2. Vandenberg, *The Private Papers of Senator Vandenberg*, pp. 513, 517.

of the Democratic campaign against Vandenberg in Michigan in 1946 had in fact provided a different sort of precedent, and Truman was accordingly condemned for his intervention against Dulles in New York. A more serious and justifiable criticism was directed at a memorandum circulated by Lehman's headquarters which characterized Dulles as a "kept Republican—by the State Department." Republican critics of "bipartisanship" did all they could to magnify these episodes and Dulles' eventual close defeat to demonstrate that the Democrats would not play fair and that association with the administration's foreign policy was only a handicap to the GOP.[3]

Vandenberg returned to Washington late in December 1949 after his serious operation, but he was able to remain only a few weeks. During that time he was publicly criticized by other important Republicans as he had not been since the end of the war. (He played little more than a passive role in the Formosan controversy which was then raging, but even his passive opposition weakened the China bloc.) Republican floor leader Wherry arrived back in Washington at the end of December and told the press he wanted no more commitments "made by bipartisan bigwigs." Senator Taft told a radio audience on January 8:

> There isn't any bipartisan foreign policy and there has not been any for the last year. [Republicans] are not consulted any more and they have not been consulted since Mr. Acheson became Secretary of State. Nobody can imagine anything that is called a bipartisan foreign policy. There isn't any such thing.[4]

Plans were being drawn for the 1950 congressional election campaign, and the evidence of the continuing popularity of the Fair Deal (and of President Truman whenever he toured the "whistlestops") was leading an increasing number of Republicans to argue privately that they could win only by capitalizing on every kind of public doubt and suspicion regarding the administration's for-

3. Arthur Krock, *New York Times*, October 25, November 11, and December 29, 1949.

4. *New York Times*, January 9, 1950.

eign policy. This viewpoint was rejected early in February when the House and Senate leaders of the GOP and the Republican National Committee drew up a statement of principles for the election year. The foreign policy plank was briefer but did not seriously differ from that in the 1948 platform.[5] At the National Committee meeting on February 6, 1950, Illinois member Werner Schroeder tried to put the group on record as opposed to continuing "bipartisanship," but on a voice vote only two others were heard to agree with him.[6]

In fact, however, the Republican congressional election campaign of 1950 did not preserve any such moderation as the statement of early February. In a word the vital new factor in the equation was Senator Joseph McCarthy. He was the demagogic culmination of the rising tide of Republican partisanship in foreign affairs.

Reaction to the Hiss Conviction. Less than a week after the Senate Democratic Conference had declared in support of nonintervention in Formosa and thus doomed for a time one Republican campaign against administration foreign policy, the GOP had been handed new and more powerful ammunition through the conviction of Alger Hiss. The charge was perjury, but the circumstances were such that it amounted to espionage for Soviet Russia. Yet four days later the Secretary of State told his news conference: "I do not intend to turn my back on Alger Hiss." Hiss had long been Acheson's friend, though only a very distant associate in the State Department itself. The Secretary explained his attitude with

5. This was the case even though Vandenberg deliberately abstained from playing a very active role in drafting the 1950 declaration. "I wanted the net result to be free of any attack based on the presumption that I 'dominated' it." Vandenberg, *op. cit.,* p. 554.

6. *New York Times,* February 7, 1950. The key paragraph agreed upon was this: "Under our indispensable two-party system, we shall be vigilant in critical exploration of administration foreign policy. We favor consultation between the Executive and members of both major parties in the legislative branch of government in the initiation and development of a united American foreign policy; and we deplore the tragic consequences of the administration's failure to pursue these objectives in many fields, particularly in the secret agreements of Yalta, subsequently confirmed at Potsdam, which have created new injustices and new dangers throughout the world."

the biblical quotation: "Inasmuch as ye have done it unto the least of these my brethren, ye have done it unto Me." [7] Unfortunately the public expression of sympathy for a convicted Communist spy was too hot an issue to be dismissed with a reverent genuflection to the Bible. A Democratic phalanx had just formed in the Senate over Formosa, but kept to its tents when Republicans assaulted Acheson over Hiss. Democrats were hoping that the attack would exhaust itself long before the November election. For that reason, as well as their lack of close ties with Acheson, it seemed preferable not to prolong the controversy by arguing back.

But at least one young Republican Senator was not disposed to keep his attack on a plain of generalities which would thus bore the public after a short period. On February 9 Joseph McCarthy started quoting figures on how many Communists and Communist sympathizers were still serving under Dean Acheson in the State Department. The specificity was startling. It certainly enlivened the Republican party rallies on the Senator's Lincoln Day speaking tour, and his charges attracted much attention in the press. The Democrats' reaction was not long delayed. For them it became a matter of high party policy to take the bull by the horns and dispose of him promptly—as far in advance of the November elections as possible. The investigation thus began in an atmosphere of partisanship from which it never escaped.

The Tydings Investigation. The Democratic Policy Committee and the Democratic Conference were convened and approved a proposal that the Foreign Relations Committee should be assigned the task of investigating McCarthy's charges. It was further decided that the Democratic panel of the subcommittee conducting the probe should consist of those Senators who were members both of Foreign Relations and of the Democratic Policy Committee. Two of them, Chairman Tydings and McMahon, were even candidates for re-election that fall. One of the Republican members of the subcommittee was also up before the voters, Hickenlooper of Iowa; on foreign affairs he had steered an uneasy course between Vandenberg and Taft. The other Republican was Lodge, definitely a Vandenberg man but hardly likely to ignore the highly

7. *Ibid.*, January 26, 1950.

partisan atmosphere in which the probe was developing on both sides.

As the technique of investigation, Tydings adopted the passive policy of listening to McCarthy's charges against named individuals and then summoning the individuals and others thought to have evidence regarding them. It was the Democrats, also, who insisted early in the investigation on having most of the hearings conducted in public, with little or no advance preparation.[8] This approach was a desperate and vain effort on their part to forestall the "whitewash" charge which soon developed anyway, mainly as part of a running fight over whether the President should open the secret loyalty files.

To be sure, the Democratic partisanship in the Tydings investigation was very largely provoked by the extravagance of McCarthy's accusations and his manner of presenting them. For weeks there did not even seem to be any central thread linking individual cases which could form the subject of a serious investigation. It was alleged that particular persons in the State Department were Communist or pro-Communist, but evidence was lacking that they had been put there by any organized conspiracy, which would at least have provided a meaningful focus for a congressional probe even if no such conspiracy were found to exist. Alternatively, an intelligible investigation could have been made with the purpose of determining whether or not Communist bias could be traced in a given line of State Department policy—as Senator McCarran undertook to do in the next session of Congress with his probe of the influence of the Institute of Pacific Relations. But it was not till late in March 1950 that McCarthy began to emphasize China policy as a particular sphere for Communist activity, and even thereafter he confused the probers with unrelated charges. McCarthy had never been a prominent member of the China bloc and it is by no means probable that he intended at the outset to concentrate his fire in support of Chiang Kai-shek, but in the

8. Senator Hickenlooper, *Congressional Record*, April 5, 1950, pp. 4832–3. A penetrating critique of the Tydings investigation may be found in William F. Buckley, Jr., and L. Brent Bozell, *McCarthy and His Enemies* (Chicago, Regnery, 1954), chs. v–x. One can generally accept the analysis contained in these chapters without sharing the authors' broader sympathy for Senator McCarthy himself.

existing political atmosphere it was almost inevitable that the material which was furnished him would gravitate in that direction (rather than, say, to an assault on the "Morgenthau policy" in Germany). By taking the pro-Nationalist line McCarthy assured himself of considerable reinforcement in his own party and a wide public hearing, despite his distasteful methods. McCarthy did not, however, positively seek to direct the probe into a full-fledged investigation of China *policy*. He was quite content to keep it personalized, as long as he could keep his charges a couple of weeks ahead of Tydings' investigation of them.

Tydings, for his part, was so anxious to bring the whole affair to a close as soon as possible, well in advance of the election, that he had no inclination to launch any orderly, penetrating, and far-reaching investigation on his own—least of all a probe of the embarrassing Far Eastern situation. McCarthy was thus able to maintain the initiative; the probe continued to appear disorganized, half hearted, and inconclusive; the Democrats were on the defensive, with no possible way of disproving every wild charge in each successive barrage. Their primary defense could only be the inherent incredibility of most of McCarthy's best-publicized accusations. But with public suspicion at a high point, only other Republicans could safely and persuasively resist him. Democratic protests would be dismissed as whitewash by the segment of the voters who really needed to be convinced that McCarthy was grossly exaggerating the problem of Communists still in government in 1950.

SURVIVALS OF EXTRAPARTISANSHIP

Republican resistance to McCarthy did appear. By implication it was sparked by Vandenberg, and it tended to follow the familiar lines of Coast-Interior cleavage on foreign affairs in the Republican party.

It was not until March 22, nearly six weeks after McCarthy's first speech and two weeks after the start of the Tydings Committee hearings, that the Senate Republican leadership moved formally toward any kind of endorsement of McCarthy. Then, after a meeting of the party's Policy Committee, Taft himself announced that McCarthy's charges were "not a matter of party policy"—McCarthy himself had not asked that they be made a "policy matter" —but that GOP Senators were helping him "in his fight" and "reaction seems to be pretty good on the whole." [9] It was a cautious statement, as policy committee statements are wont to be in the Senate; but the fact that it was made at all showed that a large faction of the GOP in the upper chamber was sympathetic to McCarthy's tactics. Three days later Bridges told reporters that a group of Republicans would "go after" Acheson in a series of public attacks, "and the parade will start next week." [10]

Vandenberg Intervenes. But that same day Senator Vandenberg, too ill to remain on Capitol Hill, published a letter to ECA Administrator Paul Hoffman which was carefully designed to reaffirm the values of "unpartisanship" in foreign affairs, without thereby unduly antagonizing his less moderate colleagues in the Senate.[11] It was a remarkably shrewd document, focused on the problems of the Economic Cooperation Administration itself—which was not at the center of the current controversy—but managing by indirection to rebuke the critics of two-party cooperation. The letter even included a concrete suggestion for establishing a sort of "second Harriman Committee" to survey requirements for the post-ERP period.

The administration responded promptly to this break in the growing partisan deadlock. Truman authorized Acheson to discuss with Vandenberg the appointment of a Republican to work on the Japanese peace treaty and other Far Eastern questions, and agreed to accept the suggestion that members of the GOP participate in a new study of the balance of trade. Vandenberg made it clear that a Republican like Dulles should be chosen, who would be capable of contributing to the formation of State Department policy, not just to its negotiation and implementation, but the administration was reluctant to use Dulles in view of the fact that he was a likely candidate to run again in November for elec-

9. *New York Times,* March 23, 1950.
10. *Ibid.,* March 26, 1950.
11. Vandenberg, *op. cit.,* p. 557.

tion to the Senate seat which Lehman was occupying. There was danger of "building him up." So the State Department first announced the choice of former GOP Senator Cooper to advise Acheson at forthcoming meetings of the Western foreign ministers. Republicans expressed resentment that Dulles was being snubbed. Truman soon yielded, and on April 5 it became known that Dulles would be appointed policy adviser to the Secretary of State at the top level of the department.[12] Dulles indicated that if he were satisfied with the scope of his new position he would pass up the autumn election campaign against Lehman, but he put the public on notice that he was going into State on a four-month trial basis.[13]

Dulles found his assignment most satisfactory. The GOP critics of two-party collaboration did not. They emphasized that Dulles himself had never been elected to any public office and that his political patrons Dewey and Vandenberg were no longer in a position to exercise much party leadership either.[14] Taft was very cool to the appointment of one who was not, as Vandenberg had been, a "responsible representative of the Republicans in Congress."[15] On April 18, however, when Truman and Acheson invited no less a Republican critic than Styles Bridges to the White House to discuss foreign policy and problems of consultation, their meeting was much worse received on Capitol Hill than Dulles' appointment had been. Members of both parties on the Senate Foreign Relations Committee resented this intrusion into their domain, and the Republicans who were most hostile to administration foreign policy were afraid that their growing ranks would be splintered if Bridges deserted. Bridges, the State Department, and the President managed to appease the jealous congressmen; but no more such dramatic attempts were made to work outside regular committee channels until after the start of the Korean

12. James Reston, *New York Times,* April 6, 1950.
13. *New York Times,* April 9, 1950.
14. Dewey did throw all of the weight he still possessed behind the re-establishment of "bipartisanship," in a formal "elder statesman" address at Princeton on April 12. He was critical of "sections of the Republican party" as well as of the administration for causing the current lapse. "Politics should 'stop at the water's edge,' and if it does not do so soon, I doubt if we will long own the water's edge."
15. *Ibid.,* April 7, 1950.

War and then mainly in the form of briefing before the public announcement of decisions already made.[16]

But a substantial measure of extrapartisan cooperation still continued despite the Far Eastern situation and Senator McCarthy.

The preliminary consultations over renewal of the military assistance program in the spring of 1950 were a model of executive solicitude and congressional collaboration. State and Defense officials outlined their problems and sought suggestions from the congressional committees before the administrators ever drafted a bill. The suggestions offered did appear in the bill ultimately submitted, to the immense gratification of congressmen.[17]

The most important legislation in foreign affairs passed in 1950 before Korea was the third-year authorization for ERP. The administration's request was cut by only $250 million, less than 10 per cent.[18] The record clearly showed an intensification of partisanship over ERP compared with 1948 and 1949. But ECA could still find GOP supporters for all but 10 per cent of its requested authorization, even though Vandenberg was no longer well enough to attend Senate sessions.

The GOP Debates McCarthyism. McCarthy too was more actively resisted—and more actively supported—by different Republican factions as the spring months wore on in 1950. The climax in the Senate came on June 1 when Senator Margaret Chase Smith read a "Declaration of Conscience" on behalf of herself and six other GOP Senators (five liberals and Hendrickson of New Jersey). All but Thye of Minnesota were from the Northeast or Northwest. (Mrs. Smith did not seek any other Republican signatures for the statement which she composed herself.)[19] The Declaration criticized the Democratic administration, but this was the key sentence:

Certain elements of the Republican party have materially added to this confusion in the hopes of riding the Republican

16. Interviews with members of the Foreign Relations Committee and persons close to Senator Bridges and the Senate GOP Policy Committee.

17. Vorys, *Congressional Record*, July 18, 1950, pp. 10529–30.

18. After the beginning of the Korean War another $450 million was cut from ERP by the Appropriations Committees.

19. Marquis Childs, *Washington Post*, August 22, 1951.

party to victory through the selfish political exploitation of fear, bigotry, ignorance, and intolerance. There are enough mistakes of the Democrats for Republicans to criticize constructively without resorting to political smears.[20]

The Republican faction which had less tender sensibilities than Mrs. Smith hit back indirectly a fortnight later with a resolution cosponsored by twenty-one GOP Senators. They asked that the *Amerasia* Communist spy case which McCarthy was currently featuring be investigated by sympathetic Senator McCarran's Judiciary Committee instead of the Tydings Committee. Of the twenty-one Republicans only four were Coastal. One of them, Hendrickson, was the only Senator who had also signed the "Declaration of Conscience." Wherry joined in the *Amerasia* Resolution, but Taft avoided committing himself.[21]

Outside Congress the annual meeting of the Governors' Conference provided a platform for three liberal Republican chiefs of sizable Coastal states to register emphatic dissent from McCarthy's methods. They were Warren of California, Duff of Pennsylvania, and Driscoll of New Jersey.[22]

Tydings Aborts. Thus on the eve of the Korean War, controversy was mounting in the Republican party regarding McCarthy's methods. To be sure, the GOP was generally agreed that the Tydings investigation of the charges was superficial and politically motivated. The probe itself had first been organized as a partisan defense mechanism against accusations made originally at a party rally. And partisan considerations became especially conspicuous right after the start of the Korean conflict, when the Democrats, desperate to end the publicity well in advance of the election, decided to capitalize on war enthusiasm to call off the hearings and "annihilate" McCarthy. Then the character of the investigation and the bitter tone of its report became the immediate issue, rather than whether or not there were actually any Communists

20. *New York Times,* June 2, 1950.
21. *Ibid.,* June 14, 1950.
22. *Ibid.,* June 19, 1950. *Washington Post,* June 19 and 20, 1950.

in the State Department. On the narrower issue both parties were able to draw their lines rigidly tight.[23]

But several of the Republican Senators were certainly voting in criticism of Tydings rather than in endorsement of McCarthy. These members of the GOP had shown sympathy for the State Department in its predicament that spring. A few of them had even raised their voices obliquely in its defense against McCarthy, despite the partisan atmosphere which had surrounded the Tydings investigation and the Far Eastern situation on which it increasingly concentrated, and those Republicans, together with many more, had continued throughout the spring to cooperate with the administration in important and varied areas of American foreign policy, especially for Europe. Their conduct showed that a considerable measure of extrapartisanship still survived the partisan fires of Formosa and McCarthy.

CONCLUSION

Neither the partisanship nor the extrapartisan survivals ended with the beginning of war in Korea in June 1950. If they had, these hundreds of pages would have only historical interest. Actually the forces which have been shown at work in the Republican party in the years between World War II and the Korean War, for and against two-party collaboration, continued to reveal themselves on other issues after mid-1950—culminating in the forthright battle between supporters of Eisenhower and Taft for the GOP presidential nomination in 1952. The advent of hostilities in Korea is our stopping place only because it was a decisive event and reintroduced special considerations which have already been noted operating in World War II—the demand for national unity in wartime and the impact of military developments on domestic politics—and because there is today a perspective on events before Korea which is lacking on particular occurrences during the later fluctuating peninsular campaign.

23. See also pp. 68–9. As a conservative from a border state, Tydings carried particular weight with the Southern Democrats.

Moreover, the survey which has here been made of foreign affairs in party politics from early World War II onward has already supplied a very broad range of examples of various forms and degrees of partisanship, extrapartisanship, and bipartisanship, and has indicated the consequences of many of them on the trend of party politics as well as on American foreign policy. Harmony between the parties has been seen generally on the increase till the end of 1948 and generally on the decline thereafter, but rarely consolidating both parties in full agreement or rigid disagreement with each other on major controversial questions in foreign affairs. Collaboration which seemed deceptively simple and popular in 1948 has shown itself vulnerable to policy failures, to the personal behavior and standing of individual leaders, and to doubts regarding its value as a political weapon. It is well to remind ourselves of these facts in the current Eisenhower era, when foreign affairs collaboration between the administration and the opposition party may once again seem deceptively simple and reliable. On the other hand, for the uncertain future we may perhaps take some comfort in recognizing that the experience of the Eighty-first Congress, confirmed in the Eighty-second, showed extrapartisanship to have great staying power even in times of widespread dissatisfaction with the administration's conduct of American foreign relations.

CONCLUSION

Conclusion

In the Introduction to this study certain criticisms were leveled at increased partisanship or full bipartisanship as desirable techniques for the democratic control of foreign relations in America; and the tentative suggestion was offered that an alternative system labeled extrapartisanship might be preferable, though it, too, posed real problems. In the subsequent chapters evidence was examined from the experience of the past decade by statistical, descriptive, and historical methods. It may be helpful now briefly to review a sample of the evidence which has been adduced to support the objections raised against partisanship and bipartisanship and to reconsider whether extrapartisanship in fact appears to be a feasible and adequate system. If so, what caveats should be offered to officials and politicians who seek to make it work?

PARTISANSHIP AND BIPARTISANSHIP

On *partisanship*—the presentation to the national electorate of true alternatives on major foreign affairs by better disciplined parties—the first criticism suggested was that the injection of such issues into national campaigns would seriously impair the appearance, and to some extent the reality, of *dependability* in foreign relations, on which America's allies—weak and frightened but probably indispensable—must count so heavily, and which may prevent the Kremlin from taking chances that precipitate hostilities. In the course of this study an outstanding example which appeared of this problem was the need for agreed determination by the official leaders of both parties to hold fast in Berlin in the crisis which unexpectedly broke out during the election campaign of 1948. The extent of collaboration between Dulles and Marshall during that summer and fall may have gone beyond what was diplomatically essential and politically prudent for the Republicans, but that some cooperation was needed seems almost certain. America's right of access to Berlin was legally, as well as physically, vulnerable. That was the fault of executive officials and military officers at the end of World War II, but if the Republicans had made political capital of the fact, Russian propaganda and bargaining power would immediately have been strengthened and serious doubt would inevitably have been cast at a delicate moment on the determination of the United States to remain in Berlin.

It was suggested as a second criticism of partisanship that not only must an appearance of dependability be preserved for the effective conduct of American foreign relations but there must also be a wide range of *flexibility* to meet changing developments in the unpredictable tactics of the Kremlin. During the period of this study the classic example of possibly harmful lack of flexibility was in American relations with China in the last months of 1949 and the first half of 1950. State Department officials and the Truman administration wanted a free hand to pursue a new policy in the Far East. But to get it they undertook to rely primarily on the party loyalty of the Democratic majorities in House and Senate. The result was not flexibility of policy—it was stalemate. As the first step, the Democrats took a firm stand not to do much *more* for Chiang Kai-shek on Formosa; the Republicans were equally insistent that no *less* should be done (and they were able to enforce such demands by attacks on administration policies *elsewhere*). Partisan suspicions in practice virtually destroyed all freedom of choice to move in any direction. The Far Eastern initiative remained in the hands of the Communists—but they chose to exercise it in a fashion which confounded the assumptions on which the partisan stalemate had been allowed to crystallize in America. They attacked Korea instead of Formosa. The administration felt compelled to reverse its abortive Formosa policy. Yet the partisan bitterness which that policy had fostered continued to grow in succeeding months, constituting a serious handicap to the President's authority to conduct the war in Korea with due regard for the delicate and shifting balance of international forces concerned.

The need to appear *united* has been offered as a third objection to partisanship, with the observation that in an emergency either coercive shock techniques or sudden drastic and disruptive concessions could be expected to be used to achieve "unity" which "transcended" the party lines. Examples can be cited of both sorts of situations. Familiar now is Roosevelt's use of *faits accomplis* to coerce greater than mere majority support for successive steps of undeclared war in the Atlantic in 1941; but the partisan Republican resistance did maintain a continuing rear-guard action till it was finally smashed at Pearl Harbor. On the other side, President Truman's decision to guard Formosa at the beginning of hostilities in Korea, June 1950, may be regarded as a move which would have been a necessary political concession whether or not it was a strategic requirement; and of course it undermined the international bargaining position which the administration had tried to establish in January, resting on Democratic partisan foundations.

It is interesting and suggestive that in the one case events made the Republican party's position untenable, in the other the Democratic party's, and that in both cases the parties suffered internally and externally for having gone so far out on a limb alone in international situations that defy prediction.

A further argument against partisanship suggested in the Introduction, in addition to considerations of dependability, flexibility, and unity, was that there was doubtful *socio-political foundation* for cleavage between disciplined responsible parties along the same lines in foreign as well as domestic affairs; increased *foreign* affairs partisanship would be likely to put further obstacles in the way of the distant realignment which would permit party responsibility at least on *domestic* problems, those in which the public is usually more interested and always better informed.[1] The statistical and descriptive analysis which has been made of the work of Congress has given evidence that these doubts are justified, and has indicated that both under the existing alignment and under a liberal-conservative realignment a major increase in party discipline on

1. The educational effects of intense partisan debate on foreign policy would at best be very distant.

foreign relations would be oppressive to important sections of the parties. Within the present Democratic coalition, cleavage on foreign relations is less obvious than it is among Republicans, but it certainly exists, and voting disagreements have been noted even among the liberals which might well be expected to persist in a future moderate left party. On the other side, the statistical evidence has accented the special difficulty of ever bringing the conservatives of the East, South, and Midwest together in the same party if the combination is to be expected to take a clear stand on foreign policy.

A special obstacle to the achievement of Republican party agreement on foreign affairs has been observed. The balance of GOP regional strength in the *Senate* greatly favors the Interior against the Coasts, whereas no such imbalance exists in the electoral votes for which Republican presidential candidates must compete in the North, nor does it exist in the National Conventions where GOP nominees are chosen. As long as Coastal and Interior Republicans differ on foreign policy, and as long as both President and Senate are major influences upon it, the GOP's imbalance in the Senate may be expected to complicate the party's inner relationships on foreign policy, in and out of power. In a *realigned* party system, the Interior Republicans, with their bastion in the Senate, might feel they could afford to be less conciliatory toward the "vagaries" of Eastern conservatives on foreign affairs, but the Midwesterners would in fact probably find themselves confronted with equally divisive recalcitrance from the Southern recruits to the conservative party coalition. The attempt to impose a foreign policy upon the party members would only be disruptive.

Mention should also be made of two other specific and obvious objections to foreign affairs partisanship under the current constitutional system: the two-thirds rule for treaty ratification in the Senate (which preoccupied the UN planners) and the possibility of divided party control of the branches of government (which was a source of special concern in the Eightieth Congress). These would have to be among the first elements of the Constitution to be altered by amendment or by custom if a determined effort were made to make partisanship an enduring system of democratic control in American foreign affairs.

As for *full bipartisanship*, it was originally suggested in criticism of such an elaborate consultative system that there are practical objections in regard to secrecy, individual ability, and available time. These problems also arise to a lesser degree with extrapartisanship, and will be discussed below. The further objection over its feasibility is related to bipartisanship's implicit requirement that party discipline must be increased to the point where representative party consultants can in fact commit their fellow partisans. This stipulation defies the obstacles (already recalled) which arise in any attempt to secure much greater party discipline on foreign affairs—obstacles no less troublesome because disciplined *a*greement rather than disciplined *dis*agreement is now the objective. The position which Arthur Vandenberg finally achieved in the Eightieth Congress was indeed semicoercive on behalf of some policies on which he had come to agree with the administration, but the related combination of circumstances in 1948 was plainly exceptional. Not necessarily so was the willingness of candidate Dewey in two election campaigns to commit himself and his campaign agents to a special, organized form of bipartisan collaboration. Any presidential nominee is regularly able to determine the procedure of his own campaign and by the resulting concentration of publicity to set the tone of his party's campaign, but he does not thereby firmly commit his fellow partisans to follow the same line even before the election—much less after it. The events of 1948 did show that a measure of full bipartisanship is possible with the existing party system under some circumstances, but developments in subsequent years emphasized how fragile and unreliable an arrangement it is with parties as they are or are soon likely to become.

The further argument was offered in the Introduction that even if bipartisanship should in fact become feasible, it would have the bad effects of excessively limiting debate and deliberately minimizing the measure of popular control over foreign relations which now results from competition of would-be "independent delegates" before local electorates (without substituting even the limited benefits of a system of national choice between partisan foreign policies). Proof of this criticism cannot be found in the experience of the past decade in America because true bipartisanship has hardly been tested, but the extreme soft-pedaling of foreign policy issues in Dewey's 1948 campaign may exemplify a tendency in that direction—albeit probably unnecessary—whenever the involvement gets as close as it then did between Dulles and Marshall. It is really not fair also to conjure up in criticism of bipartisanship the passive wartime acquiescence of both parties in the decisions of the Commander in Chief and his personal advisers. In principle, bipartisanship, by ensuring political participation in decision making, would obviate such mere passive acquiescence. But in practice there can be no assurance of that outcome—especially in times of emergency. If opposition *partisanship* in such periods is too expensive a check on the administration, at least there should be room for undisciplined agitation by individual critics in the legislature. Even when free rein exists, there may be dangerously little resistance to the executive, as was the case in America's wartime diplomacy.

EXTRAPARTISANSHIP

The tentative conclusion was offered in the Introduction that bipartisanship would be an unnecessarily drastic cure for the dangers of general partisanship, such as undependability, inflexibility, shock techniques or drastic concessions to break stalemates, and the doubtful validity of a national mandate where foreign and domestic issues are mixed; and that these risks could be satisfactorily avoided if major foreign issues could be kept out of the presidential election campaigns. For this purpose *extrapartisanship* was suggested as a possibly feasible and adequate device.

Conditions of Extrapartisanship. The experience of the recent decade which has been outlined in this study certainly has demonstrated the feasibility of such a system, and indeed that it has great staying power even under incentive and provocation to behave in a partisan manner. The divisions in both parties and the methods of Congress have been seen to lend themselves to extrapartisanship. But the evidence has revealed two particularly important general requirements if the President is to be able continuously to attract sufficiently influential extrapartisan collaborators to prevent antagonistic party lines from forming tightly.

One requirement is the actual existence of so wide a popular consensus in support of the major outlines of the existing foreign policy that the opposition party as a whole will not be deeply tempted to nominate a presidential candidate who is determined to challenge it directly. The President himself can make a major contribution to this if he is aware of the need and capable of utilizing the unrivaled potentialities of his office for epic and symbolic national leadership as well as for party leadership. A skillful President can appear to act above parties without sacrificing his party authority, if he is unostentatious about the latter. The success of Franklin Roosevelt may be cited in evidence of this, and the failures of Wilson and Truman as examples of the contrary.

In general, however, consensus is not likely to be maintained for long even by such leadership—except perhaps in wartime—unless some concessions are made to members of the opposition party on foreign relations. If the policy which the administration is advancing is so generally acceptable that no very drastic concessions are demanded by the opposition collaborators, the need to yield at some points is not a very serious matter, as witness the European Recovery Program, 1947–48.

But consensus is vulnerable not only to executive unwillingness to make any concessions at all, but also to the failure of the policy ultimately to achieve the announced objectives. This creates a dilemma in those cases where a policy which the administration regards as rationally conceived to promote American interests is in fact so widely unacceptable in the United States that even cooperative members of the opposition demand major alterations, which the executive officials are convinced will prevent ultimate success. The administration can then take the chance of going ahead on its own, "rationally," gambling that success will come and will produce consensus. But that very decision to act unilaterally is likely to encourage the opposition to throw up partisan roadblocks which prevent the policy from being successfully followed through anyway, especially if it is one which risks war and hence seems especially to require more than mere majority support; moreover, international relations are so complex and unpredictable that the officials may well have been overconfident in the first place of the wisdom of their widely unacceptable policy. (Without elaborating the particular circumstances which did not fit this pattern, it may be observed that these comments are largely derived from consideration of American relations with China in the postwar years, especially 1949 and 1950.) Alternatively, an administration may decide to make the drastic concessions demanded, thus at least forestalling stalemate opposition, and hoping that success may still be achieved in the largely unpredictable situation. In this way temporary agreement at home is secured consciously at the expense of pure rationality of policy abroad; the ultimate result may be to prevent success overseas, as was feared; then the failure abroad may in turn corrode the artificial consensus in America and put increasing strain on the extrapartisan collaboration. But at least in this case members of the opposition party will be actively implicated in the failure if it comes; and therefore intense *partisanship* will be less likely than otherwise to aggravate the loss of public confidence still further and thereby prevent the adoption of a new and more promising approach. On balance, in the long run, extrapartisanship seems most likely to survive if there is a general willingness on the part of the administration to make concessions to cooperative members of the opposition, even at the risk of policy failure. (Whether, however, the preservation of extrapartisanship is itself usually worth such risks is a question to be considered later.)

In addition to a high degree of consensus, the other general requirement for the feasibility of continued extrapartisanship relates to the awarding of political credit and blame on foreign affairs. As far as possible, for each individual politician's stand on major foreign policy, praise and attack should be leveled at him in his role as an independent delegate who is answerable on such issues to his local constituents, not as a partisan who in this field as much as in domestic affairs shares with his associates party responsibility before a national constituency. Extrapartisanship does not mean taking foreign policy out of electoral politics; it means removing the major issues as far as possible from national party campaigns, particularly the focal presidential campaigns. Senators and Representatives would still be honored or condemned for their foreign policies and voted in and out of office on issues in foreign affairs, but as *individuals* only (under ordinary circumstances).

Current examples can be adduced, but first a reference to the recent past may make the point more clearly. In a stable extrapartisan system the foreign policy brickbats in 1951 and 1952 would have been hurled at "Senator Taft of Ohio," not at "Mr. Republican," unless he had actually become the GOP presidential nominee with a program hostile to prevailing extrapartisan foreign policy. Similarly President Truman could have continued to take full credit for his personal foreign policy and praised to his heart's content individual Democrats who contributed to it, but he would not have been free to claim credit for the Democratic *party* even though he was relying heavily on the habitual willingness of Democrats to go along with his administration.

Eisenhower and his Republicans are another case in point. Relations can be improved by his willingness to praise a few cooperative Democrats as well as fellow members of the GOP; but this should not be necessary, for the Democrats are (and should remain) free to take as much credit as they may be able to get on their own for what may be accomplished jointly. Nor should they, as did some of Dulles' supporters for the Senate in 1949, expect the administration to pull its punches in a campaign on domestic issues simply because the opposition candidate was cooperating on foreign affairs. It is frequently observed that what is here called extrapartisanship cannot survive if it is made the political instrument of the majority party. That is very probably true, but it is equally unlikely to work for very long if no one, even as an individual, can make any political capital out of cooperating, or, alternatively, if those who do cooperate should demand the extreme price of a soft-pedaling of opposition to their re-election in local campaigns.

John Foster Dulles has in the past argued a contrary view:

It might be the fact—indeed, it was more or less conceded—
that on matters where we helped to hammer out foreign policy, Senator Vandenberg and I made contributions which
matched those of our opposites in the Democratic Party. The
results represented an honest and a loyal effort in a spirit of
partnership, and in reality the result bore the trade-mark of
us all. Nevertheless, when the policies finally emerged they
naturally and properly emerged as the policies of the President and his Secretary of State. In consequence, the policies
were identified in the public mind with Democrats.

The Republicans could not attempt publicly to claim credit
which might be theirs for the making of the agreed policies,
for bipartisanship would never survive if it were merely a
prelude to open quarreling as to where lay the principal credit
for origination.[2]

Certainly Dulles is right that there would be tension. But competition toward making a valuable and recognized contribution to a
joint undertaking seems far less likely to be gravely divisive than
would be the political unattractiveness of a utopian "bipartisanship" in which the electoral advantage of participating individuals
was simply ignored. Dewey in 1948 did neither his own cause nor
the future attractiveness of extrapartisanship any good by his failure to emphasize strongly the contribution of certain Republicans
to the switch from "the Grand Design" to "getting tough with
Russia."

The practices which have been indicated as needed for the
stability of extrapartisanship are obviously not drastically different
from the existing American political system. For the most part
they involve reaffirmation and formalization of familiar habits of
American politics which are brought into question only when the
ideal of party responsibility is raised. Reasons have already been
given for rejecting partisanship and strict bipartisanship in *foreign*
affairs, while affirming the distant desirability of a realignment
which would permit more disciplined party responsibility in *domestic* affairs. But friends of either of those two general systems

2. Dulles, *War or Peace*, p. 179.

will insist that extrapartisanship is not adequate, even if it is or
can be made feasible. The major objections they emphasize deserve consideration. All have some merit.

Objections to Extrapartisanship

(1) Does not the system of extrapartisanship, as described, frustrate the effective expression of minority views? This is a general
criticism leveled by advocates of *partisanship*. The answer in principle, of course, is that extrapartisanship, unlike disciplined bipartisanship, involves no conscious suppression of debate and opposition, only an effort to avoid sharp party lines. Individuals would
remain as free to resist any administration as to cooperate with it.
There certainly has been vocal opposition to Truman's foreign
policy and to Eisenhower's, even for Europe, in the last few years
and modifications have been forced.

But that is admittedly not a fully adequate answer. Presumably,
strict *partisan* debate would indeed be more intense, and the opposition to executive proposals would be more seriously regarded for
the very reason that all the "big guns" of the nonadministration
party were firing in the same direction. This kind of debate might
very well not actually produce additional information for the edi-
fication of those citizens who are attentive to foreign affairs. Extrapartisan debate largely suffices for them. But the bitterer and more
continuous barrage and counterbarrage of partisanship would
probably penetrate more deeply into the habitually uninterested
mass public. The serious disadvantage of losing this degree of
penetration must be conceded. Offsetting it are the special risks
inherent in partisanship and the fact that there would still be room
for extensive debate and for reasonably effective opposition in a
stable extrapartisan congressional system.

(2) Does not extrapartisanship frustrate simple majority action?
This is another broad criticism offered by advocates of majoritarian partisanship. As critics in (1), they resented the weakening of
the divided opposition; here they object to the administration's
having to make concessions to retain its collaborators from the
other party. The two criticisms are not inconsistent, but they do
point up the difficulty of rendering blanket judgment that in-

creased consultation would produce a "prior legislative veto" or else a "State Department transmission belt." In general, however, it does seem fair to say that the implementation of the will of a simple majority—insofar as it can be represented by the President and his party in Congress—would be inhibited by systematic extrapartisan collaboration. In reply it should be emphasized that in a democracy the level of potential sacrifice in foreign affairs usually puts a "veto power" in the hands of a large and determined minority anyway, unless executive officials are prepared to resort repeatedly to shock techniques of leadership. At least extrapartisanship may make the minority more amenable to persuasion against the exercise of its "veto" in partisan deadlock.

(3) Does not extrapartisanship impair consistent rationality in the conduct of foreign relations? This is an objection raised by advocates of full *bi*partisanship as well as friends of partisanship, and especially by those in both camps who wish to strengthen the executive over the legislature in foreign relations as the more "rational" body and are somewhat less concerned with the popularity of the resulting policies. Their arguments put emphasis on the importance of preserving the "integrity" of a foreign policy—its inner consistency in accordance with a genuine strategy—and of facilitating the exercise of foresight and sustained preparation. On this view even minor concessions to opposition collaborators are likely to be condemned as unduly disruptive. The argument is that an administration with the aid of a disciplined majority party, even if it were confronted by a disciplined and active opposition, would at least be able to prevent such vagaries as the "frittering away" of European recovery money on dried fruits and American tobacco. More important, the administration might then be able, especially if it found the minority willing to give full bipartisan support, to carry through a general mobilization lasting many months with a view to forcing a showdown with the Soviets. This is not the place to argue the merits of a policy of preventive war, but the appalling hazards involved in actually going through with an ultimatum on the basis of mere majority support are as obvious as they were before Pearl Harbor, and the likelihood of preserving full *bipartisan* agreement for such a momentous aggres-

sive decision can hardly be regarded as high in any democracy.

There is always grave risk of stalemate confronting "rational" and consistent basic policies which are so widely unacceptable that they can ultimately be maintained—if at all—only on partisan foundations. That risk at least can be minimized if there is willingness on the part of responsible officials to admit the limits of "rationality" in foreign policy—for reasons of international complexity as well as domestic politics—and so by means of extrapartisan concessions to preserve a wider range of flexible discretion which may enable them to take advantage of more favorable opportunities later on.

Actually the evidence of the postwar period suggests that extrapartisanship may normally be expected to produce a more reasonable and informative, if less dramatic, canvassing of the alternatives than would more intense partisanship. Instead of simply taking foreign policy out of the hands of the people and putting it in the hands of the experts (as some say extrapartisanship does too much and others imply it does not do sufficiently) the system should actually tend to produce *more* "experts" and utilize their skills more effectively. Robert Dahl has made this point very clear:

> As we move "up" the hierarchy of authority from expert to top administrator on the one side, and up the hierarchy of specialization from ordinary Congressman to specialized committee member on the other, the less different are the skills involved. And at the top of the pyramid, the skills of an Acheson and a Vandenberg may be of much the same kind.
>
> The solution of presidential supremacy ignores this central fact. The superior facilities of the executive-administrative for interpreting reality are important assets. But the problem is not so much one of excluding the Congressional elements of the political skill group in favor of the executive-administrative elements; the problem is to bring the highest competence of the entire skill group to bear upon the making of policy.[3]

3. Robert A. Dahl, *Congress and Foreign Policy* (New York, Harcourt, Brace, 1950), p. 104.

Moreover, there would still be room under stable extrapartisan-ship for major improvements in the bureaucratic coordinating mechanisms of the executive branch itself—on which primary re-liance should be put for the sponsoring and implementation of consistent policies. To the extent that any administration can establish a more solid front and better advance planning, its su-perior facilities may be expected to carry greater weight with Con-gress on behalf of more fully rounded programs. Of course, independent activity by members of Congress also complicates presidential efforts to coordinate the executive, but the possibil-ities have surely not been exhausted. Inside Congress much could be done to coordinate activity in foreign relations by facilitating collaboration between different committees and between their staffs through such devices as joint committees, joint hearings on particular legislation, shared staffs (including experts seconded from the Legislative Reference Service), and special select study committees—despite all the divisive jealousies which exist.

Furthermore, the *party*-control apparatus is so extraordinarily weak that it could be strengthened considerably even in foreign affairs and used discreetly when there is little risk of thereby driv-ing an enduring wedge between the parties on a major issue of foreign policy.

The argument may still be made, however, that there is simply not time for America today to shape foreign policy with such de-liberation, even though the product might well be greater wisdom as well as wider consensus. To this argument the only honest an-swer is that nobody knows—at least nobody outside the inner re-cesses of the Central Intelligence Agency, and probably no one even there, since the sure answer can hardly be had outside the Politburo in Moscow. If the West is to be attacked in the next half dozen years, even purposeful major changes in the existing politi-cal system in America could hardly become operative in time to affect the Kremlin's decision. Beyond that time they might. But as the years stretch out, imponderable elements must make Russia's ultimate choice increasingly unpredictable even to its own leaders. And the time-consuming problem of overcoming differences in the Western alliance would still remain even if new devices of partisanship or bipartisanship managed to submerge or transcend the differences in Congress. It may even be argued that if time is very short it is wiser to "tinker" with the existing system, to make extrapartisanship work more efficiently, than it would be to press immediately for drastic changes in the control of foreign relations. None of these arguments, however, is likely to convince the man who is truly oppressed with a sense of urgency about the security of the United States and is consequently impatient with the workings of American politics. To him one can only repeat that no one knows there is not time, and then recall the arguments for extrapartisanship which are especially valid if in fact there *is* time.

(4) How is it possible to distinguish between foreign and domestic policy so that the latter can become increasingly the subject of responsible party discipline and national electoral mandates, as desired, while the former remains extrapartisan? Obviously there is no clear distinction, especially in the realm of fiscal policy, as was particularly evident on the defense budget in the Eighty-first Congress. The overlap and the interaction between foreign and domestic policy is certainly very great. But the argument seems specious that no distinction at all can be recognized between the two. What is involved is a matter of emphasis. In principle, under extrapartisanship only the most important issues the primary impact of which falls on foreign relations or military affairs should, at the initiative of the President, be removed from the sphere of partisan debate by the establishment of extrapartisan mechanisms of consultation. Individual and bloc opposition could continue in those areas, and partisan debate could continue on subjects where the administration offered no invitation or was unable to find any very influential persons in the other party who were willing to cooperate.

It must be conceded, however, that if the most important foreign and military issues are also much the most interesting political issues to the public, and if they are foreclosed from partisan debate by extrapartisanship, there can indeed be little chance for the development of responsible parties with alternative programs in *any* major sphere. But such preoccupation of the public with the external concerns of the country is exceedingly unusual except in periods of great national emergency and war, when the merits of partisan debate are particularly questionable anyway. The point is simply that party responsibility and majoritarian popular mandates cannot possibly thrive in a climate of war. If American foreign relations should actually have to be conducted for indefinite periods at very high levels of mobilization, a tightly organized partisan opposition would be found intolerable. The two-party system could hardly be strengthened under such stress. But as long as domestic questions still retain some interest, there is a distant prospect for the realignment which would permit the national electorate to decide between responsible alternatives on those questions, while local electorates gave what weight they wished to the foreign policies of their individual congressmen.

LESSER PROBLEMS OF EXTRAPARTISAN COLLABORATION

The reasons have now been outlined for striking a balance at the conclusion of this study in favor of extrapartisanship over partisanship or full bipartisanship as a system for the control of American foreign relations, both on grounds of feasibility and general adequacy. But the operations of an extrapartisan arrangement also raise several lesser problems which deserve some attention.

One is the special question of mere briefing vs. real participation when congressmen are the consultants. Busy politicians of either party who are approached by executive officials on foreign affairs usually want an opportunity to take *action,* not just to learn and discuss. If information is all that is offered, most of them will give priority to other demands which are more pressing upon their limited time. When a "consultation" simply takes the form of a briefing given a few hours before an executive decision is going to be announced anyway, there can be little justification for bothering at all with a procedure which is so sure to offend congressmen (except that it may prepare them with a few reasonable arguments so that they do not explode blindly when they read the news in the papers). In general Harold Stassen's familiar observation holds true, that opposition consultants will not be satisfied unless they are "in at the take-off and not merely at the crash landing."

But this combination of the wishes of congressional consultants both to "do something" and to be "in at the take-off" raises a second special difficulty for executive-legislative collaboration, because the take-off on a problem in foreign affairs is often not an appropriate stage for legislative action. Certainly that was the view of the Far Eastern Division of the State Department regarding a new China policy in 1949. If the executive officials do try to consult with congressmen before they even have an idea what they want done, they may simply make themselves look silly and further complicate their own efforts to work out a line of policy, especially when it requires intricate negotiations between different administrative agencies. On the other hand, if the officials for that reason feel obliged to delay consultation for very long after congressmen have become concerned about a particular problem, even the normally friendly legislators will begin to criticize, as many moderate Republicans did with regard to China in the summer of 1949. Such criticism injures extrapartisan relations at the time and for the future; but under the circumstances there is no other way for interested congressmen to influence the course of policy, even to the extent of insisting that *some* policy be speedily developed. All of this shows that there is a high premium on advance planning by the experts, so that consultation may be meaningful, effective, and satisfying at the time when the seriousness of a given problem seems to warrant it, and when if possible the active contribution of legislators can be utilized.

Just what that contribution can and should be constitutes a third special difficulty in collaboration. A satisfactory extrapartisan relationship requires that the participants have a true sense of sharing in policy making. They must have a feeling that the result is the joint product of joint study, on which they have put their stamp.

If prominent members of one party actually go so far as to accept long-term office in an administration controlled by the other party, the problem of participation is solved for them. But their influence in their own party may normally be expected to decline sharply.

Extrapartisanship concerns itself more with the fruitful collaboration of politicians who intend to submit themselves to their respective local electorates, so that a measure of popular control is
preserved over their activities in foreign relations.

The most obvious and convenient opportunity for such collaboration usually will come in the drafting of specific legislative proposals which the administration is presenting. The legislative
process can be smoothed if there is consultation on the shape of
a law before it is actually put in the form of a draft bill by executive officials (but after they have formed some idea of what they are
looking for). The legislative process at best is so time consuming,
however, that even with good foresight and planning there cannot
always be time for an administration to insert a consultation-on-
drafting stage between its general formulation of policy and the
formal consideration of a bill by Congress. In that case, extrapartisan harmony may still be preserved if the officials exhibit a conciliatory attitude toward the congressional committees and early
show a willingness to make some concessions. Indeed the fact that
the points are then yielded in *public* makes it easier for the executive branch to take credit for its "reasonableness," for the legislators to take credit for their contributions, and for both groups to
be sure which concessions really are needed for harmonious congressional action. However, the normal hardening of positions
under the public spotlight may be expected to limit these last advantages and thus leave the balance in favor of *prior* consultation
wherever it is practicable on major foreign affairs legislation.

Another sometimes useful legislative contribution by congressmen in foreign affairs, besides assistance in drafting bills to make
them more palatable to the interested public, is the offering of
resolutions. If they have the indicated support of prominent members, such formal declarations will carry weight with other powers
as well as with the administration, whether or not the resolutions
are actually passed. Moreover, in the regular legislative process
congressmen can set conditions on foreign aid grants far more
freely than the traditional diplomacy is able to do, with its rules
about noninterference in the internal affairs of other countries.
Internationally the administration can shift the blame to Capitol

Hill; this is not always so inconvenient as the State Department must pretend when it deals with foreigners.

One nonlegislative field in which extrapartisan consultants from Congress have shown a capacity to participate effectively is at international conferences. Of course the major preparation has to be done by professionals in the executive branch. But congressmen can offer useful advice about the effect of proposed policies and methods of presentation on articulate public opinion in America. Moreover they are likely to have acquired considerable skills in "conference diplomacy" through their congressional experience, which also involves the reconciling of viewpoints around a committee table and in open forums, with that shrewd sense of timing and tactics which is called a "feeling for the parliamentary situation." The question does often arise—to be decided case by case, according to circumstances—whether collaborators from outside the executive branch should be utilized as formally accredited negotiators who are ultimately subject to the will of the President, or else just as regular advisers to the official delegates. Some may prefer the fuller sense of participation that goes with delegate status; others may feel that their influence in Congress is improved if they conspicuously maintain a position of independent judgment. In either case they can contribute their opinions fully and freely in the private meetings of the delegation before its policy is finally determined in detail.

The most difficult aspect of the problem of what contribution extrapartisan consultants can make arises on day-to-day "cable" questions in foreign relations, which do not require legislation. It is easy to argue that these are decisions for men who have made foreign affairs their full-time job and life work, that congressmen have neither the time nor the knowledge to participate and should not even *want* to have their "ruffled feathers smoothed" by "rituals" of consultation. Some congressmen, indeed, prefer not to be entrusted with secret information; they find its possession embarrassing and inhibiting.

But it is also true that many other able and reasonably well informed congressmen do want subjectively to participate in "secret stuff"; and objectively, if they cannot do so, they will be confronted more frequently than necessary with executive *faits accomplis* to which they have no real alternative but to subscribe—with, however, an increasing bitterness and determination to tie the administration's hands in *future* with formal legislative knots. This needs to be avoided by inviting consultation on the most important "cable" questions as well as on legislation. After all, there are a good many members of Congress who have as good a background on foreign relations as do political appointees in the top echelon of the State Department. Extrapartisan consultants can be safely furnished with much secret information for joint study with officials, since the administration fully controls the process of their selection. And the congressmen at all times, if they are seasoned practitioners of their trade, are more likely than the officials or the pollsters to be able to judge what the *politically effective* public will support in America, even discounting the capacity of the administration to alter opinion by making an impressive presentation of its case.

Besides, congressmen are not likely to want a very great deal of consultation. Busy legislators who have to worry about keeping their political fences mended for the sake of re-election are usually short of time. This has already been discussed as a criticism of full bipartisanship,[4] but it also applies as a limiting factor to extrapartisanship, although in the latter system the administration has greater freedom to pick and choose consultants who can devote more of their time to the foreign affairs task. However, even in an atmosphere of confidence as nearly complete as seems possible with a constitutional system of separation of powers, congressmen are bound to be suspicious of executive "lobbying" through the mechanisms of consultation. To appear to solicit advice too assiduously is only to increase those suspicions and impair the dignity of high office. This can often be dangerous, but no line of principle can be drawn between respectful interest and overeagerness, on the part of executive officials. This requires a tactful sensitivity to the personal reactions of individuals who differ considerably.

The relationship becomes considerably less strained to the extent that it can be made informal. Routine consultation, on a fixed

4. See Introduction, pp. 13–14.

schedule which gives little weight to the relative importance of the problems arising, is likely to go by the board after a few meetings when the legislator must choose among alternate demands upon his time. But *social* events have a special attractiveness of their own to the congressman or his wife. Especially are many of the newer members hungry for invitations to parties in the strange city of Washington, and at the same time their low seniority makes it difficult for administrators to approach them for advice, except in a social context, without arousing jealousy among the older members. Senior congressmen too, of course, are normally attracted by dinners and cocktail parties. Diplomats have long been familiar with the usefulness of social intercourse for oiling the wheels of international negotiations. State Department officials frequently have to find time to attend such diplomatic entertainments in Washington as well as during overseas missions. A similar kind of intercourse is no less desirable in the *intra*governmental negotiations which are ultimately required to carry through the major policies. Some suspicion of "social lobbying" is inevitable, but it can be minimized to the extent that the larger gatherings can be arranged by friendly and prosperous congressmen and Washingtonians rather than directly by officials.

The final special problem in extrapartisan executive-legislative collaboration to be discussed here—obviously by no means the least important—is *who* should consult.

On the side of the executive the problem is relatively less difficult than on the other side, but it is not simple. One aspect is that the outside collaborators will want to work with officials who really know something about a given subject, and also with the men who have the power of decision on that subject—and they are by no means always the same individuals. If the low-echelon expert with whom congressmen have been consulting is overruled by his superior suddenly and without warning, a fruitful relationship is likely to be destroyed. Careful intradepartmental coordination should be able to soften such transitions, but can hardly eliminate them, given the changing circumstances of foreign relations. But if congressmen go to the opposite extreme and deal only with the upper echelon, they deprive themselves of valuable information which is not to be found at the top except on paper—while most legislators by experience are in the habit of learning by ear. Ideally, it seems that conversations should be held jointly between the experts, the policy-making officials, and the extrapartisan consultants—probably after an initial briefing of the outsiders by the experts to bring them up to date with the top policy makers and thereby save the latter individuals' time. With the best of intentions such meetings are not easy to arrange on short notice. Considerable reliance must inevitably be put on full-time congressional liaison men working for the various executive agencies. Care needs to be taken by other officials to keep them informed, to give them support, to build up their prestige, and to give heed to the suggestions which they pass along.

It takes a long time to develop a relationship of genuine confidence between the congressmen and the officials with·whom it is appropriate for them to work frequently. Sometimes it is literally impossible to do so—as it ultimately became for key personnel in the Far Eastern Division of the State Department. Under those circumstances the question presents itself unavoidably whether their expertness is more valuable than the good will of Congress to the successful conduct of American foreign relations. According to the thesis of this study the answer in such cases may often be "No."

A final note on executive consultants pertains to the President himself. No stable extrapartisan collaboration can be pursued in foreign affairs except on his initiative or that of his top officials. But the extent to which any President himself participates in such conversations must depend largely upon his personal prestige with the different groups involved, the demands upon his time, and the actual extent to which he is actively controlling the foreign policy of his administration. No rule can be laid down which covers the personal qualities, attitudes, and habits here involved. It does seem fair to say, however, that there cannot often be time in the presence of the President for detailed extrapartisan discussion of individual issues in foreign affairs, except by those members of the opposition party who have actually joined his administration as regular appointees.

Outside the executive branch the problem of who should participate in extrapartisan consultation becomes more complex.

In the decentralized American party system a case might be made for the proposition that active collaboration should be sought also from *noncongressional* party leaders who wield special power in the nomination of candidates for the presidency. But such an effort would be impracticable except at rare intervals for physical reasons of time and distance and because of congressional jealousies. The exception to this rule comes during presidential campaigns, when, as was evidenced in 1944 and 1948, the opposition party's nominee has sufficient authority to appoint his personal delegate for continuous consultation.

Inside Congress it would naturally be desirable if an administration could find extrapartisan consultants who were at once competent, representative, influential, and able to keep secrets. In fact, of course, few such paragons exist. In many cases a reinforcing bridge can be provided by able personnel on the *staffs* of individual members and committees of Congress. The staff of the Senate Foreign Relations Committee is becoming deservedly renowned for the immeasurably valuable service it has performed since World War II. But its ultimate usefulness, like that of most other staffs, depends on the prestige of the members of the committee, especially the chairman. Expert assistance can supplement the effectiveness of influential politicians but is no substitute for their personal authority with their colleagues or the interested public.

Even the few regular members of Congress who do combine the qualifications most desirable for extrapartisan collaboration are often in no position, under the existing congressional system, to work closely with executive officials on foreign affairs. In seeking the cooperation of members of the opposition party it is appropriate for any administration to give more regard to their actual influence than to their formal status in the party hierarchy, but of course some of the official leaders will still be worth including, if available. Many of them will, however, be virtually barred from effective working relationships by the jealousies engendered by the committee system.

In each committee the problem of finding useful consultants is complicated by seniority, which dictates that special deference be paid to the members of both parties who have the longest continuous record of service on that committee, regardless of their ability or influence there or in Congress as a whole.

In the larger rivalry between the committees themselves, the Foreign Affairs and Foreign Relations bodies take the position with the State Department: "We're your friends. We're the ones you normally have to rely on to support you. Why go over our heads to the party leadership?" With this attitude so prevalent, it becomes particularly important that the foreign committees themselves have an influential and representative membership. The strengthening of the House Foreign Affairs Committee is the most pressing need, which is gradually being met. The composition of the Senate Foreign Relations Committee in recent years has certainly not lacked strength, but it has lacked breadth on foreign policy; that also is being remedied. Moreover, most other congressional committees have some jurisdiction in an area of foreign relations, and where such jurisdiction clearly exists it is hard for the "foreign" committees to take umbrage at executive efforts to foster collaboration with the other group concerned.

There is usually another special danger in any extrapartisan cooperation—that those who participate will be branded as administration "favorites" and that their influence in Congress will correspondingly decline. In a sense they are, inevitably, favorites, and an administration is well advised to accept that fact, if they are willing, and proceed to counteract the adverse reaction by helping to build them up through propaganda of the deed and word, as was done so skillfully with Vandenberg. Publicity is the breath of life to politicians. They can be given credit for originating various policies or for usefully modifying them, and can be given the opportunity to make the initial public presentation of new plans on which they have cooperated. But at the same time great care must be taken to minimize as far as possible the most notorious public evidence of favoritism. Ordinarily the extrapartisan collaborator himself will insist on that, knowing his vulnerability with his colleagues. But even if he does not, the administration itself must take care on this score, lest it be left with a group of cooperative consultants who in fact have lost all influence with their own party colleagues—a mere shell of extrapartisanship.

A FINAL WORD

The review which has been made in the last few pages of the special problems of extrapartisan collaboration has pointed up substantial obstacles—but no difficulties that are of themselves beyond mastery. The reforms which have been suggested in the role of political parties in current American foreign relations do not involve a general reshaping of the governmental and electoral system. For the most part what has been advocated is extension, elaboration, and improvement of practices which became familiar in the conduct of foreign affairs in the nineteen forties under the impetus of demands for collective security and resistance to Communist aggression.

No certain assurance can be offered that this American political system in fact possesses the qualities which will enable it to survive the arduous struggle against foreign totalitarianism. The possession by the United States of physical power, which is only partly the consequence of its constitutional government, may in fact be the basic presupposition without which one would not be entitled even to hope for the preservation of a measure of popular control over foreign policy through the local election of independent delegates. But the power of the nation does exist, permitting some choice of the means to exercise it, and some indeterminate time in which to make the choices. And the political system strongly induces those who immediately control that power to reach out for a very broad popular consensus to sustain their decisions. The easy access of interested minorities to political power at *some* point in the governmental system brings a constant pressure for over-all compromises that embrace far more than a simple majority of the attentive public. The resulting consensus is not only a democratic desideratum in foreign affairs. It is usually also a mighty weapon for America in her hazardous dealings with the outside world. For many years to come, the chance to secure such free consensus should not be frustrated by basic alterations in the limited function which is now performed by political parties in American foreign relations. However much an increase in party responsibility may be desirable and may prove to be practicable on domestic issues in the United States, it does not on balance appear to be either a more feasible or more adequate system for overseas policy in the foreseeable future—if the consent of the governed can in fact remain a primary consideration in the conduct of American foreign relations.

APPENDIX

Maps Depicting Congressional Voting on Foreign Affairs, 1943–50

EACH OF THE MAPS BELOW is labeled with the subject category of the roll calls with which it is concerned, and the number and house of the Congress in which they were taken. Standard regional boundaries are indicated, and within each section is a set of figures like the following example (the Northeast record on displaced persons (DP's) in the Eightieth House, map 21, page 425):

94	100	88
56	95	83
68	97	

The top line of figures represents the Democratic party's record, the second line the Republican. In each, from left to right, the first figure is the average percentage of support given to the administration by members of that party in that region; the second figure is the average percentage of support given to two-party majorities by members of that party in that region; and the third is the average percentage of support given to their own party on party-line votes by members of that party in that region. In the third line, the first figure is the average percentage of support given to the administration by members from that *region regardless of party* (Democrats plus Republicans plus minor party members), and the second figure is the average percentage of support given to two-party majorities by Democrats and Republicans in that region (minor party members ignored).[1]

1. If there were no roll calls in one of the categories, or if no member of a particular regional party made a usable record in those that were taken, that fact is indicated on the map by a heavy line. If only one member of a particular regional party made a usable record, that fact is indicated beside (his) "regional party average."

Thus regarding displaced persons in the Eightieth House, Northeastern Democrats on the average supported the administration 94 per cent of the time; they supported two-party majorities 100 per cent of the time; and they supported their own party 88 per cent of the time on party-line roll calls. Northeastern Representatives as a group, including American Labor Party members Marcantonio and Isacson, averaged 68 per cent support of the administration, while Democratic and Republican Representatives from the Northeast averaged 97 per cent support of two-party majorities.

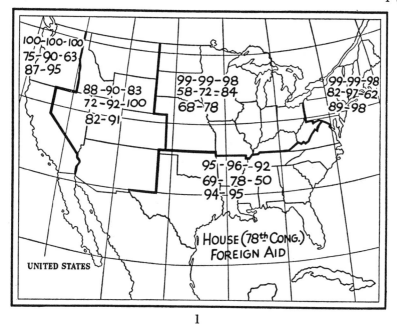

1

2

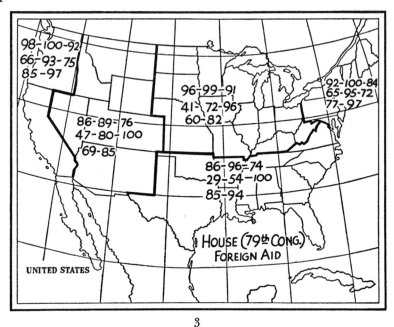

3

4

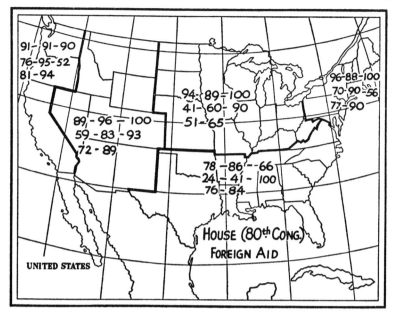

5

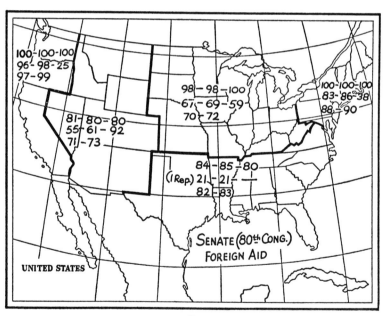

6

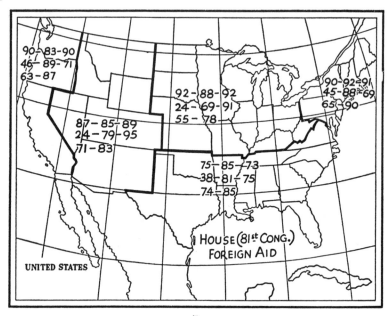

7

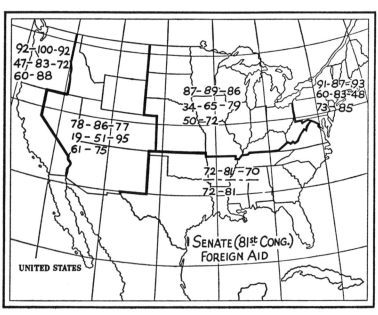

8

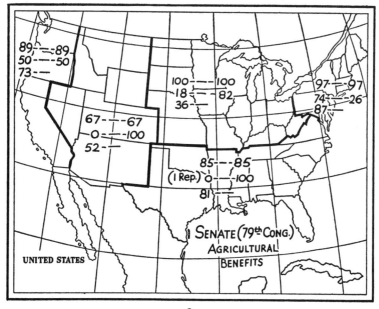

9

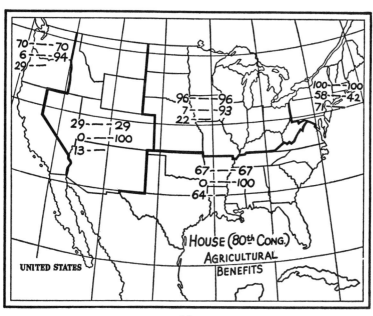

10

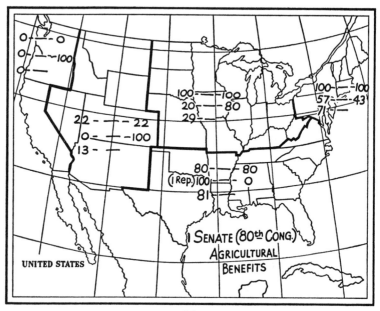

11

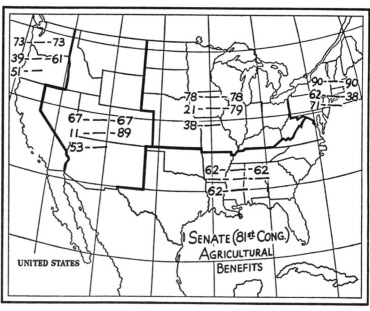

12

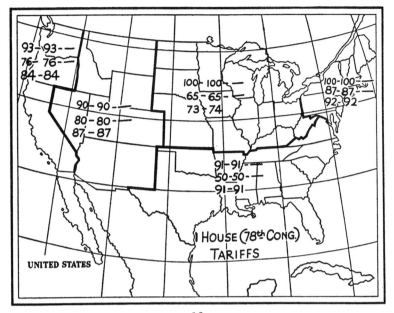

13

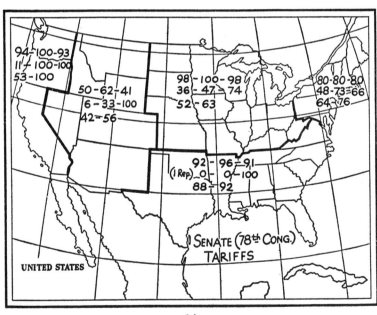

14

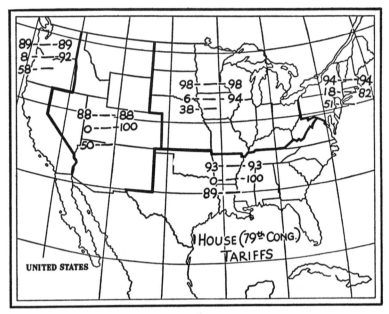

89----89
8----92
58----

98----98
6----94
38----

94----94
18----82
51----

88----88
0----100
50----

93----93
0----100
89----

HOUSE (79ᵗʰ CONG.)
TARIFFS

UNITED STATES

15

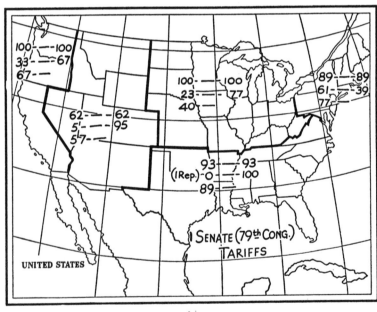

100----100
33----67
67----

100----100
23----77
40----

89----89
61----39
77----

62----62
5----95
57----

93----93
(1Rep.) 0----100
89----

SENATE (79ᵗʰ CONG.)
TARIFFS

UNITED STATES

16

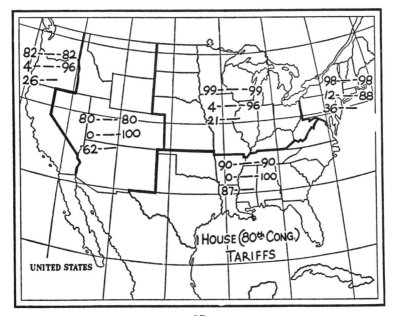

17

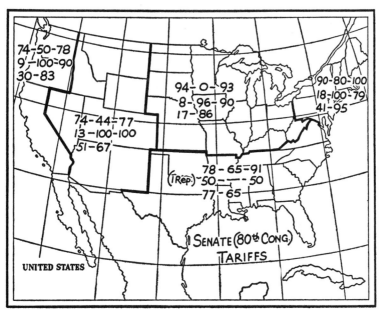

18

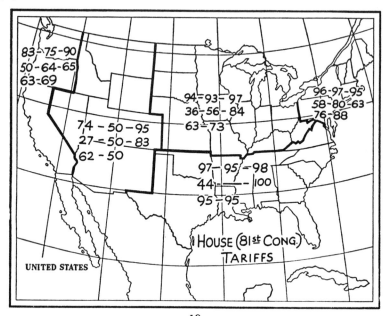

83-75-90
50-64-65
63-69

74 - 50 - 95
27-50-83
62 - 50

94-93-97
36-56-84
63-73

96-97-95
58-80-63
76-88

97- 95 -98
44- -100
95-95

HOUSE (81st CONG.)
TARIFFS

UNITED STATES

19

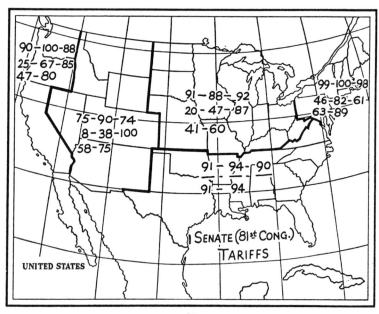

90-100-88
25-67-85
47-80

75-90-74
8-38-100
58-75

91-88-92
20-47-87
41-60

99-100-98
46-82-61
63-89

91 - 94 -90
91- 94

SENATE (81st CONG.)
TARIFFS

UNITED STATES

20

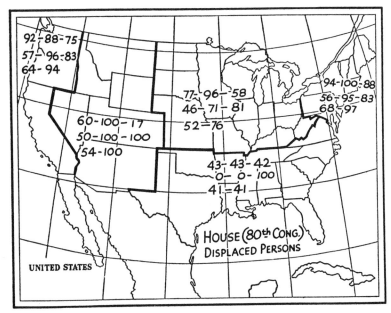

92 - 88 - 75
57 - 96 - 83
64 - 94

77 - 96 - 58
46 - 71 - 81
52 - 76

94 - 100 - 88
56 - 95 - 83
68 - 97

60 - 100 - 17
50 - 100 - 100
54 - 100

43 - 43 - 42
0 - 0 - 100
41 - 41

HOUSE (80th CONG.)
DISPLACED PERSONS

UNITED STATES

21

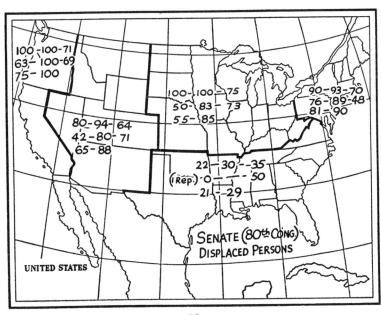

100 - 100 - 71
63 - 100 - 69
75 - 100

100 - 100 - 75
50 - 83 - 73
55 - 85

90 - 93 - 70
76 - 89 - 48
81 - 90

80 - 94 - 64
42 - 80 - 71
65 - 88

22 - 30 - 35
(Rep.) 0 - - 50
21 - 29

SENATE (80th CONG.)
DISPLACED PERSONS

UNITED STATES

22

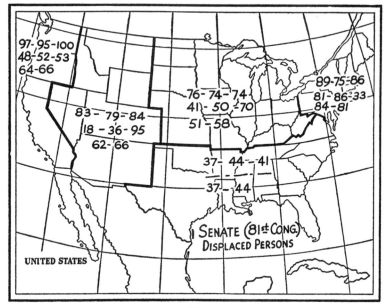

97-95-100
48-52-53
64-66

83 - 79 = 84
18 - 36 - 95
62-66

76 - 74 - 74
41 - 50 - 70
51 = 58

89-75=86
81 - 86-33
84 - 81

37- 44 - 41

37 - 44

SENATE (81ˢᵗ CONG.)
DISPLACED PERSONS

UNITED STATES

23

BIBLIOGRAPHY

BOOKS AND PAMPHLETS

ALMOND, GABRIEL A. *The American People and Foreign Policy.* New York, Harcourt, Brace, 1950.

BAILEY, THOMAS A. *The Man in the Street.* New York, Macmillan, 1948.

BALDWIN, HANSON W. *Great Mistakes of the War.* New York, Harper, 1950.

────── *The Price of Power.* New York, Harper, 1947.

BARNES, JOSEPH. *Willkie.* New York, Simon & Schuster, 1952.

BEARD, CHARLES A. *American Foreign Policy in the Making, 1932–1940.* New Haven, Yale University, 1946.

────── *President Roosevelt and the Coming of War 1941, a Study in Appearances and Realities.* New Haven, Yale University, 1948.

BINKLEY, WILFRED E. *American Political Parties, Their Natural History.* 2d ed. New York, Knopf, 1949.

BLOOM, SOL. *The Autobiography of Sol Bloom.* New York, Putnam, 1948.

BOZELL, L. BRENT, AND BUCKLEY, WILLIAM F., JR. *McCarthy and His Enemies.* Chicago, Regnery, 1954.

Brookings Institution. *The Administration of Foreign Affairs and Overseas Operations, a Report Prepared for the Bureau of the Budget, Executive Office of the President.* Washington, Government Printing Office, 1951.

BUCKLEY, WILLIAM F., JR., AND BOZELL, L. BRENT. *McCarthy and His Enemies.* Chicago, Regnery, 1954.

BUNDY, McGEORGE (ed.). *The Pattern of Responsibility, from the Record of Secretary of State Dean Acheson.* Boston, Houghton Mifflin, 1952.

BURNS, JAMES M. *Congress on Trial, the Legislative Process and the Administrative State.* New York, Harper, 1949.

BYRNES, JAMES F. *Speaking Frankly.* New York, Harper, 1947.

CARR, ALBERT Z. *Truman, Stalin, and Peace.* Garden City, New York, Doubleday, 1950.

CARROLL, HOLBERT N. "The House of Representatives and Foreign Affairs," 1952. Unpublished doctoral dissertation on file in the Harvard College Library.

CHAMBERLAIN, LAWRENCE H., AND SNYDER, RICHARD C. *American Foreign Policy.* New York, Rinehart, 1948.

CHAMBERLIN, WILLIAM H. *America's Second Crusade.* Chicago, Regnery, 1950.

CHEEVER, DANIEL S., AND HAVILAND, H. FIELD, JR. *American Foreign Policy and the Separation of Powers.* Cambridge, Harvard University, 1952.

CLAY, LUCIUS D. *Decision in Germany.* Garden City, New York, Doubleday, 1950.

Commission on Organization of the Executive Branch of Government (Hoover Commission). *Foreign Affairs, a Report to the Congress.* Washington, Government Printing Office, 1949.

———— *Foreign Affairs, Task Force Report Prepared for the Commission.* Washington, Government Printing Office, 1949.

———— *General Management in the Executive Branch, a Report to the Congress.* Washington, Government Printing Office, 1949.

———— *Overseas Administration, etc., a Report to the Congress.* Washington, Government Printing Office, 1949.

Committee on Congress of the American Political Science Association. *The Reorganization of Congress, a Report.* Washington, Public Affairs Press, 1945.

Committee on Political Parties of the American Political Science Association. *Toward a More Responsible Two-Party System: A Report.* Supplement, *American Political Science Review,* September 1950.

"Congress and Foreign Relations." Vol. *289, The Annals* of the American Academy of Political and Social Science. Philadelphia, September 1953.

Congressional Quarterly News Features. *Congressional Quarterly Almanac,* Vols. *1–7.* Washington, Congressional Quarterly News Features, 1945, 1946, 1947, 1948, 1949, 1950, 1951.

CONNALLY, TOM. *My Name Is Tom Connally.* New York, Crowell, 1954.

COTTRELL, LEONARD S., JR., AND EBERHART, SYLVIA. *American Opinion on World Affairs in the Atomic Age.* Princeton, Princeton University, 1948.

Council on Foreign Relations. Campbell, John C. (ed.). *The United States in World Affairs, 1945–1947.* New York, Harper, 1947.

———— Campbell, John C. (ed.). *The United States in World Affairs, 1947–1948.* New York, Harper, 1948.

———— Campbell, John C. (ed.). *The United States in World Affairs, 1948–1949.* New York, Harper, 1949.

———— Stebbins, Richard P. (ed.). *The United States in World Affairs, 1949.* New York, Harper, 1950.

———— Stebbins, Richard P. (ed.). *The United States in World Affairs, 1950.* New York, Harper, 1951.

DAHL, ROBERT A. *Congress and Foreign Policy.* New York, Harcourt, Brace, 1950.

DANIELS, JONATHAN. *The Man of Independence.* New York and Philadelphia, Lippincott, 1950.

DENNISON, ELEANOR E. *The Senate Foreign Relations Committee.* Stanford, Stanford University, 1942.

Department of State. Notter, Harley A. (ed.). *Postwar Foreign Policy Preparation.* Washington, Government Printing Office, 1949.

———— *United States Relations with China, with Special Reference to the Period 1944–1949.* Washington, Government Printing Office, 1949.

DILLON, MARY EARHART. *Wendell Willkie.* New York, Lippincott, 1952.

DULLES, JOHN FOSTER. *War or Peace.* New York, Macmillan, 1950.

ELLIOTT, WILLIAM Y., AND OTHERS. *International Commitments and National*

Administration. Charlottesville, Bureau of Public Administration, University of Virginia, 1949.

FAIRBANK, JOHN K. *The United States and China.* Cambridge, Harvard University, 1949.

FARLEY, JAMES. *Jim Farley's Story.* New York, Whittlesey, 1948.

FEIS, HERBERT. *The China Tangle.* Princeton, Princeton University, 1953.

—— *The Road to Pearl Harbor.* Princeton, Princeton University, 1950.

FLYNN, EDWARD J. *You're the Boss.* New York, Viking, 1947.

[FORRESTAL, JAMES F.] Millis, Walter (ed.). *The Forrestal Diaries.* New York, Viking, 1951.

GALLOWAY, GEORGE B. *Congress at the Crossroads.* New York, Crowell, 1946.

—— *The Legislative Process in Congress.* New York, Crowell, 1953.

GLEASON, S. EVERETT, AND LANGER, WILLIAM L. *The Undeclared War: 1940–1941.* New York, Harper, 1953.

GRASSMUCK, GEORGE L. *Sectional Biases in Congress on Foreign Policy.* Baltimore, Johns Hopkins, 1951.

GRIFFITH, ERNEST S. *Congress: Its Contemporary Role.* New York, New York University, 1951.

GROSS, BERTRAM M. *The Legislative Struggle.* New York, McGraw-Hill, 1953.

HAVILAND, H. FIELD, JR., AND CHEEVER, DANIEL S. *American Foreign Policy and the Separation of Powers.* Cambridge, Harvard University, 1952.

HERRING, PENDLETON. *The Politics of Democracy.* New York, Norton, 1940.

HILLMAN, WILLIAM. *Mr. President.* New York, Farrar, Straus, & Young, 1952.

HULL, CORDELL. *The Memoirs of Cordell Hull.* New York, Macmillan, 1948.

HUZAR, ELIAS. *The Purse and the Sword.* Ithaca, Cornell University, 1950.

HYMAN, SIDNEY. *The American President.* New York, Harper, 1954.

JOHNSON, WALTER. *The Battle against Isolation.* Chicago, University of Chicago, 1944.

KEY, V. O. *Politics, Parties, and Pressure Groups.* 2d ed. 1947; 3d ed. 1952. New York, Crowell.

—— *Southern Politics.* New York, Knopf, 1949.

LANGER, WILLIAM L., AND GLEASON, S. EVERETT. *The Undeclared War: 1940–1941.* New York, Harper, 1953.

LASSWELL, HAROLD D. *National Security and Individual Freedom.* New York, McGraw-Hill, 1950.

LATOURETTE, KENNETH S. *The American Record in the Far East: 1945–1950.* New York, Macmillan (for the Institute of Pacific Relations), 1952.

LAZARSFELD, PAUL F., AND OTHERS. *The People's Choice.* New York, Duell, Sloan, & Pearce, 1944.

LEAHY, WILLIAM D. *I Was There.* New York, Whittlesey, 1950.

LORD, RUSSELL. *The Wallaces of Iowa.* Boston, Houghton Mifflin, 1947.

LUBELL, SAMUEL. *The Future of American Politics.* New York, Harper, 1952.

McCAMY, JAMES L. *The Administration of American Foreign Affairs.* New York, Knopf, 1950.

MacDONALD, DWIGHT. *Henry Wallace, the Man and the Myth.* New York, Vanguard, 1948.

MacMAHON, ARTHUR W. *Administration in Foreign Affairs.* Alabama, University of Alabama, 1953.

MARKEL, LESTER (ed.). *Public Opinion and Foreign Policy.* New York, Harper, 1949.

MILLIS, WALTER (ed.). *The Forrestal Diaries.* New York, Viking, 1951.

MOLEY, RAYMOND. *27 Masters of Politics.* New York, Funk & Wagnalls, 1949.

MORGENTHAU, HENRY. *Germany Is Our Problem.* New York, Harper, 1945.

MORLEY, FELIX. *The Foreign Policy of the United States.* New York, Knopf, 1951.

NANES, ALLEN SAMUEL. "Postwar Emergency Aid Programs and American Foreign Policy," 1949. Unpublished doctoral dissertation on file in the Harvard College Library.

NEUMANN, WILLIAM L. *Making the Peace, 1941–1945, the Diplomacy of Wartime Conferences.* Washington, Foundation for Foreign Affairs, 1950.

NEVINS, ALLEN. *The New Deal in World Affairs, a Chronicle of International Affairs, 1933–1945.* New Haven, Yale University, 1950.

[NOTTER, HARLEY A. (ed.)]. Department of State. *Postwar Foreign Policy Preparation.* Washington, Government Printing Office, 1949.

NOURSE, EDWIN G. *Economics in the Public Service.* New York, Harcourt, Brace, 1953.

ODEGARD, PETER H., AND HELMS, E. ALLEN. *American Politics.* 2d ed. New York, Harper, 1947.

OSGOOD, ROBERT E. *Ideals and Self-Interest in America's Foreign Relations.* Chicago, University of Chicago, 1953.

PARKS, WALLACE J. *United States Administration of Its International Economic Affairs.* Baltimore, Johns Hopkins University, 1951.

PERKINS, FRANCES. *The Roosevelt I Knew.* New York, Viking, 1946.

PLISCHKE, ELMER. *The Conduct of American Diplomacy.* New York, Van Nostrand, 1950.

President's Air Policy Commission. *Survival in the Air Age, a Report.* Washington, Government Printing Office, 1948.

RIDDICK, FLOYD M. *The United States Congress: Organization and Procedure.* Washington, National Capitol Publishers, 1949.

ROSENMAN, SAMUEL I. *Working with Roosevelt.* New York, Harper, 1952.

SCHATTSCHNEIDER, E. E. *Party Government.* New York, Farrar & Rinehart, 1942.

—— *The Struggle for Party Government.* University of Maryland, 1948.

SHERWOOD, ROBERT E. *Roosevelt and Hopkins, an Intimate History.* New York, Harper, 1948.

STETTINIUS, EDWARD R. *Lend-Lease, Weapon for Victory.* New York, Macmillan, 1944.

—— *Roosevelt and the Russians, the Yalta Conference.* Garden City, New York, Doubleday, 1949.

STIMSON, HENRY L., AND BUNDY, MCGEORGE. *On Active Service in Peace and War.* New York, Harper, 1948.

STUART, GRAHAM H. *The Department of State, a History of Its Organization, Procedure, and Personnel.* New York, Macmillan, 1949.

TRUMAN, DAVID B. *The Governmental Process.* New York, Knopf, 1951.

TURNER, JULIUS. *Party and Constituency: Pressures on Congress.* Baltimore, Johns Hopkins, 1951.

VAN ALSTYNE, RICHARD W. *American Diplomacy in Action.* 2d. ed. Stanford, Stanford University, 1947.

VANDENBERG, ARTHUR H., JR. *The Private Papers of Senator Vandenberg.* Boston, Houghton Mifflin, 1952.

VOORHIS, JERRY. *Confessions of a Congressman.* Garden City, New York, Doubleday, 1948.

WALLACE, HENRY A. *Soviet Asia Mission.* New York, Reynal & Hitchcock, 1946.

——— *Toward World Peace.* New York, Reynal & Hitchcock, 1948.

WELLES, SUMNER. *Seven Decisions That Shaped History.* New York, Harper, 1951.

——— *We Need Not Fail.* Boston, Houghton Mifflin, 1948.

——— *Where Are We Heading?* New York, Harper, 1946.

WESTPHAL, ALBERT C. F. *The House Committee on Foreign Affairs.* New York, Columbia University, 1942.

WOODBRIDGE, GEORGE. *UNRRA, the History of the United Nations Relief and Rehabilitation Administration.* New York, Columbia University, 1950.

ARTICLES

ALSOP, JOSEPH. "Why We Lost China," *Saturday Evening Post,* January 7, 14, and 21, 1950.

ARMSTRONG, HAMILTON FISH. "Foreign Policy and Party Politics," *Atlantic,* April 1947.

BAILEY, THOMAS A. "The Dilemma of Democracy," *American Perspective,* October 1948.

BOLLES, BLAIR. "Bipartisanship in American Foreign Policy," *Foreign Policy Reports,* January 1, 1949.

——— "President, Congress, and Foreign Policy," *American Perspective,* March 1949.

BULLITT, WILLIAM C. "A Report to the American People on China," *Life,* October 13, 1947.

BURNS, JAMES M. "Bipartisanship and the Weakness of the Party System," *American Perspective,* Spring 1950.

COHEN, BENJAMIN V. "The Evolving Role of Congress in Foreign Affairs," *Proceedings of the American Philosophical Society,* October 25, 1948.

COLEGROVE, KENNETH W. "The Role of Congress and Public Opinion in Formulating Foreign Policy," *American Political Science Review,* October 1944.

"Foreign Policy in National Elections," *Editorial Research Reports,* May 1, 1944.

GROSS, ERNEST A. "What Is a Bipartisan Foreign Policy?" *Department of State Bulletin,* October 3, 1949.

HEINDEL, RICHARD H., AND OTHERS. "The North Atlantic Treaty in the United States Senate," *American Journal of International Law,* October 1949.

IRISH, M. D. "Foreign Policy and the South," *Journal of Politics,* May 1948.

KENDALL, WILLMOORE. "Bipartisanship and Majority-Rule Democracy," *American Perspective,* Spring 1950.

LEVITAN, SAUL. "Democratic Control of Foreign Policy," *Journal of Politics,* February 1945.

MACMAHON, ARTHUR W. "The Administration of Foreign Affairs," *American Political Science Review,* September 1951.

——— "International Politics and Governmental Structure," *Proceedings of the American Philosophical Society,* October 25, 1948.

MILLER, WARREN E. "Party Preference and Attitudes on Political Issues: 1948–1951," *American Political Science Review,* March 1953.

NEUMANN, WILLIAM L. "How to Merchandise Foreign Policy," *American Perspective,* September and October, 1949.

RESTON, JAMES B. "Events Spotlight Vandenberg's Dual Role," *New York Times Magazine,* March 28, 1948.

——— "John Foster Dulles and His Foreign Policy," *Life,* October 4, 1948.

——— "Memorandum to General MacArthur," *New York Times Magazine,* April 22, 1951.

——— "Prospects for Stability in Our Foreign Policy," *Foreign Affairs,* October 1948.

——— "Secretary Acheson, a First-Year Audit," *New York Times Magazine,* January 22, 1950.

ROOSEVELT, KERMIT. "The Partition of Palestine, a Lesson in Pressure Politics," *Middle East Journal,* January 1948.

ROVERE, RICHARD H. "The Unassailable Vandenberg," *Harpers,* May 1948.

RUSSELL, BERTRAND, AND OTHERS. "Can American Foreign Policy Be Democratic?" *American Perspective,* September 1948.

RUSSELL, F. H. "Foreign Policy and the Democratic Process," *Department of State Bulletin,* December 28, 1947.

SCHLESINGER, ARTHUR M., JR. "Roosevelt and His Detractors," *Harpers,* June 1950.

SMITH, BEVERLY. "The Senator [Connally] Loves a Fight," *Saturday Evening Post,* July 1, 1950.

SMITH, GEORGE H. E. "Bipartisan Foreign Policy in Partisan Politics," *American Perspective,* Spring 1950.

SMUCKLER, RALPH H. "The Region of Isolationism," *American Political Science Review,* June 1953.

WELLES, SUMNER. "Pressure Groups and Foreign Policy," *Atlantic,* November 1947.

WILLIAMS, BENJAMIN H. "Bipartisanship in American Foreign Policy," *Annals of the American Academy,* September 1948.

PERIODICALS REGULARLY CONSULTED

New York Times, 1940–51.
Newsweek, 1940–51.
Time, 1940–51.
United States News, 1945–51.
Vital Speeches, 1943–50.
Washington Post, 1948–51.

PUBLIC OPINION POLLS

American Institute of Public Opinion (the Gallup Poll). Press releases. Princeton, 1945–50.
Public Opinion Quarterly, 1945–50.
Survey Research Center publications. University of Michigan, 1947–49.

CONGRESSIONAL DOCUMENTS

Congressional Record, 1939–51.
Committee hearings, reports, and documents on all major pieces of foreign affairs legislation from 1943 through 1950.
Committee hearings and reports in the following major investigations:
    The Hurley resignation. Senate Foreign Relations Committee, 1945.
    Tydings-McCarthy. Senate Foreign Relations subcommittee, 1950.
    MacArthur removal. Senate Armed Services and Foreign Relations Committees, 1951.
    Jessup nomination. Senate Foreign Relations subcommittee, 1951.
    Institute of Pacific Relations. Senate Judiciary subcommittee, 1951–52.
Senate Document 87, 82d Congress, October 1951. *Review of Bipartisan Foreign Policy Consultations since World War II.*

INDEX

Acheson, Dean, 36, 42, 104, 169 n., 198, 215 n., 257, 330 f., 342, 368 f., 372, 377 f.; opposition to appointment, 60; and Hiss, 110, 329, 368, 373–4; his *1947* view of China, 246; and Vincent, 250; character and reputation, 327–9; attitude toward Chiang's collapse, 346 ff., 350 ff., 355–6; toward People's Republic, 360–1; toward defense of Formosa, 362 ff.

Acts. *See* Bills

Advisory Committee on Postwar Foreign Policy, 140 ff., 146, 148, 159 f.; subcommittees of, 142–3 n.

Agricultural benefits, regional division on, 54 ff.

Agriculture Committee (House), 100

Aid for Greece and Turkey, 221, 223–4, 225 f., 248, 264, 266, 273, 300, 311; roll calls on, 224

Air Policy Commission, 334

Aldrich, Winthrop, 232, 277

Alfange, Dean, 236 f.

Allen, George, 192

Almond, Gabriel, 11, 247 n.

Amerasia case, 380

American Christian Palestine Committee, 236. *See also* Zionists

American Federation of Labor (AFL), 142

American Newspaper Publishers Association, 163

Americans for Democratic Action (ADA), 219 f., 311 f.

Anglo-American Oil Agreement, 116

Appointments, Senate record on confirmation of, 59–62

Appropriations Committee (House), 86, 88, 96–8, 100, 114, 263 n., 266, 272, 274, 281 f., 287 f., 337, 340; powers, 96; subcommittee system, 97; ranking members, 97–8; weaknesses, 98

Appropriations Committee (Senate), 57, 96, 113–15, 263, 266, 280 ff., 284 f., 288 n., 289 f., 337, 340 f.; relation to other committees, 114

Arends, Leslie, 72

Armed Services Committee (House), 88, 90, 100, 337, 340

Armed Services Committee (Senate), 114, 116, 357

Arms embargo, repeal of, 131

Armstrong, Hamilton Fish, 140

Atlantic Charter, 167

Atlantic City Conference (*1943*), 155

Atlantic Pact. *See* North Atlantic Treaty

Atomic Energy Act, 201

Atomic Energy Committee (Joint House-Senate), 123

Attlee, Clement, 228 n., 229

Austin, Warren, 141, 148, 151 ff., 160, 164, 169, 178, 216, 233, 240

Badger, Oscar C., 357

Baldwin, C. B., 213 n., 314

Baldwin, Raymond E., 151 f.

Balfour Declaration, 166 n.

Ball, Joseph, 147, 162, 173 ff., 182, 284

Ball-Burton-Hatch-Hill Resolution (B_2 H_2), 147 f., 156 ff.

Banking and Currency Committee (House), 88, 100, 214 n.

Banking and Currency Committee (Senate), 214 n.

Barkley, Alben, 63, 111, 148, 160, 215, 347

Baruch, Bernard, 192, 201, 232